America's
Second Civil War

Also by Stanley A. Renshon

*The Clinton Presidency: Campaigning, Governing and the
Psychology of Political Leadership*

Good Judgement in Foreign Policy: Theory and Application

Handbook of Political Socialization: Theory and Research

*High Hopes: The Clinton Presidency and the
Politics of Ambition*
(Winner of the American Political Science Association's Richard E. Neustadt award
for the best book on the presidency, and the National Association for the
Advancement of Psychoanalysis' Gradiva Award for the best biography)

*One America?: Political Leadership, National Identity, and the
Dilemmas of Diversity*

Political Psychology: Cultural and Crosscultural Foundations

*The Political Psychology of the Gulf War: Leaders, Publics and
the Process of Conflict*

The Psychological Assessment of Presidential Candidates

Psychological Needs and Political Behavior

America's Second Civil War

Dispatches from the Political Center

Stanley A. Renshon

Transaction Publishers

New Brunswick (U.S.A.) and London (U.K.)

Library of Congress Catalog Number: 2001037345
ISBN: 0-7658-0087-X
Printed in Canada

Library of Congress Cataloging-in-Publication Data

Renshon, Stanley Allen.
    America's second civil war : dispatches from the political center / Stanley A. Renshon.
        p. cm.
    Includes bibliographical references and index.
    ISBN 0-7658-0087-X (alk. paper)
        1. political planning—United States. 2. political leadership—United States. I. Title.

JK468.P64 R46 2001 2002
303.3'4'0973—dc21   2001037345

To my wife Judith, a wonderful mother, friend,
and partner in life,
with love, affection, and appreciation

Contents

Preface

This book grows out my work on the Clinton presidency and the psychology of political leadership. In trying to understand the ways in which Mr. Clinton's psychology shaped his approach to leadership and governing, it became clear that the public issues he faced would be instrumental in defining his presidency. Mr. Clinton ran for and won the presidency as a "New Democrat," a term that implied some distance from the older kind. On a variety of issues—the economy, race, welfare reform, crime, and others—Mr. Clinton presented himself as someone who would go beyond the traditional orthodoxies of left and right. To judge the degree to which this was true required some appreciation of these positions.

Having spent many years following these debates at a distance, I began to read more widely the policy disagreements that shaped America's increasingly contentious political arguments. It quickly became clear that while many of the facts in these debates were in dispute, the disagreements ran much deeper. Indeed, it seemed the primary conflicts were not so much over facts, and not even primarily about policy—although there were certainly plenty of disagreements over both. Rather, these conflicts seemed more a product of fundamentally different views of America—what kind of country we had been, what kind of country we were, and what kind of country we should strive to become. That divide is still very much with us. The 2000 presidential election has only deepened it, and the survivor solidarity after September 11 did not surmount it.

These debates on the nature, past and future, of America represent our *basic public dilemma*. I understand that term as a primary unresolved question of public psychology that underlies and permeates the most important political issues that arise for public leadership. The basic public dilemma that faced Mr. Clinton on taking office was whether he could restore confidence in the government's ability to address and to help resolve pressing public problems, without resorting to the discredited large-scale programs that had brought about that dilemma in the first place. Paradoxically, Mr. Clinton succeeded in large part because of the unwanted and forced partnership with a Republican Congress, elected primarily because he had reneged on his promise to govern as he had run—as a "New Democrat."

Mr. Clinton's major flaw was not that he didn't see our dilemmas clearly, but rather that his own ambitions made him unable to deal honestly and effectively with them. In Mr. Clinton's first term his promise to govern as a moderate collided with his ambitions for a heroic presidency of large initiatives and great legacies.

In his second term Mr. Clinton again accurately called our attention to America's unfolding basic public dilemma, our increasing diversity and how we would handle it. In a speech at the University of California, San Diego, he outlined the issues facing this country and said he would begin a national dialogue to help address them. That initiative—optimistically named "One America"—floundered from its inception with the president's decision to define that discussion as a "black-white," rather than a multi-ethnic cultural diversity set of issues as he had first articulated it.

A number of Mr. Clinton's personal and political choices not only squandered the opportunity to help us address these issues, but also actually contributed to further dividing the country on racial, ethnic, cultural, and political lines. As a result, our basic public dilemma—how we will address and resolve these issues of common national understanding, purpose, and identity—are still very much with us. And it is a critical, but as yet unresolved, question as to whether new or different kinds of political leadership can make a constructive difference.

This volume is organized into a series of focused, substantively grounded essays of varying length. They reflect my dual training as both a political scientist and a clinical psychologist and psychoanalyst. The perspective of political psychology is regrettably lacking in most discussions of the issues addressed in this book. For example, most discussions of immigration focus on its economic aspect, do immigrants cost us more money than they contribute? This argument is based primarily on how one counts "costs" and "contributions." Yet beyond this is the much more critical question of the impact of immigration on American common values, national identity, and politics. Moreover, in the aftermath of the September 11 terrorist bombing the integration of immigrant communities has become an increasingly important question.

Many of the issues raised herein are controversial, which means that many people hold strong views on one side or another of these issues. I have tried to develop a balanced analysis of the issues involved, without avoiding the substantive judgments that follow from such work.

The essays in this book are grouped into six major sections; Foundations and Framework; American National Identity; Immigration and the American National Community; American Politics and Political Leadership; Political Leadership and the Dilemmas of Diversity; and Presidential Leadership in the New Millennium. Each chapter within these sections is self-contained, although each is separately linked, as are all cumulatively, to the major themes set out in the introduction.

This volume covers a wide range of issues—race relationships, immigration, political and presidential leadership, cultural diversity, national identity, and related topics. No author can legitimately claim exhaustive knowledge of all these issues. I certainly do not.

The knowledge that I am able to bring to bear on these issues has been greatly enhanced by those who have supported my work and from whom I have learned a great deal. My work on race relations and issues of diversity was facilitated by a fellowship from the Institute of Race Relations, Boston University. I wish to thank its director Glenn C. Loury for that opportunity. My work on immigration and diversity was greatly facilitated by a fellowship from the Center for Immigration Studies. I would like to thank its director Mark Krikorian for that opportunity and his continuing support of my work. My work on presidential leadership in the context of the 2000 election was aided by a fellowship from the Joan Shorenstein Center on the Press and Public Policy, The Kennedy School-Harvard University. I would like to thank the Center's director Thomas Patterson for that opportunity.

My work on political leadership in divided societies was also aided by a research grant from the City University Faculty Award Program. And my work on President Clinton's "One America" initiative was supported by a research grant from the Horowitz Foundation for Public Policy.

Those who have read in whole or in part the essays contained herein have assisted immeasurably my work on the topics. I would like to thank F. Fred Alford, Alexander L. George, Nathan Glazer, Eugene Goldstein, Erwin Hargrove, Kristen Monroe, Thomas Patterson, Peter Spiro, Peter Schuck, Peter Suedfeld, Stephan Thernstrom, Mark Krikorian, and especially Noah Pinkus for their helpful comments on earlier drafts of parts of the book or its constituent sections. Over the years, my many discussions with William Mac Runyan have been a continual source of understanding, perspective, and friendship. I would also like to acknowledge the valuable research assistance of Sandra Johnson and Rebecca Blanton.

I am also very appreciative of the encouragement and support of Irving Horowitz of Transaction Publishers. Mary Curtis at Transaction was very responsive, helpful, and understanding in getting this project through to completion. Anne Schneider, my editor at Transaction, was also responsive and easy to work with throughout the book's production.

Freud was right about love and work being the foundations of life. I owe so much to my family—my children David and Jonathan and my wife Judith. And I am truly blessed in being a part of their lives.

Stanley A. Renshon
New York City

Part 1

Foundations and Framework

1

America Redefined?: Political Leadership and America's Second Civil War*

Until recently, with one historical exception, America was able to take a coherent national culture and identity for granted. Successive waves of immigrants entered a country where their ultimate assimilation was considered a desirable outcome, not a contested one. The country did not prove equally hospitable to everyone, and some groups endured enormous hardships on their way to a fuller realization of America's grand vision of opportunity and freedom. Yet throughout, the dream of common purpose and community common propelled the collective desire to live up to it (Myrdal 1964) and provided the framework within which progress was understood and made.

Only the Civil War really tested the cultural and civic bonds that united the country's disparate interests. That crisis confronted America's leadership, but especially its president, with a profound but basic question: Could America share a common future without a common culture? The answer, over which the war was fought, and the recognition of which is the starting point of Lincoln's greatness, was that we could not.

Now, for the second time in its history, America faces a real question of how to maintain a stable and effective relationship between its *unum* and *pluribus*. Unlike the first, this Civil War does not pit commerce against agriculture, urban centers against rural traditions, or North against South. Rather, the new danger lies in conflicts among people of different racial, cultural, and ethnic heritages, and between those who view themselves as socially, culturally, politically, and economically disadvantaged and those whom they see as privileged. Unlike the first Civil War, conflict is not being waged by one section of the country with another, but rather it is being waged in *every* section of the country. Unlike the first Civil War, the antagonists cannot take for granted, nor take refuge in, the primary institutions in their parts of the country, such as family, or religious, social, cultural, or political organizations. These are precisely the places where the conflicts are being fought.

The consequences of these conflicts are not to found in the number of killed or wounded. Rather, they are to be found primarily in the retreat from common

3

ideals, where basic cultural values are abandoned or under siege, and institutions flounder in a sea of shrill and conflicting demands. At issue is whether it is possible or desirable to preserve the strengths of a common heritage in the face of insistence from some quarters that our past has resulted in a culture worth tearing down to build over, rather than one worth keeping and building on. The basic conflict is over the viability of American culture and identity itself.

The Decline of American National Identity

America has become the land of paradox as well as opportunity. The twentieth century has been called the American century (Evan 1998), and perhaps it is accurate to so name it. America has emerged as the predominant world power, economically, militarily, politically, and culturally. Yet, freed by the end of the Cold War from a need to focus on external enemies, America appears to have arrived at a crossroads. Even taking into account the current 2001 economic downturn, we live in a time of unprecedented prosperity. Yet, Americans continue to be uneasy about the quality of their leaders, the competence of their institutions, and the larger meaning of their lives.

Domestically, America appears to present a mirror image of its international standing. It is at once the single most powerful country in the world. Yet, it is beset domestically by fractious disagreements about its values, history, culture, and policies. Divisive issues such as affirmative action, abortion rights, English as its basic language, homosexual marriage, and many more matters of heated contemporary debate raise basic questions about the American national identity—who we are and what we ought to aspire to become.

These conflicts frame the true meaning of our "culture wars." There are many such wars. There are the abortion wars, school wars, military culture wars, gender wars, family wars, history wars, museum wars, and the classics war—not to mention the wars over flags, statues, pledges (of allegiance at school, to our country during naturalization ceremonies), and most recently a ban on celebrating Mother's Day in deference to children with gay parents.[1] Moreover, our politics, like our culture, has become mired in bi-partisan trench warfare, while all sides call for a return to civility as they plot the next defensive act to stymie, if not damage, their opponents. The attack of September 11 didn't change this.

Temporarily, it pushed "normal" politics to the periphery, and the politics of unity to the fore. Yet many divisions remain. Republicans and Democrats have disagreed about the nature of the economic stimulus package (Kessler and Eilperin 2001), whether airline security should be totally federalized (Eilperin and Nakashima 2001; Alverez 2001), and the pace of a Democratic controlled Senate in approving the judicial appointments of President Bush (Dewar 2001). The splits are such that recently the *New York Times* published an editorial (Editorial 2001; see also Clymer 2001; Lawrence 2002) entitled, "The Return of Partisanship."

Republicans and Democrats have also joined together against others in their respective parties on issues of balancing the need for wider government powers to address domestic security issues and a concern with civil rights (Toner and Lewis 2001). Yet when the house passed a substitute measure that was more closely tracked the bill passed by the Democratically controlled Senate, and many house Democrats complained (Associated Press 2001); Lancaster 2001). And, of course, many contentious issues still remain—on judicial appointments, military tribunals, energy policy which President Bush has presented as a national security issue and which Democrats have criticized him for doing (Seelye 2001), and missile defense—to name just four.

Meanwhile, as a sign that the more things change, the more they remain the same, in the midst of a surge of patriotism in the aftermath of the September 11 terrorist attack, the ACLU threatened a lawsuit against a school in California that had posted a sign on the school marquee reading, "God Bless America." Parents, teachers, and children at the school had instituted many fundraising activities to aid families of fire-fighters and police killed in the terror attack and had put up that message as a sign of their support for the country. Calling that sign and its message "hurtful and divisive" the ACLU threatened to sue in order to force its removal. As the reporter of the incident notes (Lane 2001), "The dispute illustrates how contentious the concept of national unity can sometimes be in a religiously and ethnically diverse country, even during wartime."

Fuelled by the assertive expansion of claims for group rights and acerbic debates regarding their legitimacy and limits, the country is increasingly permeated by a deep cultural divide. Every conceivable group—some deserving, others less so—has demanded legitimacy, parity, and often preference.[2] Some argue that our cultural wars are over (Sullivan 2001), but they clearly have gone deaf to the shrill accusations that masquerade as public debates. Meanwhile, political leaders attempt to finesse or make use of these controversies, rather than engage and attempt to resolve them.

Nor have matters been helped by the ways in which liberal advocates and their conservative critics have framed their differences, and characterized each other. Advocates of diversity have given more attention to pressing and expanding their claims than to the requirements necessary to build a consensus that would support and sustain them. Critics of diversity have yet to explain how to accommodate satisfactorily the reality of diversity without recourse to traditional models that rarely had to consider it.

In short, while America is undeniably more diverse than at any time in its history, it is also undeniably more fragmented and polarized; war induced unity not withstanding. Moderating and, if possible, resolving the increasingly pointed demands of these groups is *the* fundamental domestic issue, the most basic public dilemma facing American society. Success is by no means assured. Divisive issues such as affirmative action, abortion rights, English as America's basic language, homosexual marriage, the conflict between merit and equality, and many more matters of heated contemporary debate remain suffused with unresolved conflict. In these, as well as in so many matters, we are increasingly ill-served by the failure of our leadership, at every level, to address honestly the issues that separate us.

Former President Clinton (1997:509), for example, had said that it was necessary for Americans to view divisive issues, such as affirmative action and immigration, "through the prism of how we can preserve one America," and warned that our growing diversity is "potentially a powder keg of problems, and heartbreak and division and loss." He concluded that, "how we handle it (our diversity) will determine, really—that single question may be the biggest determinant of what we will look like 50 years from now and what our position will be in the world." Three months later the Clinton administration decided against adding a "multiracial" category to the 2000 Census.[3]

What Mr. Clinton did allow was the addition of a number of new classification categories and the option of allowing respondents to check more than one category. Well, isn't that the functional equivalent of having a multicultural category, you ask? Well, to some degree yes, but not really. The multicultural category would have provided a non-specific alternative to government-sponsored color-coding of the population, a goal envisioned by Clinton's idea of "One America."

On the other hand, civil rights groups worried that a multicultural category would dilute their numbers and thus their clout. There were, as well, reasonable concerns about the effect that such a non-specific category would have on the nation's ability to monitor its commitment to access and opportunity; a major question arising out of these new circumstances was how, exactly, these numbers would be counted.

The answer raised more questions than it resolved. A draft Office of Management and Budget memo (2000) for the use of such numbers established that "Responses that combine one minority race and white are allocated to the minority race." In other words, for counting purposes any person who checked the category "White," and any other minority box would become a minority. Is an American born of an Asian and Italian mother and father a minority? Apparently so. Is an American born of a naturalized American father who travelled here from Spain who also has a mother who emigrated here from Morocco a "minority?" The OMB says yes.

This approach has the effect of adding "minorities" in need of special assistance and preference. In doing so, the administration preserved untouched for another decade at least, increasingly divisive single race/ethnicity categories. And in the process, it took a step away from helping to nurture a "group that is quintessential American—emphasizing the melting pot quality of the population rather than the distinctions" (Eddings 1977), the very outcome that the President had said he championed.

Must cultural, psychological, and political diversity lead to a fragmented and dysfunctional national identity? Some worry it might. Is the opposite of fragmentation Anglo-Western domination? Some apparently think so. James Hunter (1997:52, italics his), in his book, *Cultural Wars*, argues that, "*cultural conflict is ultimately about domination.*" The word domination implies subjugation. And if Hunter is correct, it is not surprising that our culture wars are fought with no quarter given to a state of exhaustion and stalemate.

Is it true that all cultural conflict is ultimately about domination? Not necessarily. I am well aware that the United States has a mixed, in some cases, poor historical record in its treatment of American Indians, Americans of African decent, Americans of Asian decent, women, and others. Yet, the strong and ultimately more historically successful tradition in the United States has been *inclusionary pluralism*, not domination and subjugation. Those who believe otherwise have the difficult task of explaining how a "hegemonic," "dominating" elite no longer dominates.

More to the point, is it true that advocates of what we can term here "tradition" seek to dominate and subjugate those who see America differently? Do those who want English to remain our common language insist that Spanish not be taught or spoken? Do those who don't support affirmative action insist its beneficiaries never have the opportunity to compete and prosper? Do those who think assimilation to American cultural and psychological traditions afford immigrants an important vehicle to achieve their dreams here demand that they never have meaningful contact with their countries of origin or their families who remain there? Obviously not.

A better and more useful question is not whether a society must have a dominant culture, but whether, in a pluralist democracy like the United States, it is still important to have a *primary* one. Is inclusionary pluralism compatible with the cultural *primacy* of certain core American traditions like individualism, opportunity, merit, and responsibility. The wager that this country has made for two hundred plus years is that not only is it possible, but it is also necessary.

The question, "What does it mean to be an American?" has never been easy to answer. It is much less so now. A number of elements of American national identity have been identified over the years—a focus on ideals, customs, "creeds," emotional attachments, values, or psychologies.[4] In the past four decades however, new, more basic and disturbing questions have emerged.

Some ask: Is there an American national identity? Others ask: Should there be one? Some worry about how we can maintain and further develop common understandings and purpose in a diverse country. Others ask what useful purpose do such worries serve when we live in a "postmodern" era and when our allegiances ought to be global?

Those concerned with integrating large numbers of new immigrants ask: How can we best accomplish their integration into American society and culture? Immigration advocates and their political allies ask: Is it legitimate to ask immigrants to subscribe to what Americans ought to be leaving behind? Their answer is: No (Takaki 1993).

Paradoxically, arguments over assimilation assume a stable, coherent culture into which immigrants are assimilated. As the many battles that constitute our culture wars make clear, this is increasingly not the case. The major traditions and values that underlie American national culture have themselves become sharply disputed.

Some (Maharidge 1996; Isbister 1996, 1998) applaud these developments. They view the decline of key American cultural traditions, and especially its "dominant elites," as a necessary step in developing a less "hegemonic," more democratic society. Others (Schlesinger 1992; Miller 1998; Renshon 2001) worry about an America whose central traditions, many of which they see as critical to supporting a free democratic society, seem in danger of being lost, perhaps past the point of recovery.

Diversity, National Identity, and Cultural Stability

Sometimes it appears that members of the American community do not live in the same country. It is not only that "whites" and "blacks"[5] profoundly disagree about the guilt or innocence of O.J., the fairness of the criminal justice system, or whether Bill Clinton is a man who might serve as an appropriate public role model—although there are strong "racial" differences in all three areas. What is more troubling is that those whose work entails knowing the meaning of the most basic facts mirror this "perceptual divide."

Andrew Hacker (1993) examines his data and hypothetical anecdotes and finds two nations, one "black," one "white"—divisively unequal. Along similar lines, Joe Feagan (2000) entitles his book *Racist America*, with no further real analysis apparently necessary. Yet, the sociologist Arnold Rose (1964), writing a postscript twenty years after the original publication of Gunner Myrdal's Classic *An American Dilemma* (1944) at the beginning of Lyndon Johnson's presidency, detailed the great progress that American race relations had made. That analysis *preceded* the start of Johnson's "Great Society" programs.

Abigail and Stephen Thernstrom (1997), examining their data for the period following this, find enormous progress toward making Americans of African decent and others one nation indivisible. However, Orlando Patterson (1995:24-25) reaches the paradoxical conclusion that while "there is no denying the fact that in absolute terms, African Americans, on the average, are better off now than at any other time in their history…it is also no exaggeration to say that…these are the worst of times, since the ending of Jim Crow, for the African American population." How it can be both the best and worst of times for the same group is not fully explained.

The same conflicted ambiguity permeates the important and highly contentious issue of immigration. Some idealize immigrants, even as many others greet high levels of immigration with concern. Meanwhile, political leaders of all sides prefer not to deal with the large array of important concerns raised by historically unprecedented rates of legal and illegal immigration. Democrats view these rates from the vantage point of their own partisan advantage, extol the virtues of our "immigrant nation," and have been implicated in rushing to confer citizenship. Some of their allies go farther and condemn any questions about these issues as inherently racist.

Republicans are torn as well. High-tech industries crave highly skilled and computer-literate workers, which creates pressures to increase the number of "special visa" (H 1-B) workers coming to this country. These are in addition to the already large numbers coming in through traditional legal and illegal channels. Moreover, Republicans—fearful of being labelled as "anti-immigrant"—have followed the lead of former Michigan Senator Abraham (R-MI), chair of the Senate Immigration subcommittee, to "accentuate the positive" (Lewis 1977). With this view cemented in position, hard questions are not asked, and data that are inconsistent with a rosy outlook are ignored or misstated.[6]

Meanwhile political pressure is building for another amnesty for illegal, or as their advocates prefer, "undocumented"[7] aliens. Some (Sierra et al. 2000:539, italics mine) argue that "the reality of free trade and regional economic integration presents a challenge that *demands* moving beyond the confines of nationalism and addressing transnational problems with innovative solutions." In that vein, Vincente Fox, president of Mexico, has proposed solving the problem of illegal immigration from his country and region by simply making the U.S.-Mexico border an open one (Sullivan and Jordan 2000; Thompson 2000). President George W. Bush has agreed to the establishment of a bi-lateral Mexican U.S. Commission to explore immigration issues between the two countries (Thompson 2001), although he has not endorsed the open border suggestion and turned away (Hillman 2001) Mr. Fox's suggestion of a "general amnesty."

What Mr. Bush is considering is some form of what he calls "regularization" for illegal Mexican immigrants and, perhaps, other groups as well. Illegal immigration is now estimated at between 8.5 million (Porter 2001) and 9 million (Cohn 2001) and rising, with no signs of abatement. Mr. Bush's statements have been vague, but it seems clear that he wishes to regularize and exert some further control over a very porous border with Mexico's promise to help, and the price of that help is some form of regularization (Jordan and Sheridan 2001).

Some have suggested that it is part of his longer-term political strategy with Hispanics (Gigot 2001), while others (Skerry 2001) have noted that it is responsive to the business wing of the Republican Party that favors a steady supply of labor. While labor, political, and control issues have appeared to take center stage with the president's proposal, there is a much more important and rarely discussed set of issues—those dealing with cultural cohesion and integration. Put bluntly, a new regularization, with Mexico's real help, may make control of the border easier to maintain. It may also be helpful to Mr. Bush politically, although that is debatable (Gimpel and Kaufmann 2001). And it might affect some labor-intensive industries.

However, the real question that needs to be addressed is whether it benefits the country's cultural and political fabric to focus narrowly on immigration control, economics, or the future of Hispanics in the GOP. What really needs to be discussed frankly is the relationship of immigration policy to our policies concerning maintaining and improving the quality of civic- mindedness, cultural and political integration, combined with a concern for strengthening the individual traits and outlook that support them.

It is within that set of concerns that questions about dual and multiple citizenships arise. Surprisingly, given the role that porous borders and lax immigration enforcement (Brown and Connolly 2001:A17) played in allowing terrorists to enter the United States, President Bush is reported (Associated Press 2001) to have told Mexican President Vincente Fox after the attack that he "hasn't forgotten that we have commitments to work to regularize the situation of immigrants." In other words, he is still considering some form of amnesty for illegal immigrants.

There is no doubt that record levels of immigration have increased America's ethnic, "racial," and cultural diversity. More than 1.2 million immigrants, legal and illegal, now settle in the United States every year (Camarota 2001), and they have been doing so for decades. As a result, the latest figures show that "Ten percent of those living in the United States are foreign born, the majority of them from Latin America" (Rodriguez 2000). The number of immigrants living in the United States has almost tripled since 1970, rising from 9.6 million to 28.4 million today, *the highest number in American history* [8] and far out-pacing the growth of the native-born population. The new figures affirm dramatically that, "the country is going through a remarkable transformation in just a generation's time, one that will reshape the nation's demographics and social landscape for years to come" (Escobar 1999).

One of these dramatic changes concerns the "racial" and ethic composition of the country. By 2050, by some estimates, America will contain no majority "racial" or ethnic group [9] Some advocates, counting on a coalition of what they see as the oppressed, are hoping to turn James Madison's warnings about the tyranny of the majority on its head. In place of the "tyranny of the majority" they look to the day when a coalition of the minority will acquire hegemony. Others are wondering how America will manage to integrate so many culturally diverse newcomers while retaining its core identity as a country built primarily, but not exclusively, on Western European intellectual, legal, ethical, and cultural traditions.

America's traditional answer to this question has been assimilation. Yet assimilation,[10] with its implications that there is a national American identity and immigrants choosing to come here should, in good faith, try to embrace that identity, is "contested," to borrow a somewhat dainty postmodern term that hardly does justice to the fierce assault on it as a normative and descriptive model. Some sociologists see the term as harboring "deep layers of ethnocentric pretensions" and the experience associated with it a physically and emotionally harmful experience (Rumbaut 1977). Many multiculturalists see assimilation as an attempt to strip immigrants of their identity. Not unimportantly to some, this would make them less available for purposes of further deconstructing a common American identity to an amalgam of ideologically bonded advocacy groups.

This raises the question of whether it is fair to ask those who wish to live here to live within the cultural frameworks provided by these traditions. Paradoxically, it is those very traditions that have provided the framework for the many benefits those here enjoy. Most immigrants come to the United States seeking political and economic freedom. Those benefits are built on, and supported by the very same primary cultural traditions that are now being increasingly questioned—merit not group membership as a vehicle for mobility, independent thinking within a strong framework of values and ideals, moderation in character and tempered self-interest, and so on.

Assimilation to those primary American cultural traditions would seem, at face value, to be instrumental in helping immigrants achieve the goals for which they came. American cultural traditions are important as well to the country itself. Why? Because they reaffirm the viability of this traditional path through the incorporation and use of traditional American cultural values— even given assimilation's difficulties. In doing so, assimilation also reaffirms their usefulness as a path to the realization of immigrant and citizens' aspirations.

However, if there are good reasons for immigrants to assimilate and incorporate themselves into America's primary culture, there are hazards in doing so uncritically. Even immigrants who arrive in this country with values and beliefs that parallel those of traditional American culture might wonder whether assimilation to a debased national cultural is beneficial (Portes and Zhou 1994). Studies show, for example, that television and adversarial youth culture undermine the values of hard work and family values with which many immigrants arrive. Ruben Rumbaut (1977:17; see also Salins 1977:56-57) found that the length of residence for immigrant children in San Diego was associated with their spending less time on homework and more time watching television, which, not surprisingly, led to lower grade point averages (GPAs). Paradoxically then, immigrant groups who might be helpful in revitalizing such traditional American cultural values as hard work, the importance of merit, and feelings of pride and attachment to the nation are faced with becoming integrated into a culture in which these very basic ideals are themselves under attack or in decline.

Nor can Americans count on immigrant groups to answer problems here that Americans already here have not addressed themselves. A recent study, "Births of Hispanic Origin, 1989-95 (National Center for Health Statistics, February

1998) shows soaring birth rates among teens of Mexican origin that were more than twice the rate of the nation's teens as a whole, and more than three times the rate of "white" teenagers (Healy 1998; Holmes 1998). Equally disturbing is the fact that the figures revealed that Hispanics born in this country were more likely than Hispanics who moved here from their homeland (primarily Mexico) to give birth as teenagers, and to have babies outside marriage (Vobejda and Constable 1998). Indeed, these disturbing figures suggest that continuing high levels of this immigration stream may contribute along with some aspects of American culture to the development of a Hispanic/Mexican "underclass," in a country that has had little success in addressing or resolving similar problems among Americans of African decent.

As this is happening, most public debate has centered on whether, and to what extent, new immigrants are an economic asset or a liability to the country. This analysis misses a much more central issue, that is how it will be possible to integrate enormous numbers of new immigrants into a national culture and identity which, in itself is increasingly problematic.

Leaderless Politics in a Divided Society

Americans live in a country where there is enormous and increasing interconnectedness, but far less relatedness. They live in a country where indicators of economic and cultural well being go in opposite directions. And, they live in a country where, in spite of its success, many—in most polls, a majority—of its citizens, are profoundly troubled by the direction in which it appears to be going. A 1997 *Washington Post*-ABC poll (Morin 1997; see also Waysoci 1999; Pew Research Center 1999) found that in spite of a then booming national economy and a soaring stock market, 57 percent of those interviewed said the country was headed in the wrong direction, while 75 percent said you couldn't trust the government or its leaders to do what's right. Almost all who thought so, mentioned the decline of the nation's moral health and well being, as well as problems in education, race, and immigration.

Not surprisingly, America's politics are no less paradoxical than its public psychology. America is a country that hungers for policy moderation and bipartisanship, which its leaders and institutions ritually promise while engaging in the most extreme forms of partisan trench warfare. It is a country whose last president's avoidable excess diminished his authority while in office and tarnished his legacy as he departed. The Clintons' inexcusable breach in taking White House furnishings for their own, and Mr. Clinton's highly irregular and questionable pardons during the last moments of his presidency have exhausted even his most ardent supporters (Harris 2001; Cohen 2001).

And, it is a country hungry for authenticity in its leaders, but increasingly subject to large doses of spin and the politics of appearance, which is one reason why the 2000 presidential election campaign was so kind to the candidacy of John McCain. Writing of him in the *Washington Post*, Dan Balz (1999:A01) said, "the McCain rise owes to other factors as well: [including] a direct style in a year when "authenticity" has become a buzzword for what voters want." The accumulated loss of leadership capital over decades of squandered opportunity appears to have created its own public momentum for its restoration.

Divisive policy and cultural issues permeate our politics. Paradoxically however, most Americans seem to be in general agreement about many of these matters (see, for example, DiMaggio, et al. 1996; Wolfe 1996:1998). How can that be so? It also appears that the more political agreement there is among ordinary Americans, the more savage the battles become. Why? Part of the answer surely must be located in an examination of American political leadership or, more precisely, the lack of it, at least before President Bush's response to the terrorist attack.

Declining Social Capital and the Culture of Leadership

The controversies swirling around the cultural foundations of American national identity, not surprisingly, have been paralleled by debates on the decline of "social capital" (Putnam 1995:2000; Norris 1996; Ladd 1999). Decreasing levels of trust in social and political institutions, declining political participation, and declining public interest in and attention to many spheres of public life before September 11 remind us that healthy democracies are as much a function of their publics' psychology as they are of formal constitutional documents (Lasswell 1959; see also Almond and Verba 1963).

"Social capital," therefore, is a useful term because it calls attention again to the critical link between public psychology and the support of democratic social and political institutions. Yet in doing so, it risks ignoring the other half of this seminal democratic equation—*leadership capital.*

Political leadership itself is a form of social capital and, like its public psychology counterpart is indispensable to the well being of democracies. And, like social capital, evidence of its decline and the consequences of that decline permeate and complicate our present circumstances.

The term capital, as in social or leadership capital, suggests a surplus— something that you have beyond sufficiency, which enables you to do something else of value. Greater wealth for example, provides the means to support materialism, opportunity or disengagement. Social trust provides the means to find common ground or undertake common purpose. And, character and competence provide the building blocks of surplus leadership capital.

Leaders who earn, through their words and actions, a public reputation for honesty, integrity, competence, good judgment, and a steady capacity to put the public's interest first and their own, or parties' interest thereafter, will accumulate leadership capital (Renshon 2000a). Yet, the history of leadership capital accumulation in the modern presidency has not been a good one. Of the eight post-Eisenhower presidents, five were unable to gain or serve through a second term because of their own failings, and the sixth barely managed a second term in spite of them.

Mr. Johnson repeatedly lied about Vietnam and squandered his leadership capital. President Nixon committed felonies and squandered his. Mr. Ford squandered his by pardoning his predecessor. Mr. Carter failed to combine honesty with competence and squandered his, and Mr. Bush demonstrated inspired leadership abroad and listless leadership at home. Mr. Clinton managed a second term, but left a legacy so marred by scandal and controversy that his presidency can hardly be considered a success. Indeed, only Ronald Reagan managed to serve two terms and leave the office with the stock of presidential leadership capital enhanced and his reputation in tact.

So, the depletion of leadership capital is not strictly a contemporary problem. It has been under way for decades. If, as is repeatedly said, political leadership is best understood as the fit between the leader, citizens and their times-for the last decade it has been a hard one for them all.

The Decline of Leadership Capital: A Brief Political History of a Dizzying Decade

The conflicts that permeate our national culture cannot be understood apart from their relationship to contemporary American leadership capital. Our national political culture has reached an unstable plateau, paralleled and arrived at through the most wrenching, dizzying leadership reversals.

In 1991, George Bush stood at the pinnacle of his public approval. Not only had he immediately and correctly grasped the implications of Sadaam Hussein's grab for land, oil, and power, but he had successfully demonstrated that leadership that has the courage of its convictions could mobilize the support of the American public in spite of their understandable anxieties.

Unfortunately, for President Bush, after this leadership triumph, both his courage and his convictions appeared to the public, not without reason, to be less intensely stimulated by the myriad problems facing this country than in stopping Mr. Hussein.

Primarily for that reason, in 1992 Mr. Bush became another in a long line of modern presidents (Lyndon Johnson, Richard Nixon, Gerald Ford, Jimmy Carter), who was unable to serve a second term. Americans, beset by economic, political, and cultural uncertainties turned to Bill Clinton, who promised to avoid the pitfalls of the left and right and govern smartly and from the political center as a "New Democrat."

However, immediately upon his election, Mr. Clinton declared himself the heir not only to the votes he received, but to those of one of his rivals as well and declared that an overwhelming majority of Americans had voted for change. That may have been so, but it is an open question as to whether the change Americans wanted is the change they got. With a decidedly left-of-center Democratic Congress as his partner, the president temporarily lost track of his promise to govern as a "New Democrat" and began increasingly to look to many like an old one.

The result was a cataclysmic repudiation of the president and his party in the 1994 congressional, state, and local elections. Republicans gained control of both Houses of Congress for the first time since the early years of the Eisenhower administration (Berke 1994:A1). In the House they won fifty-two seats (Wilcox 1995:1). In the Senate, they added eight additional seats.

Equally, striking were Republican gains at the state and local levels. Republicans picked up twelve governorships, in addition to the eighteen they already held (Verhovek 1994:A1). No Republican incumbent who sought re-election to the House, the Senate, or to a governorship lost (Wilcox 1995:1).

At the state legislative level, the Republicans picked up at least fifteen chambers that had been in Democratic hands. In no case did Democrats pick up chambers that had been in Republican hands. Before the election the Democrats controlled sixty-four chambers, the Republicans thirty-one (three were tied). After the election the figures were forty-nine and forty-six, respectively (again, with three tied). For the first time since reconstruction, the number of Republican state legislators (3,391) approached the number of their Democratic counterparts (3,847).

There is some evidence that these changes filtered down to the local level as well. In North Carolina, for example, Republican county officials increased their numbers by fifty-six, from 217 seats from 161. Of that state's 100 counties, Republicans became the majority in forty-two local governments, up from the twenty-seven they had controlled before the election (Smothers 1995:A16).

It was clearly a Republican electoral landslide. However, its meaning was another matter. Was 1994 a classic realignment election? Or, was it just one more indication of the country's de-alignment? Was it only a repudiation of the Clinton administration, or did it represent a turning away from a government itself? Twenty-five years earlier Theodore Lowi (1969) had confidently predicted the end of the welfare state. Was this election a conformation of that assertion?

Those questions were soon answered. Republicans, flush with victory and confidence, declared that realignment was at hand, liberalism a historical relic, and a Republican in the White House just a matter of the passage of time. However, borrowing a well-worn page from Mr. Clinton's political career, Republicans, in some ways understandably, began to confuse the opportunity given to them to create a mandate with already having been given one. Americans may have wanted less government, in some areas, but, apparently, they were not prepared to do without any government. And, as a result of Republican miscalculations, and President Clinton and his parties' extremely adroit political use of them, an almost fatally weakened presidency was revived and transformed.

Democrats were immeasurably aided in this process in the 1996 presidential election by the selection of a basically decent, but terminally inarticulate Republican candidate. Democrats were now not the only political party to scarcely survive a near-death political experience. Having allowed themselves to become associated with that most dreaded of all new political words, "extremism," Republicans barely managed to hold on to their majority in the House. This insured that the newly re-elected and born-again moderated President Clinton could count on, and make use of, ample Republican anxiety at being portrayed as "harsh" every time he and they disagreed about anything.

Democrats were understandably delighted at their new-found ability to be both for balancing the budget and increasing government spending; for ending big government as we know it, even while expanding government programs; and for cutting and raising taxes at the same time. Republicans, on the other hand, are understandably distraught at their inability to agree among themselves, much less to provide an effective alternative to President Clinton. They had not yet figured out how to be for less government, but not against it; how be for affirmative action but opposed to racial preferences, and how to be favorable toward immigration while expressing legitimate concerns about economically accommodating and culturally integrating vast numbers of newcomers.

This state of acute political vertigo brought about by the dramatic and abrupt changes of the past decade has resulted in the development of a new somewhat puzzling, perhaps even bizarre, form of political extreme combat—bi-partisan trench warfare. Its purpose is to mask, as well as inflict, lethal political wounds. It requires that each party appears to accept the most publicly popular assumptions of their opponents, Democrats present themselves as prudent, and Republicans as compassionate. However, at the level of real politics, every hearing, every issue, every bill, every press conference and leak is initiated or scrutinized for what each side hopes will be decisive partisan advantage.

In these circumstances raw, often ugly, partisanship always trumps civility. Not surprisingly, public confidence in Congress, a reflection of the depletion of leadership capital, became abysmally low. For example, in February 1997, a Harris poll found that only 38 percent of the American public approved of the way Congress was doing its job. By October 1999, only 32 percent approved.[11] By September 2000, that number had climbed to 45 percent, but the highest it had ever been in the last decade had been a bare majority approving (51 percent), and its low had been a dismal 22 percent.[12]

Between 1998 and 2000, Republicans lost ground in this fight. They seemed to be biding their time, hoping that if they did not suggest, or stick with anything that appeared too controversial, or which could be mischaracterized by a president who did not hold their best interests at heart, they might—just might—hold on to their Congressional majority, and even pick up the presidency in 2000.

What they would do with the presidency seemed an unanswered question, even to Republicans. It was unclear just what the party and its leadership wished to stand for or, if necessary, stand against. In order to show the public you have the courage of your convictions, you first need to have them.

Democrats, sensing Republican vulnerability, labelled every policy difference "extremism," or accused them of favoring "the powerful" instead of "the people," a theme that Democratic presidential candidate Al Gore took up to some puzzlement and mixed results in the 2000 presidential race. Democrats feared that a tarnished president would damage their prospects—and they were right. And, they feared being put back on the wrong side of issues, such as crime or national defense. Republicans appeared fearful of being on the wrong side of any issue.

A September 2000 poll conducted by the *Wall Street Journal* and NBC found that moral standards and ethics tied with the economy as top concerns for Americans; education, health care, and social security followed. Lest there be any doubt that Americans were concerned about these qualities not only in their society but also in their leaders, consider the following evidence. Seventy percent of the American public rated the quality "being trustworthy enough to do the right thing" as very important, far outranking being knowledgeable (43 percent), being compassionate enough to understand average people (46 percent), or even having strong leadership qualities (61 percent).[13]

America's depleted leadership capital suffered another setback as a result of one of the most evenly split, bitterly fought, and unusually concluded presidential elections since 1876. The new president, George W. Bush lost the popular vote by 539, 897 votes (*Associated Press* 2000), and beat his opponent Mr. Gore in the electoral college by gaining only one more than the 270 votes needed to win. Moreover, he gained Florida's decisive twenty-five electoral votes only after thirty-six days of raw political and legal combat between the two candidates which was settled by a controversial U.S. Supreme Court decision only five days before electors were scheduled to meet and cast their state's votes for president. Small wonder that many questioned whether any president could effectively govern in such circumstances.

Public Psychology and the Decline of Leadership Capital

The decline of leadership capital in the United States owes much to the actual psychology and behavior of the leaders who depleted it. Yet, it would be unfair to attribute all our misfortunes to them. We, the public, must share a substantial part of the responsibility as well.

To understand that responsibility, we must first ask some questions about the public's psychology, or as I will argue, *psychologies*. What are the publics' expectations of our political leaders? How, if at all, have they changed? What are the implications of these changes for the accumulation or reduction of leadership capital? And, finally, how do they affect the capacity to, and the methods by which one might, govern in a divided society?

Discussions of the relationship of leaders to their "followers" repeatedly invoke the assumption of a unified public psychology. Winston Churchill, it is assumed, spoke to the need of *all* the English for heroic leadership to defend the country. Likewise, discussions of Franklin D. Roosevelt assume that *all* Americans (rich and poor) welcomed the heroic leadership necessary to save our economic and political system. In times of overriding systemic crisis, it makes sense to think in terms of a unified public psychology.

However, does it make sense to assume that in less catastrophic times? I think not. At least in the United States, it is useful to think in terms of several public psychologies rather than *a* public psychology.

People willing to take great risks to advance their personal freedom and economic circumstances founded this country. They were willing to strike out on their own, and adapt to the circumstances they encountered, which were clearly quite different from those they left behind. Yet, we are no longer a country made up primarily of rugged individualists, except in our public symbolism. Surely such people still exist. But they now share the stage with other, larger groups that are governed by different psychologies.

In a prescient book, Daniel Boorstin (1987 [1961]:3-4) pointed out a disturbing trend in American political life—the use of the country's enormous individual and public resources to "create a thicket which stands between us and the facts of life." To what was he referring? The demand of illusions that flood our experience, which, in turn, are fuelled by our extravagant expectations. Americans, he argued, have become accustomed to expect "anything and everything."

In response, no small number of political leaders (and others) has hastened to assure us that it is possible to keep both our illusions and our reality without becoming disappointed, cynical, or hopeless. Some of our leaders tell us that it is possible for government to tax less, spend more, and save. They tell us it is possible for schools to painlessly promote both merit and inclusion, and for families to be constituted in any way adults choose without harmful effects on children. It is not.

Boorstin's insight provides an important window into the forces shaping public psychology and thus leadership capital. A country whose citizens want everything, are vulnerable to leaders who promise them anything. So many hardly notice when a leader promises that the era of big government is over, while delineating a host of new government initiatives that will expand its scope. Many don't seem to care when, while searching for authenticity, they support a candidate, Mr. Gore, who assured Hispanics at a meeting that he hoped his next grandson would be born on Cinco de Mayo—their group's national holiday (Connolly 1999). And they only reluctantly notice that a president they favored has given the strong appearance of having bartered financial and personal favoritism considerations for criminal pardons, and then choose not to learn more. So, in a Gallup Poll 54 percent of the public approved of Mr. Clinton's controversial pardon of fugitive millionaire Mark Rich, before the number of his controversial pardons and other elements of his behavior on leaving office made his ratings plummet.

Public Psychology, Leadership Capital, and the Rise of Disconnectedness

The September 11 terrorist attack appears to have drastically changed the pre-attack assumption, perhaps for the long term, that no hard policy choices need to be made and that those that are avoided have no consequences. Whether Americans regain their optimism, manage their anxieties or return to partisanship seems less important, ultimately, than whether they continue to understand that choices carry consequences. And whether leaders will respond to this new appreciation with frank discussion or new language to mask partisan preferences remains to be seen.

In 1958, at the end of the Eisenhower administration, almost 75 percent of the American public thought you could trust the government in Washington to do what is right "just about always," or "most of the time."[14] By 1998, those figures had been exactly reversed with 75 percent of the public believing you could not trust Washington to do what is right "just about always," or "most of the time." The number of people who thought governmental officials looked out for the interests of the common person rather than themselves took a parallel nose-dive from 70 percent in 1958 to 20 percent in 1994.

A Pew Center analysis of the causes of the decline of trust in government concluded, "Discontent with political leaders and lack of faith in the political system are principal factors that stand behind public distrust of government. Much of that criticism involves the honesty and ethics of government leaders."[15] In other words, it is the action of leaders themselves, their integrity and morality, which affect the degree of the public's trust.

This link between the actions of leaders and the decline of trust in government is borne out by data collected after the terrorist attack by a *Washington Post* poll. Trust in government, long in decline, has surged (Morin and Deane 2001). In April 2000, only 4 percent of the public thought you could trust the government to do what is right "almost all of the time," and only 26 percent thought you could do so "most of the time." In a poll taken by the *Washington Post* on September 27, 2001, the respective figures were 13 and 51 percent! Certainly, these figures are consistent with and perhaps a result of support of President Bush's performance after the attack. And reporters, too, have made the connection. Dan Baltz and John Harris (2001) detail the connection in an article entitled, "Shock of War May Have Changed the Tone in Politics as Polls Find Public Confidence in Government Soaring. Leaders Seem to Rise to the Occasion with Bipartisan Effort."

Another piece of evidence is found in the answers to another set of questions that are ordinarily asked as part of a package of questions about trust in government. This set asks respondents to agree or disagree to the proposition that "public officials care (or don't care) about what people like me think." A September 1956 ANES poll found that 53 percent of the public thought they did care, and only 37 percent thought they did not. However, by August 1976, a CBS/*New York Times* poll found that only 26 percent of the public now thought they did, while 71 percent thought they did not. Finally, a March 1994 ABC/*Washington Post* poll found that 32 percent thought they did, and 67 percent thought not.

Finally, there is the issue of public attention in relation to civic connection. In 1997, the Pew Research Center for the People and the Press reported that in 1996 "25 percent of those they surveyed said they learned about the presidential campaign from the likes of [Jay] Leno and David Letterman, a figure rising to 40 percent among those under 30."[16] That Center also reported that among its twenty most closely watched stories in 1997 only three were concerned with politics, and none ranked higher than thirteenth. The story that headed the list was Prince Diana's death. Or as the *Wall Street Journal* (Duff 1998:A9) put it in a major headline story, "Among Factors that Influence People's Lives, Politics Ranks Toward the Bottom."

Americans' declining interest in politics can be seen in other numbers as well. In the 1992 presidential election, ordinarily a high point of the public's political interest and participation, only 55.2 percent of those eligible to vote, registered and did so. Four years later, that number had declined to 48.8 percent in spite of new laws, which made registering to vote easier than at any time in this country's history. In 1970, the first year that census forms were sent by mail, 83 percent of households responded. In 1990 that percentage had dropped to 65 percent. Disappointing results from the 2000 census left its director to doubt that he would be able to meet one of his central goals, sparking a new wave of American civic engagement (Holmes 2000).

The political trends that encourage political disassociation appear to be reinforced by economic, technological, psychological, and sociology ones. W. Lance Bennett (1988) sees economic dislocation and anxiety as the cause of the public's disconnection from traditional means of civic engagement. Geographical, occupational, and other forms of mobility also add to the loosening of traditional ties. Robert Lane (1978), in his prescient early paper, referred to this as "sociological release," the freeing of people from formerly restricting, but also connecting categories. He also worried that the "colder" market of exchange had increasingly supplanted the domain of community. Communications, mirroring politics, have become decomposed into niches (Blumer and Kavanaugh 1998).[17] And of course, the rise of the Internet certainly allows and may facilitate social disconnection from common purpose (Shapiro 1999:118-120).

As a result of these factors, Americans are more likely to rent movies than attend them. We are more likely to search for our roots on the Internet than establish them in our communities. And, we are more likely to complain about our national politics than take part in them. Small wonder Robert Putnam (2000) continues to worry that we are "bowling alone."

Public Psychology and the Politics of Avoidance

In the two centuries since J. H. St. John De Crevècoeur (1997 [1783]:43-44) asked, notably, "What, then, is the American, this new man?" there has been no shortage of answers (Renshon 2000b). The first, and most basic, was that he was motivated by the desire to do what had not been possible in his country of origin, which was to make use of his talents in the service of his ambitions to improve the material (and social) circumstances of his life.

A primary goal of achievement was "success," made possible by freedom— psychological, social, and political. And there can be little doubt that America has been wildly successful in producing it. Yet American success is not without paradox. Expanding financial security and the mass production and distribution of an increasingly large number of symbols of success through most strata of American society was a historically unprecedented accomplishment. However, with abundance came a problem. How do you tell where you stand in Levittown? The answer: You keep up with the Joneses, but you don't stand out by standing apart.

On the other hand, the achievement ethic of the 1960s was quite different. "Tune in, turn on, drop out" was an invitation to withdraw from traditional cultural codes (see pp. 53-54) surrounding achievement. From that vantage point, achievement was not measured by the accumulation of wealth, but by inner "peace" and understanding. The realization of one's own unique internal blueprint was the goal and self-enlightenment the means. Conformity to "conventional" values or views was seen as antithetical to achieving self-realization. Cole Porter's signature composition, "Anything Goes," seems an apt theme song for a cultural movement in which "do your own thing" and "let it all hang out" were taken as core personal values and which shaped how cultural codes favoring achievement would be understood and enacted.

Daniel Yankelovich (1981:163-218), surveying Americans in the 1980s, at a time of economic insecurity, found us increasingly turning away from the fusion of relentless ambition for mobility and the work ethic that had been part of American culture for centuries.[18] Following the lead of de Tocqueville, Turner, Erikson, and Riesman he found cultural values responsive to structural circumstance. He (1981: xviii-xix) viewed the turn inward as a response to diminished economic opportunities and expectations. Yet, he also saw in this turn inward a new effort to resolve the dilemmas raised by a firm commitment to ambitious self-advancement in a context of stagnant mobility. In these circumstances, the "rat race" seems less attractive than the ambiguous, but still ambitious phase, "self-fulfillment."

Avoidant Tolerance

Somewhat paradoxically, yet "emphatically," Yankelovich (1981: xviii) insisted that this form of self-fulfillment was not the middle classes' version of counter-cultural narcissism. Although, he does note that in its more extreme forms, "the new rules simply turn the old ones on their head, and in place of the old self-denial ethic [delay of gratification], we find people who refuse to deny anything to themselves—not out of bottomless appetite, but on the strange moral principle that 'I have a duty to myself.'"

How are the duties to oneself reconciled, if they are, with the traditional American commitment to community and interpersonal ideals and values? Easily. Self-fulfillment, being an entirely personal matter, requires those who pursue it to simply adapt the cultural code: "Live and let live." Or as Yankelovich (1981, 88) notes,

> Traditional concepts of right and wrong have been replaced by norms of "harmful," or "harmless," If one's action are not seen as penalizing others, even if they are "wrong" from the perspective of traditional morality, they no longer meet much opposition.

Unlike the 1960s in which counterculture adherents dismissed traditional values as bourgeois and confining, this live and let live approach to personal values and convictions has led to a new ethic that can be summed up by what has become almost an eleventh commandment, "Thou shall not judge." The "non-judgmentalism of middle-class Americans," in matters of religion, family, and other personal values emerges as the major finding of Alan Wolfe's (1998) in-depth interviews with mainly suburban clusters of Americans across the country. He attributes it to an emphasis on pragmatism rather than values in making tough personal decisions, a reluctance to second-guess the tough choices of other people, and ambivalence or confusion as the "default" moral position.

Yet, there is an important distinction to be drawn between being slow to judgment and being averse to making judgments. Why Americans now seem more averse than slow is a question left unanswered by Wolfe. However, it is nonetheless a critical question to answer if we are to understand what appears to be the paradox of a tolerant, yet avoidant public. Yet, in some ways, this is not a paradox at all. Perhaps it is precisely because Americans have become avoidant, that they are able to be endlessly tolerant. If this is true, avoidant tolerance may prove to be much more dangerous to American public life than the "repressive tolerance" about which critics like Marcuse (1965) used to worry or the "boutique multiculturalism" that now concerns critics like Fish (1998).

In his latest work, Wolfe (2001a,b) calls moral freedom the last frontier. What is moral freedom? No less than the ability to choose the specific moral commitments by which you will live.

> Should I lie or tell the truth? Is my marriage vow binding? Ought I to give in when temptation calls? To whom are my obligations strongest? To answer such questions,

Americans have traditionally relied on time-tested moral rules, usually handed down by a supreme being, that command obedience and punish defiance. Now we live in an age of moral freedom in which individuals are expected to determine for themselves what it means to lead a good and virtuous life. We decide what is right and wrong, not by bending our wills to authority, but by considering who we are, what others require and what consequences follow from acting one way rather than another.

Wolfe says that moral freedom, "is so radical an idea, so disturbing in its implications, that it has never had much currency among any but a few of the West's great moral theorists." He is right for many reasons. An argument for "moral freedom" is an odd sequel to a book that found Americans increasingly unwilling or unable to making moral or ethical judgments regarding other peoples' behavior, and even their own.

The idea of each person being his or her moral/ethical authority has a super-ficial attractiveness to it, if one doesn't think too seriously about the nature of human psychology or the foundations of human community. Most people's consideration of their own morality and ethical behavior suffers from the basic narcissistic fallacy. We tend to attribute to ourselves the best of motives, or at least good motives on balance, and we tend to underestimate woefully the amount of the not always attractive elements of self-interest that can permeate our moral/ethical calculations.

Worse, giving licence and legitimacy to such moral/ethical self-dealing runs an enormous risk to the very elements that make moral/ethical life sustainable. One need not be a modern Jonathan Edwards to know that common rules and understandings are the foundations of culture and community. The fact that affluence can purchase independence, and avoidant tolerance can facilitate unlimited personal ethical choice suggests that what Wolfe sees as moral free-dom may actually be a form of narcissistic conceit, with troubling class under-tones.

Is the new moral freedom to be available only to the wealthy? What of the segments of our society that are already having troubling harnessing a produc-tive assessment of their own self-interest in the service of developing a well-realized life? Shall we council the underclass to follow their views of their own self- interest? Isn't that partially what has placed them in a troubled social and economic position in the first place?

In a society filled with individuals who increasing have trouble drawing lines, is moral freedom a step up the mountain or off the cliff? Philip Howard (2001) argues in his recent book that Americans have given up on telling right from wrong—not in sweeping good-versus-evil ways, but in small, everyday decisions. They do not trust their judgment, or anyone else's, so they have made up rules and principles that let them evade responsibility.

The failure of the capacity to drawn reasonable moral and ethical lines was starkly evident even in the aftermath of the September 11 terrorist bombing. Susan Sontag, writing in *New Yorker Magazine* (2001) had this to say,

The disconnect between last Tuesday's monstrous dose of reality and the self-righteous drivel and outright deceptions being peddled by public figures and TV commentators is startling, depressing. The voices licensed to follow the event seem to have joined together in a campaign to infantilize the public. Where is the acknowledgment that this was not a "cowardly" attack on "civilization" or "liberty" or "humanity" or "the free world" but an attack on the world's self-proclaimed superpower, undertaken as a consequence of specific American alliances and actions? How many citizens are aware of the ongoing American bombing of Iraq? And if the word "cowardly" is to be used, it might be more aptly applied to those who kill from beyond the range of retaliation, high in the sky, than to those willing to die themselves in order to kill others.

In other words, the terrorists bombings were our fault.

Susan Sontag is not alone. Michael Lerner, writes in *Time* Magazine (2001):

We live in a society that daily teaches us to look out for No. 1, to keep our focus on our own bottom line and to see others primarily as instruments to help us achieve our goals and satisfactions....And that same insensitivity is institutionalized in the global system whose symbolic headquarters have been the World Trade Center and the Pentagon. Yet we rarely look at our lives in these larger terms. We don't feel personally responsible when a U.S. corporation runs a sweatshop in the Philippines or crushes efforts of workers to organize in Singapore. It never occurs to us that when the U.S. (with 5% of the world's population and 25% of the wealth) manages over the course of several decades to shape global trade policies, that increase the disparity between rich and poor countries, this directly produces some of the suffering in the lives of 2 billion people who live in poverty, 1 billion of whom struggle with malnutrition, homelessness and poverty-related diseases.

In other words, there is poverty in the world. We as a nation, and as individuals, have not eradicated it, therefore the chickens have come home to roost and we have experienced the understandable [and just?] consequences of our neglect.

We can see further evidence of avoidant tolerance and a failure to recognize distinctions in the response to heightened concerns about Middle East communities. Understandably, since the terrorists who attacked the United States and the organizations that supported them are anchored in Middle East politics and culture, Americans have expressed increasing awareness and concern of such groups-here and abroad. Just as understandably, American leaders from the President on down have urged Americans not to mistake the acts of a few for views of the many. And Americans have overwhelmingly, and to their credit, reacted with, for the most part (Kunkle 2001) admirable restraint in these matters during difficult times.

Yet Americans are looking more carefully at individuals who look Middle Eastern, and more carefully still at young men with such looks—especially if they are traveling in groups (Verhovek 2001). A CNN/USA Today/Gallup poll taken a few days after the attacks showed that Americans were supporting special measures intended for those of Arab descent. In the survey, 58 percent backed more intensive security checks for Arabs, including those who are

United States citizens, compared with other travelers; 49 percent favored special identification cards for such people, and 32 percent backed "special surveillance" for them.

The *Boston Globe* reports that 71 percent of Americans of African decent who responded to a Gallup Poll said they would favor more intensive security checks for Arabs, including those who are U.S. citizens, before they boarded airplanes. A smaller majority of Caucasians, 57 percent, said they would favor such a policy and, while there was no specific category for Hispanics and Asians, 63 percent of nonwhites said they, too, would favor it. A separate Zogby International poll revealed similar results, although with a narrower margin between the groups. It found 54 percent of African-Americans favored singling out Arab-Americans for special scrutiny at airport check-ins while 63 percent of Hispanics and 53 percent of Caucasians opposed it. In that Gallup Poll 64 percent of Americans of African decent and 56 percent of other nonwhites favored requiring Arabs, including U.S. citizens, to carry special identification as a means of preventing terrorist attacks. Forty-eight percent of Caucasians opposed such a drastic move.

The avoidance of judgment is also critical in understanding the public's response to the loss of leadership capital over the past two decades. Wolfe notes in another context that Washington, "is a place where the values of the 1960's and the values of corporate America have come together," both being extremely relativistic and adverse to making judgments Needless to say, a strong ethic of self-fulfillment, coupled with the view that whatever I do, or anyone else does, that doesn't directly harm anyone else is alright, "often collides violently with traditional rules, creating a national battle of cultural norms" (Yankelovich 1981:5).

It is within these overlapping layers of American cultural and public psychology that a disturbing loss of leadership capital has been and is unfolding. Leaders must be able to mobilize citizens in support for their mutual goals. However, mobilization is not synonymous with simple arousal. The capacity to harness ambition to ideals and values that resonate with, but which sometimes may require the moderation of, citizens' more unreflective "demands" or" needs" is one example of the link between leadership and citizen capital. How this is possible when Americans have become accustomed to expecting "anything and everything" (Boorstin 1987 [1961]:3-4) is no small matter as we head into the new millennium.

Political Ambition and Leaderless Politics

Ambition is a core element of any leader's success. As the building block of public accomplishment it is, as noted, a key resource for the accumulation of leadership capital. Yet, it is also necessary to distinguish among ambitions— from the simply motivational to the dangerously grandiose—but how? One answer is to examine the relationship between ambition and character integrity. A consolidated set of ideals and values for which one is willing to stand can anchor and temper ambitions, even large ones. Without them, self-interest has no constraints.

If character integrity is the capacity to maintain fidelity to ideas and values, even at the risk of personal or political harm, then it is clear that to have the courage of one's convictions you need both. In short, courage, both personal and political, is the key link between the two elements of leadership capital already discussed—ambition (and the skills to realize it) and a well grounded sense of ideals and values. The three together, ambition and ideals, consolidated by courage and other key personal resources to sustain them, are the means to the accumulation of leadership capital. I term the failure of either having convictions or the courage of them, coupled with strong ambition, *leaderless politics*.

The rise of leaders anxious for office and lacking either the skills to realize their ambitions or strong principled convictions, coupled with the courage to follow them, leads to a mismatch between ambitions and performance. Contemporary leaders often aspire to more than they are able to accomplish or willing to publicly explain. It is a paradox of our contemporary recruitment of top-level political leaders that we require of them enormous ambition to endure the rigors of gaining high office, but limit our support of their large initiatives once they are in there.

One result is that leaders are tempted to finesse their plans with spin rather than direct and honest public explanation. This was essentially Bill Clinton's problem. He was a man who believed in large plans but was forced to campaign on modest ones. Once in office he tried to mask, but still pursue, the large scope of his policy ambitions with the result that he became a moderate after the 1994 elections by necessity, not choice (Renshon 1998a).

Some believe the gap between leadership ambitions, and a combination of high but skeptical public expectations, provides room for governing in a politically contentious environment. I think not. Masking ambitions runs the risk of violating public performance standards that underlie the accumulation or depletion of leadership capital. The public appears to prefer leaders who combine competence and integrity, not those for whom the two are inversely related. Leaders unable or unwilling to risk honesty with the public deplete their own capital when caught, while also depleting the reserve of social trust and capital on which they must often draw.

American appears to have confounded large ambitions with "heroic leadership." Yet, ambition unanchored by the capacity for fidelity to deeply held values and ideals runs the risks of grandiosity or dishonesty. Torn between their ambitions and public skepticism, presidents and candidates have tried to negotiate these treacherous currents for a decade, primarily by trying to finesse them. Michael Dukakis famously suggested in 1988 that his presidential campaign was about competence, not ideology, and he was soundly trounced. Bill Clinton ran and won the presidency as a "New Democrat," governed as an old one, and Al Gore ran a divisive populist campaign while presenting himself as a moderate. While "heroic leadership" is one of the central political myths of our time, "leaderless politics" seems a more realistic description of our civic condition.

A New Beginning or a Troubled Continuation?

America begins a new millennium blessed and troubled as never before. Prior to the terrorist attack there was unprecedented economic prosperity at home and no immediate or catastrophic military involvements on the near horizon. Instead, of worrying about staggering federal deficits, both presidential candidates debated what to do with equally large projected surpluses. Yet, both major party candidates in the 2000 presidential race, Al Gore and George Bush, argued that prosperity alone cannot sustain the civic order. Their caveat to what seems like the best of times reflects a deep disease among the American public about the state of our national life.

The number of crimes committed, babies born out of wedlock, marriages that end in divorce, students performing below par, declining trust in major institutions including government, declining interest in social and political participation—these and other indicators all suggest a country whose robust economic performance was out-pacing the quality of its cultural, social, and political life.

Some see great hope in the fact that some of these trends, such as out-of-wedlock births and crime, are declining (Easterbrook 1999; Morin 1999). However, others will note that those figures do not approach the low levels evident in the 1950s. They also make use of a baseline that inflates the change, [19] and they do not include relevant information like the fact that crime rates may be falling but only 45 percent of crime is reported (Sleven 2000). This may be one reason why the American public, in spite of these improved figures, still substantially believes the country is heading in the wrong direction and is worried about its future. A *Wall Street Journal*/NBC News poll (Waysoci 1999) found that 67 percent of its respondents thought social and moral values were stronger when they were growing up and 66 percent thought that standards of acceptable and unacceptable behavior were lower today than in recent years. A report by the Pew Research Center (1999) found that," Misgivings about America today are focused on the moral climate with people from all walks of life looking sceptically on the ways in which the country has changed both culturally and spiritually."[20]

Why? Politically, the left, right, and center are united in believing that the culprit is our obsession with ourselves and our success. On the right, Robert Bork (1997) believes we neglect our culture and worship narcissism at the expense of our values. On the left, Paul Wachtel, (1994) believes America neglects its poor and worships affluence at the expense of its communities. And, from the center, Jean Elshtain (2000) criticizes the "commodification" of our most intimate relationships, as well as our more public ones.

These critics echo Daniel Bell's (1956) critical insight that one danger of successful capitalism is that it might achieve success at the cost of the foundations that support it. He worried that narrow ambitions for markets and profits, without due attention to ethical values, could undermine the moral and cultural basis of society. He did not foresee the extent to which political leaders, torn between their need to realize their ambitions and the need to respond to public concerns in order to gain office, would be tempted to sacrifice integrity for power.

He did not foresee the extent to which leaders' ambitions might weaken their commitment to making hard public policy choices. Nor did he see that many leaders, faced with a choice between alienating key supporters and responding to heart-felt public concerns, might prefer the appearance of courageous leadership to its practice.

Thus, candidate Al Gore decried a federal report (Stern 2000) documenting the targeting of violent material to under-age children and promising "harsh regulation if the [movie] industry does not shape up in six months" (quoted in Allen and Nakashima 2000). A few days later, Mr. Gore was at a lavish Hollywood-sponsored fundraiser at New York's Radio City Music Hall that raised $6.5 million for his party. A few days after that, at a Beverly Hills dinner that raised $4.2 million for his campaign, Mr. Gore promised to "nudge" (a Yiddish word which means "mildly suggest"), but never to have the government regulate the entertainment industry (Allen 2000; Seelye 2000).

The Political Contradictions of Democracy

Bell's critical insight about the cultural contradictions of capitalism, however, represents one aspect of our contemporary dilemma. The ferocious engine of successful capitalism now has an equal and parallel engine of social and political change, the ferocious engine of rights-based advocacy democracy.

Over thirty years ago, Theodore Lowi published his landmark book, *The End of Liberalism*. His title was a statement, not a question. In it, Lowi (1969:214) confidently subtitled one of his chapters, "The End of the Welfare State." With the benefit of hindsight we now know that the anomalies he pointed out in the "New Welfare" and other policies of interest-group liberalism did not result in its demise, but, paradoxically, in its expansion.

Lowi's oversight was to assume that because Americans were growing weary of the welfare state, that weariness extended to government itself. Republicans made the same mistake when they took over Congress in 1994. "New Democrats" like Bill Clinton and Al Gore have learned that committing the government to large numbers of small, but expandable, new programs is one way around the public's reluctance to support traditional large-scale government efforts.

Jeffrey Berry's (2000) study of liberal interest-group lobbies in Washington shows that contrary to conventional wisdom, such groups have flourished. He investigated major congressional proposals in 1963, 1979, and 1991, two hundred and five in all, and he found that the liberal lobby groups increasingly win their battles.

Ralph Nader, Green Party candidate, based his candidacy on the premise that Republicans and Democrats are so intent on coddling corporations that once powerful liberal advocates now go unheard. Yet, as Sebastian Mallaby (2000:19) points out, Nader's claim, is wrong, not just in portraying liberal activists as marginal. His claim that indifferent politicians have marginalized them is almost completely backward. The truth is that Republicans and Democrats disagree on many things, but advocacy groups often prevent them from making their differences count.

Mallaby notes that liberal advocacy groups have grown larger and there are more of them. They have also expanded their staffs, while becoming richer. Public Citizen, for example, has a staff of seventy-five, up from about fifty-five two decades ago. The World Wildlife Fund, started in the 1960s, is negotiating to buy a gleaming office building in Washington, complete with tree-filled atrium.

Not surprisingly, these professional outfits are good at getting their message out. What are their techniques? Ones that are basic, yet infrequently associated with liberal groups—money, professional staff and organization, and substantially funded "research" designed to support their group's position. Other resources they employ are found on both sides of the ideological spectrum—direct mail, passionate and not wholly accurate messages, stigmatizing of the opposition, and so on (Hunter 1991:135-170). However, liberal groups have been aided invaluably in one critical way that their conservative group counterparts have not. That has been in the tacit, and sometimes more explicit support of their world-view allies—the press.

This is not a complaint about a media conspiracy. It is a fact supported by empirical research. A 1995 poll of Washington reporters (cf., Samuelson 1999) found that only 2 percent rated themselves "conservative," while 89 percent had voted for Clinton in 1992 (against 43 percent of the popular vote). Only 4 percent were Republicans (50 percent were Democrats, 37 percent "independents"). The result is not a conscious effort to advance an agenda, it is more of a shared perspective that comes from shared beliefs. Journalists often see "the story" in the same way as liberal lobbyists. Business is regarded as greedy, self-interested and undemocratic. Conservative groups are "out of touch" or socially dangerous. By contrast, liberal lobbies are public-spirited "watchdogs."[21]

The causes are many. There are the hardy perennials—affirmative action, abortion rights, immigration, English as the primary language, same-sex marriage, and educational standards. But there are also dozens more that pop up periodically like bottles in a storm-tossed sea—the treatment of serious crimes committed by juveniles as adult offenses, the number of Americans of African decent working as clerks for Supreme Court justices or receiving Oscars for their acting efforts, the unfairness of "zero tolerance" policies adapted to forestall charges of disparate treatment, the building of more jails, and literally *any* disparity whatsoever, regardless of cause, between any groups that can be used to lay a claim for more attention and recognition.

As a result, basic questions that Americans thought were generally, although never fully, satisfactorily answered are now reopened. What's fair? How should we define and implement "opportunity?" How much should merit count? What does, and should, it mean to be an "American?" What is government's legitimate role in shaping or, if necessary, bending cultural traditions in light of these controversies? Given the deep cultural and political significance of these questions it is small wonder that James Davidson Hunter's (1993) subtitle, "A Struggle to Define America," captures something very fundamental.[22]

The goals sound principled—ever more justice, fairness, equality, tolerance, basic human rights, democracy, equality, legitimacy, freedom, and respect for everyone and every conceivable claim. Who could be against more democracy? Who could oppose tolerance?

What's wrong with more democracy? Nothing, so long as it is coupled with respect for obligation. Democracy without responsibility is a form of government-sanctioned narcissism.

What's wrong with more tolerance? Nothing, so long as it is balanced by a sense of cultural and personal values that frame boundaries. Tolerance without limits reflects an abdication of civic judgment.

What's wrong with more fairness? Nothing, so long as the government does not get into the business of enforcing one group's idea of what this means. Fairness is a way of approaching questions of equality, not answering them.

Bell's insight about capitalism parallels the concerns of the members of the constitutional convention who wrote the Constitution. Unrestrained capitalism not only leads to aggregations of capital that distort the democratic political process, but also undermines the very culture that supports both. The Constitution's authors had similar concerns about democracy. They, too, feared accumulations, but of political power. As a result, we operate under a system of checks and balances. They, too, were caught between the need both to expand and to constrain democracy. As a result, American is a republic. And they, too, worried about finding a proper balance between individual rights and the rules necessary to sustain a viable constitutional government. As a result, we have a "Bill of Rights," a specific listing of the powers reserved respectively to the federal and state governments and the people, and the establishment of an independent judiciary to adjudicate among them.

The political contradictions of democracy are found in the fact that unrestrained excesses of democratic virtue run the risk of compromising the political foundations from which they draw their legitimacy and gain a respectful hearing. More justice, more fairness, more equality, more redefinitions of wants into rights, more equality, more freedom and more unconditional respect for every conceivable preference do not automatically result in a better democracy.

Champions of each of these expansions address their demands, not to other citizens but to those in a position to make them civic practice—political leaders. This places our leaders in a difficult position. They are charged with the responsibility to see beyond a particular group's self interest, but also govern in a system constructed to make them responsive to it. The ability to reframe group demands, and if necessary deflect, defer, or moderate them is a core responsibility of leaders in any democracy, but especially in one in which the basic frameworks of its culture are matters of fierce debate.

Conclusion

The question this country is left with at the end of the Clinton and the beginning of the Bush presidency is whether it is possible to find and field any leader whose promises and ambitions can be honestly articulated, reconciled, and carried through. Our country faces enormous issues arising from our dramatically increased "racial," ethnic, and cultural diversity. The importance of leadership in times of national strife, is not solely, perhaps not even primarily, an ability to propose and pass legislation. But what is?

We have divisive national arguments, but on many issues there appears to be public consensus. What has been leadership's role in the development of this apparent paradox of substantial conflict and shallow divisions? How is it possible to govern, or to lead in these conditions? How can we replenish the leadership capital of this society so desperately in need of an infusion?

The question that we are left with is whether it is possible to find and field any leader who has both courage and convictions, one who is not afraid to raise and address difficult issues, even with those least likely—his political allies—to want to hear them. In our present and foreseeable circumstances, there is a need, one might say a desperate need, for post-partisan political leadership—leadership that combines principles with proportion and integrity with competence. We need leaders whose pragmatism is a function of their psychology, not their strategy and whose moderation is a reflection of their character, not their persona. This need is all the more necessary in the aftermath of the September 11 terrorist bombing and the war in Afghanistan, which is likely to be the first of a series of such combat engagements. In circumstances where white powder excites fear and the ordinary can become terrifying (Barry and Pring 2001; Nieves 2001), the country is in great need of a leader who is frank, competent, and confident. If we don't fulfill this need, we will no longer be worrying about whether democrats or republicans dominate our future, but whether as a country we have a good one.

Notes

*   This essay draws on Renshon (1996; 2000).

1.   See "Mother's Day Banned at Manhattan School," NY1 News May 12, 20001 (www.ny1.com/ny/NewsBeats/SubTopic index.html?topicintid=2&subtopicintid =4&contentintid=13368).

2.   Recently a coalition of wiccans (witches) and pagans complained in a letter to the president about his faith-based government-Church initiative (Goodstein 2001).

3.   Office of Management and Budget, 1997. Recommendations from the Interagency Committee for the Review of the Racial and Ethnic Standards to the Office of Management and Budget Concerning Changes to the Standards for the Classification of Federal Data on Race and Ethnicity; Notice, *Federal Register*, Vol. 62, No.131 (July 9, 1997), pp. 36873-36946.

4.   Historical views of American national identity coupled with a modern reformulation of the concept and its nature in contemporary American society can be found in Renshon (2000b).

5.   I placed the term in quotes to underscore that there are conceptual categories with little scientific grounding. Geneticists have argued that "race" is not a scientifically viable concept, given the mixtures of genes, and that the term and its associates (e.g., black, white, etc.) suffer from the same major drawbacks. In doing so, I depart from the adapted convention of organization like the American Psychological Association, which has reified murky scientific categories by mandating capitalization of terms like "black" and "white" whenever they are used.

    Race and its associated categories are, of course, important categories of political analysis, but that is clearly a matter of convention and politics, not molecular and genetic science. Matters are completed by the fact that the terms have some predictive validity. "Race" in the form of an observer's ascription or a respondent's self-identification does carry some predictive weight. The reason for this, however, cannot necessarily be appropriately ascribed to "race." Other possibilities include shared experience, shared outlooks, ethnicity, and strategic political self-identifications. Moreover, as rates of intermarriage in the United States increase among almost all ethnic groups the question of "pure" race categories is not only scientifically misleading but politically injurious and is also an important one to consider.

    For an analysis of how racial categories came to be used and misused in federal government's effort to count by race, see Skerry (2000). For a thoughtful examination of classification systems, including racial ones, see Bowker and Starr (1999).

6.   George J. Borjas and Richard B. Freeman (1997), two senior members of a panel examining the costs and benefits of immigration, dispute the misuse of their study by former Senator Spencer Abraham. The study in question was conducted by a panel of the National Research Council (1977).

7.   These terms reflect the attempt to control the frame of discussion, much as the "pro-choice" and "pro-life" terms have sought to do in the abortion debates. Advocates prefer the term "undocumented," because it diverts attention from the fact that these persons have entered the country in violation of our immigration laws, and have done so purposefully. Those with concerns about this type of immigration prefer the term "illegal" precisely because it places that unlawful act directly in the path of natural sympathies for those who want a "better life."

8.   The census survey counted 28.4 million foreign-born Americans, the highest number in the nation's history. They accounted for 9.7 percent of the nation's population in 1999. Of that number, 51 percent arrived from Latin America, 27 percent from Asia, 16 percent from Europe, and 6 percent from other areas of the world. America

had the highest percentage of foreign-born Americans in 1910, when 14.7 percent of the U.S. population arrived from elsewhere. But since the population itself was small, the number of foreign-born Americans was 13.5 million.

9. The relevant statistics are available from the U.S. Bureau of the Census (1992; 1995, Table 12).

10. On assimilation generally, see Kazal (1995). On the question of the demise of assimilation, see Glazer (1993).

11. The data can be found at pollreport.com(http://www.pollingreport.com/congjob.htm (October 20, 1999).

12. Data are drawn from the *Wall Street Journal/* NBC poll (Study #6008), September 14, 2000, available at: www. WallStreetJournal.com (September 15, 2000).

13. These data also are drawn from the *Wall Street Journal/* NBC poll (Study #6008), September 14, 2000, available at: www. WallStreetJournal.com (September 15, 2000).

14. For some figures, see Murray, (1997, A13; Wayne et al. 1997:216.

15. Pew Center for People and the Press, "Deconstructing Distrust: How Americans View Government," March 10, 1998; for other views of the cause of the decline of public trust, see Joseph S. Nye, Jr. (1997).

16. Cited in Kurtz (1999:A01).

17. In George Bush's campaign against John McCain in New York State, specific attacks were targeted to specific regions where they might be most effective. So Mr. McCain's vote against money to support a hospital specializing in breast cancer treatment was targeted to Long Island, cite of the hospital. Another piece of mail was sent to Republican voters in districts with a heavy concentration of farmers, noting that Mr. McCain had opposed letting New York enter the Northeast Dairy Compact, which would have provided higher payments for milk. Still another sent to the northern reaches of New York citing Mr. McCain's votes against aid to help people paying high fuel costs (Nagourney and Perez-Pena 2000: A1).

18. For example, he reports (1981:38-39) on data that in the mid-1960s,72 percent of college students agreed that "hard work always pays off. " By the early 1970s, this figure had dropped to 40 percent. These findings were paralleled in adults, for whom, between the late 1960s and the late 1970s, the percentage of adults agreeing with that aphorism fell from 58 to 43 percent.

19. Morin (1999: 34), makeing use of data collected from the National Commission on Civic Renewal (NCCR), notes that some changes since 1994 "have been nothing short of astonishing" and goes on to say that between 1994 and 1997, the number of people who said they trusted government increased from 29 to 38 percent. Left unnoted is the fact that in 1956 that number was 78 percent.

Moreover, even the rise in trust in government is somewhat paradoxical given that the proportion of Americans who voted, surely one measure of their trust in government, fell from 46.9 percent in 1992 to 42.6 percent in 1996 and 1998.

The data from which Morin draws his optimism, are themselves only marginally so. First, the report uses 1974 as the baseline, which it sets equal to zero, and then uses it to compare the years that follow. This does result in modest improvements.

However, it is highly questionable whether 1974 is the appropriate baseline, since it is a post-1960s measurement start and that period was the most volatile for all the items the scales measure. Not surprisingly, the study quietly notes (NCCR 1999:11) that "our best estimate shows that INCH (Index of National Civic Health) was far higher in previous decades." It further notes (1999: 7) that over the last three years, "the largest improvements have come in the areas of trust and personal security."

In other words, the items that measure sense of security and trust have modestly increased (are they related?), but the other items that go into the composite index have not. Moreover, viewed over time, the results are still well below the levels of all those items in 1984 and those, of course, are well below the levels of those items in 1974, and certainly well below the levels during the 1950s. The complete report may be found at: http://www.puaf.umd.edu/civicrenewal/.

20.   The complete report is available at: http://www.people-press.org/mill1rpt.

21.   A lead story in the *New York Times*, for example, indicated that business dominated Congress's last session ("Congress Leaves Business Lobbies Almost All Smiles"). Actually, the story showed that business groups won a few modest victories and played defense on minimum wage and other issues.

22.   For doubts about the "culture war" hypothesis, see Wilson (1995) and Williams (1997), the titles of whose books reflect both their premises and conclusions. Hunter's response to some of these critics of his "culture war" thesis can be found in a later paper (Hunter 1996).

References

Allen, Mike. "Democrats Stroke Hollywood At Dinner." *Washington Post*, 20 September 2000: A19.

Allen, Mike, and Ellen Nakashima. "Clinton, Gore Hit Hollywood Marketing." *Washington Post*. 12 September 2000: A01.

Almond, Gabriel, and Sidney Verba. *The Civic Culture*. Boston: Little Brown, 1963.

Alverez, Lizette. "White House Battles Plan on Airports." *New York Times*, 13 October 2001.

Associated Press. "Attacks Put U.S.-Mexico Issues on Hold." 19 September 2001.

Associated Press. "House Approves Senate Anti-Terrorism Bill." 12 October 2001.

Associated Press. "Report: Gore Won Popular Vote by 539, 987." *Washington Post*, 21 December 2000: A09.

Balz, Dan. "McCain's Rise Alters Dynamics of Race." *Washington Post*, 6 November 1999.

Balz, Dan, and John F. Harris. "Shock of War May Have Changed the Tone in Politics as Polls Find Public Confidence in Government Soaring, Leaders Seem to Rise to the Occasion with Bipartisan Effort." *Washington Post*, 14 October 2001: A03.

Barry, Ellen, and Jason Pring. "Suddenly, Everything is a Threat." *Boston Globe*, 14 October 2001.

Bell, Daniel. *The Cultural Contradictions of Capitalism*. New York: Basic Books, 1956.

Bennett, W. Lance. "The UnCivic Culture: Communication, Identity, and the Rise of Lifestyle Politics." *PS: Political Science and Politics*, December (1988) 741-761.

Berke, Richard L. "G.O.P. Wins Control of Senate and Makes Big Gains in House: Pataki Denies Cuomo 4th Term." *New York Times*, 9 November 1994: A1.

Berry, Jeffrey M. *The New Liberalism: The Rising Power of Citizen Groups*. Washington, DC: The Brookings Institution, 1999.

Blumer, Jay G., and Dennis Kavanaugh, "A Third Age of Political Communications: Where is It Heading?" Paper presented to the Roundtable on Seeking Responsibilities for Political Communication, London, 1988.

Boorstin, Daniel. *The Image*. New York: Vintage, 1987 [1961].

Borjas, George J., and R. B. Freeman. "Findings We Never Found." *New York Times*, 10 December 1997: A29.

Bork, Robert. *Slouching Towards Gomorrah*. New York: HarperCollins, 1997.

Bowker, Geoffey C., and Susan Leigh Star. *Sorting Things Out: Classification and its Consequences*. Cambridge, MA: MIT Press, 1999.

Brown, DeNeen L., and Ceci Connolly. "Suspects Entered Easily From Canada." *Washington Post*, 14 September 2001: A17.

Camorota, Steven A. "Immigrants in the United States-2000: A Snapshot of America's Foreign Born Population." Center for Immigration Studies, January 2001.

Clinton, William. J. "Presidential Debate in San Diego (October 16, 1996). "*Weekly Compilation of Presidential Documents*, October 21, 32: 42, 1996, 2091-2092.

_____. "Remarks and Question and Answer Session with the American Society of Newspaper Editors" (April 11, 1997). *Weekly Compilation of Presidential Documents*, 14, April, 33:15, 1997, 509.

_____. "Remarks at the University of California at San Diego Commencement Ceremony" (June 14, 1997). *Weekly Compilation of Presidential Documents*, 23, June, 33:25, 1997, 877.

Clymer, Adam. "Congress Resumes Partisan Warfare. *New York Times*, 14 October 2001.

Cohen, Richard. "Forsaken for a Rich Fugitive." *Washington Post*, 1 February 2001: A21.

Cohn, D'Vera. "Illegal Residents Exceed Estimate: Experts Analyzing New Census Figures Say 6 Million May Instead Be 9 Million." *Washington Post*, 18 March 2001: A01.

Ceci Connolly, "Politicians Court Hispanic Vote Census Data Show Latino Population Increased 35% in the '90s. *Washington Post*, 16 September 1999: A12.

St. John De Crevècoeur, J. H. [Susan Manning, editor]. *Letters from an American Farmer*. New York: Oxford, [1783] 1997.

Dewar, Helen. "Foreign Aid Bill Held Up by GOP Senators Demand Action on Nominees." *Washington Post*, 13 October 2001: A03.

DiMaggio, Paul, John Evans, and Bethany Bryson, "Have Americans' Social Attitudes Become More Polarized?" *American Journal of Sociology* 102 (1996) 444-96.

Duff, Christina. "Among Factors that Influence People's Lives, Politics Ranks at the Bottom." *Wall Street Journal*, 17 September 1998: A9.

Easterbrook, Greg. "America the O.K." *The New Republic*, January 4 and 11, 1999, 19-25.

Eddings, Jerelyn. "Counting a 'New' Type of American: The Dicey Politics of Creating a Multiracial Category in the Census." *U.S. News and World Report*, July 14, 1977:22-23.

Editorial. "The Return of Partisanship." *New York Times*, 13 October 2001.

Eilperin, Juliet, and Ellen Nakashima. "Security Bill Stalls in Congress House Leaders Reject Federalization of Baggage Screening." *Washington Post*, 13 October 2001: A06.

Elshtain, Jean B. *Who Are We? Critical Reflections and Hopeful Possibilities*. Grand Rapids, MI: William D. Eerdmans, 2000.

Escobar, G. "Immigrants' Ranks Tripled in 29 Years." *Washington Post*, 9 January, 1999:A01.

Evans, Howard. *The American Century*. New York: Alfred A. Knopf, 1998.

Feagan, Joe R. *Racist America*. New York: Routledge, 2000.

Fish, Stanley. "Boutique Multiculturalism," in Arthur M. Melzer, Jerry Weinberger, and M. Richard Zinman (eds), *Multiculturalism and American Democracy*. Lawrence: University of Kansas Press, 1998.

Gimpel, James G., and Karen Kaufmann. "Impossible Dream or Distant Reality? Republican Efforts to Attract Latino Voters." *Backgrounder*-Center for Immigration Studies, Washington, D.C, August 2001.

Glazer, Nathan. "Is Assimilation Dead?" *Annuals* 530, 1993: 122-136.

Goodstein, Laurie, "For Religious Right, Bush's Charity Plan is Raising concerns." *New York Times*, 3 March 2001.

Hacker, Andrew. *Two Nations in Black and White*. New York: Charles Scribner's Sons, 1995.

Harris, John F. "For Clinton's Last Act, Reviews Don't Look Good." *Washington Post*, 27 January 2001: A1.

Healy, M. "Latina Teens Defy Decline in Birth Rates." *Los Angeles Times*, 13 February 1998:A1.

Hillman, G. Robert. "Hispanic Caucus, Bush Talk Immigration Reform, Business Aide Pushed." *Dallas Morning News*, 3 April 2001.

Holmes, Steven A. "Down About the Count." *New York Times*, 9 April 2000: wk. 1.

_____. "Hispanic Births in U.S. Put at Record High." *New York Times*, 13 February 1998: A15.

Howard, Philip K. *The Lost Art of Drawing the Line*. New York: Random House, 2001.

Hunter, James Davidson. *Cultural Wars: The Struggle to Define America*. New York: Basic Books, 1997.

_____. "Reflections on the Culture Wars Hypothesis," in James L. Nolan, Jr. (ed.), *The American Culture Wars: Current Contests and Future Prospects*. Charlottesville: University of Virginia Press, 1996.

Isbister, J. "Is America Too White?" in E. Sandman (compiler), *What, Then is the American, This New Man?*" Washington, DC: Center of Immigration Studies, 1998.

_____. *The Immigration Debate: Remaking America*. New York: Kurnarian Press, 1996.

Kazal, R. A. "Revisiting Assimilation: The Rise, Fall, and Reappraisal of a Concept in American History." *American Historical Review* 100, 2 (1995): 437-471.

Kessler, Glenn, and Juliet Eilperin. "GOP Forced Bush Change on Stimulus, Democrats Say Gephardt Cites 'Failures of Bipartisanship.'" *Washington Post*, 12 October 2001: A12.

Kunkle, Fredrick. "Painful Cases of Mistaken Identity Nation on Edge Turns Ugly for Some with Ties to Mideast, Central Asia." *Washington Post*, 3 October 2001: A08.

Ladd, Everett C. *The Ladd Report*. New York: Free Press, 1999.

Lancaster, John. "Anti-Terrorism Bill is Approved, Bush Cheers House's Quick Action, but Civil Liberties Advocates are Alarmed." *Washington Post*, 13 October 2001: A01.

Lane, Charles. "Calif. School's Sign Runs Afoul of ACLU\Group Finds 'God Bless America' Message 'Divisive,' Demands Its Removal." *Washington Post*, 12 October 2001: A06.

Lane, Robert E. "Interpersonal Relationships and Leadership in a 'Cold' Society." *Comparative Politics*, July (1978): 443-460.

Lasch, Christopher. *The Culture of Narcissism: American Life in an Age of Diminishing Expectations*. New York: Basic Books, 1979.

Lasswell, Harold D. "Political Constitution and Character." *Psychoanalysis and the Psychoanalytic Review* 46 (1959): 3-18.

Lawrence, Jill. "Behind Its United Front, Nation Divided as Ever." *USA Today*, 18 February 2002:A1.

Lerner, Michael. "The Case for Peace." *Time*, 1 October 2001.

Lewis, Anthony. "Accent the Positive." *New York Times,* 10 October 1997:A23.

Lowi, Theodore J. *The End of Liberalism: Ideology, Policy, and the Crisis of Public Authority*. New York: W. W. Norton & Co., 1969.

Maharidge, Dale. *The Coming White Minority: California's Eruptions and America's Future*. New York: Times Books, 1996.

Mallaby, Sebastian. "Victim of His Success." *Washington Post*, 18 September 2000: A19.

Marcuse, Herbert. "Repressive Tolerance," in Robert Paul Wolff, Barrington Moore, Jr., and Herbert Marcuse, *A Critique of Pure Tolerance*. Boston: Beacon, 1965.

Miller, John J. *The Unmaking of Americans: How Multiculturalism has Undermined America's Assimilation Ethic*. New York: Free Press, 1998.

Morin, Richard. "Back to the Sixties." *Washington Post Weekly Edition*, 23 August 1999: A34.

_____. "Poll Finds Wide Pessimism About Direction of Country." *Washington Post*, 29 August 1997:A01.

Morin, Richard, and Claudia Deane. "Poll: Americans' Trust in Government Grows Confidence in Government More Than Doubles Since April 2000." *Washington Post*, 28 September 2001.

Murray, Charles. "Americans Remain Wary of Washington." *Wall Street Journal,* 23 December 1997:A14.

Myrdal, Gunner. *An American Dilemma*. New York: Harper & Row, 1944[1964].

National Commission on Civic Renewal. The Index of National Civic Health. College Park: University of Maryland, 1999.

Nagourney, Adam, and Richard Perez-Pena, "In New York, a Sharp Attack Awaits McCain," *New York Times*, 2 March 2000:A1.

National Research Council. *The New Americans.* Washington, DC: National Academy Press, 1977.

Nieve, Evelyn. "The Nerves of a Nation Stretch from Coast to Coast." *New York Times*, 13 October 2001.

Norris, Pippa. "Does Television Erode Social Capital? A Reply to Putnam." *PS: Political Science and Politics*, 29 (1996): 474-480.

Nye, Jr., Joseph S. et al. (eds). *Why People Don't Trust Government.* Cambridge, MA: Harvard University Press, 1997.

Office of Management and Budget. "Guidance on Aggregation and Allocation of Data on Race for Use in Civil Rights Monitoring and Enforcement." *OMB Bulletin* No. 00-02, March 9, 2000.

Page, Clarence. "Look Who's 'Profiling' Now." *Washington Times*, September 5, 2001.

Patterson, Orlando. *The Ordeal of Integration.* Washington, DC: Civitas, 1997.

_____. "The Paradox of Integration." *The New Republic* 24, 1995: 24-27.

Porter, Eduardo. "Estimate of Illegal Immigrants Reaches As Many as 8.5 Million for Some Experts." *Wall Street Journal*, 14 August 2001.

Portes, Alexander, and Min Zhou. "Should Immigrants Assimilate?" *Public Interest* 116, Summer (1994):18-36.

Pew Research Center for the People and Press. "Technology Triumphs, Morality Falters." July 13, 1999.

Putnam, Robert. *Bowling Alone: The Collapse and Revival of American Community.* New York: Simon and Schuster, 2000.

_____. "Bowling Alone: America's Declining Social Capital." *Journal of Democracy* 6 (1995): 65-78.

Renshon, Stanley A. *Dual Citizenship and American National Identity.* Washington, DC: Center for Immigration Studies, 2001.

_____. "Political Leadership as Social Capital: Governing in a Divided National Culture." *Political Psychology* 21:1 (2000a):199-226.

_____. "American Character and National Identity: The Dilemmas of Cultural Diversity," in Stanley A. Renshon and John Duckitt (eds.), *Political Psychology: Cultural and Cross Cultural Foundations.* London: Macmillan, 2000b.

_____. *High Hopes: The Clinton Presidency and the Politics of Ambition.* New York: Routledge, 1998a.

_____. *The Psychological Assessment of Presidential Candidates.* New York: Routledge, 1998b.

Riesman, David. "Egocentrism: Is the American Character Changing?" *Encounter* 55 August/September (1980):19-28.

Riesman, David, with N. Glazer and R. Denny. *The Lonely Crowd: A Study of the Changing American Character.* New Haven, CT: Yale University Press, 1950.

Rodriguez, Cindy. "Latino Influx Boosts Number of US Immigrants to All-Time High," *Boston Globe*, 12 September 2000: A1.

Rose, Arnold. "Postscript-20 Years Later," in Gunnar Myrdal, *An American Dilemma.* New York: Harper and Row [1944]1964.

Rumbaut, Rubèn G. "Assimilation and Its Discontents: Between Rhetoric and Reality." *International Migration Review* 31, 4 (1977):923-960.

Salins, Peter J. *Assimilation American Style.* New York: Basic Books, 1977.

Samuelson, Robert J. "Stealth Power Brokers." *Washington Post*, 8 December 1999:A33.

Schlesinger, Jr., Arthur A. *The Disuniting of America: Reflections on a Multicultural Society.* New York: W.W. Norton & Co., 1992.

Seelye, Katherine Q. "Before a Hollywood Crowd, Democrats Lower the Volume." *New York Times*, 20 September 2000: A1.

_____. "Bush Promotes Energy Bill as Security Issue." *New York Times*, 12 October 2001.

Shapiro, Andrew L. *The Control Revolution: How the Internet is Putting Individuals in Charge and Changing the World We Know.* New York: BBS, 1999.

Sierra, Christine Maria, Teresa Carrillo, Louis DeSipio, and Michael Jones-Correa." Latino Immigration and Citizenship." *PS: Political Science and Politics*, 33:3 (2000):535-540.

Skerry, Peter. *Counting on the Census: Race, Group Identity and the Evasion of Politics.* Washington, DC: Bookings Institution, 2000.

_____. "Why Amnesty is the Wrong Way to Go." *Washington Post*, 12 August 2001: B01.

Sleven, Peter. "Violent Crime Down 10% in 1999," *Washington Post*, 28 August 2000:A02.

Smothers, Ronald. "G.O.P. Gains in South Spread to Local Level, *New York Times*, 7 April 1995:A16.

Sontag, Susan. "The Talk of the Town." *New Yorker*, 24 September 2001:32.

Stern, Christopher. "FTC Finds Hollywood Aims Violence at Kids." *Washington Post*, 11 September 2000:A01.

Sullivan, Andrew. "Life After Wartime: Lighten Up—the Culture Wars are Over." *New York Times Magazine*, 25 March 2001.

Sullivan, Kevin, and Mary Jordan. "Fox Seeks New Cooperative Era For N. America." *Washington Post Foreign Service*, 14 August 2000: A01.

Takaki, Ronald. *A Different Mirror: A History of Multicultural America*. Boston: Little Brown, 1993.

Thernstrom, Abigail, and Stephen Thernstrom. *America in Black and White: One Nation Indivisible.* New York: Simon and Schuster, 1997.

Thompson, Ginger. "U.S. and Mexico to Open Talks on Freer Migration for Workers." *New York Times*, 16 February 2001:A1.

_____. "Fox Urges Opening of U.S.-Mexican Border to Build New Partnership." *New York Times*, 14 August 2000:A1.

Tonner, Robin, and Neil A. Lewis. "Anti-terrorism Bill: Senate Bill on Surveillance Has Broad Support." *New York Times*, 12 October 2001.

U.S. Bureau of the Census. "Projections of the Population of the United States, by Age, Sex, and Race: 1992-2050." *Current Population Reports*. P-125-1092. Washington, DC: U.S. Government Printing Office, 1992.

_____. *Statistical Abstract of the United States*, 115th Edition. Washington, DC: U.S. Government Printing Office, 1995.

Verhovek, Sam Howe. "Republican Tide Brings New Look to Legislatures." *New York Times*, 12 November 1994: A1.

_____. "Once Appalled by Race Profiling, Many Find Themselves Doing It." *New York Times*, 23 September 2001.

Vobejda, Barbara, and P. Constable. "Hispanic Teens' Birth-rate Ranks 1st of Ethnic Groups." *Washington Post*, 13 February 1998: A10.

Wachtel, Paul. *The Poverty of Affluence*. New York: Basic Books, 1994.

Wayne, Stephen et al. *The Politics of American Government,* second edition. New York: St. Martin's Press, 1997.

Wilcox, Clyde. *The Latest American Revolution: The 1994 Elections and Their Implications for Governance*. New York: St. Martin's Press, 1995.

Williams, Rhys H. (ed.). *Culture Wars in American Politics: Critical Reviews of a Popular Myth.* New York: Aldine De Gruyter, 1997.

Wilson, John K. *The Myth of Political Correctness: The Conservative Attack on Higher Education*. Durham, NC: Duke University Press, 1995..

Wirthlin Report. "Mood of the Nation." August/September 1997:4.

Wolfe, Alan. "The Final Freedom, *Sunday New York Times Magazine*, March 18, 2001.

_____. *Moral Freedom*. New York: W.W. Norton & Co., 2001.

_____. *Marginalized in the Middle*. Chicago: University of Chicago Press, 1996.

_____. *One Nation After All*. Chicago: University of Chicago Press, 1998.

Wysoci, Jr., B. "Americans Decry Moral Decline." *Wall Street Journal*, 24 June 1999:A9.

Yankelovich, Daniel. *New Rules: Searching for Self-fulfillment in a World Turned Upside Down*. New York: Random House, 1981.

Zielbauer, Paul. "Cities Failing to Heed Call of the Census." *New York Times*, 21 April 2000:A1.

Part 2

American National Identity

2

What is American Identity?

Can we define what it means to be an American, not just in terms of the hyphen showing our ethnic origins, but in terms of the our primary allegiance to the values that America stands for and values we really live by?
— William J. Clinton, June 14, 1997

In 1783, the Frenchman J. H. St. John De Crevècoeur (Manning 1997: 43-44) asked the now famous question, "What, then, is the American, this new man?" His answer: "he is either a European, or a descendent of a European."[1] However, most of all he is, "an American, who, leaving behind all his ancient prejudices and manners receives new ones from the new mode of life he has embraced, the new government he obeys, and the new rank that he holds."

The key to this transformation, De Crevècoeur thought, was this "new mode of life." Where in Europe these families had no economic or social standing or hope to acquire either, in America they did. *Ubi panis ibi patria,* he quotes as the motto of new immigrants and sums up its transition thus: "From involuntary idleness, servile dependence, penury, and useless labor, he has passed to toils of a very different nature, rewarded by ample subsistence. This is an American" ([1783]1997: 44-45).

The key then to this "new man," the American, was opportunity and mobility, both economic and political. Freed from the steel ceilings of social class and the accidents of heredity, this new man was able to pursue his labors and his destiny, on "the basis of nature and *self interest*." And, as De Crevècoeur put it, "can it want a stronger allurement?" ([1783]1997: 44, emphasis in original).

De Crevècoeur's observations are notable for another, less remarked upon, reason. They anticipate by almost two hundred years Erik Erikson's psychocultural formulation of the intersection between identity and culture. "No ego can develop outside of the social process which offers workable prototypes and roles" (Erikson 1963: 412). Or, as Kenneth Hoover (1975: 122) put it in his examination of the implications of Erikson's theories for the politics of identity, "culture largely determines the materials available for identity formation."

De Crevècoeur was not the only observer to draw an early link between a new American identity and the circumstances of a "new mode of life." In 1893,

Frederick Jackson Turner asserted that the frontier was not only the engine of American social development, but that of American character as well. Moreover, he saw it as "the line of most rapid and effective Americanization." Why? Part of his reason lay in the "perennial rebirth," "fluidity," and "opportunity" associated with it. But equally important, he argued, was the effect of this environment on habits and patterns that the newly arrived brought with them:

> The wilderness masters the colonist. It finds him a European in dress, industry, tools, modes of travel, and thought. It takes him from the railway car and puts him in the birch canoe. It stripes off the garments of civilization and arrays him in the hunting shirt and moccasin. It puts him in a long cabin of the Cherokee and Iroquois....Before long, he has gone to planting Indian corn and plowing with a sharp stick....In short, the frontier is at first too strong for the man. He must accept the conditions it furnishes, or perish....Little by little he transforms the wilderness, but the outcome is not the old Europe....*The fact is that here is a new product that is American.*[2]

Appreciating the relationship between self and circumstance in the development of identity is helpful. However, it frames our focus, without answering our questions. Consider: What is identity?

The most famous and widely employed theory, Erikson's, tells us more about its development—his eight stages—than what it is. In one place, Erikson (1968: 211) defines ego identity as "that which consists of role images." Shortly thereafter, he defines self-identity as what "emerges from experiences in which temporarily confused selves are successfully reintegrated into an ensemble of roles which also secure social recognition." Elsewhere (1980: 160), he defines the term as, "the more or less actually obtained, but forever to be revised, sense of the self within social reality."

If this sounds somewhat vague, it is. Erikson himself recognized its ambiguity, commenting, "I have tried out the term identity...in many different connotations....Identity in its vaguest sense suggests...much of what has been called the self by a variety of workers." Kenneth Hoover (1975: 116), Erikson's explicator, sums up identity as the sense of "who we are which emerges from a mutual recognition of self and others."

This definition is fine as far as it goes, but the difficulty is that it doesn't go very far. It provides no guidance for example, in gauging the relative contributions of occupational, ethnic, racial, religious, and national identities to the development and consolidation of a personal identity. Nor does it tell us very much about the process through which people balance, much less integrate, "coherent individuation" and the state "of being on the way to becoming what other people, at their kindest, take one to be" (Erikson 1963: 35). Small wonder that Robert Coles has characterized the term as "the purist of clichés" (quoted in Gilles 1994: 3; see also Gleason 1983, and Handler 1994).

Perhaps it is. Still, it is a concept with enormous psychological and political resonance worldwide. The aspiration to freely develop personal and national aspirations appears to be independent of efforts by scholars to decipher Erikson's murky, but important term.

In Search of American National Character and Identity— Three Perspectives

Since America's beginnings as a country, Americans and those interested in them have made a virtual cottage industry of trying to understand themselves (Wilkinson 1988: 1). R. Wilkinson (1988: 9-12) identifies two reasons for this. One he calls "psychology writ large," the other American intellectualism. The first reflects the fact that as a large robust country, America produces more of everything, including analyses of itself. The second, more useful reason for such interest lies in the very nature of the country. It reflects a need to understand a diverse, dynamic country whose people, culture, and experiences defy neat categories.[3] As a result, in the two centuries since De Crevècoeur first asked his famous question, there has been no shortage of answers. Foreign visitors,[4] anthropologists (Mead 1943; Gorer 1948; Hsu 1972), psychologists (Wachtel 1983) , social writers/commentators (Whyte 1963; Lerner 1957), historians (Commager 1959; Potter 1954), sociologists (Lipset 1963; Inkeles 1997a, b),[5] and psychoanalysts (Erikson 1964)[6] have all provided prospective on what, then, is this new man, the American.

The answers to De Crevècoeur's question have been diverse, as have been the methods used to obtain them. In some respects this is not surprising. Why expect that the distinctive backgrounds, intellectual and experiential, that distinguish say, a de Tocqueville from an Erikson, or a De Crevècoeur from a Lipset might result in an identical core list of what it means to be an American? Moreover, there is no theoretical reason to expect that the core elements of what it means to be an American would remain static through the enormous and profound changes that have shaped this country during its two hundred plus years of experience. Indeed, if one is persuaded by the basic insight of the culture and personality school, the opposite is more theoretically accurate (cf., Potter 1954: 62-63).

Does an examination of American history suggest that some elements of national psychology or identity have endured? Are they recognized by scholars of diverse perspectives, thus adding to our confidence in their existence and possible relevance?[7] In a word, yes. And, these elements provide a point of departure for addressing the critical questions already raised about their contemporary viability and future usefulness [8] as a basis for organizing a diverse society.

American Character Traits

Before examining what, if anything, lies at the core of being American it is well to draw some basic distinctions. The first distinction is among terms that are often used as if they were, but are not, synonymous; sometimes in the same book. For example, Wilkinson's (1988) book is titled, *The Pursuit of American Character*, but one soon encounters the following (p. 3): "By 'social character' or 'American social character'"—these two terms apparently being interchangeable and synonymous with the plain old "American character" of the title—"I mean those traits of individual personality or attitude that the population shows more frequently or in different ways than other, compared populations do."

Numerous questions immediately arise. Why is "social" used as an adjective to modify character? Is not character a term with an intra-psychic referent? And, if this is true, isn't social character unconnected to "private" (internal) character elements an oxymoron? Are "traits of personality," and "traits of attitude" equivalent, and are either or both synonymous with character? They are not so considered in the psychology literature. [9] Many searches for American "character," social or otherwise, have borrowed the term, but not the theoretical foundations that support and ought to accompany it.

A trait is simply a personal(ity) element that is sufficiently anchored in an individual's psychology, through rewarded function and experience, to become a characteristic response to diverse circumstances. Assuming it is present, it ordinarily tells us something, but not much. Indeed, torn from its cultural and psychological contexts, a single traits tell us very little.

That is one reason that the trait approach to national character has a long, but troubled history. At one time, Bulgarians were noted for their "plodding endurance and taciturn energy," Italians for their "aesthetic aptitude," and Serbs for their "warm poetic temperament" [*sic*].[10] Even if these analogies were true, would they tell us very much? Not really, unless we were willing to make the implausible assumption that everything of importance about a particular national psychology could be summed up in one trait.

Moreover, as Potter (1954, 12) points out, trait theorists sometimes confound categories. Americans are thought to be optimistic (a trait of temperament), productive (a trait of character or behavior?), and prone to joining organized groups (a behavioral tendency derived presumably from an underlying psychological trait).[11] Wilkinson (1988: 71-74) finds the content of American character in its fears, not its traits. In the tension between individualism and community (see also Lipset 1954: 101-139), he posits four historically persistent and not always conscious concerns that define American character: dependency, selfishness, social and personal entropy, and the falling away from past virtue and promise.

However national character traits are defined, their use presumes their presence. However, how are we to tell if "American traits," however defined, show up "more frequently or in different ways than those in other compared populations do"?[12] Consider the American emphasis on achievement that observers as historically and professionally diverse as de Tocqueville, Mead, Gorer, Lipset, and McClelland have emphasized. Would the overall level of, or focus on, achievement in this country, assuming we had valid measures of these items, be significantly higher than in say, Japan, Hong Kong, or Germany? Assuming valid translation of the term for cross-cultural comparability, would the level be even higher than those "less developed" countries where life is hard and making ends meet, a full-time concern? It seems unlikely.

There is, finally, the confusion that can easily develop between a national character trait(s) and its possible origins in, or association with, other categorical groupings organized along political, ethnic, religious or class lines. For example, Americans, as David Potter (1954: 18) notes, "are said to be competitive, materialistic, and comfort loving." But these are also the characteristics of the American middle class, proportionally one of the largest in the world. So, is a nation being confounded with class, or is the former a legitimately considered reflection writ large of the latter?

American Character: Creed and Values

Many lists of American traits are really descriptions of the values or beliefs by which Americans do, or aspire to, live. Such elements are not merely abstract embodiments of national ideals, although they certainly are that to some extent. Rather, they serve as a moral and behavioral compass which helps to organize the energies of individuals. They operate as well, as principles that can be, and are invoked by organizations and institutions waging political and social struggles for the groups they represent.

The fact that some individuals or groups do not abide by them or that some are not even capable of doing so, does not lessen their power. Gunnar Myrdal (1964 [1944]), commenting on American race relations, underscored the discrepancy between the American creed—a commitment to equality—and the actual conditions of Americans of African decent in the country. He pinned his hopes for the future on the inability of Americans to continue to tolerate these discrepancies, as did leaders of the civil rights movement. When movement leaders chose to march in one of the South's most racist towns, they counted on his harsh response and the larger American discomfort at seeing any group of peaceful demonstrators attacked by dogs and high-pressure water hoses (Heifetz 1996). And, they were proven correct in doing so.

There is another, less appreciated way in which values and the ideals they incorporate influence the interplay between American culture and psychology. Their internalization by individuals, groups, and institutions have consequences. Their impact can be seen in parents, who internalize the American values of achievement in relation to mobility, and shape their children's experiences (and thus their psychologies) in ways consistent with their understanding of how best to achieve and actualize those values.

To the extent that children of parents with those commitments share them, their psychologies are shaped by their own choice to pursue these values as well. Of the many accessible developmental paths in societies in which wide choice is available and valued, the internalization of values provides direction and limits. The pursuit of values, therefore, is an engine of motivation that orients individuals and groups toward a particular set of experiences. And, in doing so, it facilitates the development of particular patterns of interior psychology in the culture generally.

A number of similar values and ideals have been noted repeatedly over time. De Crevècoeur noted the fundamentally liberating role of opportunity on ambition. One hundred and forty-five years later the psychoanalyst Karen Horney (1937) made that fact the center of her analysis of the "neurotic personality of our time."[13] In 1893 Fredrick Jackson Turner noted that pragmatism and self-reliance were required values for frontier living. Eight-nine years later the psychological anthropologist Francis L.K. Hsu wrote (1972: 248, italics in original):

What we need to see is that the contradictory American "values" noted by sociologists, psychologists and historians are but manifestations of one core value. The American core value in question is *self-reliance.*

In 1848, de Tocqueville pointed out the volatile mix of private acquisitiveness and public egalitarianism.[14] One hundred and fifteen years later, Lipset (1954: 110-122) was arguing that far from having changed toward "other-directedness," as Riesman (1950) had suggested, Americans were still trying to reconcile achievement and equality on one hand, and conformity and individualism on the other.

It would be an unusual analysis of American values, in any period, that did not include or allude to those values just noted. However, many lists aspired to comprehensiveness and, as a consequence, produced mixed results. Thus Coleman's (1941: 498) early list of "American traits" included a belief and faith in democracy, equality, freedom, associational activity, individual freedom, disregard of law-direct action, local government, practicality, prosperity, puritanism, religion, and conformity. Hsu (1972: 242) notes the list is contradictory (democracy and disregard of law?), and that no attempt is made to reconcile apparent contradictory values (eg., equality and freedom). To this one might add the question of why "local government," to name just one oddity in the list, appears to carry the same weight as democracy and equality. Some years after Coleman, Cuber and Harper (1948: 369) shorten that list but add their own curious values to the first rank (e.g., monogamous marriage and science).

Almost none of these lists attempted to weigh the relative significance of the items included. Those that did (Williams 1951: 441) distinguished different kinds or levels of values orientations.[15] However, aside from providing a range of value categories into which every conceivable aspect of a culture might be placed, even these hierarchical lists provide little help in determining which values are more central and which more peripheral to a culture. Nor do they provide any theoretical guidance of how, if at all, the different value categories are related to each other, or what relationship, if any, they have to

"American psychology." And so, in the end, lists of "American values" are just that, and not theories of either American identity or psychology.

Psycho-Cultural Perspectives on American National Character

The perceptions of early visitors and observers were not informed by any theoretical understanding of either character or culture. Those did not become available until the development of the "culture and personality" school, and its legacy—national character studies. The key insight of this school was the interrelationship of the social values that characterized a culture, the reflection of these values in culture's primary institutions, and the net effect of both on the psychology and development of those who grew up within its confines.

For Margaret Mead (1942; see also Gorer 1948) a major key to understanding American character was in its emphasis on success--a double reflection on mobility. Americans could, were expected to, and expected themselves to make every effort to take advantage of the opportunities enshrined as cultural ideals and for many, though not all, actual fact. Success was measured by mobility—the distance between start and finish—or in a word, achievement.

Following Sigmund Freud, "culture and personality" theorists saw the family as the primary institution of American cultural and psychological preparation. It both prepared children for the culture into which they were born and in doing so, reflected in themselves the internalization of the culture's predominant values. Unfortunately, American culture provides no specific formulas as to how this might be accomplished other than general admonitions to work hard, do your best, and so on. So, mobility has been, and remains, infused with anxiety (the exact point made by de Tocqueville earlier).

This leads, according to Horney (1937: 14-33), to "compulsive competitiveness," and its emotional siblings, interpersonal aggressiveness and hostility. At the same time, the competitive life is a lonely one. Intimacy and competition are difficult to reconcile, another point made as well by de Tocqueville earlier. Horney notes that competition and conflict are accompanied by fear—of failure and of others. These fears weaken self-esteem and, as a result, the "neurotic" craves love.

These patterns are fueled, in part, by parents' concern for their children's success. As a result, parents tend to reward their children's performance not their existence. Given these circumstances, it is difficult for children to develop an inner-anchor for their own self-identities. Rather they are oriented in substantial part towards others—their parents, their peers, their teachers, who provide them with conditional cues of their success. In short, more than a decade before David Riesman brought the phrase "other-directed" into our analytic vocabularies, anthropologists (Mead)[16] and psychoanalysts (Horney), belonging to the "culture and personality" school, observed and documented the same feature in the unfolding circumstances of the interplay between American culture and psychology. Whether this reflected a turn from individualism, or one further reflection of it, is a key question that I will take up in the following section.

One of the key insights of early visitors to America was the extent to which the physical and psychological circumstances in which settlers found themselves shaped responses that were necessary for success. These, in turn, were instrumental in shaping the development of a particular American psychology. That interplay between external circumstances and the development and maintenance of patterns of interior psychology was, as noted, a foundation of the "culture and personality" school. So, the question naturally arises: If circumstances change, will patterns of American psychology do so was well?

The social scientist most associated with the affirmative answer to this profound question is Riesman (1950, 1951; see also Whyte 1956). Yet, as noted above, Mead and Horney had laid the theoretical basis for expecting some conformity in American psychology two decades earlier.[17] In fact, that tendency was part of very early observations of this country and its people. James Bryce (1912, quoted in Almond 1950: 35-36, italics mine) observing the power of "majority opinion" wrote that it was

> absolute, unquestioned and invoked to decide every question....Out of the dogma that the views of the majority must prevail...grows up another...that the majority is always right... *Thus, out of mingled feelings that the multitude, because it will prevail, must be right, there grows a self-distrust...a disposition to fall into line, to acquiesce in the dominant opinion, to submit thought as well as action to encompassing powers of the numbers.*

It is often not appreciated that Riesman's "other-directed" and "inner directed" are two of three forms of *conformity*. In Riesman's theory, the "inner-directed" person has simply internalized general social precepts in a society in which population and economic changes have made learning detailed social customs ("tradition directed" psychologies) too complex and cumbersome to teach individually and maintain. Such persons, of course, stand against elements of the community, but the point was that they were not often required to do so.

Internalizing the generalized standards of a community worked well, but only if those standards were relatively stable. If not, the skill most needed, and rewarded, was the ability to ascertain just what standards were expected and adapt accordingly. Riesman's postwar America was a society characterized by large-scale social and economic changes. It was also one in which these changes coincided with the development of large-scale social institutions in which efficient performance depended on teamwork. In such circumstances, being "other-directed" was an economic asset, as well as a socially valued skill and personality trait.

It is not as great a psychological distance, as it might seem at first, from Riesman's "other-directed" character to Christopher Lasch's (1979) culture of narcissism. In Riesman's "other directed" character the extensive veneer of sociability became a well-refined tool for "making it." Achievement was still paramount, and competition continues unabated, but now success is achieved in group settings, by fitting in—not by self-reliance. Autonomous thinking, or an independent sense of personal values and ideals to which one is able and willing to give primacy, or at least fidelity, generally a minority position historically, becomes a cause for others' concern, not admiration. Small wonder that Arthur Miller's Willy Loman proved a more accurate fictional representative of his time than Ayn Rand's Ned Rorak.

The lack of any firmly established internal psychological compass makes people vulnerable to the temptations of increasing abundance and repeated messages that delayed consumption is unnecessary and perhaps even odd. In the past, Lasch noted, the American penchant for self-improvement had been associated with achieving something solid and lasting. However, in an age that promised "you could have it all," or advised you to "be all that you can be," and some professional psychologists touted "self-actualization" as the North Star of psychological development, enticing images of endless and easy satisfaction trumped the hard work of building a satisfying life.[18] Consumption might well fuel an economy, but an increasing emphasis on "self-fulfillment"[19] could not quiet increasing feelings of emptiness, isolation, and dissatisfaction.

Lasch, writing in the aftermath of the "me" and "now" generations,[20] viewed American private and public life as increasingly dominated by ambitiously aggressive and self-centered individuals, a culture of selfish individualism. Riesman (1980) agreed, and while finding evidence of narcissistic elements elsewhere in American history, he nonetheless thought that what was different now was the public acceptance and even "approval" of clearly "self-serving conduct." It is not so far from Riesman's 1980 observation to the extraordinarily high approval ratings, primarily related to a booming economy, of an impeached and disgraced president.[21]

American Identity and Psychology: A Psycho-Cultural Amalgam

We are now in a better position to take up the question in the title of this chapter. Many Americans think of our democratic ideals as the cement that binds American national identity. And there is much truth in this assertion. Lipset is right when he calls attention to the historical persistence of these ideals. However, Riesman and Lasch are also correct in pointing out that the old ideals have changed. How can both be right?

A basic flaw of the values ideals approach to American national identity is not that values don't carry much actual behavioral or psychology weight. They do. However, most advocates of this approach have never really addressed the issue of how the highly abstract ideals they find embedded in American history and culture actually serve as a framework for psychological development and behavior at the level of the actual lives that people lead.

Some theorists of American values discuss these values as if they were independent and unitary—the ideal of democracy, the ideal of equality, and so on. Others have focused on the conflict between values, a commitment to achievement for example, being at odds with a commitment to equality. However, it seems more useful to focus on *clusters* of national ideals, if, as in the United States, this focus can be substantively supported. Viewed not as discrete, isolated entities, but as integrated cultural packages it would then be easier to distinguish one national cultural cluster "package" from another. It would also be easier to understand how such packages can both remain constant and change. And finally, it would be possible to more easily discern how a particular national psychology or "character" might develop in relation to a particular "package" of national ideals.

National Cultural Clusters

What then is a *national cultural cluster*? Quite simply, it is the specific sets of a country's core cultural value ideals. The origins of American national culture clusters can be traced to the twin motivations behind the establishment of the first colonies, economic and social *opportunity* on one hand and religious and political *freedom* on the other. Yet, while it is accurate to single out these values as primary motives, it would be an error to view them as isolated and discrete ends in themselves.

Freedom and opportunity came together in a particular way in the religious colonies, but in quite another manner in those searching for economic advancement, not religious freedom. Moreover, in neither was freedom or opportunity an isolated, absolute value. In the case of religious freedom, it was embedded in a community context, and in the case of economic opportunity, it coexisted with a strong belief in public, social, and political equality. In short, both freedoms (economic and political) were embedded in communities. Both religious and economically based freedom seekers confronted the issue of finding ways to live with others whose interests and motivations differed.

The third major value ideal that defines the American culture cluster grew out of the circumstances in which the other two were played out—a land rich in promise but short, at first, in the ordinary and routine. The physical realities of frontier conditions required from those living there a psychology of courage, independence, and self-reliance. However, these people were not hermits. After all, Natty Bumppo (Hawkeye) had Uncas and his father Chingachgook; and even that cultural icon of righteous individualism, the Lone Ranger had Tonto. Here we can see the third major continuum of the set that forms the American culture cluster—that of independence/self-reliance and interdependence.

So, we can now distinguish the following three core elements of the American culture cluster:

freedom for personal ambition<——>communities of others

achievement/excellence<——>social/political equality

independence/self-reliance<——>dependency

National culture clusters, then, are defined by the unique composite of specific value ideals central to a society, the relationship of these cluster elements to each other, and the range and specific location on each of the core value ideal continuum. No society has a monopoly on any particular ideal or value. For example, most societies must grapple with the dilemmas of interpersonal dependence and independence. However, a society that prizes independence and couples that with an emphasis on personal and political freedom will develop quite differently than one in which community is given precedence over both.

American Culture Clusters and National Psychology—The Role of Culture Codes

National culture clusters tell us what a society says it values. Yet cultures serious about what they value embed them in their institutions and practices. Their political, educational, and family institutions are charged with the responsibility of translating these abstract precepts—equality, freedom, and so on—into rules and understandings which can serve as a reliable guide to living in that society. Put another way, every culture must provide mechanisms for translating its ideals into real life.

The understandings of how to translate these abstractions into concrete life rules, I term *culture codes*. These codes tell a culture's members how to bridge the gap between ideals and practice. They are not "scripts," which reflect more precise rules of behavior and sequence. Rather, they are embodied, not always formally, in a culture's institutions. And they are also embedded in a culture's "folk knowledge" or cultural narratives—a term which covers stories constructed for a cultural purpose.

Consider the continuum of achievement/excellence<——>social/political equality. How can a society honor both excellence in achievement and equality? Equality of opportunity is one answer, and separating the sphere of achievement from the sphere of equality expected in general social circumstances is another.

But cultural codes tell more than how to understand and resolve the dilemmas that might appear in a culture's organizing ideals. They also provide culture's proscriptions for how to achieve its goals. Want to succeed? Put your shoulder to the wheel, or your nose to the grindstone. However, if at first you don't succeed, try, try again. And remember, the early bird gets the worm.

It is, I think, easily seen that changes in the national core cultural values are not likely to take place at the level of the elements themselves. Thus, in this respect Lipset is correct. However, change, sometimes profound change, can and does occur at the level of cultural codes that guide practice and institutions. Riesman and Lasch are correct as well.

It is also quite clear that national core cultural values and codes both reflect and facilitate patterns of national psychology. Consider just one of a highly complex set of relations among the core American culture elements and historical changes in their related cultural codes. As noted, early observers were united in the observation that "this new man,"—the American—was motivated by the desire to do what had not been possible in his country of origin. That was to make use of his talents in the service of his ambitions to improve the material (and social) circumstances of his life.

A primary goal of achievement was to acquire wealth, and the social and political freedom to do so was what made that possible. But at the same time, no man was deemed better than any other—the ethic of "democratic egalitarianism" (Lipset 1954: 123). And there was no real standard of achievement's success but wealth. In those circumstances, opportunity was bound to lead to competition and anxiety, as both de Tocqueville and Horney emphasized.

Lipset (1954: 113) argues that there is ample historical evidence of "other-directedness" which, following the lead of then contemporary commentators, he attributes to the lack of a formal American class structure. According to this theory, having no agreed-upon standards by which to judge their place, Americans were forever turning their attention outward. In short, their status anxiety made them anxious and "other directed."

However, the observations of observers are not by themselves direct evidence that status insecurity is at the root of whatever turn toward others might be evident. While status anxiety *might* lead to conformity, it can as easily lead to its opposite. Acute status anxiety coupled with intense competition for both success *and* status might lead one to try to distinguish oneself from others, not be part of the group. We might also ask why men used to making their own way, by their own means, might wish to be accepted by others, with whom they might well be in competition, at any price. Moreover, there remains the problem of why in a country devoid of widely accepted status symbols, except for wealth and its display, wealth itself did not qualify as more than enough indication that one had succeeded. It certainly must have for those who subscribed to the Protestant ethic.

The choice, of course, is not between material and structure changes in the circumstances of competition as Riesman argued, or the unchanging conflict between equality and achievement and the resulting conformity that Lipset emphasizes. Even assuming the causal link which Lipset argues between value conflict and conformity, there is no reason why changes in "material" circumstances wouldn't bring a corresponding change in the nature of the relation among the three. It represents a real change of psychological circumstances when increasing financial security and the mass production of an increasingly large number of symbols of success become more widely available though most strata of American society.

Multiple American Cultures = Multiple American Psychologies?

America's basic cultural ideals and values, like those of any country, are embedded and embodied in institutional norms and practices. Institutions primarily led, made up of, or responsive to individuals with "counter-cultural," or "self-fulfillment" ideals and values will operate very differently than those with a more traditional focus. Moreover, they also operate very differently than those with a *unified* set of value missions and practices.

Here is the core dilemma of Western democratic multicultural societies. They arrived at their present state of political, economic, and social development by providing abundant opportunity for mobility. They leveraged personal ambitions as a tool to transform individuals' social and economic circumstances. In the process, they helped develop and reinforced psychological elements that were consistent with what most considered "success." That is, an emphasis on consistency, hard work, delay of immediate gratification, and considering the consequences of one's actions or inactions.

These are, of course, the characteristics of the "Protestant ethic." However, over time, this ethic became divorced from its religious origins. Successive waves of immigrants—Irish, Hispanic, Asian, not all of them Protestant by any means—found a place by accepting and building on what then truly became a national American cultural elements. In fostering these values in the home, at school, and in occupational networks these groups not only reinforced these "traditional" American cultural elements, and the codes that supported them, but furthered the psychology that sustained them. It is in this direct way that national cultural cluster elements and national psychology are related.

Five Contemporary American Cultural Clusters and Their Associated Psychologies

It seems quite clear that almost all the elements of the American cultural cluster, have been altered by challenges to the understanding of what these elements mean, how they are to be accomplished, and how much weight is to be given to one or another element. Freedom for personal ambition, for example, which traditionally had to be reconciled with the values of community, must do so to a substantially smaller degree when the most weight is accorded to "doing your own thing." Independence and the tendency to stand apart from others has traditionally had to be reconciled with the pleasures of attachment, and raised the possibility of conformity. However, independence and self-reliance rest on a strong sense of personal identity and confidence in the personal skills that support them. However, when occupational identity trumps its intra-psychic foundation, and success in the former rests on "good interpersonal skills," individuals are more vulnerable to the evaluations and value of others. And, of course, the view that getting all that you want, when you want it, is the definition of a fully realized life, leaves little room to worry about others except as they further or impede your desires.

Finally, these changes can be seen in the cultural ideal of achievement and the cultural code of excellence and the persistent hard work to refine it. Traditionally, this ideal had to be reconciled with the value of social and political equality. As noted, this tension was addressed by making achievement and the assumption of equality somewhat independent of each other. One did not need to achieve in order to be accounted public equality. Nor did public equality require fast runners to race slowly, or smart businessmen to lose money.

De Tocqueville and others worried that the tendency to value equality over excellence would lead to mediocrity. Some modern critics equate any focus on excellence with "elitism." In truth, as Lipset (1954) points out, there has always been a tension between those willing and able to reach excellence and high achievement in their pursuits and the push to make every one equal. Resolution of these issues has become more complex and conflictual in a society in which "live and let live" and "Thou shalt not judge" vie for primacy in the cultural code. Diverse cultures further complicate these issues.

If every life-style has equal value and weight, how can we not accord parity to any person's or groups' choices? If "self-fulfillment" is the goal of achievement, of what use are traditional concerns with, and measurement of, excellence? And on what basis do we deny anyone the fruits of social equality when they fail to measure up to constructed and thus "artificial" standards. Questions like this lead to the paradox of "social promotion" policies in many major American school systems which pass children on to the next grade who cannot read, write, or do math at anywhere near their grade level.

If every disparity between individuals or groups is suspect, how can we object to decades of government-sponsored programs that reward group membership as much as or more than actual individual performance? If the full weight of vast federal, state, and local resources is placed behind mandated results rather than developing opportunity, isn't that simply a new and more democratic definition of opportunity?

These and many similar questions are at the heart of America's "culture wars." However, these wars are not solely fights between "left and "right," or "liberals" and "conservatives." There are at least five different groups in American society that are united or separated by their understanding of the relative weight to be given to each of the elements in the American cultural cluster and to their accompanying cultural codes.

There are *traditional achievers* whose cultural value views would be roughly consistent with an emphasis on freedom defined as self-interest in the pursuit of excellence and achievement. As a group, they are highly competitive, supportive of traditional culture codes that define ambition and success, and able to join up with others in pursuit of their social, economic, and political self-interest.

The *conforming achievers* are those with some commitment to traditional norms of accomplishment, but see the vehicle of their success as their skills with others. Not likely to value standing out or standing alone, their motto for achievement (to get along, go along) parallels their stance toward contentious cultural issues (live and let live).

The *self-fulfillment achievers* value accomplishment in principle, but only if it directly and immediately provides tangible personal benefit. Whether that comes in the form of self-enlightenment or self-aggrandizement, the motives are similar. In terms of contentious political or social issues, they are either tolerant or contemptuous. The first often reflects the wish to be left alone to pursue one's own interests without having to make judgments which might lead others to judge them (judge not lest ye be judged). The second comes from a supreme confidence in one's own views and values and a corresponding downgrading of those who don't agree.

The *cultural dissenters* may either be high or low achievers. They are found in the highest levels of some professions as well as at the bottom of the social ladder. These seemingly disparate groups are united by the view that current cultural values and codes must be substantially modified, if not replaced. The more cerebral of them are convinced that freedom for personal ambition is antithetical to community, excellence in achievement is subversive of equality, and independent self-reliance a mask for selfishness. The less intellectually inclined simply have no patience, aptitude, or hope to succeed as this culture has traditionally been structured, but want the enjoyment of its benefits nonetheless. They have strong convictions about all these matters. Paradoxically, while very tolerant of claims for parity and even primacy of many counterculture initiatives, their cultural flexibility, like that of some self-fulfillment achievers, is not easily extended to those with whom they disagree.

Finally, there are the *principled individualists*. This is probably by far the smallest American cultural group. It is composed of people with a commitment to pursuing excellence in their achievements but within a context of understanding that others and community count. They are capable of being self-reliant, but can as easily be comfortable with attachment and commitment, though on their own terms. They can stand apart from others if they have to, or move against them if they must, and so are not overly reliant on, or separate from, others. In matters of judgment they come to their own views and are willing to stand on them, even if it means standing out or standing apart.

American Culture and Psychology: Fragmentation or a New Synthesis?

American multicultural democracy is populated by groups with very different understandings (codes) of the major values that have historically served to integrate divergent ethnic groups. What is different now is the existence and institutionalization of organizations that are culturally "oppositional," as well as the placement of "cultural dissidents" in major leadership roles in what have been "traditional" institutions.

Institutions are not only the targets of different views of how America should culturally proceed, they are also a source of the very same tensions. America is split by political, but more basically by cultural cleavages, and these in turn are a byproduct of distinctive psychological groups.

"Traditional achievers" are a potential source of support for traditional cultural values, if they can take time out from the pursuit of their own self-interest. "Conforming," and "self-fulfillment achievers" have combined a commitment to "do your own thing" with a "live and let live" philosophy. As a result they are hardly stalwart defenders of traditional values, or indeed anything that might prove controversial. In the meantime, those with strong conviction about reversing traditional American value clusters have the benefit of their certainty, and others' timidity and self-preoccupation. Only the "principled individualists" have the strength of conviction and the capacity to take unpopular cultural stands in defense of some traditions. However, they are used to being individual not movement voices.

Abraham Lincoln, speaking to the prospect of a country "half free and half slave," said, "a country divided against itself cannot stand." He was, of course, referring as much to American culture as to its politics. Whether his insight proves prophetic has become a very troubling contemporary question.

Notes

1. De Crevècoeur's question and its answer, "have probably been quoted more than any other in the history of immigration (Gleason 1980: 31). The reason, Nathan Glazer (1993: 22) remarks, is that it appears to celebrate America's diversity and its role in forging a new national identity. Yet, modern sensibilities alert us to the fact that Indians, women, and blacks are not included in this understanding.

2. The above quotes are all taken from Turner's original presentation, "The Significance of the Frontier in American History," ([1893]1996, chapter 1, emphasis added). Similarly, Erikson (1963, 293) views the frontier as "the decisive influence which served to establish in the American identity the extreme polarization which characterizes it." Here he is referring to the need to prepare children to live in the community life which was taking root, but as well to be able to endure the physical hardships of homesteading on the frontiers. Potter (1954: 68) makes use of the term frontier in a more psychological sense and relates it to consumption and abundance.

3. Wilkinson mentions, but does not agree with, what seems the most likely explanation of this national self-concern, namely that as a country of immigrants we are more likely to be concerned with who we are as a nation, and how the many can become one (cf., Potter 1954).

4. Citations for the views of foreign visitors are found in Lipset (1963) and Inkeles (1997). These include De Crevècoeur ([1783] 1997), de Tocqueville ([1848]1998), Martineau (1837), Berger (1943), Brooks (1908), and Bryce (1912). Lipset uses the observations of Martineau and Bryce to suggest that the elements of "other-directedness" emphasized by Riesman (1950) and Whyte (1956) were, in fact, present in the earliest periods of American history. However, Inkeles (1997: 164) notes that many foreign observers reached contradictory conclusions about "this new man, the American."

5. See Inkeles' "Continuity and Change in American National Character" (1997: 161-192) and "National Character Revisited" (1997: 359-384). Both are reprinted in Inkeles (1997).

6. See his "Reflections on American Identity" (1964: 285-325).
7. A similar argument for this criteria of relevance is made by Almond (1954: 47).
8. As Thomas Sowell (1994:4-6) points out, the effectiveness of a particular cultural element or elements can only be judged in relationship to their purpose(s) and effects. We are, he notes, understandably repulsed at the idea of labeling any peoples or culture "superior," or "inferior." Yet, he also underscores a paradox contained in a wholesale reluctance to make any judgments: some cultural elements do work better. For example, the world, including the Romans, adapted Arabic numerals even though Roman rule was supreme, simply because they made calculations immensely easier.
9. There, the term character is understood as a related set of psychological elements with long developmental histories which form the foundations of, and operate across, personality structures. As Francis Baudry (1989: 656) puts it, "Our concept of character is made necessary because we find in individuals reoccurring clusters of traits with a consistency suggesting that some underlying principles, govern the selection, ordering, and relations of these traits to one another." Thus, Fenichel's (1945: 463-540) early formulation of "compulsive character" was built on the clinical findings that orderliness, stubbornness, and parsimony were dynamically united by the anxiety caused by the fear of loss of control.

    Attitudes can best be described as stable orientations toward object classes. One has an opinion about the Gulf or Korean war, but an attitude toward war itself (cf., Bem (1970: 14, or Fishbein and Ajzen 1975: 336).

    And, Greenstein's (1969: 23) lament about the large number of diverse formulations of "personality" awaiting political scientists, and others, hoping to make use of the concept is correct. However, it is extremely rare to equate attitude with personality. The "functional theory" of attitudes (Smith 1968) does, but in such an abstract way that it is virtually content free. For these reasons, equating character with personality, or worse, attitude is a categorical mistake. The psychological force, durability, and behavioral significance of the former is not matched by the latter.
10. Carleton H.J. Hayes cited in Potter (1954: 12-13). Potter refers to this approach as "a cabinet of curiosities."
11. Of course, there is no reason why any "national character," to the extent it exists, cannot consist of different kinds of psychological elements. What is necessary, however, is some recognition that the elements are not dynamically or functionally equivalent. Moreover, some attention to the psychological connections between, or among, them would also seem a necessary theoretical undertaking.
12. Wilkinson suggests that any discussion of "American traits" be undertaken in comparison only to their appearance, or lack thereof, in other equivalent populations. He suggests (1988: 3) the comparison standard be with people in "other modern industrial countries." But this is rarely, if ever, done.
13. Horney's book, entitled, *The Neurotic Personality of our Time*, is a reflection on American culture and psychology more generally than it is work focused on "clinical populations."
14. For de Tocqueville, they both sprang from the same source, the anxiety brought on by unrestrained competitiveness. To this he might well have added the volatile psychological paradox of Americans' conscientious adherence to public (and political) equality, even while devoting themselves wholeheartedly, some would say relentlessly, to their own self interest primarily reflected in the pursuit of the accumulation of wealth and the social standing that accompanied it.

    In a similar vein, Hsu (1972: 245-249, 251) argues that the ideal of unlimited equality and self-reliance, and the inability to measure up psychologically to its demands results in a tendency to embrace its opposite, in this case conformity.

15.   For example, his list includes: "quasi-values" such as material comforts; "instrumental" values such as power, work and efficiency; "universalistic values of the Western tradition" such as rationalism, justice freedom, universalistic ethics (?) and values of individual personality; and finally "particularistic, segmental, or localistic" values.

For a somewhat different approach to values as resolving "basic human problems" to which solutions must be found see Kluckhohn (1953: 246). In her analysis, these problems include: the basic nature of man, man's relation to nature, time orientations, valued personality types, and the relationship of men to each other.

There are numerous other approaches to values. For example Rokeach (1979) distinguishes between instrumental and terminal values, that is those you aspire to get to, and those that help you do so.

16.   A second key element of Mead's analysis, the fact of being a "nation of immigrants," also reinforced "conformity." Many "third generation" children of immigrants, she argued, turned their backs on their traditions of origin. As a result, parental authority was downgraded at the expense of those persons and institutions that provided much sought after cues for "fitting in." In short, the desire to belong coupled with a lack of reliable parental guides of how to do it, lead outward and elsewhere.

17.   David Potter (1962) argued for two American egalitarian traditions, one which stressed equal opportunity, the other in public domains where, regardless of measures of social standing, people expected to receive equal social deference. The latter encouraged sensitivity to others and thus an element of "other-directedness."

18.   The best book on the seductive psychology of the image and the public's role in encouraging it is still Boorstin (1992[1961]).

19.   Daniel Yankelovich's national opinion data on the growing emphasis on self-fulfillment in American culture led him (1981: xix) to conclude that, "it was not a by-product of affluence, or a shift in the national character toward narcissism, [but rather] a search for a new American philosophy of life." Of course, "philosophies of life" are themselves reflections of values and psychology and, as noted, help to facilitate the very psychologies that will buttress them.

Optimistically, Yankelovich saw (1981: 259-260) Americans growing "less self-absorbed and more prepared to take a first step toward an ethic of commitment." However, he also noted that the development of such an ethic would require direct support from "the larger society—political leadership, the mass media, institutional leadership (business, education, labor, artists and scientists, the intellectual community," in short, for the most part all the groups caught up in the ethic of relentless self-interest. Small wonder that seventeen years later, Nicholas Lehmann (1998: 38) writing in the *New York Times Sunday Magazine* lamented a new consensus which "represents an embrace of...one-way libertarianism: the average citizen has no obligation to the country, but the government has a very serious obligation to that citizen."

20.   Interestingly, as early as the 1940s psychoanalysts reported treating persons who "appeared on casual inspection as successful members of the community, as able lawyers, executives, and physicians, [but] they did not, it seems, succeed in the sense of finding satisfaction or fulfillment in their accomplishments." William Cleckely, among the first to notice this group, entitled his study, *The Mask of Sanity* (1976), reflecting the then anomalous finding that there were persons who appeared to be functioning well, even very well on a surface, conventional level, but who were seen on closer clinical observation to have areas of deep psychological disturbance which manifested itself in unstable behavior. Among the symptoms of those who would be later classified as "narcissistic" was a surface adherence to conventional moral norms, coupled with a willingness to exploit others and circumstances for their own benefit. Guilt (Riesman's other-directed super ego) seemed largely absent.

21.   An analysis of President William Clinton's high public approval ratings in the aftermath of the revelations that led to his impeachment are found elsewhere in this book.

References

Almond, Gabriel. *The American People and Foreign Policy.* New York: Praeger, 1950.

Baudry, Francis. "Character, Character Type, and Character Organization," *Journal of the American Psychoanalytic Association* 32 (1989):455-77.

Bem, Daryl J. *Beliefs, Attitudes and Human Affairs.* Belmont, CA: Brooks/Cole, 1970.

Berger, M. *The British Traveler in America, 1836-1860.* New York: Columbia University Press, 1943.

Boorstin, Daniel J. *The image: A Guide to Pseudo Events in America.* New York: Vintage Press [1961], 1992.

Brooks, J. G. *As Others See Us.* New York: Macmillan, 1908.

Bryce, James. *The American Commonwealth.* New York: Macmillan, 1912.

Cleckely, William. *The Mask of Sanity. 5th edition.* St. Louis, MO: C.V. Mosby [1941], 1976.

Clinton, William J. "Remarks at the University of California at San Diego Commencement Ceremony" (June 14 1997). *Weekly Compilation of Presidential Documents*, 23, June, 33:25 (1997), 877.

Coleman, Lee. "What is American: A Study of Alleged Social Traits." *Social Forces* 19:4 (1941).

Commager, Henry S. *The American Mind: An interpretation of American thought.* New Haven, CT: Yale University Press, 1959.

Cuber, J. F., and R. A. Harper. *Problems of American Society: Values in Conflict.* New York: Henry Holt, 1948.

De Crevècoeur, J. Hector St. John. [Susan Manning, editor]. *Letters from an American Farmer.* New York: Oxford University Press [1783], 1997.

Erikson, Erik H. *Childhood and Society.* 2nd. edition, revised. New York: W. W. Norton & Co., 1963.

_____. *Identity: Youth and Crisis.* New York: W. W. Norton & Co., 1968.

_____. *Identity and the Life Cycle.* New York: W. W. Norton & Co., 1980.

Fenichel, Otto. *The Psychoanalytic Theory of Neurosis.* New York: W. W. Norton & Co., 1945.

Fishbein, Martin, and Icek Ajzen. *Belief, Attitude, Intention and Behavior: An Introduction to Theory and Research.* Reading, MA: Addison-Wesley 1975.

Glazer, Nathan. "Is Assimilation Dead?" in Arthur M. Melzer, Jerry Weinberger, and M. Richard Zinman (eds.) *Multiculturalism and American Democracy.* Lawrence: University of Kansas Press, 1998.

Gilles, John R. "Introduction," in J. R. Giles (ed.) *Commemorations: The Politics of National Identity.* Princeton, NJ: Princeton University Press, 1994.

Gleason, Paul. "American Identity and Americanization," in Stephen Thernstrom (ed.) *Harvard Encyclopedia of American Ethnic Groups.* Cambridge, MA: Harvard University Press, 1980.

Gorer, Geoffrey. *The American People: A Study in National Character.* New York: W. W. Norton & Co., 1948.

Greenstein, Fred I. *Personality and Politics: Problems of Evidence, Inference, and Conceptualization.* Princeton, NJ: Princeton University Press, 1969.

Handler, Richard. "Is 'Identity' a Useful Cross-cultural Concept?" in J. R. Giles (ed.) *Commemorations: The Politics of National Identity.* Princeton, NJ: Princeton University Press, 1994.

Heifetz, Ronald. *Leadership without Easy Answers*. Cambridge, MA: Harvard University Press, 1996.

Hoover, Kenneth. *The Politics of Identity*. Urbana: The University of Illinois Press, 1975.

Horney, Karen. *The Neurotic Personality of our Time*. New York: W. W. Norton & Co., 1937.

Hsu, Francis L. K. "American Core Values and National Character," in Francis L.K. Hsu (ed.) *Psychological Anthropology*. Cambridge, MA: Schenkman Publishing, 1972.

Inkeles, Alex. *National character: A Psycho-social Perspective*. New Brunswick, NJ: Transaction Publishers, 1997.

Kluckhohn, Florence. "Dominant and Variant Value Orientations," in Clyde Kluckhohn and Henry Murray (eds.) *Personality in Nature, Society and Culture*. New York: Alfred A. Knopf, 1953.

Kluckhohn, Florence, and Arthur Strodtbeck. *Variations in value orientations*. Evanston, IL: Row Petterson and Co, 1961.

Lasch, Christopher. *The Culture of Narcissism: American Life in an Age of Diminishing Expectations*. New York: Basic Books, 1979.

Lehmann, Nicholas. "The New American Consensus: Government of, by, and for the Comfortable." *New York Times Sunday Magazine*, November 1, 1998:37-42, 68-70.

Lerner, Daniel. *America as a Civilization*. New York: Simon and Schuster, 1957.

Lipset, Seymour M. *The First New Nation*. New York: Basic Books, 1963.

Martineau, Henry. *Society in America*. New York: Saunders and Otlay, 1837.

Mead, Margaret. *And Keep Your Powder Dry*. New York: William Morrow & Co., 1942.

Myrdal, Gunnar. *An American Dilemma*. New York: Harper and Row, [1944] 1964.

Potter, David M. "The Quest for the National Character," in John Higgam (ed.) *The Reconstruction of American History*. New York: Harper and Row, 1962.

_____. *People of Plenty: Economic Abundance and the American Character*. Chicago: University of Chicago Press, 1954.

Riesman, David. "Egocentrism: Is the American Character Changing?" *Encounter* 55 (1980):19-28.

Riesman, David, with Nathan Glazer and Raoul Denney. *Faces in the Crowd: Individual Studies in Character and Politics*. New Haven, CT: Yale University Press, 1950.

Rokeach, Milton (ed.). *Understanding Human Values. Individual and Societal*. New York: Free Press, 1979.

Smith, M. Brewster. "A Map for the Analysis of Personality and Politics." *Journal of Social Issues* 24 (1968):15-28.

Sowell, Thomas. *Race and Culture: A World View*. New York: Basic Books, 1993.

Tocqueville, Alexander de.[translated by G. Lawrence, edited by J.P. Mayer]. *Democracy in America*. New York: Harper & Row [1848], 1998.

Turner, Fredrick J. *The Frontier in American History*. New York: Dover, [1893] 1960.

Wachtel, Paul. *The Poverty of Affluence*. New York: Basic Books, 1983.

Whyte, Jr., William H. *The Organizational Man*. New York: Simon and Schuster, 1956

Wilkinson, Ruppert. *The Pursuit of American Character*. New York: Harper and Row, 1988.

Williams, R. M. *American Society: A Sociological Interpretation*. New York: Alfred A. Knopf, 1951.

Wolfe, Alan. *One Nation, After All*. New York: Viking Press, 1998.

Yankelovich, Daniel. *New Rules: Searching for Self-Fulfillment in a World Turned Upside Down*. New York: Random House. 1981.

3

Why Not a Transnational American National Identity?*

In 1916, writing against what he saw as the excesses of the Americanization program for new immigrants, the journalist and cultural essayist Randolph Bourne called for a "Trans-national America." He envisioned the United States as a country populated by nationals with strong emotional ties to their countries of origin or, for immigrants, their home countries. In this new world, they would be united as Americans primarily by the fact that they were "international citizens."

In recent decades, it appears that Bourne's vision is being realized. The number of countries allowing, and for many immigrant-sending countries, encouraging their nationals to hold multiple citizenships has exploded. Before 1991 only four Latin American countries opted to recognize dual citizenship: Uruguay (1919), Panama (1972), Peru, (1980), and El Salvador (1983). Yet between 1991 and 1997 alone an additional six South American countries have done so (Jones-Correa 2000: 2). Once a relatively rare occurrence, there are now at least ninety-three countries to have done so. No doubt others will soon be added to that list.

Moreover, as Richard Fox and James Kloppenberg (1995: 85) point out in their recent biographical essay on Bourne, some modern theorists "have seized upon Bourne's 1916 essay 'Trans-national America' as a multicultural manifesto for a new American national identity." Alexander Aleinikoff (1998b; see also Spiro 1992), for example, specifically embraces Bourne's vision for the United States, while yet another advocate has called for dual or multiple citizenship to become a basic human right enforced by the United Nations General Assembly (McGarvey-Rosendahl 1985: 305, 321-325). The question I want to raise in this chapter is whether Bourne's vision represents a dream to which we should give our support, or whether it is a utopian fantasy with implications for this country that neither Bourne nor his contemporary advocates have thought through seriously.

Are dual citizenship and multiple nationality really an issue for the United States? An examination of the numbers (see chapter 4) suggests they are. The

latest official estimates (2000) of the number of foreign-born persons, of whatever legal status, living in the United States is over 28 million (28.4), which
represents the largest foreign-born population in our history and a 30 percent
rise (6 million) over the 1990 figures. The number of immigrants in the past two
decades adds up to the largest consecutive two-decade influx of immigrants in
this country's history.[1]

Moreover, Immigration Service official figures for 1994-1998 show that
seventeen of the "top twenty"[2] immigrant-sending countries (85 percent) allow
some form of multiple citizenship. Of the 2.6 million plus immigrants from the
top twenty sending countries, 1994-1998, 2.2 million plus (86 percent) are
multiple citizenship immigrants.[3] Historically, of the 22 million plus immigrants legally admitted into this country between 1961 and 1997, 16.3 million,
or almost 75 percent, are from dual/multiple citizenship allowing countries.

It seems clear that American immigration policy is resulting in the admission of large numbers of persons from countries that have taken legislative
steps (for economic, political, and cultural reasons) to allow immigrants to
maintain and foster their ties with the countries from which they emigrated.
One may disagree about the importance or implications of these facts, but not
with their presence. Moreover, a substantial percentage of these immigrants
arrive in the U.S. from countries with very different cultural and political traditions at a time when American cultural values are being increasingly questioned by some (see Glazer 1993). A critically important question, therefore, is
whether the unprecedented diversity brought about by recent immigration is
being achieved at the expense of a common national identity.

The consequences of allowing or encouraging the acquisition of multiple
citizenships by immigrants and citizens in the United States has rarely been
discussed outside of a small group of law-school professors and political theorists, but they deserve to be. This narrow group has generally endorsed the desirability of allowing new immigrants and American citizens to pursue their associations with their "countries of origin."[4] Some go further and advocate the
acquisition and consolidation of active attachments to other countries as a means
of overcoming what they view as the parochialism of American national identity.

Yet the basis for either endorsing or advocating the development of multiple
national attachments is based ordinarily on narrow legal analysis wherein anything permitted is acceptable, or on the "postmodern" advocates' highly abstract theoretical musings, wherein anything imaginable is suitable. The psychological implications and political consequences of having large groups of
Americans holding multiple citizenships are rarely, if ever seriously considered. Yet such questions go to the very heart of what it means to be an American
and a citizen. It also holds enormous implications for the integrity of American
civic and cultural traditions.

Just how important the implications are can be seen by asking a few basic
questions. Is it possible to be fully engaged and knowledgeable citizens of

several countries? Is it possible to follow two or more very different cultural traditions? Is it possible to have two possibly conflicting, core identifications and attachments? Assuming such things are possible, are they desirable?

Dual Citizenship and American Identity: Some Basic Questions

I would like to address these questions, doing so in a way balanced somewhere between the enthusiastic and determined and, I believe, naive embrace of massive dual-citizenship immigration as a matter of little consequence to us (Spiro 1997; Shuck and Spiro 1998), and the premature, but not unrealistic, concern of our possible evolution into a country where separate psychological, cultural, and political loyalties trump a coherent national identity (Geyer 1996).

Theory vs. Advocacy

Liberal and postmodern theorists share a support of dual citizenship, but base it on slightly different foundations. Liberal theorists emphasize America's liberal tradition and its continued failure to live up to it. They see an America indelibly stained by its treatment of Indian tribes, Americans with darker skins or accents, women—and anyone else who has a quarrel with America's distribution of wealth, influence, and public attention. The response to any disparity for these theorists is more liberalism, which is to say, more emphasis on rights— group based if necessary (Kymlica 1995)—more emphasis on government guarantees of outcomes such advocates prefer, and more mandated measures to insure that "recognition" (Taylor 1992) is not trumped by any quirky individualism. They welcome multiple citizenship because it represents a long step in the direction of insuring more democracy, defined as parity for diverse cultural traditions regardless of their degree of fit with already existing ones (Habermas 1992; for a cautionary note, see Smith 1987).

The second group of theorists are the postmodernists. Their single, partially correct insight is that social organization is a by-product of intent and is thus, to use their term, "constructed." From this they conclude that no social form has any intrinsic or functional value, except that which they advocate. Postmodernists have little, if any, regard for America's cultural and political traditions, which they see as inherently racist, xenophobic, and anachronistically nationalistic. Their remedy is to welcome, and where possible to further, the demise of American national culture and substitute "larger loyalties," which, in their view, are more "democratic" and conducive to strong "multicultural" identifications (Isbister 1996, 1998; Maharidge 1996). They welcome multiple citizenships because they believe that they weaken the ties to "hegemonic" capitalism, of which the United States is their chief exemplar.

There is much to be said of the dangers of assuming that democracy, unbalanced by a concern with the public culture and psychology that make it possible, is a virtue. Or that a preference for proven traditional cultural forms is a vice. One of the many ironies of these discussions is that those who would never dream of imposing America's so-called "dominant" cultural values on any group they feel worthy of cultural self-determination are incapable of applying the same standards to the culture that makes their own complaints possible.

Unlimited Identities—a Narcissistic Conceit

The problems with the narrow substantive basis of most theoretical discussions of multiple citizenship go beyond issues of solid substantive or theoretical grounding, or personal political views masquerading as political theory. Consider the question of multiple loyalties and national identity. Most advocates subscribe to the "Why not one more?" theory. We are reminded that we are, as in my own case, sons, husbands, and fathers.[5] We are labeled as Caucasian and Western. We are working class by background and upper-middle class by Socio- Economic Status (SES) categories. We are Jewish and reformed; New Yorkers, Manhattanites, and Upper West Siders. We are professors, scholar/ writers, psychologists, psychoanalysts, and neo-Freudians. We are economically progressive, politically moderate and culturally conservative. And we are Americans and Northerners.

Postmodern theorists see us as comprising a virtually unlimited and replaceable set of selves that can be enacted or abandoned at will (Gergen 1998). Liberal political theorists and their allies count up all the categories by which we may be understood and conclude that adding one more nationality, say Mexican or Indian, will make little, if any, difference (Martin 1999: 8-9).

The first basic fallacy of these arguments is that core identity elements are infinitely malleable. They are not. The second is that all identifications have equal weight. They do not.

In clinical work, diffused, dysfunctional or incoherent identities are always a matter of psychological concern (Erikson 1956). Politically, therefore, this state hardly seems a worthy candidate for our national aspirations. Moreover, the fact that we can have many elements in our complex modern identities does not negate the need to integrate them into a coherent and functional package. It only makes that required task more difficult. Finally, the "Why not one more?" theory fails to distinguish between the elements of personal identity that form a central core of one's psychology and those which are more peripheral. I am much more a father than a Caucasian, much more a political moderate than an Upper West Sider, and definitely more of an American than most of the categories in my list.

Consider in this context Aleinikoff's contention that multiple attachments do not produce "anomie or postmodern neurosis."[6] Indeed he argues that, "on the contrary, it appears that human beings are rather adept at living in more than one world, bringing the insights of one to bear on the other, or compartmentalizing their lives into separate spheres." He then gives as evidence the case of friends of his who adopted a Russian baby, held a dual ceremony of a Jewish ritual circumcision and, at the same time, had the baby naturalized as an American citizen, at which ceremony the parents recited the oath of allegiance for her. This, in Aleinikoff's view,

> shows that the opposite of a single fixed identity is not necessarily a loss of bearing or radical personal confusion. The two identities—Jew and U.S. citizen—are deeply significant to their relevant communities; but the assembled friends and family did not see a contradiction (or even a tension) between them.

Of course, they didn't. The parents were presumably native-born, or had lived here long enough to be naturalized, Americans. The baby would therefore be raised by parents who were themselves products of a lifetime, or many years, as Americans with all that that entails. They would speak the same language, have the same cultural patterns and outlooks, and the baby would grow up with the connection to their new country as a very early and primary experience. That these two adults chose to adopt a baby, reflects in itself the fact that what they shared was more powerful than the possible nationality-religious tensions between them.

Holding multiple identifications, even those with deep significance, does not mean they must be, or are, equal. Consider that it is certainly permissible for our political leaders to have and even to express a commitment to their faith that has deep meaning to them. However, as discussions surrounding John F. Kennedy's Catholicism in 1962 and Joe Lieberman's Judaism in 2000 make clear, we also expect that their identities as, and commitment to being Americans will take precedence.

As a practical matter however, why expect tension at all when the categories of religion and national identity have become essentially fused? As Will Herberg pointed out (1955) almost fifty years ago, the religion of America is Americanism. Or to put it another way, religion in the United States has become secularized to the extent that it has Americanized. Hence, there is little tension present in being both an American and a Catholic—or a Protestant or Jew—in contemporary American society, especially that part of it which is highly educated, affluent, and occupationally well placed.

No sensible person argues that people cannot function with multiple commitments. People are wife and mother, Catholic and professor, some child's parent and some parent's child. Most often in the United States, these commitments are tensionless and even when they aren't do not call into question fundamental values or ways of being in and seeing the world. In short, there is an important distinction to be drawn between core elements of our identity that we acquire early and which shape the reception of those other important identity elements that are developed later and those that are acquired and maintained with little trouble and less commitment.

Before we can talk sensibly about whether it is truly possible to have two or more divergent core national identities, we had better be clear about what it takes to develop and maintain a national identity that is coherent and integrated. And we had better be clear about how personal and national identities function to support the cultural and political arrangements that underlie this fabulous experiment, America.

Metaphors and Muddles

Such understanding may help us make less of a muddle of our metaphors. For example, dual citizenship is often compared to bigamy (Geyer 1996: 68).7 However, in my view, that analogy is deficient. Marriage is a voluntary union between two adults, later in their lives searching for intimacy, companionship, and partnership. It is based on a combination of similarity, complementarity, practicality, and the hope for wish fulfillment.

Nationality, on the other hand, that combination of national identification, psychology, and outlook begins with the earliest experiences of language, family, custom, and parental psychology. I want to underscore the word "outlook" in this list, because culture is deeply embedded not only in *what* we think, but in *how* we do so. Cultural frames are not interchangeable.

Furthermore, this early foundation generally develops within a relatively consistent institutional, cultural, and psychological setting which is not freely chosen, nor easily abandoned.[8] In these and other ways, nationality and national identity are quite the opposite of marriage.

Another marriage-framed metaphor that is often used compares dual citizenship to relations to one's family and one's in-laws. Advocates, like Alienikoff (1999: 39), who use this metaphor agree that conflicts can arise, but believe one can still be loyal to both. There is, of course, much that lies behind the word *can*, as in the phrase "can still be loyal." In some societies the wishes of the elders take precedence over the wishes of the couple, if they differ. In our society, it is easier to be loyal because the preferences of the couple are expected to outweigh the wishes of the parents. Yet there is a more basic question here.

What happens when both parties feel very strongly about an issue, a matter of principle for each? How does one resolve and maintain fidelity to dual loyalties in these circumstances? Not every issue between two people will involve irreconcilable principles and policies. However, they might well arise.

And what are the effects of siding with one's family at the expense of one's spouse—on the marriage and on the spouse whose views were trumped? Translated into the concerns here, what is the effect on the United States and the immigrants it seeks to integrate, when they as dual citizens give substantial weight to the policy preferences of their "country of origin"?

Nationality and national identity, therefore, seem closer to family than married life.[9] Is it possible to have equally full, deep, and enduring relationships with two spouses? I doubt it. However, if the family metaphor is more apt, it would be more accurate to begin with a basic fact and then ask some different questions.

That basic fact is the pattern of U.S. post-1986 immigration, which is heavily weighted toward immigrants with non-Western cultural and political traditions. Given that fact, questions framed through the lens of the family metaphor would be: Is it possible to have two different sets of parents, with sets of different core psychologies, different sets of values, different sets of beliefs, different world views, and the information and experiences that support them all? I don't think so.

Is it possible to give equal weight to all these elements that help form one's central emotional attachments? No, not without an extremely shallow foundation for ones' identity. Such an identity is more likely to be conflicted than functional.

The idea that individuals can integrate multiple, conflicting basic orientations toward life may well prove a form of cultural conceit. It is apparently easier for some in the privileged elite to disregard the primary attachments that most citizens have to their own countries. In so doing, they appear to have confused sophistication with a new form of modern rootlessness. Such people may go anywhere, but belong nowhere.[10]

Dual Citizenship and American Democracy

Split attention between two countries is the opposite of focused civic engagement. The American ideal of civic republicanism is, after all, the citizen not the subject. Citizenship in a democracy, especially one that is itself facing complex, divisive problems arising from its increasing diversity, and which is located in a world in which the same is true, requires much of those who enjoy its benefits.

Advocates consistently minimize the difficulties of being fully engaged, knowledgeable, and effective citizens of one political system, much less two. For example, Peter Spiro (1997: 1468) argues that "The retention of previous nationality does not necessarily detract from participation in one's newly adapted polity even if the individual remains politically active in her country of origin." What evidence is presented to support this assertion? None.

Spiro presents no evidence on levels of participation by dual citizens who are or are not active in their "home" countries. Indeed, he presents no evidence on the participation of dual citizens in this country. And, he presents no evidence on the levels of understanding and attention paid to the American political process by dual nationals regardless of their engagement in the politics of their "home countries." He is certainly entitled to his views, but they should be based on evidence beyond his own preferences before they are put in the form of declarative sentences.

Spiro further argues that

> political engagement in one polity should not preclude similar commitment in another at least to the extent that rules of political engagement in them are compatible. This possi-

bility is most clearly evidenced by the internal American construct of dual sovereignty in which citizenship in one's state is held concurrently with U.S. citizenship. (1997: 1469)

This is hardly a convincing or reassuring argument, and elsewhere in the same article he appears to take the opposite position. Spiro (1997: 1478) allows that, "as for commitment, it may be difficult fully to engage in the civic activity of more that one polity." He then endorses Michael Sandel's (1996: 343) view that whether one chooses to carry out one's commitments as an American citizen or the citizenship responsibilities of another country is a matter of personal moral reflection and choice. This is an appealing position, but one that has the most profound consequences for what has been for over two hundred years the foundation of American republican democracy—an informed and engaged citizenry.

Further, the idea that American federalism and dual citizenship between two or more different cultures and countries are similar simply does not hold up. Any American state in relationship to the national system shares critical and fundamental basic attributes. The language spoken is the same, the common culture is shared as well, the overall framework is unitary and one system in fully incorporated into the other, they operate on parallel time sequences, with parallel ranges of expected behavior, have had a long history of parallel and integrated historical experience, and so on. Does any one seriously doubt that Washington State and Washington, D.C. have more in common with each other than either has with India, Mexico, the Philippines, the Dominican Republic, Vietnam, Jamaica, El Salvador, Haiti, Pakistan, Columbia, Russia, Ukraine, Peru, Bangladesh, Poland, and Iran—to name fifteen of the top immigrant-sending (to the United States) countries that encourage dual citizenship.

There are other basic problems as well. The issue of knowledge and understanding is an important one in a republican democracy like the United States. Being informed and engaged is central to democratic citizenship (Thompson 1970). What do citizens in this country need to understand and appreciate? It would be helpful to have some knowledge of the ways in which the ideals of personal, religious, political and economic freedoms motivated those who founded this country and those who followed. It would be useful to be familiar with the courage, determination, self-reliance, optimism, and pragmatism that accompanied those motivations. And, it would be necessary to have some knowledge of the country's struggles to be aware of these aspirations.

These are large matters, but necessary ones. They apply equally to current as well as to prospective citizens. Yet we are failing badly in providing information on these matters to both groups. The "test" for citizenship requires knowledge of a number of disjointed facts that require little, if any, knowledge of the traditions, political and psychological, that have shaped this country. Many thousands become citizens and require translations of ballots on which they cast their votes. It is hardly likely that these citizens have followed the complex pros and cons of these policy issues[11] since they don't well understand the language in which these debates are conducted. More likely, they gain their information from advocacy groups who have a very particular point of view, but one which is certainly not based on dispassionate presentation of the issues so that new voters can make up their own minds.

Some ask whether it is legitimate to hold immigrants to a standard unmet by citizens. Many studies underscore that question. In a recent report by the American Council of Trustees and Alumni, a group that supports liberal arts education, a series of high-school-level multiple-choice questions were presented to a randomly selected group of graduating seniors at the nation's most elites colleges, including Harvard, Princeton, and Brown. The results were dismal. Seventy-one percent of our nation's best students did not know the purpose of the Emancipation Proclamation. Seventy-eight percent were not able to identify the author of the phrase "of the people, for the people, by the people." And, 70 percent could not link Lyndon Johnson with the passage of the historic Voting Rights Act. Yet 99 percent correctly identified Beavis and Butt-Head, and 98 percent could correctly identify Snoop Doggy Dogg (Veale 2000).

There is a legitimate case to be made for asking those seeking citizenship to be conversant with the traditions and practices of the country they are asking for entry. However, in this case the question of disparate standards seems more theoretical than practical since it could be argued that both immigrants and native-born citizens have much to learn about their country. It remains to be seen whether it is truly possible to be conversant with the traditions and policy debates of two countries. Evidence keeps mounting that doing so even in one country is a task beyond the reach of increasing numbers of American citizens.

That fact, however, does not argue for lower standards. On the contrary, the informed exercise of citizenship plays a central, critical role in this democracy. Therefore, it is extremely inconsistent for advocates to push more liberal dual citizenship policies in the name of furthering democracy, while at the same pushing for standards of knowledge and commitment that undermine it.

The dilemmas are well captured in the work of David A. Martin (1994) who first emphasized the importance of "common life," and later (1999: 4-14) said he was persuaded to support dual citizenship, albeit subject to limits. The dilemma is starkly framed by Martin's assertion that

> Democracy is built on citizen participation, and its ideal is meaningful participation—of an engaged and informed citizenry. This presupposes a certain level of devotion to the community enterprise, to approach public issues as a unified community, even while leaving much to individual choice in deciding on the aims the politic should pursue or on the specific policies to address specific public issues. (1999: 13)

Yet Martin goes on to say quite directly, that

> It must be conceded that the claims made....If pushed to their limits would argue strongly against dual nationality in the first place. If focusing primary political activity

in this fashion [by allowing the right to vote in only one place] carries such benefits for solidarity, democratic engagement, and civic virtue, how much more could these goods be expected to flow from channelling exclusive political activity? And the point is even strong if the person, by surrendering, or being required to renounce all other national ties, has thereby forsworn the use of the exit option when policies do not turn out as she favors. (1999: 27)

Yes, precisely!

Dual citizenship advocates routinely tout the beneficial effects of dual citizens living here on democratizing the politics of their home countries. No data exists to support this contention. However, it is quite possible that leaders aspiring to power will promise reforms that benefit those dual citizens abroad who might support them. They, in turn, might well support those who favor a broadening of their rights—economic or political. This narrow form of interest group politics is surely not what advocates have in mind when they discuss the virtues of multiple voting and allegiances. It seems clear then the politics of dual citizens might well be self-interested without necessarily being more widely democratic.

The Domestic Context of Dual Citizenship:
American National Culture in Transition

Countries such as the United States have become increasing diverse because of changes in its immigration laws. We are now more "racially," ethnically, religiously, and culturally diverse than at any time in our history. There are advantages to such diversity. A country can be enriched by different points of view, traditions, and contributions. However, the context of expectations, both that immigrants bring with them and those already present in their country of arrival, in which diversity increases makes an enormous difference.

Therefore, any serious discussion of the implications of dual citizenship for the United States must take into account a fundamental fact of contemporary American cultural and political life. It must consider the extent to which the fundamental personal, institutional, and cultural understandings that have provided the unum for the pluribus have increasingly become matters of contention. There is little disagreement that American national culture and identity are changing (Smelser and Alexander 1999). The question, and it is a profound one, is whether they are doing so for better or worse.

That debate is usually, and I think too narrowly, framed in terms of common values.[12] A major problem with a focus on values is that they are too abstract. Who doesn't believe in democracy? Who is against opportunity? One is reminded of the classic study that found that almost every American supports free speech, until asked about the first specific application of the principle which is controversial (Prothro and Grigg 1960).

The consequences of conducting an analysis of these issues at the rarified level of highly abstract categories leads easily to conflicts over who really is rightful heir to the values being discussed, a focus on artificial similarities, or an ambivalent and ultimately confused effort to stake out an Olympian "middle ground." So, on many contentious issues, like a permissive stance toward of dual citizenship, moderates, postmodern theorists, and liberals all argue that their views represent the best realization of "democratic values." It is difficult to make informed judgments about such matters when the analysis is presented at such a highly abstract theoretical level.

That level of abstract discussion allows ridiculous claims of commonality. Given such a stance it is even possible to argue, as one advocate does one in the case of abortion, that supporters and opponents really hold the same common values and beliefs. How is that possible? Well, according to Steven Seidman (1999: 177), they don't disagree "on a women's right to have sex, [nor] on the value of her life and the life of her children, and not on the broader social and sexual values such as the individual's right to be sexual, the linking of sex to affection or love [or] the importance of the family." I am certain those who support limits on abortion would be surprised to learn that they share the exact same reverence for human life as those who advocate abortion without limits. However, I'm not certain that most Americans, even those who believe "in a woman's right to have sex" would approve of their daughters doing so at any age, with any person or persons, and at the expense of a stable, loving, long-term relationship. In short, when they are not riddled with errors and non sequiturs, such highly abstract commonalties do little to address or resolve the real issues involved.

Finally, one can find examples of those who wish to be on both sides of the issues simultaneously. The result is confusion for anyone trying to follow their arguments. Thus, in a chapter introducing their recent book, Neil Smelser and Jeffrey Alexander (1999: 3,8,9,11) warn that a glance at earlier periods of intense polarized conflict "highlights not only the uniqueness of contemporary cultural emphasis but also the unique polarizing nature of the rhetoric." Should Americans worry? No, because "the contemporary sense of decline and anxiety about social cohesion is nothing new," and "The nation does not seem to be at a turning point." The problem with this position, as one of the book's authors John Higham (1999) points out in connection with immigration, is that in many ways the contemporary circumstances of immigrant incorporation do not resemble the past, and are much more worrisome. Nor, is the fact that the country has not yet reached a turning point, if that is accurate, reason not be concerned about the direction in which the country appears to be heading.

This might appear to be a situation worth worrying about since the authors do characterize the country as having "deep structural strains and cultural polarization." However, the authors are reassured that "common values are still a social reality." What common values are these? Highly abstract ones, such as "belief in democracy" and "the value of American life."

They are further reassured that "expanding commercialized popular culture, reflected in everything from musical hits to sports stars to fast foods and afternoon talk shows—is a homogenizing cultural focus that pervades differences of religion, ethnicity and social class." Or, as another of the book's authors, Viviana Zelizer (1999: 198), notes, "In an age of diversity, it seems, commonality can only be found at the mall." However, appearances are deceiving because homogenization is not incompatible with diversification. Even currency, that most universal of mediums, shows evidence of becoming segmented along ethnic, race, class, sexual orientation and gender lines. New monetary instruments like affinity cards are marketed as a form of multicultural money—the Rainbow card (for homosexuals), the Unity Visa Card (for Americans of African decent), and so on (Zelizer 1999: 197).

The problem here is that all these commercialized cultural markets do not necessarily lead to integrated communities. Nor is it clear that because different groups recognize and adapt specific designer labels their shared values are anything more than skin deep. Not recognizing this fact, it is easier to see evidence of our cohesion in a "shared culture and tradition—whether authentic or ersatz." Yet in coherent, integrated societies and cultures, it is former experiences that are more likely to be predominant.

Americans may agree at the stratospheric level that democracy is best. However, that hasn't exempted any of our major social, cultural or political institutions or patterns of traditional practice from acute conflicts over the specific ways in which they are constituted and operate. That is, after all, the meaning of the phrase "culture wars."

Yes, it is true that if you examine public opinion polls on a variety of contentious issues, there *is* a consensual political center (DiMaggio, Evans and Bryson 1996). Yet it is also true that in every major sphere of American life the basic agreements that allow these institutions and practices to be effective, integrated parts of social: cultural and political life are permeated by often severe conflict. The legitimacy of America's basic institutions and practices is no longer a matter of fact, but rather one of debate.

Dual Citizenship and Integration of Immigrants

What are the implications of the changes in American national culture and psychology for the very large number of dual-citizenship immigrants entering the country in these new circumstances? Two very basic consequences seem clear. First, the cultural stability of the receiving country makes a critical difference. Immigrants, whether from countries that allow or discourage multiple citizenships, enter into different cultural circumstances in countries in which the primary culture is stable and secure and in those in which it is not. Conversely, multiple citizenship has different meanings and implications in these two different circumstances. It appears quite clear that immigrants entering into a country whose cultural assumptions are fluid and "contested" will find it harder to assimilate, even if they wish to do so. And, in such a circumstance, it will be more likely for dual citizen immigrants to maintain their former cultural/country attachments than to develop newer cultural/country identifications.

Second, a country in which the institutional operation and legitimacy of assimilation to its ways of life is under attack and weakened is different than one in which it is not. In the past, assimilation, with its implications that there is a legitimate and worthwhile national identity and immigrants choosing to come here should, in good faith, try to accommodate it, was both the expectation and the reality.[13] Today, neither is true. Assimilation is equated in some quarters (Takaki 1993) with forced and unnecessary demands for conformity to a culture that has little legitimate basis for asking for it.

There is also a question as to *which* America immigrants should assimilate. Is it the traditional America of personal responsibility and initiative, hard work and an eye to the future? Or is it the America of easy narcissism, self-indulgence, and entitlement-level expectations? Both exist and operate here.

Evidence seems to suggest that if assimilation means internalizing the latter, immigrants may be correct in thinking twice. A recent study by the National Research Council (1998) found that adolescents born in the United States to immigrant parents suffer poorer health and engage in riskier behaviors than children born in other countries who then move to the U.S. with their parents. Dr. Kathleen Mullan Harris (quoted in the press release accompanying the study), who headed the study of 20,000 randomly selected students, said, "Foreign-born youth experience fewer physical health problems, have less experience with sex, are less likely to engage in delinquent and violent behavior and are less likely to use controlled substances than native-born youth." For example, foreign-born Mexican youth are less likely than native-born youth of Mexican parents to miss school for a health or emotional problem, to have learning difficulties, to be obese or to suffer asthma. They also are less likely to have had sex, to engage in delinquent or violent acts, or to use three or more controlled substances.

Arriving into a solidly assimilationist receiving culture is very different than entering into a porous and "contested" one. Yet it is also true, that arriving in a culture that contains powerful and corrosive elements raises the question: To what extent should immigrants and citizens alike assimilate to such forces. The evidence suggests that a belief that immigrant values will rescue those aspects of American culture that need reshaping is hopeful fiction.

Technology aides and abets these processes. In the past, one might be an Italian, but the ability to read Italian newspapers and keep up with the news in a local village or city were limited and the chance of seeing one's country of origin was a seminal life event. Today that is far from the case. Jet travel and its accessibility to all but the most financially marginal have erased boundaries of time and geography. Internet access to newspapers and people have likewise eroded distances. Anxiety about finding psychological grounding in a culture that allows, perhaps even encourages, the diffusion of the traditional sources of individual identity leads people to seek it somewhere, anywhere. The unprecedented search for "roots" can best be understood as a reaction to society with anxieties about rootlessness.

The desire for familiar grounding is one further reason why immigrants might well be tempted to maintain and further develop psychological attachments and loyalties to their "home" countries, and the traditions, values, customs, ways of viewing the world and the psychologies that these reflect. Technology and mobility aid these efforts. Whether one applauds or laments this development in the United States, it is important to keep this fact in mind.

The impact of the enormous numbers of multiple citizenship immigrants coming into this country varies as a function of the context in which their older and newer attachments unfold. It is within the framework of these two critically important contextual elements that the entry of enormous numbers of immigrants from countries that encourage the maintenance and deepening of ties to their "homeland" must be considered. Surely when over 85 percent of the very large number of immigrants that the United States admits each year are from such countries it is time to consider carefully the implications. When immigrants enter into a country in which the assumption that they should be motivated to adapt to the values and traditions of the country they have chosen is fiercely debated and the question of assimilation to what is increasingly difficult to answer, dual citizenship in America is, indeed, truly an issue of vast proportions and broad significance.

The United States is facing a unprecedented set of circumstances with regard to multiple citizenships. It is a country whose culture and politics were forged around allegiance to a set of principles and practices contained within a specific territory, with a specific history and a specific identity—*American*. It was not organized around a specific ethnically based nationality, as were European countries, but rather a more generalized one—American. One could come from any geographical, ethnic, racial, or religious origin and still be welcomed, though not always unambivalently, to develop an American nationality.

That American nationality has distinctive elements. It has long been associated with the American "creed," which is to say support for democracy and tolerance (Huntington 1981). Yet it is also a nationality that prefers and works to develop a specific set of psychologies. Americans prefer self-reliance to dependence, moderation to excess, optimism to futility, pragmatism to rhetoric, and reflection to impulsiveness—to name but a few of those elements.

These are, of course, the core characteristics of the "Protestant ethic." Yet critics like Aleinikoff (1999) are wrong in asserting that concerns with assimilation mask a demand to conform to what he terms "Anglo/White culture." The genius of American national culture and identity is that over time these elements have become decoupled from ethnicity, separated from religion, and detached even from "race." In all these aspects, this ethic—really these elements of national psychology—have repeatedly proved, even if not always wholeheartedly, to be open and inclusive.

Successive waves of immigrants—the Irish, Jews, blacks from Trinidad or the Bahamas, educated Hispanics of all nationalities, South Asians, Chinese and Japanese—were certainly not Protestant, definitely not Anglo, or never considered "white." Yet all of these groups have found a successful place in American society. Not, a place realized without difficulty, not a place in which everyone is a success, but a place realized nonetheless.

Becoming an American then is not simply a matter of agreeing that democracy is the best form of government. It is a commitment to a psychology and the way of life that flows from it. And it ultimately entails an appreciation of, a commitment to, and, yes, even a love of and reverence for all that it stands for and provides.

It is easy to see America instrumentally. It is a place of enormous personal freedom and great economic opportunity. America has always recognized that many arrive seeking those treasures that are in such short supply in so many of the countries from which they come. The fear that self-interest will come at the expense of a developing appreciation and genuine emotional connection to the country has, I think, always been the sub-text of attempts to insure that new arrivals become "American."

That has been the trade off. America takes the chance that it can leverage self-interest and transform it to authentic commitment. Immigrants agree in coming here to reorient themselves toward their new lives and away from their old ones. This involves some basics—learning to the extent of being at home with English, understanding the institutions and practices that define American culture, and reflecting on the ways in which *their* search for freedom and opportunity fits in with the history, with all its vicissitudes, that has shaped the idea and promise of *America*. It is only at this point, that the transformation from self-interest to genuine emotional connection can be made.

Bourne's Vision Revisited

It is important to underscore here that the recourse to "common values" as the glue that holds America together is directly contrary to the vision that Bourne (1916) enunciated of a "Trans-national America." Hyphenated Americans would retain and develop their ties to their "countries of origin or home countries and that would make each group more "valuable and interesting to each other." Moreover, these sustained and enhanced national origin differences would spur the development of an "intellectual sympathy," which gets to the "heart of different cultural expressions," and enables each person in one group to feel "as they [the other group members] feel." That, in Bourne's view would be the basis of the new cosmopolitan outlook, transnational identity, that he favored. Americans would be bound together by the sum of their differences, a remarkable psychological assertion, and further that such an "intellectual internationalism...will unite and not divide."

There are several basic inconsistencies at the heart of Bourne's vision. An "intellectual sympathy" that "gets to the heart of different cultural expressions" and allows one to feel as the other group members feel is inconsistent with known psychological theory. Empathy is primarily an emotional attunement, not an intellectual one. The idea that I know how you feel because I check with my own views of how I would feel if I were in a parallel circumstance, essentially assumes you are just like me.

Is "intellectual internationalism" only an agreement to disagree? You have your group tie and I have mine and we agree to allow each other to do so. Bourne undoubtedly modeled his idea on Americans' allegiance to common values like democracy and liberty. However, beneath the superstructure of abstract principles, there are some clear limits and mechanisms to enforce them. I may advocate the violent overthrow of the government if I am a communist theoretician in a study group, but not if I am the leader of an action cell buying guns.

Whose view prevails when different understandings of "intellectual internationalism" are at issue? Who gets to decide? This is not a matter of an abstract and ethereal belief that differences rooted in basic cultural experiences and views "will unite and not divide." These matters come up routinely in newly multicultural societies with democratic traditions. Should a democratic country committed to the equality of women allow what, to some groups, is the accepted cultural practice of female circumcision, or polygamy?

Bhikhu Parehk (1996: 254-55) has thoughtfully tried to square this intellectual circle. However, like all such attempts at theoretical alchemy, there is a large element of substantive evasion of the basic realities. Parehk lists five possible resolutions of these dilemmas: (1) the hope for universal values which will eventually transcend differences [moral universalism], (2) the primacy of core values which allows a society to distinguish those it will and will not tolerate [core values], (3) the view of society as so deeply split among class, gender and other lines that no values can hold and the uniting principle must be "do no harm," (4) "human rights" as the ultimate value, a combination of (1) and (4), (5) the encouragement of an "open-minded and serious dialogue with minority spokesmen and to act on the resulting consensus" [dialogical consensus].

Parehk focuses on each view's weaknesses and not on their strengths, and concludes (1996 255) obviously enough that none of these views is "wholly satisfactory." Nonetheless, choices must be made, as, for example, whether a democracy should allow the cultural practice of polygamy. Parehk is a tolerant democrat, which means he is loathe to impose values on anyone. Therefore, he favors "dialogical consensus." The only problem here is that conflicting, deeply held beliefs may generate more talk than agreement. What is to be done then?

Minorities, whose beliefs run directly counter to the premises on which the society operates must acquiesce. Or to put it in Parehk's (1996: 259) more gentle phrasing, "Since deep disagreements cannot be always satisfactorily solved...if the majority remains genuinely unpersuaded [after serious dialogue], its value needs to prevail." Why? The reason is found in the fact that every society develops "operative public values," those that they live by and which are embedded in their institutions, practices, and moral understandings. "They are the only moral standpoint from which to evaluate minority [cultural/social] practices" (1996: 261).

Parehk (1996: 365-83) goes to great lengths to urge a real dialogue with those whose practices are inconsistent with "operative public values," and gives a good accounting for the arguments for and against the practice of polygamy. Yet, in the end, he is both judge and jury. Of the demand from some quarters to ban arranged marriages because they are coercive, he notes that it is "unjustified" because the practice, "while it has no religious or cultural basis...means a great deal to Asians" (1996: 267).

A request for circumcision from an adult female? Well, says Parehk (1996: 271), she "should be at liberty to demand any circumcision she prefers." However, there are "complicating factors." What are these? Well, perhaps there is community pressure. How can one tell? Simple. If a single women wishes to be circumcised there is no pressure, but if more than one wishes to do so there is, and it shouldn't be allowed. Why community wishes that have no basis in group religion or culture (for arranged marriage) are not seen as coercive, while those that do have such a basis are seen as unacceptable, is not made clear.

Polygamy? After rehearsing the arguments that Muslims might make in favor of that practice Parehk (1996: 282) pronounces them "unconvincing." Assigning his own weighing system to the arguments he presents in favor of banning the practice, he says these "ought to go a long way in convincing the Muslim clerics of the value of monogamy." Perhaps. However, it is quite unlikely that a devout Muslim would weigh the arguments as has Parehk.

Parehk concludes, "Western society then, has the right to ban the practice of polygyny." What of polygamy? Well,

> *if* the current inequality of power and status, self-esteem, etc., between men and women were to end so that women could be depended upon to make equally uncoerced choices, *if* a sizable section of society were freely to opt for polygamy, and *if* the latter could be shown not to have the harmful consequences mentioned earlier, there would be a case for permitting it. Since this is not the case today, we are right to disallow it. (1996: 283, emphasis mine)

Parehk's willingness to entertain the practice rests on what can only be called a wholesale and fundamental transformation of the very culture and its practice that give authority to the claim. He is essentially saying that polygyny would be allowed when the culture reaches the stage where it no longer wishes it.

One is reminded here of Stanley Fish's complaint about "boutique multiculturalism":

> A boutique multiculturalist may honor the tenants of religions other than his own, but he will draw the line when the adherents of a religion engage in the practice of polygamy. In ...these cases (and in many analogous cases that could be instanced) the boutique multiculturalist resists the force of the appreciated culture at precisely the point at which it matters most to the strongly committed members. (1998: 69-70)

Yes. Exactly. And, doesn't it have to be exactly that way for a coherent, integrated, and functional culture? I will return to that central question at the conclusion of this analysis.

Bourne's enthusiasm for his vision is understandable. He was a social critic and he wrote well before the advent of advances in the understanding of human psychology that might have caused him to question some of his premises.The same cannot be said for his contemporary champions (Alienikoff 1998a, b). The first point to make here is that no psychological theory of identity with which I am familiar finds that the more deeply immersed and central your own cultural identity becomes, the more open you are to experience other equally strongly held and very different identities.

Literature supporting this is quite unequivocal. People who retain deeply held convictions, an identity based on common values, cultures, psychologies, world views, and so on, are much more likely to take their identities as given, as the way things are and the way they ought to be. There is no evidence historically or empirically that taking your Japanese identity seriously makes you more open-minded towards Africans. Or that growing up with a strong Italian or Moroccan identity makes you better able to feel what it is like to be an Israeli. When cultural identities are "contested," a lack of sympathy and empathy can easily turn to hostility and hatred.

Finally, in a country such as America, whose citizens are drawn from every country in the world, is it realistic and not just fanciful, to believe that Somalians will learn about and empathize with Italians, who will, in turn, do the same with Filipinos, who, in turn, will do the same with all the remaining peoples and cultures that make up this diverse country? To state that is to underscore the limits to such a vision. There are cognitive, emotional, and practical barriers to the amount of information one can take in and make use of, even if one is inclined to, which is another large presumption of Bourne's theory. To add to this burden the view that it is possible to have the desire and capacity for empathy for all the different cultures and groups that now populate America is a naive fantasy.

Many Cultures, One Nation

America reached its present state of political, economic, and social development by providing enormous personal freedom and abundant economic opportunity. In doing so, it leveraged personal ambitions as a tool to transform individuals' social and economic circumstances. In the process, it helped develop and reinforce psychological elements that were consistent with personal success and civic prudence in American democracy. An emphasis on consistency, hard work, delay of immediate gratification, prudence, pragmatism, and optimism were among these elements.

In return, it asked of immigrants that they learn the country's language, culture, and political practices. Thus oriented toward their new home, immigrants could become part of the fabric of American cultural and political life. Leaving behind a life, even one that one wanted to leave, was, of course, difficult. Yet generations of earlier immigrants thought the sacrifice worthwhile.

Multiple citizenship and its associated bifurcation of attention and commitment changes that traditional and successful recipe. Immigrants increasingly come from countries that encourage dual-citizenship. Their purposes in doing so are primarily self-interested. It may be to insure the continued flow of financially critical remittances from those working in the United States. Or it may be to organize their nationals to further the home country's policy preferences, for example, amnesty for those who enter the country illegally or the support of bilingual language policies which help to maintain and facilitate ties to the "home" country. Whatever the specific purposes, sending countries are increasingly mobilizing to retain immigrants' emotional attachments and to further develop commitment to the "home" country from which they emigrated.

This may take the form of lobbying for his country of origin's interest, for example "open borders," amnesties, maintenance of native languages—all of which the sending countries have strong self-interest in supporting. It may take the form of making American citizens and resident aliens sources of financial support for political leaders or parties in the "home" country. Or it may take the form of systematic electronic efforts to keep such immigrants in touch with developments in their "countries of origin."

These developments set the stage for a direct conflict of interest among new immigrants and citizens, many of whom retain deep attachments to their home country. Given the geographical distribution of such immigrants it is possible that whole states and certainly some localities will have a substantial portion of dual citizens with active and deep connections to their "countries of origin" being asked to put aside these experiences and connections in favor of America's national or community interest. Whether that is possible as a matter of psychology or politics remains to be seen. I intend no implication that such immigrants will be "fifth column." However, it is prudent to consider that in such circumstances they are likely to be conflicted.

This poses a dilemma for the United States, which has traditionally taken in immigrants with the assumption that they would eventually become anchored to American identity and nationality over time in a way that was not primarily instrumental. In the past this was a reasonable assumption. It no longer is.

Dual citizenship seems well suited to an age in which advocates, theorists and politicians tell us there are no limits to what we should expect to have without incurring any costs. Do you want the benefits of freedom and opportunity, buttressed by a twenty-first-century infrastructure, and unlimited access to consumer goods, but still want to maintain and further develop your emotional, economic, social, and political ties to your "home" country? No less an authority on self-interest without responsibility, former president William J. Clinton (1999) found the idea of dual citizenship publicly appealing.[14] And why not? To the immigrant it dramatically lowers the costs of immigration while raising its benefits.

Yet, in a democracy—especially one facing issues of cultural coherence and integration—the costs of dual citizenship may be high indeed. In a time characterized by enormous worry regarding the decline of social capital and its implications for American civic life, the split attachments of large numbers of dual citizens is another source of deep concern. Reforming dual citizenship in the United States is certain to be controversial. It will definitely be politically difficult. Yet such reform will have the advantage of calling all Americans home to *their* country.

This country provides so much of basic human value to those fortunate enough to call it home. Asking its citizens to have primary and relatively uncontested interest in its affairs and a concern for its welfare that is primary not conflicted seems a small and legitimate sacrifice to ask of those who ask to share its treasures—freedom and opportunity.

Efforts to welcome immigrants are important in making them feel more at ease in their new surroundings. Yet valid questions arise as to the different forms that welcoming can take, and whether or not some forms damage the very outcomes of integration they seek to foster. Do we foster attachment to American citizenship and its ideals by devaluing it? If we allow or, as some would have us do, encourage an immigrant's loyalties to his/her "home country," do we not put at risk the involvement and connection that have traditionally been the hallmarks of other immigrant groups that have become integrated into American society and culture.

Peter Shuck and Peter Spiro (1998: A22) argue that "we should encourage the assimilation of immigrants who want to be full Americans, but who naturally retain familial, emotional and economic interests elsewhere." The view that we can encourage immigrants to be "full Americans," while at the same time encouraging them to develop and consolidate their attachments to their home countries is psychologically and politically contradictory. And given that the governments of these "home countries" are mounting increasingly sophisticated efforts to strengthen these attachments, the idea that we can do both seems determinedly naïve, at best.

Shuck's and Spiro's apparent solution to this dilemma is also questionable. They report, with obvious approval, that the hyphenated Americans may also be acquiring an ampersand: Irish & American, rather than Irish-American, Dominican & American, rather than Dominican-American. But mostly, Mexican & American. In other words, in place of the now common, bifurcated attachments to this country—Italian-Americans, Hispanic-Americans, etc., they now suggest we embrace the development of citizens (e.g., Dominican & American) whose ethnic ancestry equals or trumps their identifications as Americans. If we follow Shuck's and Spiro's advice we will arrive at a most paradoxical and troubling circumstance—a United States devoid of Americans.

No country, and certainly no democracy, can afford to have large numbers of citizens with shallow national and civic attachments. No country facing divisive domestic issues arising out of its increasing diversity, as America does, benefits from large-scale immigration of those with multiple loyalties and attachments. And no country, striving to reconnect its citizens to a coherent civic identity and culture, can afford to encourage its citizens to look elsewhere for their most basic national attachments.

The question that America faces as it begins the twenty-first century is whether its cultural, psychological, and political diversity will lead to a fragmented and thus dysfunctional national identity. Mr. Clinton showed an accurate understanding of this basic public dilemma,[15] as he had when he ran for president in 1992. In a talk with reporters he said,

> It is really a potentially great thing for America that we are becoming so multi-ethnic....But it's also potentially a powder keg of problems and heartbreak and division and loss. And how we handle it will determine really—that single question may be the biggest determination of what we look like fifty years from now...and what the children of that age will have to look forward to." (Clinton 1997a: 509)

Elsewhere Clinton (1997b: 877) had warned that the central problem facing this country was whether "we define what it means to be an American, not just in terms of the hyphen showing our ethnic origins, but in terms of the our primary allegiance to the values that America stands for and values we really live by." As was often the case, however, with this president, the question was whether his actions would be consistent with his publicly stated understandings and intentions (see chapter 12).

Is the only alternative to fragmentation Anglo-western "domination?" No. Even to raise this question is to inflate a caricature. Its primary logical problem is to explain how, if "Anglo-conformity" dominates, it has been possible for the level of pluralism that has always been part of this country's heritage to exist, must less to prosper (Abramson 1980; see also Gleason 1980). The truth is that there have been pressures for immigrants to conform, but they have been to national political values more often than to parochial cultural ones. Moreover, some of the pressures to conform to "Anglo-values," as for example in the case of learning English, have much more to do with wanting newcomers to become integrated into the society in which they have chosen to belong than they do with "subjugating" their cultures of origin. There are obviously strong arguments as well on the side of those who hold that uniting diverse peoples, an early understood task of the new American republic, requires some basic uniformities, with language being an obvious candidate.

Is it true that the goal of all cultural conflict is domination? Not necessarily. Must America insist on a dominant culture? Perhaps a better question to ask is whether in a democratically pluralist country like the United States, is it still important to have a *primary* culture?

Notes

*   This chapter builds on Renshon (2000). I would like to thank Nathan Glazer, Eugene Goldstein, Peter Spiro, Peter Schuck, Stephen Thernstrom, Mark Krikorian, and especially Noah Pinkus for their helpful comments on earlier drafts this paper or its constituent sections. I would also like to acknowledge the valuable research assistance of Sandra Johnson.

1.   The figures are drawn from the U.S. Department of Commerce (1997: 52-53).

2.   See U.S. Department of Justice/Immigration and Naturalization Service, 1999: 8; also U.S. Department of Justice/Immigration and Naturalization Service (1999: 9).

3.   Keep in mind that while seventeen of the "top twenty" immigrant-sending countries are multiple citizenship allowing countries, that number (17) represents only a small percentage of the total number (92, not including the United States) of such countries. And, of course, many of these remaining seventy-five (75) countries allowing multiple citizenship send the United States many thousands of immigrants. Adding those countries to these figures suggests that almost 90 percent of all immigrants come from countries that allow or encourage multiple citizenship.

4.   Typical are the positions of law professors Peter H. Schuck (Yale Law School) and Peter J. Spiro (Hofstra Law School) who write (1998: A22), "dual citizenship poses little threat to U.S. national interests, and efforts to combat it would be futile and counterproductive."

5.   For an eloquent formulation of this view, see Levinson (1986).

6.   The quotes in this paragraph are drawn from Aleinikoff (1999).

7.   David Martin (1999: 8, fn 24) points out that the bigamy metaphor was made in the context of dual citizenship debates in the early nineteen century.

8.   An example of the confusion that accompanies failure to think clearly about these distinctions can be seen in the recent article by David Martin. He begins his discussion of dual citizenship by informing the reader that he will use the terms citizenship and nationality interchangeably, and elsewhere refers to "mere "nationality." He terms (1999: 8-11) the distinction between citizen(ship) and national(ity) a "technical one," which is "rarely important for my purposes." He then goes on to discuss the issue of multiple and conflicting loyalties in which, of course, the distinction between national and citizenship are central, not mere technicalities.

9.   The metaphor linking family life and national identity suggests certain parallels. There are, of course, differences as well. The nation is not a parent writ large. Nor does it have the primary responsibilities for nurturing, guidance, and socialization. On the other hand, the nation, like the family, is present from the child's earliest experiences. It is to be found in language, cultural practices, and the national cultural identifications of the parents. However, the nation is also the consistent context in

which her development unfolds and provides the institutions (e.g., schools, civic and community experiences) and objects (flags, rituals like the pledge of allegiance) through which the child's personal and national identity becomes fused at an early age.

10. Waltzer (1997: 87) notes that "In immigrant societies people have begun to experience what we might think of as a life without clear boundaries and without the security of singular identities."

11. What David Martin (1999: 31) refers to as "simple voting," is, in fact, anything but simple (Kelley and Mirer 1974).

12. Or as Alexander and Smelser (1999: 3; see also Huntington 1981: 23) put it, "The core of the complaint concerns common values in American society. " For a disclaimer from the view that common American political values are enough, see Lind (1996: 242-43) and Smith (1988).

13. In an early work on American national character, the English psychoanalyst Geoffrey Gorer (1964: 25) wrote,

> With few exceptions, the immigrants did not cross the ocean as colonists to reproduce the civilization of their homes on distant shores; with the geographical separation they were prepared to give up, as far as lay in their power, all their past: their language, and the thoughts which that language could express; the laws and allegiances they had been brought up to observe, the values and assured ways of life of their ancestors and former compatriots; even to a large extent their customary ways of eating, of dressing, of living.

This is the immersion into the "melting pot" that colors the myths of both assimilation's advocates and critics. The former see that process as natural and desirable, the later see it as little better that the cultural rape of immigrant identity. Yet both sides would do well to keep in mind Gorer's answer to the question he raised of why early immigrants might not wish to reproduce their homelands here. The answer was to be found in the fact that most immigrants had

> ...escaped...from discriminatory laws, rigid hierarchical structures, compulsory military service and authoritarian limitation of the opportunities open to the enterprising and the goals to which they could aspire.

On assimilation's discontents, see also Skerry (2000).

14. Jerry Rawlings, president of Ghana mentioned in a news conference with President Clinton that he was sponsoring a bill to allow present and former nationals of Ghana dual citizenship. Part of that exchange follows:

Q: Would it be dual loyalty?

President Rawlings: Well, I guess that's what we have a bit of—we don't have any problem with that...I have a problem with you because you're demanding loyalty to the American Constitution and yet I cannot command the same type of loyalty in my country.

President Clinton: ... Almost all countries allow some form of dual citizenship...it certainly won't hurt to get more Americans interested in Ghana and contribute to Ghana's future. I thought it was quite a clever idea myself.

15. Elsewhere, I (Renshon 1998: 3-33) have described the basic public dilemma as a fundamental unresolved question concerning public psychology and governance facing the president on taking office. It is not a specific question about public policy,

but rather the public's psychological connections to its institutions, leaders, and political process. This unresolved public concern underlies and frames more specific policy debates.

References

Abramson, Harold J. "Assimilation and Pluralism," in Stephen Thernstrom (ed.), *Harvard Encyclopedia of American Ethnic Groups.*" Cambridge, MA: Harvard University Press, 1980.

Aleinikoff, T. Alexander. "Between National and Post-National: Membership in the United States.*Michigan Journal of Race and Law* 241 (1999).

_____. "A Multicultural Nationalism?" *The American Prospect,* January/February (1998b):80-86.

Alexander, Jeffery C., and Neil J. Smelser. "The Ideological Discourse of Cultural Discontent: Paradoxes, Realities, and Alternative Ways of Thinking," in Neil J. Smelser and Jeffrey C. Alexander (eds.), *Diversity and Its Discontents: Cultural Conflict and Common Ground in Contemporary American Society.* Princeton, NJ: Princeton University Press, 1999b.

Bourne, Randolph S. "Trans-National America." *Atlantic Monthly* 118 (1916):86-97.

Clinton, William J. "Remarks and Question and Answer Session with the American Society of Newspaper Editors" (April 11, 1997). *Weekly Compilation of Presidential Documents* 14, 33:15 (1997a):501-510.

_____. "Remarks at the University of California at San Diego Commencement Ceremony" (June 14, 1997). *Weekly Compilation of Presidential Documents* 23, 33:25 (1997b): 876-882.

_____. "Remarks at a Welcoming Ceremony for President Jerry John Rawlings of Ghana" (February 24, 1999). *Weekly Compilation of Presidential Documents*, March 1, 35:8 (1999):298-299.

DiMaggio, Paul, John Evans, and Bethany Bryson. "Have Americans' Social Attitudes Become More Polarized?" *American Journal of Sociology* 102 (1996):444-496.

Erikson, Erik H.. "The Problem of Ego Identity." *Journal of the American Psychoanalytic Association* 4:1 (1956):58-121.

Fox, Richard Wrightman, and James T. Kloppenberg (eds.). "Randolph S. Bourne," in *A Companion to American Thought*. Cambridge, MA: Blackwell, 1995.

Gergen, Kenneth J. *The Saturated Self.* Cambridge, MA: Harvard University Press, 1998.

Geyer, Georgie Anne .*Americans No More :The Death of Citizenship.* New York: Atlantic Monthly Press, 1996 .

Glazer, Nathan. "Is Assimilation Dead?" *The Annals of the American Academy of Political Science* 530 (1993):122-136.

Gleason, Philip. "American Identity and Americanization," in Stephen Thernstrom (ed.), *Harvard Encyclopedia of American Ethnic Groups.*" Cambridge, MA: Harvard University Press, 1980.

Gorer, Geoffrey. *The American People: A Study in National Character.* Revised edition. New York: W.W. Norton & Co., 1964.

Habermas, Jürgen. "Citizenship and National Identity: Some Reflections on the Future of Europe." *Praxis International* 17 (1992).

Herberg, Will. *Protestant, Catholic, Jew: An Essay in American Religious Sociology.* Garden City, NY: Doubleday, 1955.

Higham, John. "Cultural Responses to Immigration," in Neil J. Smelser and Jeffrey C. Alexander (eds.), *Diversity and Its Discontents: Cultural Conflict and Common Ground in Contemporary American Society.* Princeton, NJ: Princeton University Press, 1999.

Huntington, Samuel P. *American Politics: The Promise of Disharmony*. Cambridge, MA: Belknap Press, 1961.

Isbister, J. " Is America Too White?" in *What, Then is the American, This New Man?"* Compiled by E. Sandman. Washington, DC: Center of Immigration Studies, 1998.

_____. *The Immigration Debate: Remaking America*. New York: Kurnarian Press, 1996.

Jones-Correa, Michael. "Under Two Flags: Dual Nationality in Latin America and Its Consequence for the United States." Working Papers in Latin America (no. 99/00-3), The David Rockefeller Center for Latin American Studies, Harvard University, 2000.

Kelley, Stanley J., and T. Mirer. "The Simple Act of Voting," *The American Political Science Review* 68 (1974):572-591.

Kymlica, William. *Mutlicultural Citizenship: A Liberal Theory of Minority Rights*. Oxford: Clarendon Press, 1995.

Levinson, Sanford. "Constructing Communities Through Words That Bind: Reflections on Loyalty Oaths." *Michigan Law Review* 1440 (1986):1463-1470.

Lind, Michael. *The Next American Nation*. New York: Free Press, 1996.

Maharidge, Dale. *The Coming White Minority: California's Eruptions and America's Future*. New York: Times Books, 1996.

Martin, David A. "New Rules on Dual Nationality for a Democratizing Globe: Between Rejection and Embrace." *Georgetown Immigration Law Review* 14 (1999):1-34.

_____. "The Civic Republican Ideal for Citizenship, and for Our Common Life." *Virginia Journal of International Law* 301 (1994).

National Research Council. *From Generation to Generation: The Health and Well-Being of Children in Immigrant Families*. Washington, DC: National Research Council, 1998.

McGarvey-Rosendahl, Patricia. "A New Approach to Dual Nationality." *Houston Journal of* Parehk, Bhikhu. "Minority Practices and the Principle of Toleration." *International Migration Review* 30:1 (1996):251-287.

Prothro, J. W., and C. M. Grigg. "Fundamental Principles of Democracy: Basis of Agreement and Disagreement." *Journal of Politics* 22 (1960):276-294.

Renshon, Stanley A. *High Hopes: The Clinton Presidency and the Politics of Ambition*. New York: Routledge, 1998.

_____. *Dual Citizenship and American National Identity*. Washington DC: Center for Immigration Studies, 2001a. *(http://www.cis.org/articles/2001/renshondual.pdf)*

Sandel. Michael J. *Democracy's Discontent: America in Search of a Public Philosophy*. Cambridge, MA: Belknap Press, 1996.

Schuck, Peter H., and Peter J. Spiro. "Dual Citizens, Good Americans." *Wall Street Journal*, 18 March 1998:A22.

Seidman, Steven. "Contesting the Moral Boundaries of Eros," in Neil J. Smelser and Jeffrey C. Alexander (eds.), *Diversity and Its Discontents: Cultural Conflict and Common Ground in Contemporary American Society*. Princeton, NJ: Princeton University Press, 1999.

Skerry, Peter. "Do We Really Want Immigrants to Assimilate?" *Society*, March/April 2000:57-62.

Smelser, Neil J., and Jeffrey C. Alexander (eds.). *Diversity and Its Discontents: Cultural Conflict and Common Ground in Contemporary American Society*. Princeton, NJ: Princeton University Press, 1999a.

Smith, Rogers M. "The 'American Creed' and American Identity: The Limits of Liberal Citizenship in the United States." *Western Political Quarterly* 41 (1987):225-251.

Smith, Tony. *Foreign Entanglements: The Power of Ethnic Groups in the Making of American Foreign Policy*. Cambridge, MA: Harvard University Press, 2001.

Spiro, Peter J. "Dual Nationality and the Meaning of Citizenship" *Emory Law Review* 46:4 (1997):1412-1485.

Takaki, Ronald. *A Different Mirror: A History of Multicultural America*. Boston: Little Brown, 1993 .

Taylor, Charles. *Multiculturalism and the Politics of Recognition*. Princeton, NJ: Princeton University Press, 1992.

Thompson, Dennis F. *The Democratic Citizen*. New York: Cambridge University Press, 1970.

U.S. Department of Commerce. "Current Population Reports: The Foreign-Born Population in the United States: March 1999" (P20-519). Washington DC: U.S. Government Printing Office, 2000.

U.S. Department of Commerce, Economics and Statistics Administration, U.S. Census. "Profile of the Foreign-Born Population in the United States: 1997" (P23-195). *Current Populations Reports Special Studies*. Washington, DC: U.S. Government Printing Office, 1997.

U.S. Department of Justice. Immigration and Naturalization Service. "Statistical Yearbook of the Naturalization and Immigration Service-1998." Washington, DC: U.S. Government Printing Office, 2000.

_____. Immigration and Naturalization Service. "Annual Report: Legal Immigration, Fiscal Year, 1998," No. 2, May 1999b.

_____. Immigration and Naturalization Service. "Annual Report: Legal Immigration, Fiscal Year, 1997," No. 1, January 1999a.

Walzer, Michael. *On Toleration*. New Haven, CT: Yale University Press, 1997.

Veale, Scott. "History 101: Snoop Doggy Dog Roosevelt." *New York Times*, 2 July 2000, wk.5.

Zelizer, Viviana A. "Multiple Markets, Multiple Cultures," in Neil J. Smelser and Jeffrey C. Alexander (eds.), *Diversity and Its Discontents: Cultural Conflict and Common Ground in Contemporary American Society*. Princeton, NJ: Princeton University Press, 1999.

Part 3

Immigration and the American National Community

4

Dual Citizenship in America: An Issue of Vast Proportions and Broad Significance*

Fueled in part by the numbers of new immigrants, the United States is becoming dramatically more diverse—racially, ethnically, and culturally. The latest census figures show that the number of legal and illegal immigrants living in the United States has almost tripled since 1970, rising from 9.6 million to 28.3 million today and far out-pacing the growth of the native-born population (Escobar 1999; U.S. Department of Commerce 2000.[1]

Moreover, a substantial percentage of these immigrants arrive here from countries with very different cultural and political traditions. This scenario is unfolding at the same time that American cultural values are increasingly being questioned by some.[2] An important question, therefore, is the relationship between dual citizenship and American national identity. It is within this context that questions about the impact and advisability of allowing or encouraging dual or multiple citizenships arise.[3]

Some argue that it is desirable for new immigrants to pursue their continued associations with their "countries of origin." Some go further and advocate the acquisition and consolidation of active attachments to other countries as a means of overcoming what they view as the parochialism of American national identity. Yet the basis for either endorsing or advocating the development of multiple national attachments is ordinarily based on theoretical and sometimes abstract arguments about such terms as democracy, citizenship, and rights.

However, before we can address these important questions, there are several prior ones. How many countries allow their nationals to have multiple citizenships? Solid numbers are in short supply. In a 1996 paper, Jorge Vargas (1996: 2) put the number at forty. One year later, a 1997 draft memorandum on dual citizenship prepared for the United States Commission on Immigration Reform (Morrison & Foerster 1997: 9) indicated that "at least thirty-seven and possibly as many as forty-seven countries allow their nationals to possess dual nationality." Goldstein and Piazza's list (1998; see also 1996) of countries allowing multiple citizenship countries published in 1998, put the number at fifty-five. Several other authors who have written on multiple citizenships have mentioned a few as illustrations.

How many Americans are eligible for, or claim, multiple citizenship status? We do not know. As the *Wall Street Journal* (Zachary 1998) puts it, "no one knows just how many citizens claim a second nationality," or are entitled to do so. Why? According to Peter Spiro (1997: 1455, fn 199; see also Hammer 1985: 445), an enthusiastic advocate of multiple citizenships, "Statistical surveys of the number of dual nationals appear never to have been undertaken, nor have the United States or other governments sought to collect such information." Yet, he estimates that Mexico alone, which recently passed a law allowing its nation dual-citizenship rights, could create in the United States, "almost overnight a concentrated dual-national population numbering in the millions." How many millions? He doesn't say.

According to T. Alexander Aleinikoff (1998a: 27), another advocate of multiple citizenships, "The U.S. Government does not record and has not estimated, the number of U.S. dual citizens, *but the total may be quite large.*" How large? He doesn't say.

I first briefly discuss the concept of multiple citizenships, and then turn to an enumeration of those countries that allow it, and examine them in the context of American immigration policy from 1986 to 1997. I then turn to two additional sources of multiple citizenship eligibility in the United States, illegal immigrants and their children, and those who are already eligible to become citizens. Finally, I close with some questions regarding the implications of multiple citizenships for American politics and society.

What is Dual Citizenship?

At its most basic level, dual or multiple citizenship involves the simultaneous holding of more than one citizenship or nationality. Dual or multiple *citizenship* is not the same as dual *nationality*, although they are sometimes confused or used interchangeably. Citizenship is a political term. It draws its importance from political, economic, and social rights and obligations granted to a person by virtue of having been born into, or having become a recognized or certified member of a state.

Nationality, on the other hand, refers primarily to the attachments[4] of members of a community to each other and to that community's ways of viewing the world, its practices, institutions, and allegiances. Common community identifications develop through several or more of the following elements: language, "racial" identification, ethnicity, culture, geography, historical experience, and identification with common institutions and practices.

In many culturally homogenous countries nationality and citizenship coincide, yet they are not synonymous. Or as a *Harvard Law Review* editorial states (1997: 1817), "an individual's national identity is not necessarily the same as the passport she holds." This, of course, is precisely one of the questions raised by multiple citizenships.

Dual citizenship allows such a person to have many or, in some cases, all of the rights and responsibilities that adhere to a citizen in each of the several countries in which he or she is a citizen regardless of length of time or actual residence in a country, geographical proximity, or the nature of their economic, cultural, or political ties. There are variations among countries in which specific citizenship rights are allowed and under what conditions. Some European countries, for example, Sweden, Denmark, Norway, and Finland grant foreign citizens voting rights in local and regional elections. Some Latin American countries that permit or encourage their nations to gain second citizenships in the United States allow those citizens to vote in elections in their country of origin (e.g., Peru, El Salvador, Columbia), some (e.g., Honduras, Brazil, and Mexico) do not.[5]

The idea seems on the surface counterintuitive. How could a person owe allegiance or fully adhere to the responsibilities of citizenship in several or more countries at the same time? In the United States, the legal answer is: easily.

The United States does not formally recognize dual citizenship, but neither does it take any stand—politically or legally—against it. No American citizen can lose his/her citizenship by undertaking the responsibilities of citizenship in one or more other countries. This is true even if those responsibilities include obtaining a second or even a third citizenship, swearing allegiance to a foreign state, voting in another country's election, serving in the armed forces (even in combat positions, and even if the state is a "hostile" one), running for office, and if successful, serving.[6] Informed constitutional judgment suggests Congress could legislatively address any of these or other issues arising out of these multiple, perhaps, conflicting responsibilities.[7] Yet, to date, it has chosen not to do so.

Aleinikoff (1998a: 26-27; see also O'Brien 2000: 57) notes that a person in the United States may acquire multiple citizenships in any one of four ways. He or she may be born in the United States to immigrant parents. All children born in the United States are U.S. citizens regardless of the status of their parents (*jus soli*) . Second, a person may be born outside the United States to one parent who is a U.S. citizen and another who is not (*jus sanguinis*). A child born to an American citizen and British citizen in the United Kingdom, for example, would be a citizen of both countries. Third, a person can become a naturalized citizen in the United States and that act is ignored by his or her country of origin.[8] This is true even if the country of naturalization requires, as does the United States, those naturalizing to "renounce" former citizenship/nationality ties. In the case of the United States, failure to take action consistent with the renunciation carries no penalties, and other countries can, and often do, simply ignore that oath of allegiance. Fourth, a person can become a naturalized citizen of the United States and in doing so lose his/her citizenship in his/her country of origin, but can regain it at any time, and still retain U.S. citizenship.[9]

There is also a fifth and in some ways newly emerging vehicle for developing multiple citizenships unremarked upon by either Alienikoff or O'Brien. A country like the United States that does not formally recognize dual citizenship, but does not dissuade it either, may have citizens whose countries of origin has dual citizenship agreements with third, fourth and even fifth countries. For example, a number of Latin American countries recognize dual nationality with Spain, as Guatemala does with other Central American nations (Jones-Correa 2000: 2). The common citizenship status towards which the European Union is moving is another example of what might be called *block multiple citizenships*.

Countries that Allow Multiple Citizenship: A Large and Fast-Growing Group

People, even those who are attentive to public life and affairs, are genuinely surprised at the number of countries that allow and encourage multiple citizenships. It is a large number and it is growing rapidly. A 1996 survey conducted by a Hispanic advocacy group found that seven of seventeen (41 percent) Latin American countries allowed some form of multiple citizenships. As of 2000, only four year later, fourteen out of seventeen Latin American countries in that survey (84 percent) were allowing multiple citizenships, and another, Honduras, had a bill to do so pending before its legislature (De la Garza, et al. 1996)

A list of countries allowing or encouraging multiple citizenships is listed in Appendix I. Drawing on several helpful,[10] but sometimes inconsistent,[11] lists in conjunction with my own inquiries[12] I have established that there are currently ninety-three countries, including the United States, that allow some form of multiple citizenship. It is important to underscore, however, that the specific rights and responsibilities that accrue to such citizens vary.

Some countries allow their citizens to become dual citizens but balk at allowing immigrants to their country to do so (Germany).[13] New Zealand now permits dual nationality unless, in a specific instance, this "is not conducive to the public good." The French Civil Code formerly provided that any adult who voluntarily accepted another *nationality* would automatically forfeit French *citizenship*, but this provision was amended in 1973 so that now "any adult, habitually residing abroad, who voluntarily accepts another *nationality* will only lose the French *nationality* if he expressly so declares" (italics mine). Some countries, such as Algeria and France, allow their nationals to chose in which country's armed forces they will serve. Others do not.[14] Irish citizens in Britain may vote and sit in Parliament. The Irish Constitution was changed in 1984 to permit Britons living in the Republic to vote in elections to the lower house of the Irish National Parliament. Spain does not permit those who hold other Latin American citizenships to vote or stand for election.[15] Peru, Argentina, and Columbia allow absentee voting by their dual citizen nationals. El

Salvador, Panama, Uruguay, and the Dominican Republic do not (De la Garza et al. 1966: 2-3; see also Jones-Correa 2000: 3, 5). The new Mexican law creates dual citizenship (but not nationality) and regulates it. Holders of Declaration of Mexican Nationality IDs will not be able to vote or hold political office in Mexico, to serve in the Mexican Armed Forces, or to work aboard Mexican-flagged ships or airlines (Martin 2000; see also *Migration News* 2000).

This brief survey is not meant to be exhaustive. However, it is meant to underscore one important point. Countries that allow multiple citizenships vary substantially in the specific ways and the extent to which they encourage or limit the responsibilities and advantages of their multi-citizenship nationals. It is possible both to permit and to regulate dual citizenship. Most countries that allow dual citizenship, also restrict it. The United States does not.

It would be useful to have an up-to-date survey of the practices of all dual-citizenship allowing countries. Yet if additional evidence is consistent with the limited survey above, the United States would surely be among the most, if not *the* most permissive dual citizenship allowing country—having no restrictions whatsoever in any of the wide range of practices that other countries regulate. This seems not to have been so much a matter of conscious public or political choice but a lack of awareness and the result of one core Supreme Court case.[16] That case has made it virtually impossible to lose one's American citizenship coupled with the economically, politically, and cultural motivated acts of other countries acting in their own self-interest.

Multiple Citizenship and American Immigration

Why should Americans care how many other countries allow their nationals to hold multiple citizenships, their motivation for doing so, or the specific ways in which they regulate, encourage, or limit specific responsibilities and entitlements? The answer to this question is complex and cannot be fully analyzed here. However, surely one key element of any answer has to do with recent patterns of American immigration.

The numbers noted at the beginning of this chapter are reflect the well-known and major changes in the rates and nature of immigration to the United States following Congress' 1965 landmark changes in the country's immigration law. No single number, of course, can do justice to the complex array of changes this law has promoted. However, some perspective can be gained from the most recent Census Bureau figures.[17]

As noted in chapter 3, the latest official estimates (Camorota 2001) of the number of foreign-born persons, of whatever legal status, living in the United States is more than twenty-eight million (28.3). This is the largest foreign-born population in our history and represents a thirty percent rise (6 million) over the 1990 figures. The number of immigrants for the last few years of the decade stretching from 1990, coupled with the total number of immigrants in the previous decade (19980-90) add up to the largest consecutive two-decade influx of immigrants in the country's history. The area of origin of the foreign-born population is as follows: 50.7 percent were born in Latin America, 27.1 percent were born in Asia, 16.1 percent were born in Europe, and the remaining 6.2 percent were from other parts of the world. The foreign-born population from Central America (including Mexico) accounted for two-thirds of the foreign-born population from Latin America and for one-third of the total foreign-born population (U.S. Department of Commerce 2000).

We have now reached the threshold necessary to begin answering the question: So what? The answer to that question, however, begins with the asking of another. What is the relationship between the countries that provide the vast pool of immigrants to the United States and the multiple citizenship status of those they send us? Some data are presented in Appendix II.

Appendix II presents a list of twenty selected, high immigrant-sending countries from Immigration and Naturalization Service official figures for 1994-1998. Those countries that allow their nationals to hold multiple citizenships status are highlighted in bold print. These data show that seventeen of these "top twenty"[18] immigrant-sending countries (85 percent) allow some form of multiple citizenship. One of the remaining three, Korea, is actively considering adapting such legislation.

The numbers for specific years are even more graphic. In 1998, of the 443,058 immigrants admitted that year from the "top twenty" sending countries, 361,437 (84.5 percent) were from multiple citizenship allowing countries. In 1997, of 552,556 immigrants from the "top twenty" sending countries, 474,559 (89.3 percent) were from multiple citizenship allowing countries. The figures for the years 1996, 1995, and 1994 are comparable, with multiple citizenship allowing countries accounting for 86.1 percent, 85.4 percent, and 84.8 percent, respectively, for each of these years. Overall, of the 2.6 plus million immigrants from the top twenty sending countries, 1994-1998, 2.2 plus million (86 percent) are multiple citizenship immigrants.

Recall too, that while seventeen of the "top twenty" immigrant-sending countries are multiple citizenship allowing countries, that number (17) represents only a small percentage of the total number (92) (not including the United States) of such countries. And, of course, many of these remaining seventy-five (75) multiple citizenship allowing countries send the United States many thousands of immigrants. A more detailed analysis might well find that numbers approaching or exceeding 90 percent of all immigrants come from multiple citizenship allowing countries.[19]

These numbers establish a basic and important fact: *American immigration policy is resulting in the admission of very large numbers of persons from countries that have taken legislative steps (for economic, political, and cultural reasons) to maintain and foster these persons' ties with the countries from which they emigrated.* One may disagree about the importance or implications of these facts, but not with their presence.

It is possible to argue, of course, that these figures are not really representative because they cover only the "top twenty" or because they cover a limited period of time. A wider frame of focus coupled with a longer historical analysis effectively allows us to dismiss this argument. An historical perspective on all current dual/multiple citizenship sending countries is found in Appendix III.

Appendix III presents data on immigration to the United States by nationals from all dual/multiple citizenship allowing countries for the three decades beginning in 1960 and then for every year beginning in 1991 and extending through 1997. Figures in bold beneath the dates represent the total level of legal immigration of that period. Figures in bold at the bottom represent the total contribution of dual/multiple citizenship allowing countries for that same period and their percentage of the total for that period. Given that data for some countries in some periods is not available (N/A), these figures under-represent the actual numbers. However, even so, they clearly show the extent to which immigrants to the United States are disproportionately from countries that allow or encourage dual/multiple citizenship and the retention of ties to their countries of birth/origin. Of the twenty-two million plus immigrants legally admitted into this country between 1961 and 1997, 16.3 million, or almost 75 percent, are from dual/multiple citizenship allowing countries.

There are several ways in which to gain some fuller appreciation of these figures. For example, if you examine the countries of birth that contribute 500,000 or more persons to America's foreign-born population in both 1990 and 1997, ten of thirteen (76 percent) are dual/multiple citizenship encouraging countries. In six of these countries there has been a substantial, statistically significant increase in the numbers of citizens from these countries in the seven years between the two sets of figures. In 1990, the last enumerated census year, seven of the top ten countries of birth of the foreign-born population in the United States were dual citizenship encouraging countries.[20]

All of these figures represent different ways of viewing a set of numbers that have been gathering size and importance since the profound changes in American immigration law in 1965. These numbers have been accumulating by the millions. Yet they have done so largely without notice or analysis.

Further, as substantial or surprising as these figures may be, they do not tell the whole story of the number of dual/multiple citizens arriving and living in the United States. To further deepen our understanding we must turn to two other categorical sources: illegal immigrants and immigrant fertility rates.

Legal Immigration of Multiple Citizenship Nationals: Not the Whole Story

Legal immigration is an important element in understanding the numbers that fuel the importance and implications of dual/multiple citizenship in the United States, but by no means the only one. A fuller understanding requires us to look at two other sets of figures. The first figures estimate the number of illegal immigrants that arrive in this country. The second concern the children of dual/multiple citizenship nation immigrants, whether legal or not, since all are by law American citizens.

Illegal Immigration [21]

One source of dual citizens in the United States is not often discussed—illegal immigrants. Illegal immigrants are relevant to the total dual citizenship in the United States in two ways. First, the children of illegal immigrants born in the United States are American citizens by birth and dual citizens by parental nationality. And second, illegal immigrants can be, and have often become, legalized through various "amnesty" programs that the government has enacted over the years.

The Immigration Reform and Control Act of November 6, 1986 (IRCA) authorized legalization (i.e., temporary and then permanent resident status) for aliens who had resided in the United States in an unlawful status since January 1, 1982 (those who entered illegally or as temporary visitors with authorized stay expiring before that date or with the government's knowledge of their unlawful status before that date were not eligible). The Triennial Comprehensive Report of Immigration (INS) estimates that in addition, 2.676 million persons gained lawful permanent residence as a direct result of IRCA.

In 1997, President Clinton considered making use of a rarely exercised executive authority, to exempt 20,000 illegal Haitian immigrants from deportation (Schmitt 1997) . In 1997, he did sign a law extending amnesty provisions for Guatemalans and Salvadorans (INS 1997). Two years later, he made a decision to grant eighteen months of amnesty to Hondurans and Nicaraguans living illegally in the United States because of storm damage in their countries of origin. That period was later extended for Nicaraguans (U.S. Government 2000).

In 2000, proposals were made, which President Clinton supported (Associated Press 2000), allowing anyone who came to the United States illegally before 1986 to apply for legal residence. That bill (Schmitt 2000; Nakashima 2000), the Latino and Immigrant Fairness Act, would have allowed at least 400,000 people who came into the United States before 1986—and most likely more—to apply for permanent residency. It would also have offered legal status to 300,000 immigrants who fled wars and political chaos in Haiti, El Salvador, Honduras, Guatemala, and Liberia and applied unsuccessfully for refugee status.

And, of course, after his election in 2000, President Bush proposed an amnesty for an undetermined number of illegal Mexican immigrants (Eggen and Fears 2001). Criticized for not including the illegal immigrants of other countries, President Bush said he "would consider granting legal residency to all undocumented immigrants, not just Mexicans, who came to the U.S. to work" (*Wall Street Journal* 2001). Democrats in Congress immediately upped the ante. They called for raising visa ceilings to reunite immigrant families, allowing most, if not all, immigrants living in the United States unlawfully to earn permanent legal status, and enhancing temporary worker programs with greater legal protections (Schmitt 2001).

Illegal immigration then, whether through the various amnesties that have been implemented over the years or because the children of illegal immigrants are citizens, or both, does have a bearing on dual citizenship numbers. And it does so on an ongoing basis. However, what exactly are the numbers and countries involved?

By its very nature, illegal immigration is hard to quantify accurately. Nonetheless, various estimates have been made, some relying on quite sophisticated methodology. In 1995, the INS attempted to estimate the number of illegal immigrants in the United States and arrived at a figure of about 5.0 million undocumented immigrants as of October 1996, with a range of about 4.6 to 5.4 million. The population was estimated to be growing by about 275,000 each year, which is about 25,000 lower than the annual level of growth estimated by the INS in 1994.

Although undocumented immigrants come to the United States from all countries the world, relatively few countries add substantially to the population. The annual growth of the illegal population can be grouped into four disparate categories: (1) Mexico, with more than half of the annual growth, adds just over 150,000 undocumented residents each year; (2) six countries—El Salvador, Guatemala, Canada, Haiti, Honduras, and the Bahamas—each add between 6,000 and 12,000 annually; (3) thirteen countries each add about 2,000 to 4,000 annually; and (4) the remaining approximately 200 other countries add a total of about 30,000 undocumented residents each year (see Table 4. 1). A large majority of the additions each year, more than 80 percent, are from countries in the Western Hemisphere. As we shall see, almost all of those countries encourage dual citizenship.

The figures above, however, proved much too low. As a result of reporting of the 2000 census, the bureau drastically revised its estimates. It now reports that the number of illegal immigrants in the country as of 2000 was over 8.4 million, with a range of 7.6 million and 8.8 million (U.S. Department of Commerce 2001; see also Cohn 2001). For the illegal population to have grown so much since the last estimates it would have to have been increasing by between 400,000 and 500, 000 people per year. These figures have important implications for domestic policy and national identity, but here I would like to maintain the focus on dual citizenship.

How many illegal immigrants come from dual-citizen countries? Complete figures for the revised 2000 census numbers are not yet available. However, the INS did provide estimates of the top twenty sending countries of illegal immigration in its 1996 estimates. They are given in Table 4.1 with dual citizenship countries in bold.

It is clear from the data in Table 4.1 that 19 of 20 (95 percent) of the top illegal immigrant sending countries are dual-citizenship allowing. This means

Table 4.1
Estimated Illegal Immigrant Population for Top
Twenty Countries of Origin (Estimate* 1996)

Population
All countries (Total, estimate)   5,000,000

Country of origin (Dual citizenship countries in bold)

1.	**Mexico**	2,700,000
2.	**El Salvador**	335,000
3.	**Guatemala**	165,000
4.	**Canada**	120,000
5.	**Haiti**	105,000
6.	**Philippines**	95,000
7.	**Honduras**	90,000
8.	**Poland**	70,000
9.	**Nicaragua**	70,000
10.	**Bahamas**	70,000
11.	**Colombia**	65,000
12.	**Ecuador**	55,000
13.	**Dominican Republic**	50,000
14.	**Trinidad & Tobago**	50,000
15.	**Jamaica**	50,000
16.	**Pakistan**	41,000
17.	**India**	33,000
18.	**Dominica**	32,000
19.	**Peru**	30,000
20.	Korea	30,000
	Other	774,000

*Source: U.S. Census: http://www.ins.gov/graphics/aboutins/statistics/illegalalien/index.htm

that every amnesty proposed and acted upon is highly likely to produce larger numbers of dual citizens in the United States. One might argue that the actually numbers involved here are, compared to regular legal immigration, relatively small. Consider Mexican illegal immigration, which represents 54 percent of all illegal immigration—almost three million persons. However, these estimates are now recognized as too low. Assume for the moment that illegal Mexican immigration represents the same 54 prcent of the new 8.4 million figure. That represents over 4.5 million illegal immigrants from this single source. These numbers are not small.

Yet the greatest impact of illegal immigration on dual citizenship numbers may not be found in looking at these numbers alone. Rather it is necessary to examine these numbers in the context of what we know about fertility rates of new immigrants. We turn to that analysis in the following section.

Fertility/Birth Rates

The Census Bureau estimates that the proportion of the foreign-born population is likely to increase in future years given that group's relative youth and high fertility rates. For example, the average foreign-born household had larger numbers of children under eighteen than the native-born household (1.02 vs. .067) Or, to put it another way, 60 percent of those with at least one foreign-born householder had one or more children under eighteen compared with 45 percent of native households. Foreign-born households were more likely to have two (44 versus 36 percent) or more (16 versus 9 percent) children than native-born households. Twenty-five percent of families with a foreign-born-householder from Latin America had three of more children, and among married couples, with householders from Mexico, this figure is 79 percent. And of course, illegal immigrants have children who are American citizens.

The latest census figures are even more striking (U.S. Department of Commerce 2000: 3). In 1999, 25.4 percent of family households in which a foreign-born person was the householder consisted of five or more people. In contrast, only 13.2 percent of native family households were this large. Among foreign-born households, the proportion with five or more people varied from 40.1 percent when the householder was from Central America to 11.1 percent when the householder was from Europe. For Latin America, generally, the figure was 33.0 percent.

So What? Revisited: Some Implications of Multiple Citizenships

The subtitle of this chapter of multiple citizenships is "An Issue of Vast Proportions and Broad Significance." We've examined the proportions, but what of the significance? What are the possible implications of having vast and increasing numbers of residents in the United States with multiple citizenships? Surely when over 85 percent of the very large number of immigrants that the United States admits each year are from such countries it is time to consider carefully the implications. When immigrants enter into a country in which the assumption that they should be motivated to adapt to the values and traditions of the country they have chosen is fiercely debated and the question of assimilation to what is increasingly difficult to answer, dual citizenship in America is, indeed, truly an issue of vast proportions and broad significance.

Notes

*   This chapter builds on Renshon (2000). I would like to thank Nathan Glazer and Mark Krikorian for their helpful comments. I would like also to acknowledge the valuable assistance of Sandra Johnson.

1.   The figures are drawn from the U.S. Department of Commerce (1997: 52-53).

2.   Nathan Glazer, "Is Assimilation Dead?" *The Annals of the American Academy of Political Science*, 1993, 530, pp.122-136.

3.   Americans may be slightly more familiar with the term dual citizenship, which denotes holding official citizenship status in at least two separate countries. Yet the

      term multiple citizenship is the more accurate one since it covers the holding of two, *or more* citizenships. No country that allows its nationals dual citizenship has any prohibition against holding more than one other. For example, Michael Jones-Correa notes that a number of South American countries (Argentina, Chile, Guatemala, Honduras, Nicaragua, and Paraguay) have dual citizenship agreements with other central American countries or with Spain, which, itself, is part of the European Union whose common citizenship treaties are being implemented. These countries, in turn, have more robust dual citizenship laws for their own citizens and foreign-born nationals (Jones-Correa 2000.) The terms dual and multiple citizenship(s) are therefore used interchangeably throughout this paper.

4.   Nationality is often thought of as expressed primarily through emotional attachments, and these are important. Yet, it would be a mistake to divorce a person's emotional attachments from the understandings and knowledge which both reflect and inform them.

5.   On these differences, see the work of Tomas Hammer (1998), Rodolfo De la Garza, et al. (1996: 2-3), and Jones-Correa (2000: 3, 5).

6.   While the Department of State now takes the position that acceptance of policy-level employment with a foreign government *will* be presumed a basis for denaturalization, a number of American dual citizens have held high positions in a foreign government without loss of citizenship. Raffi Hovannisian became Foreign Minister of Armenia, and stated publicly: "I certainly do not renounce my American citizenship," thus closing off a legal challenge to what he had done. Muhamed Sacirbey, Foreign Minister of Bosnia in 1995-96, is an American citizen and dual national. The chief of the Estonian army in 1991-95, Aleksander Einseln, also was an American. Many Americans have served at the United Nations as ambassadors of their other countries' citizenship (Franck 1996).

7.   For example, in 1986 following the Supreme Court's decision in Afroyim v. Rusk (387 U.S. 253) Congress repealed parts of the statutory provisions of the American citizenship law by adding the key requirement that loss of citizenship could occur only on the citizen's "voluntarily performing any of the following acts with the intention of relinquishing United States nationality" (Act of Nov. 14, 1986, § 18, 100 Stat. 3655, 3658 [codified as amended in 8 U.S.C. § 1481 1988]). With that, the onus shifted to the government to demonstrate that a designated act had been performed both voluntarily and with the specific intent to renounce U.S. Citizenship (Franck 1996).

8.   The reasons for ignoring these circumstances vary. A country may simply not perceive the practice as sufficiently important or widespread to merit attention or action. Or it may serve its own purposes—political, economic, or cultural by ignoring other ties from which they benefit. Or, the country may have legal prohibitions against the practice, which are weakened by another of that country's political institutions. For example, as Thomas Franck (1996) points out, Australian law as legislated in 1948 appeared to withdraw citizenship from any Australian who "does any act or thing: (a) the sole or dominant purpose of which; and (b) the effect of which; is to acquire the nationality or citizenship of a foreign country." Yet a recent court case there held that this provision did not apply to an Australian of partly Swiss origin who applied to the Swiss Government for recognition of her *jus sanguinis* status as a Swiss citizen. The case thereby opened the door to recognition of dual nationality since the court held that to lose Australian citizenship, the citizen's motive must have been to *acquire* Swiss citizenship, rather than to obtain recognition of an already-existing status of foreign nationality.

9.   Jones-Correa (2000: 32) offers Bolivia, Honduras, and Venezuela as examples of Latin American countries that allow repatriation upon return. Eugene Goldstein and

Victoria Piazza (1998: 1630) add Haiti to this list. This is, of course, a form of *de facto* dual citizenship. This form does not allow the exercising of formal political rights in the immigrant's country of origin, but to the extent that repatriation is the person's ultimate goal, it may very well effect attachments to a new country.

10.   These include: Capriotti & Associates-International Law, Portland, OR 97208-2792 [www.capriotti.com] (ND); Aleinikoff (1988a: 28-29); Goldstein and Piazza (1996: 517-521;1998: 1629-1632); Kalvaitis (1998: fn 184); Kang (1998: 1); Kempster (1999: 8); Schuck (1998: 223); Spiro (1977: 1455, 1457-58); Vargas (1996: 50, fn 198); Zappala and Castles (1999: 273); and Jones-Correa (2000: 3, 5).

11.   Most discussions of dual citizenship do not attempt comprehensive listings. Those discussions that do are often limited by those countries that do and those that do not respond to inquiries, or those for which information is otherwise unavailable. So for example, Goldstein and Piazza do not list Ireland (which does permit dual-citizenship). More troublesome are inconsistencies that arise from conflicts between what two or more different authors assert or from erroneous information.

Thus, Goldstein and Piazza (1996) list the Philippines and India as a non-dual citizenship countries, while Peter Schuck (1997: 11; 1998: 222) says they are, for American-born children of Filipino and Indian nationals. Along similar lines, Jones-Correa (2000) lists Argentina as having limited dual citizenship (with other treaty countries), while Goldstein and Piazza (1998) make no such distinction. And finally, Goldstein and Piazza list the Netherlands as a non-dual citizenship country, while the Schmitter-Heisler (1998) article discusses the effects of the Dutch dual citizenship law passed in 1992. In all cases of differences, inquiries were made of the appropriate embassies. In the few cases, where this did not produce clarification preference was given to the views of authors with established records of scholarship.

12.   The strategy employed for this study was to accept as accurate countries listed as allowing dual citizenship by reputable academic authorities in the study of immigration. Where a country was not listed as accepting multiple citizenships by previous studies, but which was important for our purposes in the analyses which follows, we emailed and called the embassies of those countries directly. After explaining our general interest in the subject and saying we would greatly appreciate their help we asked:

1. Whether your country now permits the children born of your nationals living abroad (for example, in the United States) to obtain or retain their citizenship in your country.

2. Whether your country now permits adult nationals living abroad to retain their citizenship in your country if they also become a citizen of another country (for example, the United States).

13.   This and the examples that follow are drawn from Franck (1996). A new German citizenship law and its implications are detailed in appendix I, footnote 1.

14.   Hammer (1985: 446) notes that some dual nationals face the risk of having to serve in two different armed forces if they travel to the country in which they hold citizenship/nationality but did not serve. He further notes that some countries, like Turkey, mandate in the Constitution that service in the army is a requirement for all Turks, period.

Later evidence however, suggests Turkey may have modified its position on this somewhat. Mark Miller reports that at a conference organized by the Alien Commission of the West Berlin Senate in 1989, the Turkish counsellor in Berlin said that his government permitted Turkish males living in Germany to pay 10,000 Deutsche Marks over a ten-year period to reduce their active time of service in Turkey to two months (Miller 1991: 948) .

15.   See Miller (1991: 948).

16.   There are a number of cases relevant to the circumstances through which American citizens may give up or lose their citizenship: Perkins v. Elg (1939); Kawakita v. U.S. (1952); Mandoli v. Acheson (1952); Perez v. Brownell (1958);Trop v. Dulles (1958); Schneider v. Rusk (1964); Afroyim v. Rusk (1967); Rogers v. Bellei (1971); Vance v. Terrazas (1980); and Miller v. Albright (1998).

However, by far the most important case is Afroyim v. Rusk, 387 U.S. 253 (1967), decided by the U.S. Supreme Court on May 29, 1967. In that ruling, the court held that to sustain a finding of citizenship loss under the [then current] Statement and the rules, there must have been forthcoming persuasive evidence establishing that the action taken by the citizen was accompanied by an *affirmative intention* to transfer allegiance to the country of foreign nationality, abandon allegiance owed the United States, or otherwise relinquish United States citizenship (emphasis mine).

What does "affirmation intention" mean? On April 16, 1990, the State Department adopted a new set of guidelines for handling dual citizenship cases which assumes that a U.S. citizen intends to retain his U.S. citizenship even if he or she: (1) is naturalized in a foreign country; (2) takes a routine oath of allegiance to a foreign country; or (3) accepts foreign government employment that is of a "non-policy-level" nature.

So, taking an oath of allegiance to another country is no longer taken as firm evidence of intent to give up U.S. citizenship, even if that oath includes a renunciation of U.S. citizenship. These assumptions do not apply to persons who: (1) take a "policy-level" position in a foreign country; (2) are convicted of treason against the U.S.; or (3) engage in "conduct which is so inconsistent with retention of U.S. citizenship that it compels a conclusion that [he] intended to relinquish U.S. citizenship." The third is unspecified and decided on a case by case basis.

For the law regarding this, see Immigration and Naturalization Service, Interpretations of the Citizenship and Naturalization Law, 350.1 Expatriation in the absence of elective action by persons acquiring dual nationality at birth prior to repeal of section 350.

17.   The figures that follow are drawn from the U.S. Department of Commerce, Economics and Statistics Administration, U.S. Census, "Profile of the Foreign Born Population in the United States: 1997," *Current Populations Reports Special Studies* (P23-195), pp. 8-49. Definitions of terms used are found in Appendix A, pp. 52-53.

18.   U.S. Department of Justice/Immigration and Naturalization Service.1999. "Annual Report: Legal Immigration, Fiscal Year, 1998," No. 2, May, p. 8. U.S. Department of Justice/Immigration and Naturalization Service, 1999. "Annual Report: Legal Immigration, Fiscal Year, 1997," No. 1, January, p. 9.

Both reports provide legal immigration figures for *selected* countries for the years they cover. As a result, some additional information is necessary to understand why the term "top twenty," while essentially accurate, is in quotes. One anomaly is that neither of the two documents include the countries making up the former Yugoslavia (Serbia and Montenegro, Croatia, Bosnia-Herzegovina, Macedonia, and Slovenia), all multiple-citizenship allowing countries, in their list of top immigrant sending countries. Yet with 10,750 immigrants in 1997 and 11,854 in 1996 coming from these countries in those two years, they certainly send more immigrants than several of the countries included in document's list of high-sending countries. For these reasons, the numbers and percentages of multiple citizenship country immigrants as a function of the total number of listed "top twenty" countries tends to *under-report* their magnitude.

One other anomaly of the table should be noted. The May 1999 report of 1995-1998 immigration figures includes one country (Bangladesh) that is not included in the top sending country list in the January 1999 document reporting the immigration figures for 1994-1997. The reports follow each of the countries listed back through several previous years. So the May 1999 report contains figures for Bangladesh for the years 1995-1998, even though it is not listed as a top sending country in the earlier January 1999 report, which covered the years 1994-1997. In that latter report, Ukraine is listed as a top immigrant-sending country and its immigrant-sending history is traced back from 1994-1997. However, in that report Bangladesh is *not* listed. Otherwise the specific countries listed are the same.

To more accurately reflect the realties of the data on high ("top twenty") immigrant sending countries, I have reported the Bangladesh data for 1998, but not for previous years when the numbers are well below those of Ukraine, which is listed in that "top twenty" group in the January 1999 report.

19. See the discussion that follows on illegal immigrants and immigrant fertility rates.
20. U. S. Census, "Profile of Foreign Born Population, 1997, p.12.
21. The two categories, illegal and legal, are separable, though often confounded by advocates on both sides of the many questions raised by American immigration policy. The difference may be succinctly stated. Illegal immigrants are those who enter this country with the intention of, and by, evading the administrative reviews that would accompany legal claims for residence. An example of undocumented legal immigrants would be ethnic Muslims who were stripped of their identification and other papers before being allowed to leave Serbia during the conflict in 1998. Many were offered an opportunity to resettle in the United States and other countries. They did so having lost their documentation, but they nonetheless went through an administrative review process before gaining admission. The same lack of documentation can be found in some case of authentic requests for asylum, yet it must also be said that some lack of documentation is meant to make verification of asylum claims difficult.

Some immigrant advocacy groups prefer the term "undocumented" rather than "illegal" for obvious reasons. It helps make it sound as if the many millions of illegal immigrants living here all accidently left their entry application and identification materials at home in their bureau drawers. And, of course, the legal and political standing of those who have gained entry by breaking U.S. laws differs from those whose genuine and dire (non-economic) circumstances have left them without full documentation.

References

Aleinikoff, T. Alexander. "Between Principles and Politics: The Direction of U.S. Citizenship Policy." Washington, DC: Carnegie Endowment for International Peace, 1998.

Camorota, Steven A. "Immigrants in the United States—2000: A Snapshot of America's Foreign Born Population." Washington, DC: Center for Immigration Studies, 2001.

Capriotti & Associates-International Law. Portland, Oregon [www.capriotti.com] April 16, 2000.

Castles, Stephen. "Multiculturalism Citizenship: A Response to the Dilemma of Globalisation and National Identity?" *Journal of Intercultural Studies* 18: 5 (1997).

Cohn, DJ'Vera. "Illegal Residents Exceed Estimate Experts Analyzing New Census Figures Say 6 Million May Instead be 9 Million." *Washington Post*, 18 March 2001: A01.

Editorial. "The Functionality of Citizenship." *Harvard Law Review* 110 (1997): 1814-1831.

Eggen, Dan, and Darryl Fears. "Bush Weighs Legal Status of Mexicans Illegal Immigrants May Get Residency." *Washington Post*, 16 July 2001: A01.

Escobar, G. "Immigrants' Ranks Tripled in 29 Years." *Washington Post*, 9 January 1999: A01

Franck, Thomas M. "Clan and Superclan: Law Identity and Community in Law and Practice." *American Journal International Law* 90 (1996):359.

De la Garza, Rodolfo O., Miguel David Baranoa, Tomas Pachon, Emily Edmunds, Fernando Acosta-Rodriguez, and Michelle Morales. " Dual Citizenship, Domestic Politics, and Naturalization Rates of Latino Immigrants in the U.S." The Tomas Rivera Center: Policy Brief, June 1966.

Glazer, Nathan. "Is Assimilation Dead?" *The Annals of the American Academy of Political Science* 530 (1993): 122-136.

Goldstein, Eugene, and Victoria Piazza. "Naturalization and Retention for Foreign Citizenship: A Survey," *Interpreter Releases* 73:16 (1996).

_____. "Naturalization and Retention for Foreign Citizenship: A Survey," *Interpreter Releases* 75:45 (1998), Appendix I.

Hammer, Tomas. "Dual Citizenship and Political Integration." *International Migration Review* 19: 3 (1985): 438-450.

INS: Statement Regarding the Nicaraguan Adjustment and Central American Relief Act. Washington, DC, 20 November 1997/PRNewswire.

Jones-Correa, Michael. "Under Two Flags: Dual Nationality in Latin America and Its Consequence for the United States." Working Papers in Latin America (no. 99/00-3), The David Rockefeller Center for Latin American Studies, Harvard University, 2000.

Kalvaitis, Ruta M. "Citizenship and National Identity in the Baltic States." *Boston University International Law Journal* 16:231 (1998).

Kang, K. Connie. "Dual U.S.-Korean Nationality Nears." *Los Angles Times,* 14 June 1998.

Kempster, Norman. "Crises in Yugoslavia; 3,000 to 4,000 U.S. Civilians Believed Stuck, Many of Those Living in the Two Republics Hold Dual Citizenship." *Los Angeles Times*, 3 April 1999.

Martin, Philip. "U.S. and California Reactions to Dual Nationality and Absentee Voting." Foreign Ministry of Mexico, February 17, 2000.

Migration News. "Mexico: Dual Nationality." March 2000. Vol. 7. No 3. http://migration.ucdavis.edu.

Miller, Mark J. "Dual Citizenship: A European Norm?" *International Migration Review* 33:4 (1991):945-950.

Morrison & Foerster LLP. "Issues Raised by Dual Nationality and Certain Reform Proposals," draft memorandum prepared for the U.S. Commission on Immigration Reform, July 13, 1997.

Nakashima, Ellen. "President Pressures GOP on Immigrant Aid Measure." *Washington Post*, 25 October 2000: A02.

O'Brien, Jeffrey R. "U.S. Dual Citizenship Voting Rights: A Critical Examination of Aleinkoff's Proposal." *Georgetown Immigration Review* 13:533 (1999): 573-595.

Renshon, Stanley A. "American Identity and the Dilemmas of Cultural Diversity," in Stanley A. Renshon and John Duckitt (eds.), *Political Psychology: Cultural and Cross Cultural Foundations*. (London: Macmillan, 2000).

Schmitt, Eric. "Clinton Expected to Spare Haitians from Deportation." *New York Times*, 17 December 1997.

_____. "G.O.P. Fight with Clinton on Immigrants Splits Party." *New York Times*, 22 October 2000.

_____. "Democrats Counter Bush Proposal on Immigrants." *New York Times*, 3 August 2001.

Schmitter-Heisler, Barbara. "Contents of Immigrant Incorporation," in Herman Kurthen, Jurgen Fijalkowski, and Gert. G. Wagner (eds), *Immigration, Citizenship, and Welfare in Germany and the United States: Welfare Policies and Immigrants' Citizenship*. Stamford, CT: JAI, 1998

Schuck, Peter M. *Citizens, Strangers, and In-Betweens: Essays on Immigration and Citizenship*.Boulder, CO: Westview Press, 1998.

_____. "The Re-Evaluation of American Citizenship." *Georgetown Immigration Law Journal* 12:1 (1997): 1-34.

Senders, Stephan. "National Inclusion in Germany." *New German Critique* 67 (1996): 147-175.

Spiro, Peter J. "Dual Nationality and the Meaning of Citizenship." *Emory Law Review* 46:4 (1997): 1412-1485.

Triennial Comprehensive Report on Immigration—1999/Executive Summary. Washington, DC: Immigration and Naturalization Service. h*ttp://www.ins.gov/graphics/aboutins/repsstudies/execsum.html*

U.S. Department of Commerce, Economics and Statistics Administration, U.S. Census. "Profile of the Foreign Born Population in the United States: 1997. *Current Populations Reports Special Studies* (P23-195). Washington, DC: U.S. Government Printing Office, 1997.

U. S. Department of Congress, Bureau of the Census. "Executive Steering Committee for Ace Policy II, Report #1-Appendix A, 13 October 2001. http:/www.census.gov/dmd/www/pdf/Report1.PDF

U.S. Department of Justice/Immigration and Naturalization Service. "Annual Report: Legal Immigration, Fiscal Year, 1998," No. 2, May 1999b.

_____. "Annual Report: Legal Immigration, Fiscal Year, 1997," No. 1, January 1999a.

U.S. Government Federal Register: 9 June 2000 (65:112), pp. 36721-36722.

Vargas, Jorge A. "Dual Nationality for Mexicans? "*Chicano-Latino Law Review* 18:1 (1996): 1-58.

Wall Street Journal. "Bush Will Consider Giving Residency to All Undocumented Immigrants." 27 July 2001.

Zachary, G. Pascal. "Dual Citizenship is a Double Edge Sword" *Wall Street Journal*, 25 March 1998: B1.

Zappala, Gianni, and Stephan Castles. "Citizenship and Immigration in Australia." *Georgetown Immigration Law Journal* 13: 273, 1999.

Appendix I
Countries/Territories Allowing Dual Citizenship in Some Form

1. Albania
2. Antigua & Barbuda
3. Argentina
4. Australia[1]
5. Bahamas
6. Bangladesh
7. Barbados
8. Balsarius
9. Belize
10. Benin
11. Bolivia
12. Brazil
13. Bulgaria
14. Burkina Faso
15. Cambodia
16. Canada
17. Cape Verde
18. Chile
19. Colombia
20. Costa Rica
21. Croatia
22. Cyprus
23. Cyprus (North)
24. Dominica
25. Dominican Republic
26. Ecuador
27. Egypt
28. El Salvador
20. Fiji
30. France
31. Germany [2]
32. Ghana
33. Greece
34. Grenada
35. Guatemala
36. Guyana
37. Haiti
38. Hungary
39. India[3]
40. Iran
41. Ireland
42. Israel
43. Italy
44. Jamaica
45. Jordan
46. Latvia
47. Lebanon

48. Lesotho
49. Liechtenstein
50. Lithuania[4]
51. Macao (with Portugal)
52. Macedonia
53. Madagascar
54. Malta
55. Mexico
56. Montenegro (Yugoslavia)
57. Mongolia
58. Morocco
59. Netherlands[5]
60. New Zealand
61. Nicaragua
62. Nigeria
63. Northern Ireland+
64. Panama
65. Pakistan
66. Paraguay
67. Peru
68. Pitcairn+
69. Philippines
70. Poland
71. Portugal
72. Romania
73. Russia
74. Saint Kitts (Saint Christopher) & Nevis
75. Saint Lucia
76. Saint Vincent
77. Serbia (Yugoslavia)
78. Slovenia
79. South Africa
80. Spain
80. Sri Lanka
82. Sweden
83. Switzerland
84. Taiwan
85. Trinidad/Tobago
86. Thailand
87. Tibet
88. Turkey
89. United Kingdom
90. United States
91. Ukraine
92. Uruguay
93. Vietnam

+=limited sovereignty, under UK law

Appendix II
Dual Citizenship Status of Top Twenty Immigrant-Sending Countries: 1994-1998

Country of birth	Number/% 1998	Number/% 1997	Number/% 1996	Number/% 1995	Number/% 1994
1. **Mexico**	**131,575(19.9)**	**146,865(18.4)**	**163,572 (17.9)**	**89,932 (12.5)**	**111,398 (13.8)**
2. China	36,884 (5.6)	41,147(5.2)	41,728 (4.6)	35,463 (4.9)	53,985 (6.7)
3. **India**	**36,482(5.6)**	**38,071(4.8)**	**44,859 (4.9)**	**34,748 (4.8)**	**34,921 (4.3)**
4. **Philippines**	**34,446(5.2)**	**49,117(6.2)**	**55,876 (6.1)**	**50,984 (7.1)**	**53,535 (6.7)**
5. **Dominican Republic**	**20,387(3.1)**	**27,053(3.4)**	**39,604 (4.3)**	**38,512 (5.3)**	**51,189 (6.4)**
6. **Vietnam**	**17,649(2.7)**	**38,519(4.8)**	**42,067 (4.6)**	**41,752 (5.8)**	**41,345 (5.1)**
7. Cuba	17,375(2.6)	33,587(4.2)	26,466 (2.9)	17,937 (2.5	14,727 (1.8)
8. **Jamaica**	**15,146(2.3)**	**17,840(2.2)**	**19,089 (2.1)**	**16,398(2.3)**	**14,349 (1.8)**
9. **El Salvador**	**14,590(2.2)**	**17,969(2.3)**	**17,903 (2.0)**	**11,744 (1.6)**	**17,644 (2.2)**
10. S. Korea*	14,268(2.2)	14,329(1.8)	18,185 (2.0)	16,047 (2.2)	16,011 (2.0)
11. **Haiti**	**13,499(2.0)**	**15,057(1.9)**	**18,386 (2.0)**	**14,021(1.9)**	**13,333 (1.7)**
12. **Pakistan**	**13,094(2.0)**	**12,969(1.6)**	**12,519 (1.4)**	**9,774 (1.4)**	**8,698 (1.1)**
13. **Colombia**	**11,836(1.8)**	**13,004(1.6)**	**14,283 (1.6)**	**10,838 (1.5)**	**10,847 (1.3)**
14a. Russia	**11,529(1.7)**	**16,632(2.1)**	**19,668 (2.1)**	**14,560 (2.0)**	**15,249 (1.9)**
14b. Ukraine	**NR**	**15,696(2)**	**21,079(2.3)**	**17,432(2.4)**	**21,010(2.6)**
15. **Canada**	**10,190(1.5)**	**11,609(1.5)**	**15,825 (1.7)**	**12,932 (1.8)**	**16,068 (2.0)**
16. **Peru**	**10,154(1.5)**	**10,853(1.4)**	**12,871 (1.4)**	**8,066 (1.1)**	**9,177 (1.1)**
17. **United Kingdom**	**9,011(1.4)**	**10,651(1.3)**	**13,624 (1.5)**	**12,427 (1.7)**	**16,326 (2.0)**
18. **Bangladesh**	**8,621(1.3)**	**NR**	**NR**	**NR**	**NR**
19. **Poland**	**8,469(1.3)**	**12,038(1.5)**	**15,772 (1.7)**	**13,824 (1.9)**	**28,048 (3.5)**
20. **Iran**	**7.883(1.2)**	**9,642(1.2)**	**11,084 (1.2)**	**9,201 (1.3)**	**11,422 (1.4)**
Total "Top Twenty" Immigration	443,058	552, 556	624,460	476,592	559,282
DC "Top Twenty" immigration	374,531	493,493	538,081	407,145	474,559
% DC of	(84.5%)	(89.3%)	(86.1%)	(85.4%)	(84.8%)
Other** Immigration	217,419	245,822	291,440	243,869	245,134
Total Immigration	660,477	798,378	915,900	720,461	804,416

Key: Dual citizen countries in bold

NR/not reported

* Dual-citizenship legislation pending in legislature

** Includes both dual and non dual-citizenship allowing countries

Appendix III
DC COUNTRIES ONLY - LISTED IN ALPHABETICAL ORDER
1961-1997- Immigrants Admitted by Region and Country of Birth

Country	1961-1970	1971-1980	1981-1990	1991	1992	1993	1994	1995	1996	1997	TOTAL
	3,221,677	4,493,314	7,338,062	1,827,167	973,977	904,292	804,416	720,461	915,900	798,378	21,997,644
1 Albania	N/A	N/A	N/A	6,713,934	682	1,400	1,489	1,420	4,007	4,375	6,727,307
2 Antigua & Barbuda	N/A	12,900	N/A	944	619	554	438	374	406	393	16,628
3 Argentina	42,100	25,100	25,700	3,889	3,877	2,824	2,318	1,762	2,456	1,964	111,990
4 Austria	N/A	N/A	N/A	589	701	549	499	518	554	487	3,897
5 Australia	9,900	14,300	13,900	1,678	2,238	2,320	2,049	1,751	1,950	1,630	51,716
6 Bahamas	N/A	N/A	7,300	1,062	641	686	589	585	768	641	12,272
7 Bangladesh	N/A	N/A	15,200	10,676	3,740	3,291	3,434	6,072	8,221	8,681	59,315
8 Barbados	9,400	20,900	17,400	1,460	1,091	1,184	897	734	1,043	829	54,938
9 Belize	N/A	N/A	18,100	2,377	1,020	1,035	772	644	786	664	25,398
10 Belarus	N/A	N/A	N/A	N/A	3,233	4,702	5,420	3791	4,268	3,062	24,476
11 Benin	N/A	N/A	N/A	24	10	21	18	23	38	48	182
12 Bolivia	N/A	N/A	12,300	3,006	1,510	1,545	1,404	1,332	1,913	1,734	24,744
13 Brazil	20,500	13,700	23,700	8,133	4,755	4,604	4,491	4,558	5,891	4,583	94,915
14 Bulgaria	N/A	N/A	N/A	623	1,049	1,029	981	1,797	2,066	2,774	10,319
15 Burkina Faso	N/A	N/A	N/A	8	16	11	16	17	17	13	98
16 Cambodia	1,200	8,400	116,600	3,251	2,573	1,639	1,404	1,492	1,568	1,638	139,765
17 Canada	286,700	114,800	119,200	13,504	15,205	17,156	16,068	12,932	15,825	11,609	622,999
18 Cape Verde	N/A	N/A	N/A	973	757	936	810	968	1,012	920	6,376
19 Chile	11,500	17,600	23,400	2,842	1,937	11,778	1,640	1,534	1,706	1443	75,380
20 Colombia	70,300	77,600	124,400	19,702	13,201	12,819	10,847	10,838	14,283	13,004	366,994
21 Costa Rica	17,400	12,100	15,500	2,341	1,480	1,368	1,205	1,062	1,504	1,330	55,290
22 Croatia	N/A	N/A	N/A	N/A	77	370	412	608	810	720	2,997
23 Cyprus	N/A	N/A	N/A	243	262	229	204	188	187	148	1,461
24 Cyprus (North)	N/A	N/A	N/A	N/A	N/A	N/A	N/A	N/A	N/A	N/A	0
25 Dominica	N/A	N/A	N/A	982	809	683	507	591	797	746	5,115
26 Dominican Rep	94,100	148,000	251,800	41,405	41,969	45,420	51,189	38,512	39,604	27,053	779,052
27 Ecquador	37,000	50,200	56,000	9,958	7,286	7,324	5,906	6,397	8,321	7,780	196,172
28 Egypt	17,200	25,500	31,400	5,602	3,576	3,556	3,392	5,648	6,186	5,031	107,091
29 El Salvador	15,000	34,400	214,600	47,351	26,191	26,818	17,644	11,744	17,903	17,969	429,620
30 Fiji	N/A	N/A	N/A	1,349	807	854	1,007	1,491	1,847	1,549	8,904
31 France	34,300	17,800	23,100	2,450	3,288	2,864	2,715	2,505	3,079	2,568	94,669
32 Germany	200,000	66,000	70,100	6,509	9,888	7,312	6,992	6,237	6,748	5,723	385,509
33 Ghana	N/A	N/A	14,900	3,330	1,867	1,604	1,458	3,152	6,606	5,105	38,022
34 Greece	90,200	93,700	29,100	2,079	1,858	1,884	1,440	1,309	1,452	1,049	224,071
35 Grenada	N/A	N/A	10,600	979	848	827	595	583	787	755	15,974
36 Guatemala	15,400	25,600	87,900	25,527	10,521	11,870	7,389	6,213	8,763	7,785	206,968

Appendix III (cont.)

	Country	1961-1970	1971-1980	1981-1990	1991	1992	1993	1994	1995	1996	1997	TOTAL
37	Guyana	7,100	47,500	95,400	11,666	9,064	8,384	7,662	7,362	9,489	7,257	210,884
38	Haiti	37,500	58,700	140,200	47,527	11,002	10,094	13,333	14,021	18,386	15,057	365,820
39	Hungary	17,300	11,600	9,800	1,534	1,304	1,091	880	900	1,183	949	46,541
40	India	31,200	176,800	261,900	45,064	36,755	40,121	34,921	34,748	44,859	38,071	744,439
41	Iran	10,400	46,200	154,800	19,569	13,233	14,841	11,422	9,201	11,084	9,642	300,392
42	Ireland	42,400	14,100	32,800	4,767	12,226	13,590	17,256	5,315	1,731	1,001	145,186
43	Israel	12,900	26,600	36,300	4,181	5,104	4,494	3,425	2,523	3,126	2,448	101,101
44	Italy	206,700	130,100	32,900	2,619	2,592	2,487	2,305	2,231	2,501	1,982	386,417
45	Jamaica	71,000	142,000	213,800	23,828	18,915	17,241	14,349	16,398	19,089	17,840	554,460
46	Jordan	14,000	29,600	32,600	4,259	4,036	4,741	3,990	3,649	4,445	4,171	105,491
47	Latvia	N/A	N/A	N/A	86	419	668	762	651	736	615	3,937
48	Lebanon	7,500	33,800	41,600	6,009	5,838	5,465	4,319	3,884	4,382	3,568	116,365
49	Lesotho	N/A	N/A	N/A	4	15	5	8	10	11	6	59
50	Liechtenstein	N/A	N/A	N/A	3	1	3	0	2	1	1	11
51	Lithuania	N/A	N/A	N/A	157	353	529	663	767	1,080	812	4,361
52	Macao(w/ Portugal)	N/A	N/A	N/A	267	320	334	287	373	453	277	2,311
53	Macedonia	N/A	N/A	N/A	N/A	N/A	N/A	367	666	863	783	2,679
54	Madagascar	N/A	N/A	N/A	23	41	32	27	42	43	33	241
55	Malta	N/A	N/A	N/A	83	85	52	75	72	52	54	473
56	Mexico	443,300	637,200	1,653,300	946,167	213,802	126,561	111,398	89,932	163,572	146,865	4,532,097
57	Mongolia	N/A	N/A	N/A	2	6	8	21	17	17	22	93
58	Montenegro	N/A	N/A	N/A	N/A	N/A	N/A	N/A	N/A	N/A	N/A	0
59	Morocco	N/A	N/A	6,700	1,601	1,316	1,176	1,074	1,726	1,783	2,359	17,735
60	Netherlands	27,800	10,700	11,900	1,283	1,586	1,430	1,239	1,196	1,423	1,059	59,616
61	**New Zealand	N/A	N/A	N/A	793	967	1,052	918	727	800	655	5,912
62	Nicaragua	10,100	13,000	44,100	17,842	8,949	7,086	5,255	4,408	6,903	6,331	123,974
63	Nigeria	1,500	8,800	35,300	7,912	4,551	4,448	3,950	6,818	10,221	7,038	90,538
64	Northern Ireland	N/A	N/A	N/A	N/A	N/A	N/A	N/A	N/A	N/A	N/A	0
65	Panama	18,400	22,700	29,000	4,204	2,845	2,679	2,378	2,247	2,560	1,981	88,994
66	Paraguay	N/A	N/A	N/A	538	514	668	789	559	615	304	3,987
67	Pakistan	4,900	31,200	61,300	20,355	10,214	8,927	8,698	9774	12,519	12,967	180,854
68	Peru	18,600	29,100	64,400	16,237	9,868	10,447	9,177	8,066	12,871	10,853	189,619
69	Philippines	101,500	360,200	495,300	63,596	61,022	63,457	53,535	50,984	55,876	49,117	1,354,587
70	Pitcairn	N/A	N/A	N/A	N/A	N/A	N/A	N/A	N/A	N/A	N/A	0
71	Poland	73,300	43,600	97,400	19,199	25,504	27,846	28,048	13,824	15,772	12,038	356,531
72	Portugal	79,300	104,500	40,000	4,524	2,748	2,081	2,169	2,615	2,984	1,665	242,586
73	Romania	14,900	17,500	38,900	8,096	6,500	5,601	3,444	4,871	5,801	5,545	111,158
74	*SU/Russia	15,700	43,200	84,000	56,980	8857	12079	15249	14,560	19,668	16,632	286,925
75	Saint KittsNevis	N/A	N/A	N/A	830	626	544	370	360	357	377	3,464

Appendix III (cont.)

	Country	1961-1970	1971-1980	1981-1990	1991	1992	1993	1994	1995	1996	1997	TOTAL
76	Saint Lucia	N/A	N/A	N/A	766	654	634	449	403	582	531	4,019
77	Saint Vincent	N/A	N/A	N/A	808	687	657	524	349	606	581	4,212
78	Yugo/Serbia	46,200	42,100	19,200	2,713	2,604	2,809	3,405	8,307	11,854	10,750	149,942
79	Slovenia	N/A	N/A	N/A	N/A	8	50	67	65	77	62	329
80	South Africa	4,500	11,500	15,700	1,854	2,516	2,197	2,144	2,560	2,966	2,093	48,030
81	Sri Lanka	N/A	N/A	N/A	1,377	1,081	1,109	989	960	1,277	1,128	7,921
82	Sweden	16,700	6,300	10,200	1,080	1,463	1,393	1,140	976	1,251	958	41,461
83	Switzerland	16,300	6,600	7,000	696	1,023	972	877	881	1,006	1,063	36,418
84	Taiwan	N/A	N/A	N/A	13,274	16,344	14,329	10,032	9,377	13,401	6,745	147,652
85	Thailand	5,000	44,100	64,400	7,397	7,090	6,654	5,489	5,136	4,310	3,094	152,670
86	Tibet	N/A	N/A	N/A	N/A	N/A	N/A	N/A	N/A	N/A	N/A	0
87	Trinidad/Tobago	24,600	61,800	39,500	8,407	7,008	6,577	6,292	5,424	7,344	6,409	173,361
88	Turkey	6,800	18,600	20,900	2,528	2,488	2,204	1,840	2,947	3,657	3,145	65,109
89	UK	230,500	123,500	142,100	13,903	19,973	18,783	16,326	12,427	13,624	10,651	601,787
90	Ukraine	N/A	N/A	N/A	N/A	14,383	18,316	21,010	17,432	21,079	15,696	107,916
91	Uruguay	N/A	N/A	8,300	1,161	716	568	516	414	540	429	
92	Vietnam	4,600	179,700	401,400	55,307	77,735	59,614	41,435	41,752	42,067	35,519	942,039
		2,594,700	3,298,600	5,777,500	1,678,064	806,103	720,194	633,847	564,291	736,269	628,039	
		%DC=80%	%DC=73%	%DC=78%	%DC=91%	%DC=82%	%DC=79%	%DC=78%	%DC=78%	%DC=80%	%DC=78%	

1961-1997 %DC= Total DC (174, 376, 077)/immigration total (21,997,644) = 79%

Appendix I Notes

1. For information on Australia, see Gianni Zappala and Stephan Castles (1999: 273, fn 137; see also Castles 1997) who quote the Australian Citizenship Act of 1948 as follows: "People must have deliberately sought and acquired the citizenship of another country in order to lose their Australian citizenship; if they acquire it automatically rather than by taking some action to acquire it they do not lose their Australian citizenship."

2. In July 1999 the Citizenship Law Reform Act was published in the German official gazette. This act entered into force on January 1, 2000. Under the new law, German citizenship has always been and will continue to be passed on by parents to the children. Any child of a German national (mother or father, married or not married) will be considered a German citizen by birth, whether born inside or outside Germany. The Reform Act introduces an aspect of "territorial acquisition": any child born inside Germany to parents of foreign nationality will acquire German nationality by birth if at least one parent has been lawfully residential in Germany for at least eight years and has for at least three years been the holder of a certain higher form of residence permit. This new provision will apply to most children of migrant workers who have been living in Germany for at least eight years. Those children, however, once they have grown up will have to decide between keeping German citizenship and renouncing their other citizenship (i.e., that of their parents) or keeping the foreign nationality and losing the German nationality. Under the existing German Citizenship Law (which in this respect corresponds to that of many other countries). German nationals lose their German citizenship if and when they acquire a foreign nationality upon their own application, i.e. by naturalization.

    It has always been possible in theory to be granted a waiver by German authorities for keeping German citizenship when acquiring a foreign nationality. Under the new law this waiver will be granted more easily. The relevant section of the Act reads: When deciding upon an application in accordance with sentence 1 (waiver), the public and private interests will have to be balanced. In the case of an applicant with residence abroad, it will have to be taken into consideration whether he/she can make the case for continuing links to Germany."

    That means in effect, that in terms of the naturalization of foreigners as well as the acquisition of foreign citizenship by Germans the threshold of tolerance of dual citizenship (which has never been a problem in the case of acquisition of several nationalities by birth) will be made much more flexible.

    While there is a provision requiring renunciation, Stephan Senders says that in the past there has been no requirement to prove that it was done. He reports that according to unofficial government estimates 8 percent of naturalizing Turks retain their Turkish citizenship. Ethnic Germans who have other citizenships were allowed, even under the old law, to retain their German citizenships even when they were naturalized in other countries. A 1993 government study estimated that 1.2. million Germans legally held a second foreign citizenship. See Senders (1996: 158-159).

    The fact that the United States makes no effort to follow through on the renunciation clause in its own oath of allegiance essentially renders any such provisions in the laws of other countries a moot point.

3. See Schuck (1997: 11; 1998: 222).

4. Ruta Kalvaitis (1998: 231, fn 184: 227, footnote 184) reads: "Members of the Latvian diaspora, however, are allowed to hold dual citizenship. See Law on Citi-

zenship (Lat.), supra note 175, transitional provisions 1, 2. Footnote 227 reads: "Lithuania, however, allows members of its Western emigre community to hold dual nationality, despite the fact there is no established law to this fact."

5.   See Barbara Schmitter-Heisler (1998:103-104, fns 14, 15).

5

Do Multiple National Loyalties Equal Conflicted National Loyalties?*

America has entered a period in which the acquisition of multiple national identifications are legal, technologically feasible, and from the standpoint of individuals and some states—politically and economically advantageous. The question that arises is whether multiple national identifications are equally advantageous or even desirable for the relatively small number of Western industrial democracies, most notably the United States, that are being called upon to accept and embrace such developments.

Advocates of dual citizenship and multiple nationalities look to the past, and reassure us that we are unlikely to go to war over dual citizenship, as we did with the British in 1812 (Spiro 1997: 1422-1423; see also Martin 1999: 20). That conflict arose when the British, then following the "perpetual allegiance" theory of citizenship, forcibly tried to repatriate American citizens at sea. It is hardly imaginably that we would go to war with any country over its claim on any citizens who happen to have more than one nationality.

So, yes, it is true that we will not go to war with Britain, or anyone else over these kinds of matters. Neither will we use forceful coercion to require Israel to return one of its dual citizens who committed a murder in the United States and fled the country. It is a fact of contemporary international politics that democracies rarely go to war with one another (Russett 1993).

Still, that does not end the matter and may not even constitute a proper focus of the question. If multiple citizenships and loyalties no longer raise the prospects of war between countries, is not the same as saying they raise no troubling conflicts. If war between democracies is unlikely, this does not mean that war or armed conflict between democracies and states organized on other political principles is still not possible. And finally, the fact that war between states of whatever political persuasion is unlikely *over* these issues, does not mean that such concerns do not raise profound domestic concerns for countries so affected.

In this chapter I take up the question of whether multiple national loyalties necessarily result in conflicting national loyalties. I begin with the question of conflict between nations, which has historically been the cause of much of the conflict over multiple nationalities and loyalties, and agree that dual citizenship per se is unlikely to lead to war. However, I argue that this is at best a very shallow consideration of the issues at stake given a focus on conflict.

Loyalty and identification to a country are complex concepts, and I distinguish between primary and secondary attachments. I then present some evidence from studies of the acquisition of national identity and loyalty in children, which suggests that early attachments are not so easily discarded or modified. These data present a cautionary message to those who argue that many important identity elements can easily coexist with the same psychology.

Yet, the question of how individuals integrate or fail to integrate multiple identity elements is not solely a matter of interior psychology. An individual's loyalties, attachments, and identifications unfold in the context of the society and culture in which he develops. A changing national psychology (see chapter 2) or a changing national culture (see chapter 2) both provide the basis for a different configuration of identity. In this chapter, I want to focus on another feature of the current political international and American environment that has a profound impact on the extent to which we might worry about multiple nationalities and loyalties. That feature is the conscious and strategic decision of other national governments to recognize and make use of international migration patterns for their own state and political purposes. Mexico provides a useful case study of why such developments may be of some domestic American national concern.

What evidence is there that even if foreign government do wish to make use of their dual citizen nationals, there is reason for concern, much less alarm? Again, the case of Mexican-Americans is instructive and I examine some data relevant to trying to answer this question. And finally, advocates of multiple nationalities and loyalties ask a fair question: What's different now? Haven't Americans of different national descents such as the Irish and the Jews, lobbied in favor of their particular home counties throughout American history? Obviously, the answer to that question is yes (Smith 2001), so why should it be more of a concern now? There are at least five answers to that question.

Dual Citizenship and Political Conflict: The War of 1812 Redox?

Peter Spiro, who argues that we should "embrace dual nationalism, says,

> The prospective spectacle of millions of Mexican American dual nationals lining up at their consulates to vote in Mexican elections, on the one hand, and the possibility of their voting in high concentration in some U.S. Elections on the other suffices to justify the enterprise [e.g., reappraising dual nationality]...however the oddity of these developments should not by itself provoke resistance. In fact, *under the standard of earlier times*, dual nationality now poses little threat to the polity. (1997: 1460; see also 1468, fn 246)

What are these standards of earlier times to which he refers? Spiro argues that (1997: 1461) now "democracies rarely make war on each other," and, it was war that ultimately made dual citizenship so problematic in a hostile world. In a maligned incarnation they [nationals] could undermine from within by doing the command of their other allegiance, threatening the polity at a fundamental level.

Spiro is raising the specter here that dual citizens might be treasonous because of their mixed loyalties in wartime, but asks us not to worry about this because democracies now rarely go to war. This is an extremely odd argument for an advocate of dual citizenship to make. If mixed loyalties are so dangerous to this republic that treason is a major issue, and I am *not* arguing that it is, then the fact that we rarely go to war with other democracies is small comfort.

The fact of the matter is that many of the ninety-two (not including the United States) immigrant-sending, dual-citizenship encouraging countries are not democracies. Of the top twenty immigrant-sending countries to the United States (see chapter 4) which account for 84 percent of our total number of immigrants each year, only three—Canada, the United Kingdom and India— are mature democracies. Most are not democratic (e.g., Iran, Pakistan, Vietnam etc.) and the rest are fledgling democracies often with large and deeply rooted authoritarian strains (e.g., Mexico, the Dominican Republic, Russia, Ukraine, etc.).

However, democracies do still have armed conflicts with non-democracies. And as David Martin (1999: 8, fn 23) points out, "If relaxed rules on dual nationality are adapted or expanded over the coming decades, persons with such a mix of citizenship (one democratic and one non-democratic) will undoubtedly make up a significant percentage." Martin adds that the "especially worrisome cloud" of the rise of ethnic tensions and identity politics will increase the structural fault lines in a large number of what he terms "polyglot nations," of which the United States is surely now one.

Martin is not wrong to worry. In Santa Ana, California, former Vietnamese communists and their non-communist counterparts scuffled during a protest against an art show's positive depiction of the communist regime (*New York Times* 1999). In another similar incident, the decision of a Vietnamese immigrant to drape a communist flag across the front of his store sparked thousands to protest (Sanchez 1999).

In Miami, in the Elian Gonzalez case, residents of South Miami, backed by their local government, said they would defy federal orders to hand the boy over to immigration authorities. The *New York Times* reporter (Bragg 2000) who covered the story wrote,

> To many people here, some who cheered and some who shuddered, it was a declaration of independence for a part of the country that is, increasingly, a nation apart. People have even begun to greet each other with: "Welcome to the Independent Republic of Miami." Latin Americans make up the overwhelming majority, and English has faded from homes, offices and stores. But it is the Cuban exiles who drive the county's economy, politics and culture, and it is Cuba's flag, not the United States,' in the windows of shops, on car antennas and on the mural behind the Chevrolet dealership on Le Jeune Road.

During the outbreak of violence in the Middle East in the last six months of 2000 large groups of anti-Israeli/pro Arab demonstrators held noisy protests at which several were arrested (Waldman 2000; see also Barry and Christian 2000). During this period several Jewish synagogues were vandalized (Chivers 2000).

Given these facts, the optimism of multiple-citizenship advocates that inter-nation conflict that has implications for dual citizens is an historical relic is wishful thinking. The evidence simply does not support such naive optimism. Yet, while international military conflicts that engage or test the loyalties of dual citizens in this country can not be easily ruled out, the real problem is not war, but cohesion.

Do Multiple Loyalties Equal Conflicted Loyalties?

Loyalty is a complex concept and an even more complex emotion. Psycho-logically, it is basically an attachment to, a sense of identification with, and feel-ings "toward a person, place or "thing."[1] These can run from the shallow to the profound, from the episodic to the immutable, and from the singular to the diverse.

Primary nationality, the one that we are born into, begins to take root very early, indeed even before a child is born. The history and practices that brought a particular couple together are themselves influenced by the cultural expecta-tions and understandings that the couple acquired while growing up in their country and culture. How they prepare for and how they relate to their child is also conditioned by the same cultural factors. And, of course, the parents speak to the child in their own language, soon to be his, and as he grows they are the guides and interpreters of the cultural he must learn and traverse. Being embed-ded in and attached to one's country of origin begins early.

Children begin to incorporate the symbols of their nationality and country at an early age. E. L. Horowitz (1940) found that 25 percent of a sample of first graders in Tennessee chose the American flag as best, and that by seventh grade the number doing so was 100 percent. Lawson (1963) later replicated that study in an urban-suburban New York sample and found that from kindergarten chil-dren put the stars and stripes first. Eugene Weinstein (1957) found that children's first notions of viewing their country as "good" and other countries as "bad" surfaced as early a five years old. The emotional attachments to country clearly begin much earlier than the cognitive development level necessary to sustain an intellectual understanding of the concepts (Jahoda 1973). Indeed, that is precisely the fulcrum of their life-long power.

Summing up a variety of such early studies, A. F. Davis (1968: 114) con-cludes:

> the main lesson ...is how early and closely they conform to a relatively stable and complex order of preferences appropriate to their American nationality...it runs through all grades, it is common to boys and girls, impervious to the syllabus and remarkably resistant to background factors like family social status or region.

What is the point of these studies? Just this: Loyalty to a nation and the feelings of attachment begin at a primal age and become increasing consolidated as the child develops. That is why people are willing to die for their country, why great national accomplishments bring pride, and why the symbols of a country—the flag, a constitution—carry such great emotional weight and political power.

It is why a *New York Times* reporter (Waldman 1999) , covering the attitudes of African immigrants to this country could write, "Many African Immigrants say that whether they stay here for 2 or 20 years, Africa is, and always will be, home." It is why Funeraria Latina—owned by funeral industry giant Service Corporation International—transports 80 percent of the bodies out of the United States (Finley 1998). Alejandro Ruiz, who left Mexico and began working on landscaping crews around Denver, became a U.S. citizen, raised ten children, has forty grandchildren and three great-grandchildren here, and can still say he wants to be buried at "home," meaning Mexico. He says (quoted in Finley 1998),

> My heart is here, but it's also there.... Even though here I made money, enough to feed my family—it was easier for me to make a living here—I will go back to Mexico. When I die, I must go back to Mexico.

It is why Lan Samantha Chang (1999), a novelist writing in response to the Wen Ho Lee case could say in a *New York Times* Op Ed piece entitled "Debunking the Dual Loyalty Myth, "True, many immigrants have strong ties to their countries of birth....But cultural or familial loyalties are on a different level from political allegiances....I love China, but I am a citizen of the United States." Chang appears to want to distinguish between a love for one's "home" country and being willing to commit treason against one's adopted country. This is obviously a fair, reasonable, and appropriate distinction.

Yet in the process of making such a distinction, Chang acknowledges the duality of her feelings. The issue is not between love of one's country of origin and treason, but rather the multiple loyalties that appear to be part of many immigrants' psychology. Consider the case of Aida Ridanovic, an immigrant from Bosnia. She says (quoted in Finley 1998),

> On one hand, I've become so American that, if I go back, there will be tons and tons of things I'll miss. On the other, I am so much a Sarajevan that every day I pray to God that somebody will offer me a job there.... I live my life on two tracks, one here, one there. And I am assimilated. I have a quite ordinary American life. I have a job. My husband has a job. We have our kids in day care. We pay taxes. We have a new holiday, Thanksgiving, which I really do care about. And we celebrated the Fourth of July...[however]I want to die in Sarajevo.

Ridanovic adds, refugees forced to leave their homes "may not like America, but all of them agree on one fact: They have a better life in America."

Or, consider the reactions of some Mexican Americans interviewed about whether they would apply for U.S. Citizenship in light of Proposition 187. Some of the answers were included in Corchado and Anderson (1994):

(1) Never, I was born in Mexico, raised in Mexico, and I want to die in Mexico.... (2) [G]iving up my Mexican citizenship is like giving up a child of mine.... (3) Its as though I'm betraying my country, my people and my culture.

The point here is not that immigrants are disloyal. They are, however, conflicted. And increasingly, governments of dual-citizen-sending countries are taking steps to insure that the loyalties and attachments that many immigrants feel for their country of origin are maintained and even stimulated. A good illustration of the issues involved in these developments can be found in examining the case of Mexico and its immigrants to the United States.

Mexico's Dual Citizenship Decision:
A Mix of Self-Interested Motivations

Mexico, which shares a long border with the southwest and western United States, is one of the single highest sending countries of immigrants into the United States. Half of the foreign-born population in the United States is from Latin America, and more than a quarter (28 percent) are from Mexico.

Or, consider that in 1960, 1970, 1980, and 1990 Mexico was one the top ten countries that sent immigrants to the United States (U.S. Department of Commerce 1997: 13, Table 3-1). In 1980 and 1990 it was *the* highest immigrant-sending country. This will no doubt be true as well for the 2000 figures. In 1980, there were 2.1 million Mexicans living in the United States. By 1990, that figured had doubled to over 4.2 million. By 1994, that figure had jumped to 6.6 million (de la Grazia 1997, 2). And by 1997, that figure had jumped to over 7 million (U.S. Department of Commerce 1997: 12).

Mexican Americans, in particular, have significantly high birth-rates. The Census Bureau estimates that the proportion of the foreign-born population is likely to increase in future years given that group's relative youth and high fertility rates. As previously noted, the average foreign-born household has larger numbers of children under eighteen than the native-born household (1.02 vs. .067). Twenty-five percent of families with a foreign-born householder from Latin America has three or more children, and among married couples, with householders from Mexico, this figure is 79 percent.

As Steven Holmes (1998: A12) points out in his analysis of the 1998 National Center for Health Statistics study:

[M]uch of the increase in Hispanic-origin births is a result of high fertility rates among Mexican Americans, particularly recent immigrants. About 70 percent of the babies born to Hispanic women 1995—up from 61 percent in 1989—were born to women of Mexican heritage....The study provides further evidence that people of Mexican heritage have an increasing demographic significance in American society. The study's findings strongly imply that, as a result of high levels of immigration and a high birth rate, people of Mexican heritage are poised to become a major economic, political, and cultural force in the coming decades.

These facts have not been lost on the government of Mexico. As Paula Gutierrez (1997; see also Vargas 1996: 7-10) points out in discussing Mexico's new dual nationality laws, "The dual nationality amendments radically depart from Mexican tradition and laws." The change requires that three articles of the Mexican constitution be amended and at least fifty-five secondary laws be repealed or revised. This enormous undertaking represents, "a sharp reversal after decades in which successive governments either ignored Mexican expatriates or referred to them as pochos, or cultural traitors" (Dillon 1995). What changed?

The full story of that change has yet to be written, but it will surely entail self-interested strategies on the part of the ruling Mexican party, the opposition party trying to make inroads against it, and a growing chorus of Mexican-Americans who want to further their economic, political and cultural claims in their country of origin. Each of these parties has their own versions of self-interest, but it is instructive to note that the interests of the United States were clearly absent.

This does not by itself make Mexican dual-citizenship an adverse development for the United States. However, it does underscore the extent to which the calculations that led to Mexico's decision to enact dual citizenship were taken with the self-interests of the three Mexican groups wholly in mind. Its impact on the politics, economy, and culture of the United States counted for very little, if at all, in these calculations.

And what are these calculations? Several seem quite clear. Mexico has always depended on the northward movement of immigrants into the United State to reduce population and economic pressures, and the political consequences that flow from them. Encouraging northward migration operates, therefore, as a "safety valve" for Mexican society and, not incidently, for its governing elites.

Mexico, like other immigrant-sending countries, benefits economically from sending many of its nationals to the United States to work. The reason is that Mexican nationals, working in the United States, are a key source of national income, which itself helps to relieve economic and thus political pressures on the governing elites. A recent study (de la Garza et al. 1997: 1-2) on the binational impact of Latino financial remittances found that because of "the very large number" of new arrivals from Latin America remittances have "dramatically increased" and "represent a substantial contribution to the national economies of the receiving countries."[2]

Specific figures for Mexico are themselves startling. For example, in 1990 the five countries that one study examined (Columbia, Dominican Republic, El Salvador, Guatemala, and Mexico) received over $1 billion in remittance income, however, "remittances to Mexico account for over half of the total amounts sent to the five countries combined (De la Garza et al. 1997: 2)." As the authors (p. 3) point out, the World Bank figures they used are "conservative estimates, and others indicate that Mexican remittances account for between $2 to $4 billion." Moreover, Mexico was one of three countries in which the increase in rates of remittances was greater than its immigrants' income (p. 4). Finally, the amount of remittances to all five countries exceeds the amount of U.S. aid, and this is true even for countries like El Salvador, which received the largest amount of such aid in the 1980s.

From the standpoint of Mexican economic incentives, the advantages of dual citizenship to Mexico are clear. The more closer ties to the "homeland" can be encouraged and stimulated, the more stable the flow of remittances will be and the more likely they are to increase over time. Removing barriers that keep Mexican Americans alienated from their home country is another plus from this standpoint. Dual-citizen Mexican Americans can now send their money home and have use of it when they spend time, retire, or even die there. From the self-interested economic perspective of Mexican Americans, this is a positive development.

However, powerful economic incentives are—and they are substantial—it would be a severe error to underestimate the political importance of Mexican Americans to the Mexican government. Spiro has argued (1997: 1470) that, "Mexico and other countries would have no concrete means to use their nationals as instruments, at least not consistent with international law..." I am not sure what international law making use of multiple loyalties is inconsistent with, but it is clearly part of the strategic thinking of Mexican leaders.

In a private meeting with U.S. Latino leaders in 1995, former Mexican President Zedillo said (quoted in Vargas 1996: 3)[3] that his government would support the then pending constitutional and other legal changes, allowing dual-citizenship to "increase the political clout of Mexican Americans." Why was he interested in doing that? For one reason because his goal was to "develop a close relationship between his [Mexico's] government and Mexican Americans, one in which *they could be called upon to lobby U.S. Policy makers on economic and political issues involving the United States and Mexico*" (Corchado 1995a: 11A, emphasis mine; see also Vargas 1996: 3).

Or, as Jorge Vargas notes, "the many recently developed Mexican government programs now in operation[4] to reach out to the Mexican American Community in the United States have a clear purpose:

> The government of Mexico is investing in Mexican Americans now and plans to collect tomorrow. Recognizing their political and economic power in the United States, but aware of their familial and spiritual links they continue to maintain with Mexico, the country of their ancestors, *the Mexican government is hoping to contribute to the development of a powerful and effective lobby ready to represent and defend the interests of Mexico in this country.* (1996: 9; emphasis mine)

Speaking of the Mexican government change in its approach to Mexican Americans, Raul Izguirre, president of the National Council of La Raza, said in an 1996 interview (quoted in Corchado 1995b: A1; see also Vargas 1996: 7, fn 23, emphasis mine):

For Many years there was an aversion by Mexico to deal with our community. *Now they realize we represent a long term interest.*

What interests are these? Writing before the changes became law, Vargas says,

> Mexicans with dual nationality would raise an array of novel and delicate questions in the United States. Such questions may address international law in general, and specific areas of domestic legislation of these two countries. Taxation, labor issues, acquisition of real estate and other business transactions, inheritance, domicile, military service, family law and minor's rights, deportation and other immigration law aspects, political rights and diplomatic protection may be among the long list of technical legal questions directly affected by this contemplated legal change. (1996: 3)

To this substantial list, one might add newly elected Mexican president Vincente Fox's call (Jordan 2000; Thompson 2000) for essentially open borders between the two countries. Since almost all the traffic would go in the south to north direction, this suggestion would appear to be highly advantageous to Mexico. It would insure more Mexican Americans to send more remittances, further defuse Mexican population problems, economic, and social pressures, and insure the mobilization of ever larger groups of dual citizens in Mexico's behalf. Its overall benefits for the United States appear economically modest. Politically, however, this suggestion would be potentially destabilizing.

Dual citizens and those with multiple loyalties might be used to organize in favor of other policies the Mexican government might favor, for example, bilingual language policies that help to maintain and facilitate ties to the "home" country. Or, they might be used to promote amnesty for those who enter the country illegally (Greenhouse 2000), another policy that furthers Mexico's interests much more than those of the United States. The Mexican president was quite clear in his remarks to the Mexican Federal Congress in May 1995:

> The Mexican nation *goes beyond the territory contained by its borders.* Therefore an essential element of the "Mexican national program" will be *to promote the constitutional and legal amendments designed for Mexicans to retain their nationality.* (quoted in Vargas 1996: 5; emphasis in original)

It is not possible to read this as anything other than a straightforward statement that Mexico considers individuals who have emigrated, and even obtained citizenship elsewhere, as still being Mexican nationals. Of course, the fact that the Mexican government so considers Mexican American citizens in this way does not mean that Mexican Americans necessarily reciprocate the feeling. Yet there is certainly enough theory and evidence to support the view that many Mexican immigrants retain an important attachment to their country of origin.

Vargas agrees, noting that one set of "sociological" arguments in favor of dual citizenship for Mexicans is that,

Mexicans are very proud of their culture. In principle, any Mexican is a true nationalist. They love their history, culture and traditions, and especially they love their beautiful country. Accordingly Mexicans remain Mexicans anywhere they are. (1996 10)

Mexican American Dual Citizens: Ambivalent Loyalties

Some of the most direct manifestations of issues that can arise with multiple loyalties are seen in the case of Mexican Americans. Other research data suggests that Vargas's "sociological arguments" have substantial real-world manifestations. As a result, they are not just a matter of abstract controversies. Rather, they directly raise basic questions about issues of cultural coherence and attachment in American politics.

On many empirical measures, Mexican Americans stand apart from traditional or even contemporary patterns of integration into American society. Ruben Rumbaut (1996), for example, surveyed over 5,000 people in California. Half were U.S.-born children of immigrants, half were foreign-born children who immigrated here before they were twelve (the 1.5 generation). He offered each child the opportunity to self-identify by either (1) national origin (e.g., Jamaican, Hmong); (2) hyphenated identity (e.g., Mexican American, Filipino American; (3) a plain American identity; and (4) a pan racial/ethnic identity (e.g., Hispanic, Latino, "Black").[5] Rumbaut finds a definite trend toward adopting a hyphenated American identity from the foreign-born children compared to those born here (from 32 percent to 49 percent). These findings, he correctly states are indicative of a significant "assimilative trend." He notes the most assimilative groups appear to be the Latin Americans,

> with the very notable exception of Mexicans. Among the U.S. born less than four percent of Mexican American-descent youth identified as American (the lowest proportion of any group). (1994: 765, emphasis mine)

Moreover, among second-generation Mexicans, "a very substantial number identified as Chicano, virtually all of them U.S. born and all of them in California; in fact a quarter of all Mexican-descendant second-generation students self-identified as Chicano, a historical and problematic identity unique to that group...." In other words, compared to other second-generation immigrant children, Asians, for example, Mexicans were far more likely to select a pan racial/ethnic identity that did not include some American component.

The same kind of differences showed up in language use—one of the key elements of integration into a new society. Rumbaut measured facility by relying on self reports, a method ripe for methodological errors like those brought about by social desirability factors.[6] However, even so he found a Mexican difference:

> Three quarters of the total sample preferred English, *including substantial majorities in every group...the single exceptions are the Mexicans who are the most loyal to their native tongue,* although even among them 45 percent preferred English. More than one-

third speak English only with their parents, although, interestingly a smaller proportion speak English only with their close friends (who are also children of immigrants). (1994, 767 emphasis added)

And finally, when one examines the rate of naturalization for those qualified to seek it, Mexicans again stand out. The proportion of naturalized citizens among the foreign-born population in 1997 was 53 percent for those from Europe, 44 percent for those from Asia, and 24 percent for those from Latin America. Why are the Latin American naturalization rates so low? Primarily, *"because of the low figure for the population from Mexico (15 percent)"* (U.S. Department of Commerce 1997: 20, emphasis mine).

Does dual citizenship inhibit naturalization in the United States? Hispanic advocacy groups argue it does not. De la Garza and his associates (1996) compare a group of Central and Latin American countries which do and do not grant dual citizenship and ask whether dual citizenship affects naturalization rates. They conclude it does not. However, they erroneously include six countries that do grant dual citizenship (Bolivia, Chile, Guatemala, Costa Rica, Ecuador, and Brazil) in their list of ten that do not.[7] Moreover, they are only able to conclude that there is no difference by excluding the single largest immigrant-sending country with (at the time) no dual citizenship provisions—Mexico—from their analysis.

A more careful analysis of the impact of dual citizenship on naturalization rates was undertaken by Philip Yang (1994) as part of a large empirical analysis of naturalization, using national census data. He notes,

In spite of the [statistical] significance of its coefficient, the negative effect of dual citizenship also contradicts the dual citizenship hypothesis that dual citizenship encourages naturalization. The odds of naturalization for immigrants from countries which recognize dual citizenship are about 20 percent (-.201=.799-1) smaller than the odds for those from countries which do not. Perhaps, immigrants may...have confusion about and difficulty in maintaining dual allegiances to both the country of origin and the host country. Thus, immigrants may be reluctant to identify themselves with Americans and are therefore much less likely to naturalize. (1994, 473-74)

The ambivalence that immigrants feel because of the pull of dual loyalties can be resolved in several different ways. The pull of the old country can recede, and the attachment to the newer one can grow. The pull of the old country can retain its original strength and even grow, given modern technology and/or efforts by the "old country" to stimulate them. Or the immigrants can continue to have strongly mixed feelings essentially making them feel never truly at home.

Multiple Loyalties: Then and Now

We are now in a better position to answer a question that arises in connection with the spread of dual-citizenship. Plainly stated, the question is: Is it not true that other immigrants have come here, established themselves, and yet still retain an active interest and involvement in the affairs of their home countries, even after several generations? Irish and Jewish Americans come easily to mind here.

It's a fair question. Certainly many Irish Americans were concerned with "the troubles" and some provided financial support for the positions they favored. In the annals of lobbying, the efficacy of those lobbying for the state of Israel is legendary and a model for those who wish to use their dual citizenship to emulate it. So why isn't what's "good" for Irish and Jewish Americans equally good for Mexican or Muslim dual nationals?

While no one answer is likely to be definitive, it seems that there are at least five differences between then and now:

(1) *American Culture in Transition*

As I previously suggested (see chapter 2), American culture has been going though a difficult and contentious transition. Yes, culture is always in transition. However, when transition arises from a questioning of the basic legitimacy and fairness of core social and political institutions it reflects quite a different set of circumstances. Ongoing and expected cultural evolution and development that builds on and refines basic cultural and political institutions are one matter. Building on the ruins of what was previously accepted is another.

So, when Irish and Jewish Americans expressed and acted on their continuing interests in their "home" countries[8] they did so in a context in which one set of basic elements of an American identity, a commitment to its core institutions, cultural arrangements, and their desire to be part of them was not in doubt.

(2) *Changes in American National Psychology*

The term American national psychology does not mean that here is one American psychology or an indelibly etched American "national character." It does reflect the fact that the blend of opportunity and freedom framed by a constitutional republic, which reflected and encouraged both, created a group of citizens who were determined to realize their ambitions and make use of the opportunities, who were independent, optimistic and secure enough to take risks, but temperate and fair-minded enough to allow pragmatism to temper them.

Obviously, not every American displayed these characteristics in whole or in part. However, America would not have been built without these characteristic being substantially distributed in its population. As previously noted, American public psychology has evolved and become more differentiated. We are no longer a nation of rugged individualists, although that characteristic remains a clear presence here. Echoes of those earlier characteristic survive and have been adapted to our new millennial circumstances, but the number of Americans who combine them appears to be shrinking. Other-directedness saps independence, and "thou shall not judge" provides a cover for not doing so.

Hence, in the past whatever interests Irish and Jewish Americans had in their respective "home countries," it was filtered through the lens of a more widely shared national psychology which didn't shy away from independent-minded judgments. What kinds of judgments might these be in these circumstances of multiple attachments? One such set of judgments would surely involve setting boundaries and priorities regarding one's attachments.

(3) *Multiple Loyalties then and Now: The Psychology of Identity Primacy*

Consider the hyphenated Irish or Jewish American identity. Does that mean such a person is an *Irish*-American, a Irish-*American*, an *Irish-American,* or an *American* of Irish descent? Each of these possible permutations reflects a psychological identification with, and arrangement of, some of the basic building blocks that form our identity.

It seems very unlikely that for most Irish and Jewish Americans their "home country" identifications were either equal to, or more important than, their American identity. Moreover, had any of their fellow countrymen suggested that they should be, it seems fair to say that most would respond clearly, straightforwardly, and without much self-doubt: No. They might be interested in some aspects of their "home countries," but most, if not all, would say they were American first and primarily.

Consider further the hypothetical case in which the Irish and Jewish American equivalents of "black," or Chicano (Hispanic) were available. Let's call them "white" and "European." In fact, those terms, while available, have never been embraced by Irish and Jewish Americans. Such an embrace would effectively decouple one's identity from any specifically stated identification with America.

Can anyone seriously argue that such an identity would be chosen as Rumbaut (1994: 764 Table 2) found was the case in second-generation immigrants from Mexico? He found that almost half selected a racial/panethnic identity, or that another 8 percent of such adolescents would select an identity exclusively allied with national origin. Would a random sample of Irish or Jewish American second-generation children find over 50 percent whose *selected* self-identification did not include an American element? I think not.

(4) *Ninety-Three and Fast Rising: The Problems of Scale*

The number of multiple citizenship encouraging countries is rapidly rising. More countries will be added to that list. Yet, there is an asymmetry in the movement of immigrant populations. The flow is from economically struggling, often less republican political countries to the more economically secure liberal democracies. The weight of cultural economic and political adjustment falls on the latter, not the former.

Few Americans, not of Mexican origin, seek to become nationalized in Mexico. And if they did, they would learn that Mexico, unlike the United States, requires those who would do so to renounce their former citizenship, and are serious about it. If the foreigner makes such an affirmation, but does so in a "fraudulent manner or without true intent *to be definitely and permanently obligated by them*," the result can be a stiff fine (Vargas, 1996: 32-33, emphasis mine). Who decides when and whether the taking of an oath is done in this matter? The issue is "exclusively dependent on the absolute discretionary powers of the Mexican authorities." Moreover, the Mexican government does not even issue birth certificates for the children of non-Mexicans born in Mexico (Vargas 1994: 35).

Even if Mexico, were to liberalize there nationalization laws for other that their nationals living abroad, it would have little discernable impact on the nature of their political, cultural, and social institutions. The same cannot be said of the circumstances of the United States.

The United States takes in the greatest number of immigrants, from more countries, of any country in the world. No other country does so. It is also the destination of substantial numbers of illegal immigrants, which, because of the new census figures, is now estimated to be closer to 10 or 11 million rather than the 5 to 6 million previously estimated (Cohn 2001; Rodriguez 2001).

These three facts, coupled with the reality of ninety-two immigrant-sending countries, that encourage dual citizenship for their nationals (but not necessarily for the nationals of other countries), lead to one inescapable conclusion. No other country in the world takes in so many immigrants, from so many dual citizenship allowing countries, and as a result has a vast and swelling population of citizens with dual citizenships and multiple loyalties.

In the past, Irish and Jewish Americans, to the extent they had interests and some level of attachment to their "home countries" were the numerical exception, not the rule. Today, with 85 percent of the large number of immigrants the United States has accepted in the last four decades from dual citizenship encouraging countries, the situation is fast being reversed. Dual citizens are increasingly becoming the rule, not the exception in certain geographical areas in the United States.

(5) *Compatibility of Interests Then and Now: Some Distinctions*

Immigrant involvement in "homeland issues," as Mona Harrington (1980: 680-686) terms them, is not new. The Irish in the United States made "U.S. relationships with Ireland's archenemy England, a campaign issue as far back as the 1840s" (Harrington, 1980: 682). Ancestral quarrels like those between Greece and Turkey have periodically spilled over into American legislative politics. Yet, is it inaccurate to say as Peter Spiro does (1997: 1477) that a "dual Mexican American who advocates policies that benefit Mexico is little different from a Catholic who advocates policies endorsed by the church or by a member of Amnesty International who writes his congressman at the organization's behest."

The first question that needs to be asked pertains to the relationship of the policy advocacy to the person's (or group's) self-identity. Any American citizen who espouses a policy position is likely to be in accord with one advocacy group or another. Does the citizen who agrees with the Amnesty International position define himself as a "world citizen" and not a U.S. one? Or, is he basically an American citizen who supports the position of an international organization? Is every American citizen who supports the work of the United Nations an example of dual loyalties, about which we should worry? Obviously not. Neither Amnesty International nor the United Nations is a "home country" with all the emotional attachments that follow from that experience.

A second question that needs to be asked concerns numbers, assuming those who wrote in favor of Amnesty International positions were self-identified as "world citizens." How many such "world citizens" are there who do not primarily identify as Americans? Are they the same numbers of possible dual citizens as Mexico possesses, over 7 million? Further, are they concentrated in a few states and metropolitan areas where their combined weight might tip the scales of deliberative policy, as is the case, for example, with Mexican Americans (U.S. Department of Commerce 1997: 14-17)?

What of Catholics voting in accordance with the Vatican position on an issue? This example begins to get closer to the issues raised by dual loyalties to another country, but falls far short as a accurate model. Few, if any, Americans were born, raised, and emigrated from the Vatican. As a result, whatever doctrinal beliefs that were learned in church were also learned in an American community, embedded in American cultural and social institutions, and surrounded by others with the same core American experiences. Moreover, policy positions of whatever sort are primarily cognitive while attachments to one's country are more fully affective. Policy preferences are not often deeply held, and even when they are, rarely organize the person's sense of core identity.

Moreover, to my knowledge, the Vatican has never sought to substitute its positions on say, birth control, for the more general, fundamental, and important set of beliefs that constitute the "American Creed." One can easily be an American Catholic who supports the Vatican's position on this issue or an American Catholic who does not, but will remain an American.

Well, don't Irish and Jewish Americans lobby on behalf of what is, in fact, a foreign government or group? Yes; but again it pays to make distinctions. The Irish have certainly successfully labored to involve the American government in the solution to the "troubles." And Jewish Americans have lobbied the American government to support the establishment of, and more successfully, the continued existence of Israel. These, however, do not constitute lobbying for policies that are against the interests of the United States. Resolving tensions between the Irish and our historic allies, the British, is not against American interests. And supporting the right of existence of a democratic state of Israel isn't either. Can the same be said of organized efforts for major amnesty programs which subvert the attempt to make immigration an orderly, fair, and supportable policy? Can it be said, too, of organized efforts in support of open borders with countries that stand to reap many more advantages from that policy than the United States? Can it be said of organized efforts to make the United States a multilingual country where there is no longer a common language and understanding? I think important differences are clear in these cases.

And, there are others. Does it matter that the results of such policies, if successful, would change the basic cultural, psychological, social, institutional, and political organizations that have been the foundations of this country's republican democracy for over two hundred years? Yes. Of course it matters.

Notes

*   This chapter builds on Renshon (2000b). I would like to thank Nathan Glazer, Eugene Goldstein, Peter Spiro, Peter Schuck, Stephen Thernstrom, Mark Krikorian, and especially Noah Pinkus for their helpful comments on earlier drafts this chapter or its constituent sections. I would also like to acknowledge the valuable research assistance of Sandra Johnson.

1.   In psychoanalytic theory the term that would cover all three is "object," which can refer to concrete (specific people, places) and categorical entities (like nation or America).

2.   The authors also argue that remittances to "home countries" benefit the United States nationally. Their argument is based on the fungibility of financial figures. Thus, if country X buys products from the United States and its immigrants abroad send money home, this money can be viewed as helping to pay for such imports. Examining the few studies adduced (and their data) to support this claim is beyond the purposes of this chapter.

   However, the authors do acknowledge that the vast majority of remittances come from five states where such immigrants are generally located (California, Texas, Florida, Illinois, and New York), and they are substantial. The authors estimate (p.8) that over $3.1 billion in remittances were sent home by immigrants from these five states. They note (p. 8): " Clearly, this constitutes a major resource, which if invested locally [in the United States] could significantly improve state and local economies in general, and the personal conditions in which these immigrants live in particular.

3.   Jorge A. Vargas is of Mexican nationality and a former professor of Law in Mexico City, now visiting at the University of San Diego Law School.

4.   These include aggressive government strategies to develop and maintain contact with important groups of Mexicans abroad, the creation and proliferation of sixteen Mexican Cultural Institutes and Centers, a promotional campaign in the favor of NAFTA (North American Free Trade Agreement), a considerable increase in the number of Mexican Consulates, the development of special programs to provide legal and diplomatic protection to both documented and undocumented workers, and the publication of a new bilingual newsletter, "La Paloma."

5.   The quotation marks are mine and reflect the findings of biologists and anthropologists which suggest that race is a socially constructed political category. Rumbaut (1994: 763) says that the last two categories (three and four) are exclusively identities "made in America," and the last (four) represent, "a denationalized identification with racial ethnic minority groups in the country of destination, and self-conscious differences in relation to the white [*sic*] Anglo majority

population." He then counts together those who select a plain American identification (11 percent) and those who select a pan racial/ethnic identification (21 percent) and concludes they are not connected to their origins but to their "American present."

He is certainly incorrect to state that the hyphenated identity is not also a "made in America" one. Yet, a larger and more important question arises from his characterizations of his identification data. From the standpoint of national coherence and integration, the major question of these data is how much identification with an American identity each category represents. It is quite clear that the plain American identifications (11 percent) are that. It is also likely that the national origin identifications (27 percent) are not. It is unclear how much identification with the United States is contained in the largest category, the hyphenated American identity (40 percent). And the same is also very true for those who eschew any category with the name American in it (21 percent).

6.   There are reliability and validity problems with such data as well. For example, Rumbaut (1994: 760) reports correlations of the respondents' self reports with performance with the objective Stanford reading achievement test score. He reports there was a "strong correlation" of .42 (p=.0001).

What these number don't reveal is that in a sample of over 5,000 respondents it is fairly routine to get findings of such magnitude. Moreover, a correlation of .42 sounds high, but it means that of all the variance in the relationship between self-report and object test measures, only 16 percent is actually explained. Or to put it another way, the objective test results "explain" or account for only 16 percent of the level of proficiency reflected in the self-report.

7.   They base their list on a publication by Blaustein and Flanz entitled *Constitutions of the World*, but give no date for the publication.

8.   Of course, the number of immigrants from Israel to the United States is low, both in numbers and percentages in comparison to, for example, Mexico or the Philippines. The dual citizenship/loyalty issue arises primarily because of the historical circumstances preceding the establishment of the state of Israel and the fact that the "law of return" promises any Jew Israeli citizenship on immigration. So, for most American Jews the question concerns not their returning to a state from which they once lived, but emigrated, but rather their attachment to the existence of a Jewish homeland after a 2000-year diaspora.

References

Barry, Dan, and Nichole M. Christian. "Thousands March to U.N. to Support Palestinians." *New York Times*, 14 October 2000: A1.

Blaustein, Albert, and Gizbert Flanz (eds). *Constitutions of the World*. Dobbs Ferry, NY: Oceana Publications, n.d.

Bragg, Rick. "Stand Over Elian Highlights a Virtual Secession of Miami." *New York Times*, 1 April 2000: A1.

Chang, Lan Samantha. "Debunking the Dual Loyalty Oath." *New York Times*, 1999.

Chivers, C. J. "Police Investigating Vandalism at Door of Bronx Synagogue." *New York Times*, 9 October 2000: A1.

Clinton, William J. "Remarks at a Welcoming Ceremony for President Jerry John Rawlings of Ghana," (February 24, 1999) *Weekly Compilation of Presidential Documents*, March 1, 1999, 35:8, 298-99.

Cohn, D'Vera. "Illegal Residents Exceed Estimate." *Washington Post*, 18 March 2001: A01.

Corchado, Alfredo. "Zedillo Seeking Closer Ties with Mexican Americans." *Dallas Morning News*, 8 April 1995a: 11A.

_____. "Mexicans Study Dual Citizenship, Implications of an Idea Intriguing to Many." *Dallas Morning News*, 5 July 1995b: 1A

Corchado, Alfredo, and K. Anderson. "Mexican's Internet in Citizenship up as Proposition 187 Prompts Increase." *Dallas Morning News*, 1 December 1994: 27-A.

Davis, A. F. "The Child's Discovery of Nationality." *The Australian and New Zealand Journal of Sociology* 4 (1868):107-125.

Dillon, Sam. "Mexico Wants to Make Dual Citizenship Legal." *New York Times*, 11 December 1995: A6.

Finley, Bruce. "Hearts Torn between Old, New Worlds." *Denver Post*, 23 August 1998.

Garza De la, Rodolfo, Manuel Orozco, and Miguel Barona. "The Binational Impact of Latino Remittances." Policy Brief, The Tomas Rivera Policy Institute, 1997.

Greenhouse, Steve. "Coalition Urges Easing of Immigration Laws." *New York Times*, 16 May 2000: A1.

Gutierrez, Paula. "Comment: Mexico's Dual Nationality Amendments: They Do Not Undermine U.S. Citizens' Allegiance and Loyalty or U.S. Political Sovereignty." *Loyola L.A. International and Comparative Law Journal* 999: 19 (1997).

Harrington, Mona. "Loyalties: Dual and Divided," in Stephen Thernstrom (ed.), *Harvard Encyclopedia of American Ethnic Groups*." Cambridge, MA: Harvard University Press, 1980, pp. 676-686.

Holmes, Steven A. "Hispanic Births in U.S. Reach Record high." *New York Times*, 13 February 1998: A12.

Horowitz, E. L. "Some Aspects of the Development of Patriotism in Children." *Sociometry* 3 (1940) 329-41.

Jahoda, Gustav. "The Development of Children's Ideas about Community and Nationality," in Charles G. Bell (ed.), *Growth and Change: A Reader in Political Socialization*. Belmont, CA: Dickenson, 1973.

Jordan, Mary. "Mexican President Touts Open Borders." *Washington Post*, 25 August 2000:A01.

Lawson, E. D. "The Development of Patriotism in Children: A Second Look." *Journal of Psychology* 55 (1963): 279-86.

Martin, David A. "New Rules on Dual Nationality for a Democratizing Globe: Between Rejection and Embrace." *Georgetown Immigration Law Review* 14 (1999):1-34.

National Assessment Governing Board. *Civics Framework for the 1998 National Assessment of Educational Progress*. Washington, D C, 1998.

National Research Council. *From Generation to Generation: The Health and Well-Being of Children in Immigrant Families*. Washington, DC: National Research Council, 1998.

New York Times. "Exhibit of Vietnamese Art Arouses Immigrant Anger." 7 July 1999: A19.

Renshon, Stanley A. "American Identity and the Dilemmas of Cultural Diversity," in Stanley A. Renshon and John Duckitt (eds.), *Political Psychology: Cultural and Cross Cultural Foundations*. London: Macmillan, 2000b.

Renshon, Stanley A. *Dual Citizens in America: An Issue of Vast Proportions and Broad Significance*. Washington, DC: Center for Immigration Studies, 2000a.

Rodriguez, Cindy. "The Impact of the Undocumented." *Boston Globe*, 6 February 2001.

Rumbaut, Ruben. "The Crucible Within: Ethnic Identity, Self-Esteem, and Segmented Assimilation Among Children of Immigrants." *International Migration Review* 28: 4 (1994):748-794.

Russett, Bruce. *Grasping the Democratic Peace: Principles for a Post-Cold War World*. Princeton, NJ: Princeton University Press, 1993.

Sanchez, Rene. "Days of Rage in Little Saigon: Portrait of Ho Chi Minh Incenses Vietnamese Immigrants." *Washington Post*, 5 March 1999: A02.

Slambrouck, Paul. "Sweeter Holiday for Mexican-Americans." *Christian Science Monitor*, 12 December 2000.

Smith, Tony. *Foreign Entanglements: The Power of Ethnic Groups in the Making of American Foreign Policy*. Cambridge, MA: Harvard University Press, 2001.

Spiro, Peter J. "Dual Nationality and the Meaning of Citizenship." *Emory Law Review* 46:4 (1997):1412-1485.

Thompson, Ginger. "Fox Urges Opening of U.S.-Mexican Border to Build New Partnership." *New York Times*, 14 August 2000: A1.

U.S. Department of Commerce, Economics and Statistics Administration, U.S. Census. "Profile of the Foreign Born Population in the United States: 1997." *Current Populations Reports Special Studies* (P23-195). Washington, DC: U.S. Government Printing Office, 1997.

U.S. Department of Education. Office of Educational Research and Improvement. National Center for Education Statistics. *The NAEP 1998 Civics Report Card for the Nation* (NCES 2000-457). Washington, DC, 1999.

Vargas, Jorge A. "Dual Nationality for Mexicans?" *Chicano-Latino Law Review* 18:1 (1996):1-58.

Veale, Scott. "History 101: Snoop Doggy Roosevelt." *New York Times*, 2 July 2000. Sec. wk. 5.

Waldman, Amy. "Killing Heightens the Unease Felt by Africans in New York." *New York Times*, 14 February 1999: A1.

Weinstein, Eugene A. "The Development of the Concept of Flag and the Sense of National Identity." *Child Development* 28 (1957):167-74.

Yang, Philip Q. "Explaining Immigrant Naturalization." *International Migration Review* 28:3 (1994):449-477.

Part 4

American Politics and Political Leadership

6

Character Issues in the
2000 Presidential Campaign

Traditionally, candidates' stands on public issues have been the focus of making choices in presidential selection. In recent decades, however, an important change has taken place. Now, rather than asking candidates where they stand, the public wants to know who they are and how they will lead.

Reflecting an awareness that integrity, vision, judgment, and skills are important measures by which to judge those who would lead us, the public has increasingly focused on the personal qualities of presidential candidates. These concerns are not new.[1] Yet, the question remains: By what standards might these elements be judged? One answer to this question has been the rise of "character issues."

As the term implies, "character issues" lie at the intersection of psychological and political theory. Yet they are also firmly situated in the arena of partisan politics. Although character questions are often raised as a form of accusation, they purport to tell us something important about those who would lead us. The question is: Do they?

The answer to that question would appear to be: Yes.[2] Honesty, integrity, and trustworthiness may well be virtues in themselves, but they are also important for the nation's political life. This is primarily so because they are a key resource of leadership capital (Renshon 2000). That, in turn, affects the president's capacity to govern and lead. Leadership involves the mobilization, orchestration and consolidation of public-mindedness for common purposes. A dishonest president forfeits the assumption of public trust that underlies social capital. A president whose positions do not reflect his convictions leaves us wondering which, if either, we should credit. And a president whose political self-interest can be counted on to supersede his public-mindedness raises the question of whether we are being enlisted for his, or our, purposes.

These large issues are critical, yet the public also finds itself trying to address a host of other, perhaps surrogate issues. Is an idealist with lofty policies (Bill Bradley) necessarily a better candidate than a practical politician armed with a policy for every problem (Al Gore)? Are "gentleman Cs at Yale" (George

W. Bush) necessarily inferior, from the standpoint of a successful presidency, to a degree from Harvard as Al Gore has suggested (even if Gore's overall records shows signs of underachievement) (Maraniss and Nakashima 2000: A1; see also Turque 2000, 44, 93-94, 111)? Is the public looking for heroic leadership, as their attraction to the McCain candidacy seemed to suggest? And if so, is heroic leadership what the times require?

These and other questions speak to the broader issue of psychological suitability (Renshon 1998a). The major questions raised by this terminology are not only those regarding a candidate's specific character traits, but the fit, or lack thereof, between them, the responsibilities of presidential leadership, and the public's expectations and preferences. No formula exists to answer these questions. A heroic candidate biography may well require us to expect the same kind of leadership, or it may be an outstanding element of an otherwise complex and not wholly suitable presidential psychology. A public preference for heroic leadership may coexist with an equally strong preference for moderation.

In this chapter I ask: Does character still matter? An examination of a range of data[3] suggests that it does. More specifically, I examine the impact of the Clinton presidency in helping to set the frame within which character issues are being considered.

Yet, if character matters, how will we know it? One traditional answer has been the characterizations that candidates' campaigns and allies make against their opponents. The public has roundly condemned these, even as they reluctantly take in what is being said. However, few who have condemned character attacks have considered that they give the public valuable information about the candidates. I suggest at least four reasons why character attacks and the responses to them help the public make important judgments about the psychology and leadership of those who would govern us.

Finally, I turn to the question of the broader cultural and political contexts in which the search for leadership takes place. I argue that the public's experiences and leadership preferences have an important effect on the kinds of leadership that develop and are supported in a society. Further, the controversy over the 2000 election outcome has obscured an important sea of change unfolding in American society. I distinguish between two models of leadership in contemporary American society. One, the *heroic,* has become traditional; the other, *reflective* leadership, is emerging in response to structure and psychological changes in the American public. I close by suggesting how each of these two models of leadership affected the 2000 presidential campaign.

Does Character Still Matter?

Asking whether character still matters is really two questions. First, does it still matter to the public? And, second does character matter in some empirically and substantively grounded way, regardless of the public's view? We can answer both questions, and the question posed in the above title, with one word: Yes.

True as this may be, it does not explain *why* character issues have continued to play an important role in the presidential selection process. Nor does it tell us in what ways they have done so.

Questions about character in a presidential election are framed by three circumstances. They reflect larger public yearnings stimulated by the recent historical presidential experience.[4] They are framed by the state of the country and the public's view of it. And, they are responsive to the public's acceptance of the form and content of such information.

Character Issues as a Legacy of the Clinton Presidency

Any discussion of the role of character issues in the 2000 presidential campaign must begin with the presidency of William J. Clinton. The Clinton presidency is virtually unique in having at its helm a man whose performance evaluations were strong and whose personal standing was dismal. Up until the time Clinton left office with a cloud of suspicion and public disapproval for his conduct during his last days in office, Americans consistently rated his performance in the 60 percent range, while saying in a variety of ways that they disapproved of his morals and ethics.

A January 27, 2000 ABC poll found that 58 percent of the public approved of Clinton's performance as president, but 61 percent disapproved of him as a person (Langer 2000).[5] Seven in ten Americans said they were tired of the problems associated with the administration, and fewer than one-third of Americans wished that Clinton could run for a third term.[6] Fifty-four percent said (Langer 2000) they would be "glad to see him go," and only 39 percent said they would be "sorry to see him go."[7]

One of President Clinton's immediate legacies to the public's view of the presidency was to reframe the "moral" and "rhetorical" dimensions of the presidency in the 2000 election campaign. There are several strands of evidence to support this view. One could take note of the covers of major news magazines such a *Newsweek*'s, entitled "Straightshooters: How Bradley and McCain are scoring with the Politics of Authenticity" (November 15, 1999). One could read the story headings of major news articles like that in the *Washington Post* (Broder 1999: A6), subtitled, "Americans yearn for a president with character and leadership." Or one could read one of the many columnists from all sides of the political spectrum who proclaimed the importance of authenticity (Gigot 2000: A26; see also Cooper 1999: 48). One could also listen to the explanations for unsuccessful campaigns from high officials such as Dan Cal, campaign spokesman for Steve Forbes, who said (quoted in Wayne 2000: A26),

> While a lot of people may have liked our message, it didn't translate into votes. You have a healthy economy and not the anger you had in 1992 and 1996. With the Clinton White House, issues of morality and character were important. This became more of a race about biography and character, and Steve's strength is as an issue candidate.

Or, one could look at some survey data. In a 1995 Pew survey, 54 percent of those polled thought the president could/should deal with low moral standards, and by 1999, that number had risen to 60 percent. How? In 1995, 25 percent of the national sample said the president "can best deal with low morals/ethics by 'serving as a role model.'" By 1999, that figure had risen to 38 percent. Correspondingly, in that same period, the number of citizens who thought the president could accomplish this task by proposing policies dropped from 18 to 11 percent, and the number who thought the president could accomplish this task by using the "bully pulpit" to draw attention to moral issues dropped from 10 to 9 percent.[8]

Given these findings it is not surprising that during the campaign the issues that topped voters' concerns were those having to do with a candidate's ethics and morality.[9] A poll taken by the Tarrance Group for Voter.Com found that when people were asked which was *the* most important issue for the next president to deal with, moral values topped the list (18 percent). That was followed by education (13 percent), social security (11 percent), health care (10 percent), taxes and crime tied (at 6 percent), and on down the list into single digit items.[10] A Gallup Poll taken in January 2000 found that Americans were more interested in the style and leadership capabilities of the candidates than their positions on the issues. Fifty-one percent of likely voters interviewed in the January 7-10 poll chose "leadership skills and vision" as being more important than "where the candidates stand on issues that matter to you"—chosen by just 36 percent. This was true for both "likely voters" and for a national sample of adults.[11] It was true for Republicans, Independents, and Democrats alike.[12]

Another way in which Mr. Clinton's presidency shaped the 2000 presidential campaign was through public exhaustion and weariness with the Clinton administration and its effects on the candidacies of both Republicans and Democrats alike. From the start of the Lewinsky scandal and the president's impeachment there was much discussion of the effect of these events on Al Gore's presidential campaign. Some have dismissed the idea of any Clinton fatigue as a "fraud" (Wilentz 2000a: 6; 2000b: 8) or a "cliché" (Dionne 2000: A31). At one point there was even talk of Clinton nostalgia, but not much evidence to support its existence (Harris 2000: A01).[13]

Clinton fatigue, however, was real enough. A February 2000 ABC news poll found that 51 percent were tired of President Clinton, 49 percent thought Mr. Gore too close to him, and 48 percent felt the country needed a new direction. Combining these items as an index and using multiple regression analysis, the strongest predictors of the likely vote were the candidates' favorability ratings. However, after controlling for favorability and party identification, Clinton fatigue again emerged as a key predictor of the vote. Its impact went significantly above and beyond political predisposition and views of the candidates.[14] A further indication of its significance is found in a special analysis of Gallup poll results among likely voters in January, and again in February-March. That analysis suggested that the "Clinton fatigue factor" might indeed be significantly hurting Gore's campaign, and that the net effect might be about 8 percentage points in the difference between Gore's and Bush's support.[15] And finally, Ted Koppel in a *Nightline* interview with George W. Bush reported that 50-percent of those polled by ABC said that Mr. Gore was too close to President Clinton to provide the country with the fresh start that it needs.[16]

Clinton fatigue, like the importance of character issues, did not affect all voting groups equally. Indeed, it appeared to effect swing voters of both parties and moderate and conservative Republican voters more than traditional Democratic voters. In a series of studies leading to the development of new categories of stable public opinion group placement, the Pew Research Center identified nine separable groups: Staunch Conservative (95 percent) , Moderate Conservatives (86 percent), Populist Republicans (86 percent) New Prosperity Independents (73 percent), The Disaffected (68 percent), Liberal Democrats (58 percent), Socially Conservative Democrats (59 percent), New Democrats (58 percent), and the Partisan Poor (59 percent).[17] The percentage of each group that felt "Clinton fatigue" is in parentheses.

Not surprisingly, the groups differed with regard to the qualities they thought important in presidential candidates. Good judgment was supported to a substantial degree by all nine groups, but when it came to the importance of high moral standards, the groups differed dramatically. The percentage agreeing that such high standards were necessary are as follows: Staunch Conservative (84 percent), Moderate Conservatives (81 percent), Populist Republicans (75 percent), New Prosperity Independents (61 percent), The Disaffected (67 percent), Liberal Democrats (46 percent), Socially Conservative Democrats (58 percent), New Democrats (56 percent) , and the Partisan Poor (53 percent).

The same holds true for views about the importance of different elements of presidential psychology and character. The Pew survey, noted above, found that in both 1995 and 1999, high ethical standards were seen as the second most important quality to have in a president, after sound judgment. Yet seven out of ten voters who preferred Mr. Bush said that personal integrity was very important, and 50 percent of Gore supporters believed it was important. Sixty percent of Bush supporters thought it essential for a candidate to say what he believes, while 50 percent of Gore supporters thought this essential. On the other hand, more Gore than Bush supporters thought it essential for a candidate to have compassion for others (67 percent vs. 59 percent) and be willing to compromise (37 percent vs. 29 percent).

In 1996 Bob Dole plaintively asked, "Where's the outrage?" It is now possible to provide one probable answer: Among Democratic loyalists, Clinton's behavior elicited either a yawn, a wink or an averted gaze. Among Republican loyalists, it was transmuted into personal distaste. Among "independents" Clinton, and by implication his chosen successor, Al Gore, is in some trouble.

Just how this might unfold in the general election obviously became an important matter. One set of clues could be gleaned from the primaries. In the nonpartisan California primary vote, 61 percent held a low personal opinion of the president, while 58 percent of them approved of his performance. These figures paralleled national opinion samples.

Yet among the committed (primary) voters a different story emerged. Democratic voters in Ohio rated the president's performance as far superior (77 percent) to their concerns with him as a person (42 percent). Among Missouri Democrats the figures were 80 percent (performance) and 45 percent (morals), respectively, and among New York Democrats 85 percent and 35 percent.

Some sense of the Republican view of Mr. Clinton is found in the nonpartisan California exit poll. Of course, large percentages of the Bush and McCain supporters did not rate Mr. Clinton's presidential performance highly. But their ratings of him as a person were even much lower, especially for supporters of Mr. Bush. As R. W. Apple (2000 A20) put it,

> No doubt Mr. Bush's strategists took considerable comfort from the fact that McCain voters, like Mr. Bush's supporters expressed strong disapproval of Mr. Clinton as a person, as contrasted to their favorable opinion of his performance as president. The governor clearly intends to accuse Mr. Gore of faulty moral leadership, saying 'I will repair the broken bonds of trust between Americans and their government.' Lest anyone think he was only talking about Mr. Clinton, he appropriated an unfortunate phrase of Mr. Gore's and turned it against him. "I will remind Al Gore," he said, "that Americans do not want a White House where there is no controlling legal authority."

However, less expected and more interesting than either the views of the Democratic or Republican party faithful toward Mr. Clinton, were the voters who backed the insurgent campaigns in either party, those of Mr. Bradley and Mr. McCain. In a complicated way, these candidates certainly attracted "swing" voters and appeared to represent some portion of the larger swing vote in the general election. Since the exit polls for Republican primaries did not ask for a rating of either Mr. Clinton's performance or character, we have to look to other polls.

In the nonpartisan California poll, Bradley voters were much more likely than Gore voters to hold an unfavorable view of the president personally. Among McCain voters who made personal evaluations, many more viewed Clinton unfavorably than favorably. In the Ohio democratic poll, Bradley supporters were much more likely to rate Clinton personally in an unfavorable way than Gore supporters. The same was true in Democratic primaries in Missouri, New York, and New Hampshire.

Certainly in the Republican primaries, and to some extent in the Democratic primaries as well, the personal qualities of the candidates played a major choice in voter preferences.[18] Of course, primary voters are more ideologically informed and engaged than the general electorate (S. Wayne 2000), so these numbers may have tended to *underestimate* the importance of personal issues and overestimate the weight given to policy positions. Yet, even so, the numbers present a convincing picture that to voters, character counts.

The Ohio Republican primary exit polls showed that 55 percent of the voters said that a candidate's leadership and personal qualities were more important to them than a candidate's stand on the issues. In Missouri that number was 52 percent, and in New York 54 percent. In California's nonpartisan election exit polls, the relative weight of personal qualities and policy stands were approximately even.

Among Democrats, the relative weight of policy stands and personal qualities in candidate preference was somewhat more heavily weighted to the former, but personal qualities still played a substantial role. In Ohio, Democrats weighed policy more heavily, as did Democratic primary voters in Missouri and New York.

Even among Democrats, the importance of personal qualities in relationship to policy issues can be seen in another set of exit poll questions. Asked to select a policy issue or issues that affected their choice and then to select a personal quality or qualities that "mattered most in deciding how you voted for president," personal qualities and specific policy issues were equally strong. In Ohio, Democrats said that standing up for what you believe was more important (30 percent) than the highest ranking policy issue, race relations (28 percent). The importance of having the right experience (27 percent) and knowledge of the economy (27 percent) were similarly weighted. Similar results were reported in other democratic primaries.[19] Among Republican primary voters, comparable data show a similarly pronounced weighing of personal qualities over specific policy issues.[20]

And how did Clinton fatigue affect the actual presidential vote? Richard Morin and Claudia Deane (2000; emphasis mine) poll directors for the *Washington Post,* writing about Clinton fatigue found,

> The majority of voters—about seven in 10–said their vote had nothing to do with the First Bubba. But among those who were trying to send a message to 1600 Pennsylvania Ave., the edge went to those who didn't have anything nice to say. In all, about two in 10 said their vote was meant to express opposition to Clinton, and about one in 10 said their vote was meant to express support. We were watching those voters who like Clinton's work but not his persona. As predicted, one in three of these voters defected to Bush. *Moreover, "honest" ranked as the single most important trait voters this year were seeking in the next president*—and eight in 10 of these voters supported Bush.

In an analysis of exit polling data reported by the *New York Times*, Robin Toner and Janet Elder (2000) found,

> Voters were generally in a contented mood as they cast their ballots, but there were also signs of Clinton fatigue: in their negative judgment of the president's character and in the priority many put on straight talk and honesty. When given a choice, a plurality of voters—about a fourth—rated honesty a more important consideration than experience or an understanding of the complex issues of the day, according to the voter polls. And

those people tended to vote for Mr. Bush, who also had an edge among those who considered strong leadership most important...two-thirds of respondents said the country, enjoying a record economic boom, was going in the right direction over all. But 6 in 10 said it was on the wrong track morally. Mr. Clinton's job approval rating stayed fairly high, but his personal unfavorability rating was equally high in the surveys....Most voters said they would remember Mr. Clinton more for the scandals of his presidency than for any leadership he provided.

In his examination of the Lewinsky scandal, John Zaller (1998: 188) argued that, "the public is, within broad limits, functionally indifferent to presidential character." The data presented herein suggests he is mistaken. But the actual contours of public concern with character issues must be examined in the context of the changing public ambivalence about the politics of character attacks and the changing nature of political leadership in American society.

What We Can Learn from Character Attacks

Americans did not wish to chance repeating the ethical lapses that helped define the Clinton presidency. And the evidence is that their feelings about those lapses helped to cause Al Gore's election loss. Yet, it would be a mistake to conclude that Americans were ready to hear the candidates hurl disparaging words toward each other. On the contrary, the word that best describes the public's view of character issues, is *ambivalence*.

Consider the following interview in which a woman was asked in 1988 about Gary Hart's private life:[21]

Woman: Well, I think his private life is his own business.

Interviewer: It wouldn't affect whether or not you would vote for him?

Woman: Yeah, it makes a big difference to me.

Interviewer: His private life does?

Woman: Yes.

Interviewer: Should the press report on his private life?

Woman: No.

Interviewer: How are you going to know about it?

Woman: I would have felt better if I didn't know about it.

Interviewer: You don't want to know?

Woman: No, I don't.

Interviewer: But it does affect the way you vote, right?

Woman: It certainly does.

Along similar lines, but equally paradoxical, although the public disapproved of Mr. Clinton's behavior, it preferred not to hear about it. Consider the case of President Clinton's relationship with a twenty-one-year-old intern. Sixty-four percent of the public thought it a private matter having little to do with his job as president. The same 64 percent said that the public doesn't need to know the details of the president's relationship with the intern. However, 61 percent of the public thought it important to know if the president encouraged Ms. Lewinsky to lie (Bennet and Elder, 1998: A14). How it would be possible to find this out without learning more of the details of their relationship is unclear.

It is difficult to recall that the 2000 campaign started out with warm, glowing ads from candidates Bradley, Bush, and Gore (Marks 1999: A1). It is also hard to recall how well all the candidates spoke of each other (Kurtz 1999: A16), or how fast that changed (Balz 1999: A14) One reporter stated that the warm and fuzzy ads were a direct result of the fact that "The public's patience with attack ads has worn thin" (Marks 2000a: A28).

Public patience may have worn thin, but not its susceptibility. Like the woman discussing reports of Gary Hart's infidelities, the public doesn't like what they hear. Yet it cannot help being affected by it. As long as this is true, character attacks, in their many forms will be with us.

However, this is not to say that character attacks haven't evolved. Candidates now call their opponents' psychology into question by reference to either their policies or biographies. Bradley's characterization of Gore policies as "timid," and himself as "bold" is not only a comment on their respective policies (Balz 1999: A14) but on the psychology each would bring to the White House. Mr. Gore's charge that Bradley "abandoned" the Democrats when he left Congress not only reinforces Mr. Gore's image as someone who stays and fights, but Bradley as someone who quits when the going gets tough. When George Bush accused John McCain of running an "angry" campaign, he was not so subtly reminding voters of questions regarding the latter's temperamental suitability for high office (Nagourney and Perez-Pena 2000).

One defense that has become standard is to accuse your opponent of running a negative campaign. Kathleen Hall Jamieson reports that although Mr. Clinton complained about his opponent's negative attacks, he actually used more of the them in the campaign (Jamieson 2000: 115-120). When, after months of indecision, Mr. Bradley finally raised the issue of Mr. Gore's visits to the Buddhist temple, Mr. Gore accused him of "divisive, manipulative attacks," which use "personal vilification, challenging the integrity of those who disagree with him," and asked, "Why did Senator Bradley raise this issue to divide Democrats, which only helps Republicans, who are the true impediments to campaign finance reform?" (Clymer and Nagourney 2000: A24).

When Mr. Bush introduced an ad that accused Senator McCain of distorting his statements on his tax cuts (which was true).[22] McCain aired a counter ad which accused Mr. Bush of reneging on an agreement, sealed with a public handshake, not to run a negative campaign. The implication was that Bush could not be trusted. As one observer noted, "the bottom line in both spots is the suggestion that 'going negative' in a campaign is not simply a tactic, it is a moral flaw (Marks 2000b: A20).

With so many charges and counter charges, some have given up any hope of making meaningful distinctions among campaign assertions. The *Wall Street Journal* (Editorial, 2000: A16) said, flatly, "The distinction between positive and negative campaigning, in fact, no longer has much meaning." Others like Ramesh Ponnuru (1999: A16) have argued there is nothing wrong with "accentuating the negative," and some have difficulty articulating any meaningful standard whatsoever. One noted academic despaired in print about Mr. Gore's "shameless" introduction of Willy Horton into the 1988 Democratic primary contest.[23] Yet, apparently not fully familiar with the campaign on which he was commenting, he went on to say that Mr. Gore had not run any negative ads because he hadn't used a picture of Mr. Bradley, attacked him by name, or made personal remarks that belittle him." If such elements were not present, then accusations of negative campaign ads were a "complete and utter fabrication," and he added, the Gore campaign "isn't there" (Sabatto quoted in Davis 2000: A17).

There are distinctions to be drawn between positive and negative campaigning, but the more important distinction is among the various forms of the latter. There may well be things "wrong" with accentuating the negative, but one cannot make a judgment about this issue "in general." There are standards that *can* be applied, but what are they?

We can ask whether ads are positive ("good") or negative ("bad"). We can ask whether or not they are accurate. And, we can ask whether ads have or have not crossed some boundary of political propriety. However, a better question to ask is: What do they tell us?

Negative ads, like other aspects of a campaign and the choices made within it, tell us some important things about the candidate. I am not referring here to whether the ads are truthful or accurate. Instead I want to suggest that by their ads, candidates tells us something psychologically about themselves. Although ads are obviously a team effort, they do reflect some important aspect of the candidate's personal psychology, the character of the campaign that he mounts, and the people with whom he surrounds himself.

Question 1: What is your starting stance toward the kind of campaign you wish to run?

One starting point is to ask how a candidate initially positions his campaign. Mr. Bradley declared that he would run a different, loftier campaign, one that would not respond to "politics as usual" with attack ads (Hunt 2000: A23; see also Dao 2000: A25). This established him as a candidate with lofty ideals, which fit the campaign theme he was developing around "big ideas." It also reinforced his self-image as a leader above politics, not mired in it. A less desirable by-product was that it reduced his options when his opponent attacked.

Along similar lines, both Mr. Bush and Mr. McCain began by viewing themselves as above "politics as usual," and publicly shook hands on a promise not to go negative. Mr. Bush had already promised a campaign that appealed to "our better angels and impulses" (Quoted in Bruni 2000: A14) For John McCain, this approach reinforced his credentials as a "different" kind of leader, one who would reform not only by policy (campaign finance reform), but by example (which was important since he could not, or would not, set a personal example during the campaign by rejecting "soft money"). For George Bush, as well, this was a chance to reinforce the point that he was a "uniter," someone who could bring people together.

On the other hand, Al Gore's campaign managers were very clear. They said (Marks 2000a: A28), "things may get rougher, if circumstances warrant," and "we're going to fight for the voters in New Hampshire and Iowa." And, they did. One reporter(Cummings 1999: A24) noted that, "Mr. Gore's aggressive stance stands out in the 2000 campaign season that has, for most presidential candidates, remained soft."

One might well ask why a candidate sets out with such an unrealistic standard in the first place.[24] It might reflect well on his idealism, but not on the acuity of his judgment. Mr. Gore's response, reserving the right to make clear "differences" may not have been idealistic, but it was realistic. It allowed him the latitude to define those circumstances without, as Bill Bradley and John McCain did, becoming involved in questions of whether his reversal, when it came, violated a central campaign pledge.[25]

Question 2: What kinds of ads do you use?

The essence of choice is the appreciation of difference. Even so-called positive ads are comparative by strategy and implication. Assuming that there is a tactical or other political reason to call attention to differences, the question is: How is it done? When John McCain ran an ad touting his experience and readiness for command, Bush forces complained that McCain was going negative (Review and Oulook 2000: A16). But McCain had merely touted his own preparation, the rest was implied. Mr. Gore was more direct after he clinched the nomination in questioning Mr. Bush's preparation for the presidency. In an interview aboard Air Force One, Mr. Gore asked (quoted in Berke and Seelye 2000: A1), "You have to wonder, does George W. Bush have the experience to be president?" He then went on to link Mr. Bush to a risky tax scheme," saying, "I think that these two issues are closely related. The people of this country overwhelmingly reject this risky tax scheme that would put Social Security and Medicare at risk and threaten our prosperity."

Negative? Well, it certainly wasn't meant as a compliment, but it is a legitimate question asked directly and forthrightly. The same seems true of Mr. Bush's questioning of Mr. McCain acceptance of large corporate contributions from those whom he regulates, and as the champion of campaign finance reform.

A more difficult case arises when an opponent takes part of a record and, by focusing on it, "distorts" it. The problem here, of course, is that every ad focuses on something to the exclusion of others, and thus "distorts." Consider John McCain's ad touting his readiness to take presidential command. It assumes that commanding a fighter wing is good training for the presidency, and not surprisingly fails to mention questions about how you can lead if you can't develop good working partnerships with your Senate colleagues after seventeen years.

Or, consider a tougher case. When George Bush ran an ad in New York State saying that John McCain had voted against money for breast cancer research, McCain was outraged at the distortion of his record. Yet that project did appear on his website under the heading, "wasteful, unnecessary and low-priority spending." The McCain campaign countered that in many of those votes, he did not object to the projects themselves, but the way they were approved without being considered in committee and competing with other projects on their merits (Nagourney and Perez-Pena 2000: A1). That information was not made clear before Mr. Bush called attention to the issue.

Still, some ads do cross a line. The question is: Which line? When John McCain accused George Bush of "twisting the truth like Clinton" (Marks 2000b: A14), he was accused of crossing several lines. First, the ad was hard-hitting, but inflated, harsh, and rhetorically overheated. William Bennett who advised both candidates said (quoted in Bruni 2000: A14) that the ad crossed the line between "fair play and unwarranted warfare." Republicans anxious to gain the White House could be excused for worrying that one of their candidates was neutralizing a very powerful issue for the fall campaign. Shortly after the negative response to these ads, McCain promised, again, to conduct a positive campaign.

It is likely that McCain's campaign realized that the ads were "detracting" from his image as reformer and hero, which had propelled him to that point. McCain may have been influenced as well by research that found after watching George W. Bush and John McCain attack each other in negative ads, six in 10 Republicans surveyed nationwide said they were more likely to vote for the Texas governor (Kurtz and Morin 2000: A14). Yet, in retrospect, that ad also revealed something about John McCain's psychology that ultimately destroyed his campaign. Questions had already been raised about his temper and temperament. That ad revealed a person who would lash out, in a very personal and overcharged way, against someone he thought had wronged him. He had already done so before, but the incident was not widely reported or discussed.

In December 1999, Senator McCain's campaign finance reform was attacked by the Americans for Tax Reform group. According to the report:

> The McCain campaign struck back in highly personal terms with a blistering attack on ATR and its president, Grover Norquist, calling him "one of Washington's most noto-

rious special interest group leaders" whose only concern was that "the soft money spigot flowing into his group's coffers" would be cut off. But McCain, who is leading Texas Gov. George W. Bush in New Hampshire polls, didn't stop there. He attacked Norquist's character, saying he had lobbied in the past for the "Marxist" president of the Republic of the Seychelles and "against a government crackdown on Internet porn."(Neal 1999: A32)

When McCain lashed out again (Von Drehle 2000: A07) against the "evil" influence of Jerry Faldwell and Pat Robertson with highly personal, overheated charges the transition from hero to hothead was consolidated.

Question 3: What do you do when you are attacked?

Assuming lofty ideals run into "politics as usual," what do you do? Let's say you are a Democrat, deeply concerned with the plight of poor people, and have devised a plan that will replace Medicaid with a better program. Assume further that your opponent distorts, misrepresents, and mischaracterizes your plan by accusing you of trying to "destroy Medicaid." In doing so, your opponent portrays you as a man without principle, willing to turn your back on the poor, whose well being you have made central to your campaign. Just in case anyone missed the implication, let's say this candidate sends his campaign manager Donna Brazille to appear on *Face the Nation* and she says your reform has "serious implications and risks in the African American Community."[26]

This is no mere "policy difference." This is a direct and inaccurate attack on a basic premise of your campaign. It accuses you of being uncaring toward those you say you care about, the old, the poor, and the minorities. It accuses you of having a poorly thought-out proposal. What do you do in such circumstances? Well, if you are Mr. Bradley and your opponent aggressively questions your figures, you shrug your shoulders and say (quoted in Balz 1999: A12), "We each have our own experts."

In so doing, Mr. Bradley conveyed that he was "above the fray," but he failed to demonstrate that he was willing, or able, to get into the fray. Moreover, he showed he was unwilling to do so on an issue that was central to his campaign and the issues on which that he had staked his candidacy. Worse, he gave the impression not of lofty idealism, but of passivity and a man who could be pushed around.

The Gore campaign did not miss these signals. When someone in the Bradley campaign released a flier accusing Mr. Gore of lying, Mr. Gore personally and forcefully complained to Mr. Bradley who ordered two of his (Mr. Bradley's) aides to publicly apologize. The retraction was barely noted elsewhere, but in the Gore campaign "it became a symbol of how easy it was for the Gore campaign to shove Mr. Bradley without getting pushed back" (Dao and Kristof 2000: A1).

Neither, apparently, did the public miss the larger implications of Mr. Bradley's behavior. In a talk before high school students and their parents, Mr. Bradley said, "I hope over the next week New Hampshire will send a message that politics as usual is out."[27] They did. He lost, and never recovered.

Question 4: Are you willing to go for the jugular, and if so, how do you do it?

Going for the jugular is code for "killing off your opponent," which in politics means you win the nomination (office) and he doesn't. Often it is equated, wrongly, with other psychological traits. For example, the *New York Times* (Hitt and Davis 2000: A24) reported growing doubts among Democrats that Mr. Bradley "had what it took to win—especially the ruthlessness and the furious uncompromising tenacious lust for power."

Going for the jugular in politics does not literally mean cutting someone's throat. The symbolism is rich and evocative, but the facts are a different matter. Principled leaders who are not ruthless, and who are not driven by a "lust for power" at whatever costs, can occasionally "go for the jugular" and remain principled. This does not require a knife, only a keenly felt ideal (other than self-interest) and the capacity to press it. It entails making use of an issue that you know will be effective and using that issue forcefully. It requires that you be able to make use of the tools (arguments) at hand, and use them directly, without being inhibited by conflict avoidance or guilt. It must reflect a conviction that this is a fair and appropriate issue.

When Bob Dole debated Bill Clinton, he raised the issue of Mr. Clinton's ethics only once, in passing, and while looking away. For all his reputation in some quarters as a "hatchet man" he was incapable of looking Mr. Clinton in the eye and pressing him on what was clearly a major and appropriate issue. Mr. Dole asked of the public "Where's the outrage?" He might have first considered why they should show any in his behalf if he couldn't show any himself.

Mr. Bradley was the 2000 presidential campaign's Bob Dole. Mr. Gore was deeply implicit in the questionable excesses of the Clinton fund-raising. He led a cheering session for the president after his impeachment and continued to insist Mr. Clinton was a "great" president. Yet, for all this, Mr. Bradley refused to raise the issue directly or consistently. When given opportunities to comment on these facts Mr. Bradley would say only (quoted in Allen 1999: 15), "I think there were obviously some similarities that have been addressed, I'm not going to get into the details at this stage of the game."

After his joint appearance with John McCain, Mr. Bradley did note that "a lot of people in politics were embarrassed" by these activities, but then softened his remarks by adding, "the lessons you learn" from such an experience are important. Compare this with John McCain's statement (quoted in Hitt and Davis 2000: A24) the same day attacking Mr. Gore for having asked "monks and nuns to violate their vow of poverty in order to pay thousands of dollars so they could spiritually commune with him." In doing so, Mr. Bradley proved himself the nicer candidate, but not the more effective one.

Political Leadership for a New Age: Heroic or Reflective?

Every presidential race brings with it candidates whose psychologies reflect different assemblies of experience and qualities. Strong ambition has become the modern standard, but the link between personal and political ambitions becomes fused at different ages, around different skills, and with different implications for leadership style. Al Gore's father remarked (quoted in Bruni 2000: wk.1; see also Maraniss and Nakashima 1999: A6; Zelnick 1999) when his son had become the vice president that "we raised him for it." In a family dispute about whether young Al Gore should be made to plow a steep slope on the family farm, his mother acquiesced to his father, Senator Gore, with the comment (quoted in Zelnick 1999: 30), "Yes, a boy could never be president if he couldn't plow with that dammed hillside plow." George W. Bush, on the other hand, made his first official foray for himself into politics in 1978 at the age of thirty-two (Minutagio 1999). And John McCain did so in 1982 at the age of forty-six, although there are indications he had political office on his mind well before that (McCain 1999).

Nevertheless, the analysis of candidates' psychologies and their relationship to the responsibilities of public leadership mask an important question. Has the nature of leadership itself, and the public expectations surrounding it, changed? I want to suggest here, that it has, and draw some implications from the 2000 presidential campaign.

Leadership is a notoriously vague concept.[28] Some associate it with charisma—that vaguely defined term which includes the ability to generate political excitement. Others view it as a personal quality akin to *gravitas*, which allows the leader to command respect and, above all, compliance. Still others see leadership as the act of faithfully representing constituent views and goals. Political leadership may involve all of these elements to some degree.

Political leadership in a democracy is essentially found in the capacity to direct and exercise power for public purpose. However, what it entails and how it is accomplished, when it is, are key questions. Elsewhere (Renshon 1998b: 226-228), I have proposed three distinct aspects of political leadership: mobilization, orchestration, and consolidation. *Mobilization* refers to the president's ability to arouse the public. *Orchestration* refers to channelling of public arousal, understanding, and support in the effective application of policy achievement. Lastly, *consolidation* refers to the skills and tasks necessary to preserving a set of supportive relationships and institutionalizing the results of one's policy judgments.[29]

These three elements suggest *what* leadership is, but they don't address the question of *how* they are enacted. Consider mobilization. Any leader who aspires to exercise his power for public purpose must engage the public. This means he must get the public's attention, translate their policy intentions to acceptable public purpose, and secure the legitimacy derived from the honest enactment of this process.

Sometimes, this is easily done. External crisis like severe economic down-turns or major involvement in foreign conflict make leadership purpose and public need almost synonymous. At other times, mismatches between a leader's knowledge or ambitions may lead to a form of indirect or masked leadership. Eisenhower's indirect, behind-the-scenes, "hidden-hand" presidency (Greenstein 1984) and Bill Clinton's use of the "New Democrat" slogan to mask "Old Democrat" ambitions (Renshon 1998a: 74-75) are two illustrations of this point.

The state of the public and its degree of consensus also make an enormous difference to the how of leadership enactment. "Hidden-hand" leadership may be more acceptable in times of cultural and political consensus, and masked leadership more necessary in times of sharp political or cultural conflicts. As both the external circumstances and the public's psychology change, it is not surprising that the meaning and means of "successful" leadership also changes. These changes have important implications for how we select and judge our lead-ers. And, they also hold important implications for the best fit between assem-blies of experience and qualities that define leaders' interior psychology and the circumstances which they govern.

I want to frame my point here by articulating two very different understand-ings of political leadership in this country, one traditional and well known, one emerging and not yet well articulated. These models of leadership are, respec-tively: the *heroic* and the *reflective* (see chapter 14 for a fuller explanation).

Heroic leadership in American society is the traditional. Its archetype is Franklin D. Roosevelt, its metaphor the hierarchy, and its motto: decide and command. The task of the heroic leader is to convince the public of what it is that he already thinks they *must* do. *Reflective* leadership, on the other hand, is personal and diffuse. Its prototype, but not its archetype, is Bill Clinton. Its metaphor is the prism, and its motto is: select and reflect. It is not introspective, but externalized. The task of reflective leadership is to gather the disparate elements of frayed or fractured political and cultural consensus and mirror them so that publics can see the basis for their common purposes. The reflective leader diffuses conflict, not sharpens it. It is leadership whose purpose is not to choose and impose, but to engage and connect.

Conclusion: Heoric and Reflective Leadership and the 2000 Presidential Campaign

As leadership theorists never tire of pointing out, there is a close connection between the leader and her times. Dire circumstances call for heroic leadership. However, our times may well call for a different form of leadership, one that is based less on command and more on the articulation of common concerns.

Americans flirted with heroic leadership in the 1992 and 1996 presidential campaigns with Ross Perot and Pat Buchanan. Both articulated, encouraged, and tried to make use of grievance, coupling it with their own strong claims for heroic leadership status. Pat Buchanan in 1992, like Alan Keyes in the 2000 campaign, ran on the premise of his own strong consistency. Whether leading a "pitchfork revolt," (Buchanan) or finding dignity in a mosh pit jump (Keyes) neither candidate could promise Americans more than uncompromising conflict in a society already weary of it. In 1992 and 1996, Ross Perot emphasized "straight," but not particular insightful, talk coupled with a promise to open up the hood of government and get in there and fix it—period! Having come from the quintessential command and control experience (his own company), he was ill prepared, ill-suited, and in the end mismatched for the position to which he aspired. Americans may have been responsive to his apparent, but limited candor, but not at the price of his temperament and control.

Bill Clinton was successful in both elections because he represented a new, less sharp-edged leadership. Promising to "put people first," he seemed to care and connect with many Americans, and they, in turn, connected with him. He did not promise to command, but to respond. He reassured Americans that as a leader he would not aspire to grand plans, but rather sensible policies. His political stance as a "New Democrat" promised to heal the cleavages that permeate our society and to do so in a way which would bring left and right, Democrat and Republican together in new common efforts. In short, he was the prototype, yet until he was forced to work with a Republican Congress, ultimately a flawed exemplar, of a new reflective leadership style.

It is now clear in retrospect that Mr. Clinton had adopted a reflective style to mask some very basic heroic tendencies. And, as a result, far from diminishing conflict, he escalated it. Far from bringing people together, he divided them. During his presidency the country was not at war, but it was not at peace.

That was part of his legacy as Al Gore and George W. Bush campaigned to take his place. If this analysis is correct, a number of Americans are not looking for a fighting leader, but a leader who could, if necessary, fight. They prefer someone who reconciles rather than divides, and they prefer someone with common plans, not large ones.

If this analysis is correct, Al Gore's psychology and campaign may well have represented a mismatch between him and the new, emerging climate of American leadership. Mr. Gore is very programmatic, a reflection of his interest and experience in government. His strong support of government programs reflects a very robust view of their role.

Mr. Gore's relentless pursuit of traditional core democratic constituencies and his inability, or disinclination, to distance himself, even symbolically, from them raised the issue of how fairly Mr. Gore would represent groups across the board and not only the constituent pillars of the Democratic party. Mr. Gore noted his support of free trade as an example of his capacity to distance himself from labor unions that support him. Asked about reverberations among unions, he replied (quoted in Berke and Seelye 2000):

> Some of them have not yet endorsed me because of the fact that I'm in favor of this legislation. Others have endorsed me in spite of our disagreement on this legislation because I agree with them on 90 percent of the issues. And George Bush disagrees with them on 100 percent of the issues. I think it's the right thing.

Nevertheless, the reporters pointed out in the same article that on the campaign trail, Mr. Gore hardly mentioned the trade agreement. And in an appearance before seeking their endorsement, Mr. Gore never brought up his position, but instead spoke of their essential agreement on all other issues important to them.

Mr. Gore is an aggressive, ferocious sometimes savage political street fighter. As he demonstrated with Bill Bradley, he will mislead and sometimes demonize his opponents. His campaign theme "fighting for you"[30] represents a good fit between his psychology and leadership style, but it was sometimes done in a harsh way.

George W. Bush, on the other hand, represents a different kind of leadership. He is certainly not as programmatic as Al Gore, and assuredly not as well versed on the details of policy complexities. Perhaps as a result of having entered politics later in life, his record in Texas seemed to indicate he is not a man of large agendas. That is a decided drawback to those who look to government to solve the host of problems we confront, but keep in mind that such a view basically represents a heroic view of leadership. Bush's commitment to facilitating institutions in the "civil society" to stimulate horizontal public connections appears to be more consistent with reflective rather than heroic leadership.

Vice President Gore is a very smart man. He is deeply versed in policy issues. There is no doubt that on grounds of experience, he is well qualified for the presidency. However, he was a candidate whose determination and earnestness can easily shade off into insistence.[31] He is a man who *very* much wants to be president and gives the impression of being willing to do almost anything to get it.[32] In one article Mr. Gore is quoted as saying "you have to rip your opponent's lungs out and then move on." He is also very easily drawn to harsh demagoguery. This is apparently an update of early political advice given to him by his mother. Ceci Connolly noted that, "The first time Al Gore ran for president, his mother slipped him a note as he prepared for an Iowa debate: 'Smile, Relax, Attack.' Twelve years later, the dutiful son is still following her advice." In a relatively peaceful period in which the public says it is tired of intense conflict, this might well have been a drawback. And, there may well have been a mismatch between the heroic leadership his candidacy espouses and his personal qualities and biography.

Mr. Bush, on the other hand, is certainly intelligent, but nowhere near as versed or as immersed in policy as his opponent. He is as interested in building relationships as in building policy monuments. On domestic policy, he cares deeply about education and as one observer noted "running against the sixties." However, no one can reasonably argue that he sees himself proposing, much less providing a solution to the many problems that one could address. Mr. Bush envisions a government of limits and that reflects something about his ambitions for accomplishment in office. They are certainly not grand, but it remains to be seen whether they might prove to be, as they were in the case of Ronald Reagan, more important than profound.

Notes

1.   Peter G. Petterson (quoted in Raines 2000: A22) recalls doing polling and interviewing for a group called Citizens for Eisenhower. The interviews showed, he recalled, that people would say of Ike, "here's someone I can really like," "someone I'd trust," "someone who would do the right thing." He then wrote Eisenhower a memo that "talked about the transcendent importance of character and trust and how it was a far better strategy for Eisenhower to build on that rather than get into overly gritty nuances of his positions and Taft's positions, because he was seen as a transcendent figure."
2.   This view is not universally shared. Thomas Patterson (1993) argues that concerns with "character" have drawn attention away from more important policy issues and should be downplayed. Others (Lichtenberg 1989: 6) have argued that such concerns are irrelevant. Consider the following syllogistic *non sequitur* by a media pundit writing on Gary Hart's withdrawal from his candidacy because of his lies, poor judgment, and womanizing with Donna Rice:

> "Gary Hart's sex life was thought by many to indicate a lack of respect for women; yet *Ms.* Magazine gave him a 94 percent rating on civil rights and women's issues. Personality traits should be irrelevant to our judgment of the person qua politician."

In other words, if you agree with a candidate's political views, his psychology ought not matter.
3.   The analysis developed in this section of this book is guided by theories of presidential leadership, political psychology, and comparative psychoanalytic theory. However, the raw information used to support these analyses is all "public data." That term, and its implications, deserves a brief explication.
    Public data is simply information that is available to any interested person and which resides in the public domain. Included are multiple, cross-checked news accounts of events, multiple and cross-checked biographical accounts, the words of the candidates themselves, and of others about them. Each kind of public data is used in a specific way for a limited purpose with recognition of each method's advantages and limitations.
    Newspaper and other journalistic accounts are primarily used as documentation of the major facts concerning a particular event, e.g., a presidential candidate made a particular pledge, a particular event took place within a certain sequence of events, and so on. The accounts themselves are, for the most part, concerned with *describing* events and the circumstances surrounding them. This material is an important part of the attempt to use specific "contexts" and "circumstances" in a theoretically useful way. In attempting to answer the question of what happened (as a prelude to trying to answer, why), a presidential researcher might depend on many types of data including presidential news conferences and interviews with major actors, documentary evidence, and so on.

None of these various data are without flaws. Each can be viewed as a form of commentary designed to influence the framing and understanding of particular narrative lines or incidents. Thus, a presidential press conference can be viewed as the president's narrative of his behavior, and the reasons for it. Likewise, interviews with other actors, provide their own narrative perspective. Even the release of what seems to be less subjective data like a report released by the White House (or its opponents) on the number of welfare mothers helped to find employment is part of a narrative based on a particular sample with a particular program operating with a particular definition of work and of success.

A detailed analysis of the major sources, along with the advantages and limitations of their use, can be found in Renshon (1998a 401-408; 1998b: 307-318).

4.   Donald Kinder and his colleagues (1980) found that presidential candidates are judged mostly on the strengths and weakness of the incumbent.
5.   See www.abcnews.com (March 15, 2000).
6.   The Pew Research Center for the People and the Press, "Retro-Politics, The Political Typology: Version 3.0, Section V: The Clinton Legacy and the Next President, November 11, 1999." See www.peoplepress.org/typo99sec5.htm (March 12, 2000).
7.   See www.abcnews.com (March 15, 2000).
8.   The Pew Research Center for the People and the Press, "Retro-Politics."
9.   For an exception to this general trend, see Dalia Sussman," Issues Trump Character in New Poll," ABCNews, March 2, 2000. See http://www.abcnews.go.com/sections/politics/DailyNews/poll000301_1.html (March 15, 2000).
10.   The Terrance Group and Lake/Snell/Perry Associates, "Battleground 2000: A Survey of Voters Attitudes for Voter.Com, March 12-13, 2000. See http://www.voter.com (May 18, 2000).
11.   The Gallup Poll Editorial Staff, "Setting the Stage: Election 2000 Part I: Mood of America," January 22, 2000. See http://www.gallup.com/poll/releases/pr000122.asp (March 12, 2000).

The question reads: Which of the following do you think will be most important to you when you decide who to vote for — [ROTATE: Where the candidates stand on issues that matter to you (or) the leadership skills and vision you think the candidates would have as president]?

Stance on issues	Neither	Leadership skills/vision	No opinion	Both equally	
Likely Voters (LV) Jan 7-10 2000	36%	51%	12%	1%	*
National Adults (NA) Jan 7-10 2000	37%	49%	10%	1%	3%

12.   The Gallup Poll Editorial Staff, "Setting the Stage: Election 2000 Part I: Mood of America," January 22, 2000. See http://www.gallup.com/poll/releases/pr000122.asp (March 12, 2000).

	Republicans	Independents	Democrats
Leadership and Vision	51%	54%	44%
Stance on Issues	33%	33%	42%
Both Equally	13%	12%	11%

13.   Harris's anecdotal information was not supported by more representative data. The Pew survey reported,

"Despite talk that the public is longing for an extended Clinton era, the president's favorability ratings have dropped significantly since last year. Less than half of the public (48%) now rates Clinton very or mostly favorable compared to 55% in March, 1999. These are among the lowest ratings the president has received since he took office in 1992. Clinton has lost some ground among most major demographic groups. Most notable, perhaps, is Clinton's loss among core Democrats. One year ago, 85% of Democrats said their overall opinion of Clinton was very favorable or mostly favorable. Today, that number is 73%. Young men and African-Americans view Clinton more favorably than members of other demographic groups. Almost six-in-ten men age 18-29 (59%) give Clinton a favorable rating, compared to only 46% of men over age 50. A strong majority of blacks (84%) also continue to view Clinton in a positive light."

See The Pew Center for the Press and the Public, "Voter Preferences Vacillate," May 11, 2000, http://www.peoplepress.org/may00rpt2.htm (December 8, 2000).

14.   Daniel Merkle, "Clinton Fatigue Is Still a Drag for Gore," ABCNews, March 1, 2000. See http://www.abcnews.go.com/sections/politics/DailyNews/poll000301.html (March 16, 2000).

Significant Factors Predicting Gore/Bush Vote (Beta Weights)

	2/27/00	9/2/99
Candidate favorability		
Bush	.36	.29
Gore	.26	.29
Party identification	. 22	.24
Clinton fatigue	.18	.20

15.   David W. Moore, "'Clinton Factor' May Be Hurting Gore in Presidential Race," The Gallup Organization, March 16, 2000. See http://www.gallup.com/poll/releases/pr000316.asp (March 17, 2000).

16.   Transcript, "Interview with George W. Bush," *Nightline*, March 14, 2000. See www.abcnews.go.com/onair/nightline/transcripts/n100314_trans.html (March 15, 2000)

17.   Using factor and cluster analysis to place individuals, respondents were asked a series of questions in eight areas: environmentalism, religion and morality, social tolerance, social justice, business sentiment, financial security, anti-government sen-

timent, and patriotism/militarism. More specific descriptions of the methodology and of the groups may be found at: www.people-press.org/typo99sec.1.htm (March 1, 2000).

18.   Data reported in the paragraphs that follow are drawn from exit polls conducted by a consortium of news organizations and reported on ABC news. These data may be found at http://abcnews.go.com/sections/politics/2000vote (March 8, 2000).

19.   In Missouri, Democrats said that social security and medicare issues weighed relatively heavily (30 percent), but personal qualities like standing up for what you believe (25 percent), having the right experience (22 percent), being a strong and decisive leader (19 percent) and not being a typical politician (10 percent) carried a greater overall weight than the remaining policy issues that voters selected as important.

    In New York the same pattern emerged among Democrats. Personal qualities such as having the right experience (25 percent), standing up for your beliefs (23 percent) being a strong and decisive leader (13 percent), generally carried more cumulative weight than the most important issues (social security/medicare (21 percent), education (16 percent), and health care (12 percent).

20.   Ohio Republicans thought that standing up for what you believe (33 percent), and being a strong and decisive leader (24 percent) carried more weight than the top policy issues, including reflecting moral values (33 percent) tax reform (15 percent). In Missouri, standing up for what you believe (34 percent) and being a strong and decisive leader (18 percent) outweighed the two top policy issues, moral values (34 percent) and tax reform (12 percent). While in New York, standing up for what you believe (36 percent) and being a strong and decisive leader (19 percent), outweighed the top two policy issues, moral values (26 percent) and social security/medicare (17 percent).

21.   Transcript, *MacNeil/Lehrer NewsHour*, December 18, 1987, p. 8.

22.   Some of the details are examined in Allison Mitchell with Frank Bruni (2000: A17; see also Calmes and Rogers 2000: A24).

23.   Gore has had a long history of harsh attacks on his opponents. Some of this material is covered in J. Cummings (1999: A24).

24.   One of Bradley's supporters was quoted in Gellman et al. (2000: A01) as saying the candidate held a "view of American politics which is somewhat stilted and perhaps unrealistic—and I mean that in a positive way."

25.   Predictably, Gore campaign spokesman Chris Lehane characterized the change (Dao 2000: A1) as "a sign of desperation. After 12 months of above-it-all politics, he's clearly started listening to his pollsters and consultants and decided to wage a negative campaign."

26.   Transcript, *Face the Nation*, November 13, 1999.

27.   Quoted in Greg Hitt and Bob Davis, "Bradley, Despite Wound, Refuses to Open 'Scandals' Box for Strong Weapons Against Gore," *Wall Street Journal*, 26 January 2000: A24.

28.   Representative works on political leadership include: Burns 1978, George 1969, Greenstein 1984; 1998, Heifetz 1994, Janis 1989, Neustadt 1990 [1960], Paige 1977, Skowronek 1993, Tucker 1981, and Tulis 1987.

29.   Consolidation also involves setting up and into motion policy structures or procedural regimes which solidify the results of the president's policy judgments. It may involve the creation of new agencies, working groups or other institutional forms. Or it might combine refocusing the functions or direction of existing policy structures. These methods of consolidation also represent ways in which a president's policy decisions can have an enduring effect. They are, in essence, a legacy of a president's judgment and leadership.

30.   Gore's campaign bus had a banner on its side proclaiming: "AL GORE FIGHTING FOR US" in three-foot-high letters. At a campaign speech in Albany, New York, Gore used the word "fight" twelve times in ten minutes (Allen 2000: A09).

31.   One reporter covering Al Gore noted the connection as follows:

> Gore doesn't so much ask for a vote as insist on it. He starts every town meeting by promising to answer every voter's question, no matter how long it takes. It is a shtick—wherever he goes, he says, "If necessary, I'll stay here till March 7"—but he follows through with earnestness...he took questions at a gymnasium in Spring-field, Mass., for more than three hours. By that time, all but a dozen of the 300 audience members had filtered out. "Would you like to add comments about any-thing I might have overlooked in my treatment of this?" he asked a woman who had just heard an exhaustive account of his views on homeless people. Later, he asked, "Did that sound like a good agenda to you? I'm trying to convince you all to vote for me. (Allen 2000: A09)

32.   One *New York Times* reporter captured this element in comparing the motivations of Mr. Gore and Mr. Bush. He (Bruni 2000: A23) quotes Mr. Bush as saying:

> "the most difficult part of that endeavor [the campaign] was being on the road." According to Bruni it all made for an interesting contrast. Vice President Al Gore comes off as one of the most ardent, ambitious aspirants to the Oval Office in quite some time, a man who would crawl across broken glass to get there. Mr. Bush comes off as a man who wants it, but not at any price, and sometimes not as much as he wants to wake up in his own bed at the Governor's Mansion in Austin, Tex., wander downstairs to make a pot of coffee, let out the pets and fetch the newspaper.

References

Allen, Mike. "Road Trips in Northeast Put Contrasts Into Focus Gore's Full Force Makes Bradley Seem Subtle." *Washington Post*, 21 February 2000: A09.

_____. "Will the Shining Armor Get Tarnished?" *Washington Post National Weekly Edition*, 29 November 1999:15.

Apple, R. W. Jr. "Bush Needs McCain Backers, but Winning Their Votes Won't Be Easy." *New York Times*, 9 March 2000:A.20.

Dan, Balz, "Getting Down and Dirty." *Washington Post National Weekly Edition*, 13 December 1999:A 12.

_____. "Largely Similar Democrats May Use Meeting to Cite Differences." *Washington Post*, 27 October 1999:A14.

Bennet, James, and Janet Elder. "Despite Intern, President Stays in Good Graces." *New York Times*, February 24, 1998; A15.

Bennett, W. Lance. "The UnCivic Culture: Communication, Identity, and the Rise of Lifestyle Politics." *PS: Political Science and Politics,* December 1988: 741-761.

Berke, Richard L., and Katherine Q. Seelye. "With a Convert's Passion, Gore Pledges Campaign Finance Reform. *New York Times*, 12 March 2000.

Blumer, Jay G., and Dennis Kavanaugh. "A Third Age of Political Communications: Where is it Heading?" Paper presented to the Roundtable on Seeking Responsibilities for Political Communication, London, 1988.

Broder, David S. "The Satisfied but Skeptical Voter." *Washington Post*, 15 November 1999:6.

Bruni, Frank. "Bush and McCain, Sittin' in a Tree, D-I-S-S-I-N-G." *New York Times*, 9 February 2000b: A14.

_____. "Campaign Notebook: A Wistful Bush Reflects on Hearth and Home." *New York Times*, 28 January 2000a: A23.

Burns, James M. *Leadership*. New York: Harper and Row, 1978.

Burns, James M., and Georgia J. Sorenson. *Dead Center: Clinton-Gore Leadership and the Perils and Moderation*. New York: Charles Scribner's Sons, 2000.

Calmes, Jackie, and David Rogers. "Tax Tussle of Bush and McCain Gets More Combative." *Wall Street Journal,* 20 January 2000: A24.

Clymer, Adam, with Adam Nagourney. "Bradley Questions Buddhist Temple Donations, and Gore Complains of Divisive Attacks." *New York Times,* 31 January 2000:A24.

Connolly, Ceci. "'New' Gore Bears Striking Resemblance to '88's." *Washington Post*, 11 December 1999

Cooper, Matthew. "The Search for Authenticity." *Time,* 1 November 1999: 48.

Cummings, Jeanne. "Attack on Bradley Tax Ideas Shows Gore's Skills at His Own Sport: Taking Jabs at Candidates." *Wall Street Journal*, 8 December 1999:A24.

Dao, James. "Bradley's New Message to Voters: Gore Can't Be Trusted," *New York Times*, 28 January 2000:A1.

_____. "Throwing an Elbow at 'Old Politics.'" *New York Times*, 6 February 2000: A25.

Dao, James, and Nicholas D. Kristof. "Early Promise Vanished, Bradley Plans to Quit Today." *New York Times*, 9 March 2000:A1.

Davis, Bob. "Gore's Barbs Sting Bradley, Stay in Bounds." *Wall Street Journal,* 28 January 2000: A17.

DiMaggio, Paul, et. al. "Have American Attitudes Become More Polarized? *American Journal of Sociology* 102:3 (1996): 690-755.

Dionne, E. J. Jr. "A Return to Political Civility?" *Washington Post*, 28 April 2000:A31.

Duff, Christina. "Among Factors that Influence People's Lives, Politics Ranks at the Bottom." *Wall Street Journal,* 17 September 1998: A9.

Editorial. "Positive Negatives," *Wall Street Journal,* 17 February 2000: A16.

Gellman, Barton, Dale Russakoff, and Mike Allen. "Where Did Bradley Go Wrong? Many Believe Wounds Were Self-Inflicted." *Washington Post*, 4 March 2000: A01.

George, Alexander L. "The 'Operational Code': A Neglected Approach to the Study of Political Leadership and Decision Making." *International Studies Quarterly* 13 (1969): 190-222.

Gigot, Paul A. "A Vote for Character." *Wall Street Journal*, 3 February 2000: A26.

Greenstein, Fred I. (ed). *Leadership in the Modern Presidency*. Cambridge, MA: Harvard University Press, 1998.

_____. *The Hidden Hand Presidenc.y.* New York: Basic, 1984.

Harris, John F. "As Term Wanes, 'Clinton Fatigue' Yields to Nostalgia," *Washington Post*, 1 May 2000: A01.

Heifetz, Ronald. *Leadership without Easy Answers*. Cambridge, MA: Harvard University Press, 1994.

Hitt, Greg, and Bob Davis. "Bradley, Despite Wound, Refuses to Open 'Scandals' Box for Strong Weapons Against Gore." *Wall Street Journal*, 26 January 2000:A24.

Hunt, Albert R. "People and Politics: Two Decidedly Different Insurgents." *Wall Street Journal*, 27 January 2000: A23.

Hunter, James Davidson. *Culture Wars: The Struggle to Define America*. New York: Basic Books, 1993.

Jamieson, Kathleen Hall. *Everything You Think You Know About Politics...and Why You're Wrong*. New York: Basic Books, 2000.

Janis, Irving. *Crucial Decisions: Leadership in Policy making and-Crisis Management*. New York: Free Press, 1989.

Kinder, Donald R., M. D. Peters, Robert P. Abelson, and Susan Fiske, "Presidential Prototypes." *Political Behavior* 2 (1980): 314-337.

Kurtz. Howard. "Mr. Nice Guy for President." *Washington Post Weekly Edition,* 29 November 1999:A16.

Kurtz. Howard, and Richard Morin. "Shown TV Spots Via Internet, Republicans Nationwide Lean Toward Governor." *Washington Post*, 16 February 2000: A14.

_____. "Americans Wait for the Punch Line on Impeachment as the Senate Trial Proceeds, Comedians Deliver the News. *Washington Post*, 26 January 1999: A01.

Kurtz, Howard, and Ben White. "Forbes Signals He Will Withdraw Delaware Defeat was Key, Aides Say." *Washington Post*, 10 February 2000: A06.

Lane, Robert E. "Interpersonal Relationships and Leadership in a 'Cold' Society." *Comparative Politics*, July (1978) :443-460.

Langer, Gary. "Analysis: Public to Clinton: Nice Job. See Ya." 27 January 2000. See www.abcnews.com (March 15, 2000).

Lichtenberg, Judith. "The Politics of Character and the Character of Journalism," Discussion Paper D-2, The Joan Shorenstein Center, Harvard University, October 1989, p. 6.

Maraniss, David, and Ellen Nakashima. "Gore's Grades Belie Image of Studiousness." *Washington Post*, 19 March 2000: A01.

Marks, Peter. "McCain Launches a New Salvo." *New York Times*, 9 February 2000: A14.

_____. "Bush and McCain Vie on Truth." *New York Times.* 8 February 2000: A20.

_____. "In Ads, Candidates Gloves Stay On." *New York Times*, 1 January 2000:A28.

_____. "In New Hampshire Ads, an Audible Warmth." *New York Times*, 6 December 1999: A1.

McCain, John, with Mark Salter. *Faith of My Fathers*. New York: Random House, 1999.

Minutagio, Bill. *First Son: George W. Bush and the Bush Family Dynasty. New York: Times Books*, 1999.

Merkle, Daniel. "Clinton Fatigue is Still a Drag for Gore." *ABCNews*, March 1, 2000.

Mitchell, Allison, with Frank Bruni. "McCain and Bush Find a Fght in the Details of the Tax Cut." *New York Times*, 20 January 2000:A17.

Morin, Richard, and Claudia Deane. "Why the Fla. Exit Polls Were Wrong. *Washington Post*, 8 November 2000.

Murray, Charles. "Americans Remain Wary of Washington." *Wall Street Journal,* 23 December 1997: A14.

Nagourney, Adam, and Richard Perez-Pena. "Bush and McCain Trade Bitter Criticism as Campaigns in New York Gather Steam." *New York Times*, 3 March 2000: A1.

_____. "In New York, a Sharp Attack Awaits McCain, *New York Times*, 2 March 2000: A1.

Neal, Terry M. "Tax Reform Group Attacks, McCain Fires Back." *New York Times*, 26 December 1999: A32.

Neustadt. Richard. *Presidential Power and the Modern Presidents: The Politics of Leadership from Roosevelt to Reagan*. New York: Free Press, 1990 [1960].

Nye, Joseph S. Jr., et al. (eds.). *Why People Don't Trust Government*. Cambridge, MA: Harvard University Press, 1997.

Paige, Glenn D. *The Scientific Study of Political Leadership*. New York: Free Press, 1977.

Patterson,Thomas E. *Out of Order.* New York: Alfred A. Knopf, 1993.

Ponnuru, Ramesh. "Accentuating the Negative." *New York Times*, December 4, 1999: A 17.

Putnam. Robert. *Bowling Alone: The Collapse and Revival of American Community*. New York: Charles Scribner's Sons, 2000.

Raines, Howell. "When Personal Appeals Trump Party Labels." *New York Times,* 9 February 2000: A22.

Ramerzez, Anthony. "McCain's Ethnic Slur Gone but not Forgotten." Associated Press story reported in the *New York Times,* 5 March 2000:A23.

Renshon, Stanley A. "Political Leadership as Social Capital: Governing in a Divided National Culture." *Political Psychology* 21:1 (2000):199-226.

_____. *The Psychological Assessment of Presidential Candidates*. New York: Routledge, 1998a.

_____. *High Hopes: The Clinton Presidency and the Politics of Ambition*. New York: Routledge, 1998b.

Review and Outlook. "Positive Negatives." *Wall Street Journal*, 17 February 2000:A16.

Shapiro, Andrew L. *The Control Revolution: How the Internet is Putting Individuals in Charge and Changing the World We know*. New York: BBS, 1999.

Skowronek, Stephen. *The Politics that Presidents Make*. Cambridge, MA: Harvard University Press, 1993.

Sussman, Dalia. "Issues Trump Character in New Poll." *ABCNews*, March 2, 2000.

Toner, Robin, and Janet Elder. "An Electorate Largely Split Reflects a Race So Very Tight." *New York Times*, 14 November 2000.

Transcript. *Face the Nation*. November 13, 1999.

Transcript. *MacNeil/Lehrer NewsHour*. December 18, 1987, p. 8.

Tucker, Robert C. *Politics as Leadership*. Columbia: University of Missouri Press, 1981.

Tulis, Jeffrey. *The Rhetoric Presidency*. Princeton, NJ: Princeton University Press, 1987.

Turque, Bill. *Inventing Al Gore* .New York: Houghton Mifflin, 2000.

Von Drehle, David. "Trying to Erase 'Evil'; John McCain's Rhetorical Grenades Have Stirred Anger in the GOP and Raised Allegations That He is Exploiting Religious Differences." *Washington Post*, 2 March 2000:A07.

Wayne, Stephan J. *The Road to the White House 2000: The Politics of Presidential Elections*. New York: St. Martin's Press, 2000.

Wayne, Stephan J., et al. *The Politics of American Government, s*econd edition. New York: St. Martin's Press, 1997.

Wayne, Leslie. "Forbes Spent Millions, but for Little Gain." *New York Times*, 10 February 2000:A. 26.

Wilentz, Sean. "Yawn." *The New Republic*, 28 February 2000: 6.

_____. *The New Republic*. 6 March 2000: 8.

Wolfe, Alan. *Marginalized in the Middle*. Chicago: University of Chicago Press, 1996.

_____. *One Nation After All* .Chicago: University of Chicago Press, 1996.

Yardley, Jim, with Fran Bruni. "Bush Takes Tougher Line and Emphasizes Reform." New York Times, 8 February 2000: A20.

Zaller, John. "Monica Lewinsky's Contribution to Political Science." *PS: Political Science & Politics*, 1998, 31:182-89.

Zelnick, Bob. *Gore: A Political Life*. Washington, DC: Regnery, 1999.

Zielbauer, Paul. "Cities Failing to Heed Call of the Census." *New York Times*, 21 April 2000: A1.

7

Assessing Judgment and Leadership in the 2000 Presidential Campaign— An Introduction

The Presidency is basically a place of decision; its important that you work hard...But in the end hard work is not enough. You also have to make good decisions, and that requires a certain level of experience, a certain level of judgment, a certain instinct.—William J. Clinton (2000: 2585)

Whom would you prefer to serve in the White House making life and death decisions about matters of war and peace? Would you prefer a president with a well-deserved reputation for good judgment, or would you prefer someone who has demonstrated in his public life that his judgment is open to serious question? What about making important decisions regarding domestic policy that could have serious implications? Would you prefer someone with good judgment or someone whose judgment you found questionable?

If you answered both questions to yourself—"Good judgment, of course"—you validated in a personal way the premise of this and the following chapters. But, equally important, you share that view with a large majority of the American public. In 1995, 76 percent of Americans thought that "sound judgment in a crisis" for a president was "absolutely essential."[1] Twelve percent thought it "essential." By 1999, 78 percent thought "sound judgment" an "absolutely essential" trait for a president while 12 percent more thought it "essential."

On that basis you might have expected that judgment, sound or otherwise, would have received substantial direct attention during recent presidential campaigns. It did not. Judgment, when it comes up at all, ordinarily does so indirectly, through surrogate issues like "temper," "experience," and even intelligence. The extent to which surrogate terms and discussions really clarify judgment issues raised by each candidate's psychology is questionable.

In this chapter and those that follow, I explore the question of whether it is possible to reach any understandings of a presidential candidate's judgment before he enters office. If it is possible, on what basis might it proceed? What are the most promising frames of analysis through which to view these issues, and what cautions might be observed in doing so? I begin by focusing on the two respective 2000 election party nominees, George W. Bush and Albert Gore, Jr. I then turn to an examination of the issues surrounding Republican party presidential hopeful John McCain's temper and psychology in relation to his judgment. Although my focus is on American presidents and candidates, I hope that the analysis that follows will provide useful perspectives to those whose interest in these issues lies in other geographical, political, and cultural domains.

Is the issue of judgment in the presidency important to the American public? I present data that answers that question with an emphatic *yes*. Is it possible to make use of an unfolding presidential campaign process to draw some inferences about a candidate's judgment? I present some material drawn from the 2000 presidential election which suggests that it is. Before turning to those issues, however, a central theoretical question involving the possible dual nature of the office and the judgments of the person who occupies it must be raised.

Two Presidencies or One? The Dual Judgment Problem

Aaron Wildavsky (1966: 7) begins his well-known paper on the presidency with the following statement: "The United States has one president, but two presidencies; one presidency is for domestic affairs, and the other is concerned with defense and foreign policy." Wildavsky's point is that the president has more control over his foreign policies than his domestic ones. This is a result of having to share institutional and political power domestically and having less need to do so internationally.

Wildavsky's argument in favor of two presidencies raises the issue of whether there is a parallel dualism in presidential judgment. I term this the *dual judgment problem*. The most basic formulation of the question involved is this: Do presidents make substantially different kinds of calculations, go through substantially different procedures, both in their own internal weighing processes and in those that take place in the advisory context to reach judgments, or make use of substantially different judgment frameworks when dealing with foreign policy than they do with domestic policy?

Perhaps foreign policy operates by a wholly different judgment calculus. Perhaps paralleling Wildavsky's two presidencies argument, presidents have two sets of judgment frameworks, one for domestic and one for foreign policy. Perhaps the lack of constraint on presidents in foreign policy, again momentarily accepting Wildavsky's argument, means that we get to see the president's "real" judgment in foreign affairs because he doesn't have other centers of power to inhibit or otherwise temper them. Or perhaps, foreign policy judgments, especially those having to do with armed conflict provide their own inhibitions on poor judgment because of the consequences of making errors. Wildavsky (1966: 13) quotes President Kennedy: "domestic policy...can only defeat us; foreign policy can kill us."

Obviously, it is not possible to settle these issues here. But they are important to raise and address, even if preliminarily, for reasons having to do with one purpose of this chapter. If foreign policy judgments are of a substantially different sort than domestic or personal political judgments, then there is not much substantive traction on the issues of good judgment to be gained by looking at presidential election campaigns.

Why is it that the questions that public opinion polls ask regarding candidate "experience" are not a reliable substitute and guide for answering such questions? Primarily, because most recent modern presidential candidates have not served in positions where their judgments about foreign policy have been put to the acid test of command. Examples include Georgia governor Jimmy Carter, Arkansas governor Bill Clinton, Colorado senator Gary Hart, Massachusetts governor Michael Dukakis, Minnesota senator Walter Mondale, Texas governor George W. Bush, California governor Reagan, and so on.

Even in cases in which an incumbent is running for reelection, as was the case with Mr. Clinton in 1996, Mr. Reagan in 1980, and to some degree Mr. Gore in 2000, foreign policy may be crowded out of the public discussion by domestic concerns. In an October, 1999 poll Americans rated social security/medicare (17 percent), the economy (16 percent), education (15 percent) moral breakdown (13 percent) and health care (12 percent) as the top five double-digit problems facing the country. Only one foreign policy issue, nuclear proliferation was mentioned at all in the top tier of ten issues and this by only 7 percent of respondents.[2]

Needless to say, trying to gauge a candidate's judgment by his answers to hypothetical circumstances is little better than reading tea leaves. Moreover, any discussion of foreign policy differences between two candidates, even when they do arise, is not the same as direct inquiry about the qualities of judgment that a candidate might bring to bear on foreign policy questions. Does it show good judgment to be for more aid to the United Nations? Perhaps that depends on your view of that organization's purpose, effectiveness, and responsiveness to reform. What about continuing American aid to the Soviet Union? Is being in favor of that an illustration of good judgment? Perhaps that depends on your views of American interests in the area, the purposes for which the aid is given and spent, and the nature and monitoring of the expected results.

Trying to divine judgment from policy positions is a difficult and highly questionable undertaking that invites partisan definitions. Equally unsatisfactory is the fact that it confounds legitimate policy disagreements with a different, more basic set of psychological skills and capacities that enter into making good judgments *in unfolding circumstances.* The same problem arises when trying to impute "character" from being for or against particular policy positions. Both Democrats and Republicans with different convictions, and the courage of them, can be principled people psychologically.

The two presidencies and their dual judgment counterpart represent one possible framing of the issues, but there is another. It is found in the seminal work of Richard Neustadt (1991[1960]). Neustadt's paradigm-changing insight was that while the president might wear many hats, they are all worn on the same head. Rather than standing on the outside looking in at the president, Neustadt suggested that it was better to look over his shoulder. Doing so, Neustadt concluded, left one inescapable conclusion: Whatever roles the president played, his purposes were unitary. They were to preserve his policy prerogatives and enlist others to act on behalf of them.

From the perspective of Neustadt's framework, one can no more easily separate the "two presidencies" than one can argue the president becomes a different person when he ends a discussion with the Secretary of State and leaves for a fund-raising event at which he puts on his "party leader hat." The argument is not that the two activities are the same, only that they are carried out by the same person in the service of the same general purposes.

Neustadt had been criticized for focusing too much on power and bargaining, but no one has suggested that his insight about the singularity of the person occupying the office is wrong. Similar arguments occupied psychology at one time: Is it the person or the circumstances that determines behavior? The answer is obviously both with the additional caveat that the latter can have no effect without the former. Another version of this time-consuming, but not enlightening, debate asks: Are we different people with different people? Well, yes. We don't often treat our children like our spouses and most adults can discern some difference between their parents and their co-workers. However, that doesn't mean there can't be, or is not, an underlying set of psychological patterns clearly evident in almost all people, if you were able to see them over time and across circumstances.

The person at the center of all these relations remains who she is, with her own core ambitions, ideals, and ways of relating with others—even as these are and must be somewhat adjusted to circumstance. It is the same person who is parent to his child and child to his parent. Little substantive or theoretical traction is gained by positing an ever expanding multiplicity of selves, as postmodern theorists have done. The person unencumbered either by the consistent and effective functioning of his own character psychology, or the consolidated psychological lessons drawn from experience, is—in a very elemental way—psychologically adrift not adroit.

It seems logical to suggest that it is possible to tell a fair amount about a candidate's judgment from his behavior during the unfolding campaign and a focused look back over his record. It also seems fair to say that this is not often done. And so we are faced with a paradox.

A candidate's judgment is very important to most voters, but they are not helped in reaching their own good judgment about these matters by the reporting that covers important campaign issues. This is one more area in which there appears to be a disconnection between voters and media reporters. Voters, of course, are able to reach their own conclusions on these matters in cases like Mr. Hart's obvious lack of judgment. However, one is probably ill-advised to depend on such flamboyant episodes since poor judgment does not always advertise itself so blatantly.

One way to address this problem is to have media analysts become more aware of the links they need to explore and report. This, in turn, will require a step back, away from the 'horse race' aspect of the campaign, to a more substantively oriented focus on the things that matter to governing. This approach might appear similar to odes that tout the virtues of motherhood and apple pie. And, to some extent, it is. However, judgment may well be in the same position as "character issues" were ten years ago—recognized as important, but technically difficult to translate into concrete behavioral or career terms for non-clinicians.

In the chapters that follow I will present evidence that a leader's interior psychology can play an important role in his political and policy judgments. John McCain's personal ethical lapses as the basis for his emerging as a champion of campaign finance reform policy tell us something about his judgment. Al Gore's support for the minuteman missile, and how and why he came to it, also reveal some aspects of his judgment.

Yet, as important as such evidence might be, it is an error to try and reduce policy judgments to characterological psychology. Yes, it is probably true that the historical analogies one selects reflect the lessons that are most personally salient to the person doing so, and are therefore personal in that sense. However, it is also true that analogies and the history they rest upon have their own independent factual weight. And it is very true that reality in the form of the current circumstances that exist and are unfolding do, and ought to have enormous weight in the calculations of foreign policy judgments. What to do in the Middle East may have a lot to do with Mr. Clinton's search for an historic legacy, but the facts on the ground exert their own inexorable presence as well. Can we analyze the failed Camp David Summit in 2000 without asking about the impact of Mr. Clinton's historical and political ambitions on his judgments? I think not. Can we assign them primacy? Perhaps. Can we then say that because of this we can therefore safely disregard the facts on the ground and the knowledge of how these parties acted in the past? Absolutely not.

Is Presidential Judgment Important? The Public's View

There are a number of ways to establish the importance of good judgment in presidential candidates. We can rely on experiences with ourselves and others regarding the benefits of good judgment and the costs of not exercising it. We can also look to literatures in psychology and political science which establish judgment as an important element to consider. We can look to historical experience to suggest that judgment plays a role, on occasion an absolutely critical one, in the making of decisions with the most profound consequences. The process of judgment in the Cuban missile crisis would appear to qualify as evidence here. And, finally, given that democracies take citizen concerns seriously, we can examine public sentiment for signs of judgment's relevance.

Of course, the fact that the public believes that judgment should be considered and is important does not establish that in any particular case it *is* important. On the other hand, if the public does believe judgment is important, two issues would be raised immediately: (1) to what extent, and in what circumstances, does judgment enter into the voting calculus? and (2) to what extent do campaigns provide information about it to the voters who think it important?

How important is the good judgment of candidates to the American electorate? The answer found in Table 7.1 appears to be: Americans find the judgment of presidential candidates extremely important. As noted earlier, in 1995, 76 percent of Americans thought that "sound judgment in a crisis" for a president was "absolutely essential," and, by 1999, 78 percent thought "sound judgment" an "absolutely essential" trait for a president. Twelve percent in each year thought it "essential."

A look at data suggests that sound judgment was more important to Americans in a president than high ethical standards (67 percent), compassion (64 percent), saying what one believes in (59 percent), having consistent positions

Table 7.1
Public Views of Most Important Presidential Qualities

Presidential Qualitites	Absolutely	Essential
	1995	1999
	%	%
Sound judgement	76	78
High ethical standards	67	63
Compassion	64	63
Saying what one believes	59	57
Consistent positions	51	50
Forcefulness & decisiveness	50	46
Experience in public office	30	38
Willingness to compromise	34	33
Party loyalty	25	33
Experience in Washington	21	27

(51 percent), forcefulness and decisiveness (50 percent), experience in public office (30 percent), willingness to compromise (34 percent), party loyalty (25 percent), and experience in Washington (21 percent). Indeed, from 1995 to 1999, of the top six personal attributes wanted by the American public in a president only "sound judgment" increased in the percentage of people who thought it important. The other five declined in percentage.

Does this hold for groups across the ideological spectrum? Yes. In a series of studies leading to the development of new categories of stable public opinion group placement, the Pew Research Center identified nine separable groups:[3] Staunch Conservatives, Moderate Conservatives, Populist Republicans, New Prosperity Independents, The Disaffected, Liberal Democrats, Socially Conservative Democrats, New Democrats, and the Partisan Poor.[4] The primary importance of "sound judgment" was confirmed among almost all groups across the ideological spectrum.

An examination of these data suggest some rather strong findings. The importance of sound judgment was evident across all ideological groups. Staunch Conservatives, Populist Republicans, New Prosperity Independents, Disaffected Voters, Liberal Democrats, Socially Conservative Democrats, and New Democrats all thought sound judgment in a president more important than high ethical standards and compassion, often by substantial margins. Across all groups but one, "sound judgment" was on the average twenty three percentage points more important than compassion. The only exception to his rule was found among the Partisan Poor who saw compassion more important than sound judgment. Yet, even in this group, 64 percent thought sound judgment extremely important. Somewhat surprisingly, "sound judgment" just beat out high ethical standards among Staunch Conservatives.

Table 7.2
Important Presidential Qualities by Political Viewpoints

	Staunch Conservs %	Moderate Reps %	Populist Reps %	New Prosperity Indeps %	Disaf- fecteds %	Liberal Dems %	Socially Conserv Dems %	New Dems %	Partisan Poor %
Sound judgment	85	81	78	82	82	79	82	77	64
High ethical standards	84	81	75	61	67	46	58	56	53
Compassion	44	62	67	53	67	66	70	61	76

From Importance to Appraisal: No Easy Matter

The fact that the public considers a matter important is no guarantee that the issues will be directly raised and covered during the campaign. And this appears to be the case with good judgment. Even when the campaign coverage focused on the personal attributes of the candidates, a concern with judgment was nowhere to be found.

Evidence for this comes from an unusual study conducted by the Pew Research Center for the People and the Press and the Project for Excellence in Journalism and the Committee of Concerned Journalists. The study, entitled "A Question of Character,"[1] examined five weeks of stories in newspapers, television, radio, and the Internet that spanned the five months between February and June 2000. The study identified six lines of character analysis in the articles, three each for candidates Bush and Gore. For George Bush they were: (1) Bush is a different kind of Republican, (2) Bush lacks the intelligence or knowledge for the job, and (3) Bush has relied heavily on family connections to get where he is. For Mr. Gore the three were: (1) Gore is experienced and knowledgeable, (2) Gore is scandal tainted, and (3) Gore exaggerates or lies.

Of these six major story lines, four appear related to good judgment. They are Bush's intelligence, Gore's experience/knowledge, Gore's being scandal tainted, and Gore's exaggerations or lies. These major story lines refer only to the frames that journalists used repetitively to cast their stories. They do not constitute the universe of possible story frames related to judgment that might have been used. With that caveat in mind, let us examine in the following chapters how they might possibly be related.

Notes

1.   All figures in this and the following paragraphs on sound judgment are drawn from the Pew Research Center for the People and the Press, The Political Typology-Version 3.0, Section V: The Clinton Legacy and the Next President (http://www.people-press.org/typo99rpt.htm) (November 11, 2000).

2.   Pew Research Center for the People and the Press, "Candidate Qualities May Trump Issues in 1999," October 18, 1999 (http://www.people-press.org/oct99mor.htm) (November 1, 2000).

3.   Using factor and cluster analysis to place individuals, respondents were asked a series of questions in eight areas: environmentalism, religion and morality, social tolerance, social justice, business sentiment, financial security, anti-government sentiment, and patriotism/militarism. More specific descriptions of the methodology and of the groups may be found at www.peoplepress.org/typo99sec.1.htm (March 1, 2000)

4.   The groups and their descriptions are as follows:

Staunch Conservatives: Pro-business, pro-military, pro-life, anti-gay and anti-social welfare with a strong faith in America. Anti-environmental. Self-defined patriot. Distrustful of government. Little concern for the poor. Unsupportive of the women's movement. Predominately white (93 percent), male (62 percent) and older. Married (74 percent). Extremely satisfied financially (54 percent make at least $50,000). Fifty-seven percent are white Protestants.

Moderate Republicans: Pro-business, pro-military, but also pro-government. Strong environmentalists. Highly religious. Self-defined patriots. Little compassion for poor. More satisfied than Staunch Conservatives with state of the nation. White, relatively well-educated, and very satisfied financially.

Populist Republicans: Religious, nationalistic, and pro-life. Negative attitudes toward gays and elected officials. Sympathetic toward the poor. Most think corporations have too much power and money. Tend to favor environmental protection. Roughly six-in-ten are dissatisfied with the state of the nation. Heavily female (61 percent) and less educated. Fully 31 percent are white evangelical Protestants compared to 15 percent overall.

New Prosperity Independents: Pro-business, pro-environment, and many are pro-choice. Sympathetic toward immigrants, but not as understanding toward black Americans and the poor. Somewhat critical of government. Tolerant on social issues. Well-educated (40 percent have a college degree), affluent (almost four-in-ten earn at least $75,000), young (70 percent less than age 50), and male (64 percent). Less religious (only 15 percent go to church weekly).

The Disaffecteds: Distrustful of government, politicians, and business corporations. Favor creation of third major political party. Also, anti-immigrant and intolerant of homosexuality. Very unsatisfied financially. Less-educated (only 8 percent have a college degree) and lower-income (84 percent make less than $50,000). Half are between the ages of 30-49. Second only to Partisan Poor in number of single parents.

Liberal Democrats: Pro-choice and supporters of civil rights, gay rights, and the environment. Critical of big business. Very low expression of religious faith. Most sympathetic of any group to the poor, African-Americans, and immigrants. Highly supportive of the women's movement. Most highly educated group (48 percent have a college degree). Least religious of all typology groups. One-third never married.

Socially Conservative Democrats: Patriotic, yet disenchanted with the government. Intolerant on social issues. Positive attitude toward the military. Think big business has too much power and money. Highly religious. Not affluent but satisfied financially. Slightly less-educated, older (32 percent are women over age 50).

New Democrats: Favorable view of government. Pro-business, yet think government regulation is necessary. Concerned about environmental issues and think government should take strong measures in this area. Accepting of gays. Somewhat less sympathetic toward the poor, black Americans and immigrants than Liberal Democrats. Many are reasonably well-educated and fall into the middle-income bracket. Nearly six-in-ten (59 percent) are women and 17 percent are black.

Partisan Poor: Nationalistic and anti-big business. Disenchanted with government. Think the government should do even more to help the poor. Very religious. Support civil rights and the women's movement. Have very low incomes (39 percent make under $20,000), and nearly two-thirds (63 percent) are female. Thirty-six percent are African-American and 13 percent are Hispanic. Not very well-educated. Largest group of single parents.

Bystanders: Somewhat sympathetic toward poor. Uninterested in what goes on in politics. Rarely vote. Young (46 percent under 30), less-educated and not very religious.

5.   Available at: http://www.journalism.org/publ_research/character1.html, July 27, 2000. (October 3, 2000).

References

Clinton, William J. "Remarks at a Reception for Representative Maurice D. Hinkley in Kingston, New York (October 22, 2000)," *Weekly Compilation of Presidential Papers.* 36:43 October 30, 2000: 2582-2589.

Neustadt, Richard E. *Presidential Power and the Modern Presidents: The Politics of Leadership from Roosevelt to Reagan.* New York: Free Press, 1991 [1960].

Wildavsky, Aaron. "The Two Presidencies." *Transaction,* December (1966): 7-14.

8

Is George W. Bush Smart Enough
to Be a Good President?

George W. Bush is a president with guilelessly inexact syntax, or as Maureen Dowd (2001) put it, a president "not known for his linguistic precision." He is a president whose intelligence became a public question during the presidential campaign he won, and even. thereafter. His caricature as a dim bulb is a staple of late-night monologues. And, certainly, he is the only president to inspire a sitcom, "That's My Bush," whose main character, "is a crude portrayal of Mr. Bush as President Dumbass" (Millman 2001).

Nonetheless, he is also the president of the world's only superpower. And in that role, he is responsible for addressing complex, important, and sometimes critical international issues. He is also the president of 200 million plus Americans, a group that is increasingly diverse and in many ways divided. Therefore, the question of whether Mr. Bush is "up to the job," as Mr. Gore and Senator McCain both asked during the campaign, is a matter of no small importance to all Americans.

In asking whether Mr. Bush is smart enough to be a good president, it is important to be clear at the outset exactly to what the words refer. First, we need to have some understanding of the word "smart." Secondly, we need to have some idea of how we will gage "smartness." Third, we need to have some appreciation of the level of "smartness" that is necessary. That, of course, raises the question: Necessary to do what? The answer in this chapter's title is: to be a good president. However what does that mean? What is a "good president?

In this chapter, I first take up a key question: What does being smart mean? I then take the related question of how being "smart" is related to be a "good president." I then turn to the key question that frames this essay: Is Mr. Bush smart enough to be a good president?

What Does Smart Mean?

Smart is a word that stimulates intuitive understanding. Many think they know what it means. However, a glance at any thesaurus ought to make clear— quickly—that there is much more complexity to this term than we ordinarily allow. A primary synonym for smart is *clever*, a word that has several synonyms associated with it: intelligent, sharp, quick. Another primary synonym for smart is *intelligent*. However, this word, too, has a series of synonyms, which are not quite synonymous, associated with it: clever, bright, gifted, intellectual, sharp, quick, able. Many of these words, in turn, carry with them associated synonyms that may or may not covey what we ordinarily mean by the word smart. Able, for example, has as its synonyms: proficient, capable, competent, skilled and adept. Clever has as related synonyms—talented, intelligent, bright, and gifted. Knowledgeable has a number of synonyms, including: able, bright, gifted, sharp, quick, up to date, familiar, well informed, brilliant, intense and clear.

Pundit Questions

Smart, in short, is an imprecise word, and like other imprecise words requires of its users some specificity. Newspaper columnists and pundits who use the term in connection with Mr. Bush are regrettably imprecise. Timothy Noah (2001), writing in *Slate*, titles his column, "Dubya: Smart? Or Dumb." In Noah's intellectual world there are only two categories and Mr. Bush fits into the latter. Conservative columnist Michael Kelly called Bush a "pinhead"—twice (Kelly 2000a, b).[1]

The New Republic certainly seemed to agree. It ran two cover stories on Mr. Bush's lack of intelligence. The first cover depicted Mr. Bush as a scarecrow figure from the Wizard of Oz, with the story line— "The Hardest Jobs in Politics." What job is that? The article's cover story—"The Woman Who Has to Get George Bush a Brain" (Cottle 1999). Less than a month later, *The New Republic* did another cover story on the same subject, featuring George Bush wearing a dunce cap with his hands up, palms out, in an " I don't know" pose, alongside the title of the cover story, " Why Americans Love Stupid Candidates (Chait 1999: 26-29).

Washington Post columnist Mary McGrory (2000: B01) is was quite certain that,

> Bush doesn't know much, and he doesn't know what he doesn't know. He's not a dummy, but he has absolutely no curiosity, an alarming deficit in a world leader. He is also tongue-tied on the stump, like his father before him.

She allowed that he is "no dummy." Yet she also says that he doesn't know much and doesn't know how much he doesn't know. This might well serve as an operational definition of stupidity.

Indeed, the question of Mr. Bush's intelligence seemed to permeate public concern, that is if media attention is an indicator. One could hear debates on Bush's intelligence on CNN (*Crossfire* Transcript 1999) entitled, "Is Bush a Lightweight or Does the Media Treat him Unfairly?" You could read news accounts in any major newspaper with titles such as: "George W. Bush: Is He or Isn't He Smart Enough?"(Merida 1999), or "Bush on Stage: Deft or Just Lacking Depth?" (Allen 1999). You could get the results of multiple public opinion polls to see just what the public thought of Mr. Bush's intelligence (e.g., Langer 1999). You could hear Mr. Bush asked directly by a *Time* (CNN transcript, 2000) correspondent whether he was smart enough to be president—his answer: "I'm confident of my intellect"[2] You could read what many pundits on both sides of the issue said (e.g., Kinsey 1999; Will 1999). And you could read that Mr. Bush's mother Barbara had assured the public that her son was "no dummy" (Fox News On Lline, 1999).

While the public in general gave Mr. Bush high marks for his intelligence and capacity to be president (see below) the question was asked during Bush's campaign. David Von Drehle (1999: A1) described one such incident:

Certain questions come up in town meetings year after year, primary after primary. Taxes. Education. Abortion. Health care. This was one rarely put into words: A supporter of Texas Gov. George W. Bush rose to ask–in the nicest possible way, hemming and hawing and obviously uncomfortable–whether Bush is, you know, well...dumb. "Intellectually curious" was the gentle phrase the man used. But Bush did not miss the point of the question. "They're saying I'm not, uh, very smart," he said, and the audience in Bedford's whitewashed old Town Hall laughed. Was it a nervous laugh? A laugh of amazement–hey, who ever thought they'd hear a presidential candidate say that? Maybe it was an expression of relief, to hear Bush put into words the fact that was on everyone's mind.

And how did Mr. Bush respond?

[Speaking] to his usual packed house, answering questions in a relaxed, rambling, free-associative kind of way–and the IQ question was laid out for everyone to hear. "I'd rather be underestimated than overestimated," Bush answered. He flashed a grin and paused. "I've been underestimated before." Another grin, another pause. "And Governor Richards regrets it!" That would be Ann Richards, the liberal stem-winder who was, once upon a time, governor of the great state of Texas. She wanted to be governor again. It was 1994 and Richards was running for re-election against George W. Bush, with whom she was not terribly impressed. She liked to call him "shrub." On Election Day, Shrub had the last laugh. (Von Drehle 1999: A1)

The New Republic article, entitled "Why Americans Love Stupid Candidates," actually raised an interesting point. Its author (Chait 1999: 26) argued that, "What Bush understands, and the pundits do not, is that he is a brilliant candidate not despite his anti-intellectualism but because of it." Jonathan Chait's point was that at the time of the election Americans were more interested in character than they are in detailed policy knowledge. He notes as one of the many examples in his article that the media hardly ever gave coverage to John McCain's actual ideas, but rather treated his ideas as reflections of his heroic biography—and I would add psychology.

Chait (1999: 29) closed by noting that,

unless presidential candidates campaign on a pledge to address specific problems, they have great difficulty in rallying the people and their representatives in Congress once they in office....What are candidates elected on the basis of character and personal history empowered to achieve? Nothing much.

It isn't clear at all whether Chait is right about "character candidates" having no political empowerment. Indeed, I think (Renshon 2000) the evidence is clear that character can translate into political capital. However, Chiat's suggestion that Mr. Bush's focus on "character" came at the expense of issues is simply wrong, and he clearly had not listened carefully, if at all, to Mr. Bush's many very substantive policy addresses. Mr. Bush campaigned on a number of issues—tax reduction, educational reform, social security reform and privatization, faith-based initiatives, a different stance toward China (as strategic competitor), the Soviet Union, and deployment of United States forces abroad, the building of a missile defense—to name some, but not all.

Still, the question that Chiat and others raise is an important one. Is George Bush smart enough to be president? What does being smart actually mean? And, how did this question arise in the first place?

Is Mr. Bush Smart?: The Origins of a Question

The view that President Bush is "not up to the job" owed its continuing traction to several elements. Some of them have to do with his background. Some of them have to do with his style. And some of them have to do with the use that has been made of these elements by others for their own purposes.

Readiness vs. Capacity

It is useful at the outset to distinguish between questions of *readiness* and *capacity*. As will become clear, critics and commentators on this subject tend the mix the two terms somewhat indiscriminately. Questions related to the former raise issues of experience. Questions regarding the latter raise questions of ability and competence, independent of experience. The first can be "cured" by exposure and increasing familiarity, the second can not.

Nevertheless, experience and familiarity can lead to the unsubstantiated impression of knowledge. That someone has developed policy views is often taken to be an indicator of their capacity. However, that does not necessarily follow. Finally, and most importantly, having experience and policy views do not necessarily translate into good judgment about policy solutions.

Questions about George W. Bush's readiness and capacity to assume the office of the presidency owe their origin to a number of factors. Like most governors who have won the presidency—Ronald Reagan, Jimmy Carter, and William Clinton—Mr. Bush had little actual foreign policy experience. However, the questions raised about him go further than his lack of experience.

His relatively brief political career is certainly an important element in the questions that are asked. So, too, are elements of his political style—his tendency to focus on a limited policy agenda, the fact that he is a man of few words, the view of him as a leader strongly influenced by his advisors and as a leader with limited policy interests. Added to these elements is the view, put forward, primarily, but not solely by his critics, that Mr. Bush has risen to the top because of family connections and in the process has displayed a certain motivational and intellectual laziness.

George W. as "Shrub"

In the analysis that follows, all these issues will be examined. Let us, however, begin with the first public airing of these allegations—his first successful political campaign. Recent questions about George W.'s intelligence owe their origin to a narrative line, which had its origins in Mr. Bush's first campaign for governor. His opponent, Ann Richards had a 60 percent approval rating and took to calling Mr. Bush (quoted in Merida 2000: C1) "Shrub" a reference to a stunted, misshapen bush that grows in the dust and dirt of the Texas plains and that will never amount to a tree.[3] She referred to him as "Prince George," a reference to his famous father and family.[4] The attendant implication was that his privileged position was a substitute for real ambition and achievement. And she often said, "he didn't have a clue," a reference to her assumption that he was out of his league and out of his depth. He won the election.

A Man of Sometimes Puzzling Words

These questions, no doubt, have been helped along by the fact that Mr. Bush, as noted, is a man of relatively few words—certainly compared to say Bill Clinton. And those words are not the standard, or even occasionally the correct words for what he wishes to describe. He has called Greeks "Grecians," and Kosovars "Kosovians," and he has famously mixed tenses and concepts. Indeed, several Bush critics have now published books of "Bushisms" (Weisberg 2001; Begala 2001), examples of his not always successful battle with the nuances of the English language. There are many examples. Asked by *Times* columnist William Safire about whether he would run for president Bush is quoted (in Balz 1999: A03) as replying, "I am a candidate and I'm going to be the nominee." Asked later about the quote Bush appeared puzzled by it and replied, according to the *Austin American-Statesman*, "Then I misquoted, then I misspoke myself."

Verbal fluency is often taken as a indicator of intelligence, which it often can be. Yet it can also reflect a glib superficiality. It can easily mask an inability or disinclination to speak directly and honestly to the choices one will have to make. And for a president, governing in a divided culture, that kind of intelligence can be fatal both to his leadership and to the people he is supposed to represent.

A Man of Few Words, But What Does That Mean?

Mike Allen (2001: A8) of the *Washington Post* asks of Bush, is he "Deft or Just Lacking Depth?" Why lacking depth? Because Mr. Bush repeated the word "routine" three times to describe the air strikes against Iraq," and because, "throughout his first month in office, the president's remarks on substantive issues have been consistent, but in every case brief, leading policy analysts and congressional leaders to question whether the pattern is more indicative of an exceptionally disciplined politician, or one with a shallow grasp of the issues at hand." Leaving aside momentarily just who the unnamed policy analysts and congressional leaders are (Clinton appointees, the Democratic leadership?), the question raised in the article seems to turn on whether Mr. Bush is disciplined or shallow.

Had Allen been alert he might have come across an article by a colleague of his (Von Drehle 1999: A1) which said this of Mr. Bush's campaigns for the Texas governorship, and his behavior once in there:

> Bush likes to run on a very simple platform. In Texas in 1994, he repeated the same four ideas in every speech he gave, in every answer to every question. When he gave his first address to the legislature, he gave them the same four points. Then, for those who might be bored by the repetition, he offered a fifth program: "Pass the first four."

It is possible, of course, that Mr. Bush is both focused and shallow. Yet, this idea is never raised by the reporter, or his sources. Contained therein are also other assumptions, namely that a brief answer cannot possibly reflect an adequate, even good, appreciation of the problems at hand and that long answers are synonymous with good policy solutions. Of course, this is a glaring *non-sequitur*. Long answers and elaborate explications are not necessarily better, and may even be worse than a short, crisp insight into a problem which is summarized with crisp clearly communicated understanding.

Dana Milbank (1999: 18) argued that Mr. Bush's silence was not a reflection of his being dumb—Milbank thought Bush "smart and savvy." Rather he thought it stemmed from the cautious strategy of a front-runner. Clarence Paige (1999) of the *Chicago Tribune* agreed:

> I have a theory. I don't think Dubya is dumb as he sounds. For one thing, I don' think Texans are that dumb. You can't be the governor of one of the nation's biggest states without somebody noticing whether you're a few bricks shy of a load. Most likely, I suspect he has dumbed himself down. Front-runners typically avoid saying anything that could get them into trouble, which means they avoid saying much of anything original. They stick to their stump speech. They stick their chins up, throw out a few cheery bromides, crack a few one-liners and smile a lot. In sports, this ploy is called "freezing the ball." In politics, it is called "staying on message."

Yes, But is He Curious?

Critics of Mr. Bush's readiness to be the president raised questions about his level of involvement in the decisions he makes. This actually has two elements: (1) the view of Mr. Bush as a passive puppet of smarter men, and (2) his interest and involvement in learning what he needs to know in order to reach good judgments. The latter issue has been raised by allies of Mr. Gore (McGrory 2000), under the heading of "curiosity." McGrory is certain that curiosity is necessary to being a good leader and that Mr. Bush, "has absolutely no curiosity, an alarming deficit in a world leader."

It is unclear just what McGrory and others who make this criticism substantively, not politically, have in mind when they raise this issue. If they mean by this that Mr. Bush does not raise the kind of deep philosophical questions that can lead to long discussions about the meaning of things, she is undoubtedly correct. Yet, there is a growing body of evidence that Mr. Bush does indeed ask questions.

Bruni and Schmitt (1999: A30) write after interviewing people who have worked with Bush that,

> Mr. Bush has demonstrated a particular fondness for asking his advisors hypothetical questions about possible developments in the world's hot spots. Several advisors said that he seemed to prefer discussions to in-depth reading, although he has been known to needle his advisors when something they say diverges from something they wrote.

Elizabeth Mitchell (2000: 333) writing of Bush's preparation for his 1990 campaign for governor, states that he,

> maintained a regular schedule of policy meetings where he gathered disparate voices in the Republican party to hash out issues. According to many who attended, George W. took great glee in assembling the most diverse group he could find and then let the discussion fly for several hours. He would ask hundreds of specific questions, demonstrating the same intense curiosity he displayed on the backroads of Texas.

During the confrontation with China over the downing of the U.S. reconnaissance plane, David Sanger and Steven Lee Myers assembled a preliminary analysis of Mr. Bush's policy decisions that emerged from days of background briefings, anecdotes related on the fly by officials in the midst of negotiations, and a White House timeline of the diplomatic exchanges. They write (Sanger and Myers 2001), "From the first moment, Mr. Bush was constantly peppering his closest aides, particularly Ms. Rice and her deputy, Stephen J. Hadley, with questions about the state of the crew, the strategy, their interpretation of what was going on within the Chinese leadership."

Once the Chinese had agreed to return the crew, Mr. Bush turned to more detailed matters (McGeary 2001): "How long would it take to refuel the pickup plane in China? What would be the flight path? How long would the plane be on the ground?" This does not seem like the behavior of a disengaged, disinterested, or uncurious leader.

One of the few attempts to gauge Mr. Bush's decision-making style (Berke 2000b; see also Merida 2000 for an independent confirmation of many of these points) confirmed that Mr. Bush carefully selected his advisors, worked with them to develop confidence in their loyalty and judgment, and then relied on them. Among Berke's findings drawn from wide ranging discussions with Bush advisors were the following: (1) Mr. Bush prefers to speed through meetings to get to the heart of the matter; (2) both candidates [Mr. Gore and Mr. Bush] tend to be stubborn, often not yielding to their advisors' suggestions; (3) [M]r. Bush is not inclined to alter a speech sharply or a schedule on the fly; (4) when he was beaten by John McCain in the New Hampshire primary he told his aides that the campaign had to become more aggressive and not be passive as Mr. McCain claimed the reformer mantle. Bush asked his aides to come up with suggestions, which they did, and he accepted a number and rejected some; (5) He does not hesitate to overrule his advisors, and when he does he is often guided more by instinct than policy; (6) At staff meetings Mr. Gore is more like a sometimes overbearing teacher, while Mr. Bush often plays the impatient student. "I've heard the governor say, 'Why don't you close the book and tell me what you think is most important?'; (7) "His classic question is, 'Have you told me everything I need to know?'"; (8) "If he doesn't know, he'll say, 'Hold it.'" "If somebody uses an acronym he doesn't know, he'll stop them and say, 'What does that mean?'" Sometimes he says, "Use plain English."; (9) Mr. Bush made no excuses for his gaps in knowledge saying,

> I don't think anybody knows everything about every subject, and anyone who pretends they do is someone I don't want to be the president, because this is a complicated world....The key to the presidency is to set divisions, to lay out the parameters by which decisions will be made and to encourage really good, competent people to serve the country for the right reasons and to build a team.

Richard Berke's analysis suggests not only that Mr. Bush asks questions, but that he asks important ones. "Is this all I need to know?" raises the issue of whether important elements of a problem have been left out in the discussion/briefing. "What does that mean?" or "Use plain English" are the challenges of a person who is not afraid to admit he doesn't know, but wants to understand.

Perhaps the most important question that Mr. Bush continually asks is, "Will it work?" It is clearly more a practical than an intellectual question. As Mr. Bush has often said of himself, he is a man who likes results. This would appear to be an important trait in a president.

As to whether Mr. Bush is a man who is a passive puppet, the evidence that is emerging is quite to the contrary. John Harris and Dan Balz (2001)interviewed a great many people in preparation for their 100-day assessment of the Bush presidency. They found,

> The most striking [contradiction]is the tension between the private Bush and the public one. Within the confines of the White House, Bush emerges as a man of supreme self-confidence. In meetings, briefers never get through their presentations; Bush interrupts without hesitation when he feels he has heard enough. On several occasions, he has casually issued edicts with little concern that he has undercut members of his Cabinet. There is little doubt that it is Bush—his personality, his likes and dislikes, his political values—who is the animating force of this White House. At the same time, he is perhaps the least confident public performer of the modern presidency.

Harris and Balz write that when the president met with the German chancellor, Gerhard Schroeder made clear his government objected to Bush's declaration that the United States no longer supported the Kyoto agreement aimed at limiting greenhouse gases.

> Rather than smoothing over the disagreement, one White House aide recounted, Bush challenged Schroeder, "Where are you going to get your energy in 20 years?" In the minds of many critics, there remains the suspicion that Washington is witnessing a scripted presidency, with Bush delivering lines crafted by the vastly more experienced vice president, Cabinet secretaries, and senior staff. But the Schroeder session suggests a president who will not be stage-managed.

The Politics of Intelligence

Character issues are not the same as analyses of character. The first are conducted with primarily political ends in mind. The latter are undertaken to analyze and understand. So, too, the politics of intelligence are different than the analysis of it, and questions raised about George W.'s capacity have been at least, if not more, political than analytical.

Obviously, questioning someone's intellectual capacity and whether they are "up for the job" is a profoundly political question. It is also one that was raised repeatedly by everyone who ran against George W. in the 2000 election campaign. Senator Orin Hatch made a broad joke based on the assumption that he would win his party's nomination, saying to Mr. Bush at a Republican forum (quoted in Bruni 1999: A1): "You should have eight years with me, and boy, you will make a heck of a president after eight years."

Alan Keyes offered his unspecified criticism of candidates who seemed merely to read scripted lines. McCain made condescending comments to Bush about his "not having any idea of how important campaign finance reform could be in restoring public trust." And he also questioned Mr. Bush's readiness to step into the role of commander in chief by arguing (quoted in Mitchell 2000) both in person and in his media ads that, "I am fully prepared to lead. I do not need on-the job-training."

Such charges were routinely made by Al Gore, indirectly, and his surrogates directly. For example, in an interview with the *Washington Post* (Balz and Connolly 2000), Mr. Gore was asked:

> *Post*: Do you think Bush is smart enough to be president?

> *Gore*: "I have not questioned his intelligence. And I don't think anyone should question his intelligence. I don't have any doubt about his intelligence. And I don't think anyone should question his intelligence. I have raised the question that flows naturally out of his $2 trillion tax scheme, that a proposal like that raises the question naturally does he have the experience to be president. In proposing a law to permit concealed weapons in churches and synagogues and school facilities, I think that naturally raises the question, does he have the judgment to be president."

Mr. Gore's running mate, Senator Joe Leiberman (quoted in Seeyle and Prez-Pena 2000), had this to say about the relationship of experience to being up to the job, "I don't think Governor Bush is ready based on his experience, his record, his proposals in this campaign to be the kind of president that the American people need at this point in our history." Another of Mr. Gore's supporters had this to say:

> [A]l Gore delivered a provocative foreign policy speech Sunday that raised an important question: Does George W. Bush have the experience, the gravitas and, by implication, the brains to run U.S. foreign policy? (Friedman 2000)

By the end of the campaign there was no pretense either by Mr. Gore or his campaign that Mr. Bush's intelligence and capacity to perform as president were not a major issue.[5]

In early November, Mr. Bush was speaking of his plan to allow workers to invest a fraction of their Social Security payroll taxes, and said (quoted in Seelye 2000):

> This frightens some in Washington because they want the federal government controlling Social Security, like it's some kind of federal program. We understand differently, though. You see, it's your money, not the government's money. You ought to be allowed to invest it the way you see fit.

Mr. Gore never allowed that Mr. Bush's comment might have been a slip of the tongue or a poorly worded thought, instead milking the idea that it was just plain dumb—and that it was further evidence that Mr. Bush is blank on the basics and not equipped to be president. "Four days before the election, he doesn't even know that?" the vice president asked (quoted in Seelye 2000) in an interview with television station KCCI, the CBS affiliate in Des Moines. "I think that's outrageous."

In Mr. Gore's last televised campaign ads, which focused on the theme of "Is he [Bush] ready to lead America?" His deputy campaign manager Mark D. Fabiani remarked, "I think people, not just in the Gore campaign but in the country, have known for a while that Bush's readiness to lead has been the elephant in the room for this entire election" (quoted in Sack 2000).

Foreign Policy Experience and Intelligence

As noted, most governors who run for the presidency have very little foreign policy experience. It would not be surprising that they would be less familiar with or ill at ease conversing on say—American policy toward the IMF or the intricacies of our policies in Macedonia. However, the public does expect and often receives from such candidates their views of general policy stances toward major players in the international system. Thus, every presidential candidate is expected to express he his or her views on relations with the Soviet Union, policies toward "rogue states," and so on.

And Mr. Bush had done so. In a September 1999 speech at the Citadel, Bush gave a speech entitled, "A Period of Consequences." On November 19, he gave a well-received speech at the Reagan Library on defense issues entitled, "A Distinctly American Internationalism," and on November 21 he had an hour-long interview on his foreign policy with Tim Russert on *Meet the Press*.

Against this background on November 3, 1999, while Mr. Bush was still involved in wresting the Republican nomination from the determined efforts of Mr. McCain, among others, a news reporter gave Bush a surprise test in the middle of an interview. He was asked to name the leaders of the following countries—Taiwan, India, Pakistan, and Chechnya (Bruni 1999a). Bush could name only the leader of Taiwan. That same reporter noted that a week before this incident, Senator John McCain twice referred to the Czech Republic as Czechoslovakia, a nation that had ceased to exist after January 1, 1993, when it had become two separate republics—the Czech Republic and Slovakia.

Moreover, Mr. McCain "flunked" his own pop quiz on naming leaders several weeks later (Mitchell 1999). Asked by a reporter if he could name the president of Ireland, he couldn't. Nor could he name the governor of Vermont, where he was campaigning at the time he was asked the question. Of course, Senator McCain had a long career in politics and had been involved in major foreign policy issues as a senator. On the other hand, McCain's academic record at the Naval Academy was worse than Bush's at Yale. Clearly, failing a pop quiz of names has different meanings depending on the range of other elements that enter into the evaluation of the particular leader who doing so.

Vice President Gore raised a much more useful query at the time when he questioned Mr. Bush's characterization of the newly installed coup leader in Pakistan as someone who would contribute to the stability of the region (Neal 1999). Mr. Gore's point was the Mr. Bush seemed to be supportive of a coup that had overthrown a democratically elected leader, albeit one with which the Clinton administration had expressed growing frustration. A *New York Times* editorial (Editorial 1999: A16) called this "un-nuanced formulation,"

> [a] novice mistake in presidential politics and comes as a reminder that Mr. Bush...is still a newcomer to high-level campaigning. He has time—and a clear need—to master his foreign policy briefings.

Mr. Gore's well-taken point, echoed by others (Friedman 1999), was that rather than focus on isolated facts to indicate understanding, it would be better to address questions of foreign policy understanding directly.

Mr. Bush's response to this incident was somewhat instructive. As might be expected under the circumstances, Mr. Bush argued that

> America understands that a guy doesn't know the name of every single foreign leader. People are making their choice based upon judgment, based upon vision, based upon philosophy. (quoted in Sawyer 1999)

Yet, several weeks later in an interview, George W. had this to say:

I think the American people have questions about every person running for President in terms of foreign policy, and they should.

Then speaking of his advisors he said that they had helped him to translate his bedrock beliefs about the United States' role in the world into specific policies:

they help me understand the nuance—a word I'm learning. In Texas politics, we don't spend much time on nuance. But there's nuance in foreign policy. I'm beginning to learn that. (quoted in Bruni and Schmitt 1999)

This is a brave admission, but what is one to make of it? It certainly contains an admission that his critics had a point. Mr. Bush admits that he lacks a nuanced view of foreign policy and that he has been gaining that nuanced understanding from his advisors. However, this comment also contains an important piece of information about Mr. Bush's psychology, which is equally relevant to his performance as president.

Mr. Bush is not afraid to say he doesn't know, when it's a point that his critics have used against him. Contrary to critical comments that he is so "dim" that he doesn't even know what he doesn't know, he seems to be well aware. More importantly, he is clearly willing to do something about it.

Wouldn't it be better if a candidate had a more nuanced view of foreign policy before he ran for office? Perhaps. Does not having a nuanced understanding of foreign policy before running for office preclude having good judgment about foreign policy issues once in office? There is no evidence of that. Indeed, Barbara Farnham's (2002, in press) study of Ronald Reagan's judgments regarding the cold war suggest he should get high marks for his insights there in spite of his reputation as a "hands-off," not particularly engaged president.

A more nuanced view and understanding of foreign and domestic policy issues would certainly appear preferable, to a point. Why isn't this a case of more always equals better? Several reasons seem relevant here. First, more nuanced and less nuanced views of a matter can still lead to good judgments. Second, an accurate fundamental understanding may trump nuance in making good judgments. And third, too much nuance can be paralyzing—the opposite of good judgments and decisions.

Consider in this regard Leon Panetta's characterization of Bill Clinton's decision process. Mr. Clinton was certainly one of the most knowledgeable and nuanced presidents to serve in that office. Yet in an interview conducted for *Nightline*, Mr. Panetta (*Nightline* 1999) had this to say:

...there often wasn't a final firm decision, and no closure. Yes. He would say, "Gosh, did I make the right decision?" and he would start to really think about it and he would ponder it because it is his nature is to not to bring closure. His nature is to constantly assess and assess again, depending on who's talking to him and depending on the thoughts that are presented. So he would sometimes go into a very torturous process, trying to come to closure on something. And the problem is that if you are trying to move legislation, you're trying to get something to the hill, or if you're trying to tell a congressman or senator what has to be done, or what the administration's position is, you could be floundering for a while, trying to get a decision. So that was a problem.

Sometimes, less nuance leads to better decisions and more effective leadership.

George W. Bush: Experience Does Seem to Count

In a December 1999 *New York Times* analysis Frank Bruni had a different insight into the dynamics of Mr. Bush's tentativeness and caution. He noted (1999b: A1) that Mr. Bush has yet to exude the kind of confidence and comfort that he has in some of his policy speeches. One day later, his colleague Richard Berke (1999: A32) noted that before the Republican primary debates in which he had performed unimpressively the previous week, Bush had taken part in only two other campaign debates in his whole political career, one when he ran for governor in 1994 and the other when he sought re-election in 1998.

Mr. Bruni's observation coupled with Richard Berke's history suggests another possible explanation for Mr. Bush's tentativeness and caution: inexperience and the anxiety that accompanies it. Berke (2000a: A17) called the Republican primary debate on January 5 in Durham, North Carolina, "the most spirited and at times, the most entertaining of the campaign. In it Bush managed not only to hold his own against his hour rivals, but to score some points on his own behalf. At one point Mr. McCain, alluding to Mr. Bush's lack of preparation, or perhaps understanding said,

> I don't think you have an idea of how important campaign finance could be to restoring the confidence of young Americans in the government. Mr. Bush shot back: "What you don't need to do is tell me what I have no idea about." (quoted in Berke 2000a)

The most important of Mr. Bush's debates took place against Al Gore in December 1999. Pundits, following the stupidity/shallowness line of thinking wrote that Mr. Gore would eviscerate Mr. Bush. Typical was Mary McGrory who wrote (2000), "The vice president is a demon debater who would eat George W.'s lunch." That didn't happen. Immediately after the first debate Berke wrote,

> Many lawmakers, governors and strategists in both parties were unusually measured, saying that neither man had put in a performance compelling enough to force many voters to immediately reconsider whom they would support. Such admissions are rare; the tradition after presidential debates is for operatives to rush out of the auditorium to declare their candidate "won." (2000c: A1)

David Broder agreed. He wrote,

> ...both candidates accomplished most of their goals. Their performance reinforced my feeling that Al Gore and George W. Bush have developed into capable contenders, with

clearly defined policy differences and leadership styles. They are giving the country the kind of choice it deserves. (2000: A35)

Public opinion polls showed a decided edge going to Gore immediately after the debate. A *New York Times* poll reported (Kagay 2000) that 43 percent of voters thought that Mr. Gore "won" the debate, 30 percent said that Mr. Bush "won." And 19 percent thought it was a tie. That makes 49 percent who thought that Mr. Bush did at least as well as Mr. Gore. One could argue, and some (e.g., Safire 2000) did, that simply by standing toe to toe with Mr. Gore a seasoned and aggressive debater, Mr. Bush had begun to allay questions about his capacities.

Interestingly, that same poll found that the support of Mr. Gore's supporters had softened, while that of Mr. Bush's supporters had become more robust. Before the debate 45 percent of Mr. Bush's supporters were enthusiastic while 44 percent had reservation. Forty-one percent of Mr. Gore's supporters were enthusiastic while 45 percent had reservations. After the debate, 54 percent of Bush voters described themselves as enthusiastic.

Yet, Gore's performance undercut his advantages with an aggressive style, and moved in the reverse direction as reporters commented on some Gore misstatements, and the Bush campaign successfully linked them to other times in which Mr. Gore had been factually inaccurate. As Al Hunt (2000) noted, "Following last week's debate, snap polls gave the nod to Al Gore, but there was a delayed negative reaction to the Democratic nominee's style."

The second debate produced more intense reactions from the two campaigns, especially that of Mr. Bush's campaign. Kevin Sack (2000) wrote,

> The mood of the Bush campaign was ebullient after Wednesday's debate in which aides felt that Mr. Bush had survived prolonged questioning about foreign policy, his biggest weakness The confidence seemed to exceed the first two debates' traditional post-debate spin. About an hour after the debate ended, an ABC News producer overheard Karen P. Hughes, Mr. Bush's communications director, speaking on the telephone to another who was with Mr. Bush, about instant polls showing that Mr. Bush had won the debate. "Tell him that he just became president of the United States," Ms. Hughes instructed the aide. Mr. Gore's campaign chairman William M. Daley, predicted that the instant polls would prove meaningless. He pointed out that such polls favored Mr. Gore after the first debate last week in Boston, but that the numbers quickly turned toward Mr. Bush as news reports focused on Mr. Gore's factual mistakes.

In several surveys, including one for ABC news and another for CNN a plurality of the public gave Mr. Bush a clear edge (Hunt 2000).

The capacity to learn from experience and then do so is a key finding of several 100-day assessments of Mr. Bush. David Sanger and Lacy(2001: A1) summing up a wide range of observations on the president note, "But even his critics say he is a far more confident leader than he was on Jan. 20, something he demonstrated in Quebec last weekend, when he handled questions on Latin American politics, drugs and trade issues with a degree of subtlety that was missing in his first days in the White House." Apparently, Mr. Bush is not only able to learn—he does.

Ambition and Intelligence

One part of the conventional view of whether Mr. Bush is smart has to do with his ambition. By many reasonable and balanced accounts (Mitchell 2000; Minutaglio 2000), George W. Bush was not consumed with it. Indeed a strong case can be made that he was under-motivated given his capacities. The reasons why this might be so are beyond the scope of my focus here, but it is very likely related to the expectations that children, who grow up in families with very accomplished parents, feel, not necessarily directly from their parents, and the ways in which they deal with these pressures. It is also true that sometimes the children of highly accomplished parents, like their counterparts in more conventional families, may take a while to get their life bearings.

At any rate, Mr. Bush's adolescent, college, business school and early business career were not marked by outstanding success, although in his Midland, Texas oil business ventures there was plenty of evidence of hard work. This was a period as well, when, by his own admission, he drank too much (Mitchell 2000: 203-207). The view of Mr. Bush as the privileged son of a wealthy family that had cushioned his struggles, and a young man not wholly in control of himself, has a reasonable basis.

It is an important, but difficult and necessary task, however, to distinguish arrested ambition from intelligence. It is also a necessary but difficult task to distinguish developmental drift or delay from intelligence as well. Both ambition and developmental drift are primarily matters of psychology, not intelligence. Smart underachievers are fairly common, and there is no good evidence that Mr. Bush lacked the capacity to achieve when he set his mind to doing so.

The relationship of intelligence of developmental drift is a bit more difficult to disentangle. Certainly, a person who drifts instead of focuses can be said to be somewhat self-indulgent. The same characterization can be made of someone who chooses not to take charge of or responsibility for his or her behavior. You could say someone who is self-indulgent is not acting intelligently and in his or her own self-interest. Yet, the question here too, is whether we are talking about psychology or intelligence. The operating assumption here appears to be that if somebody were "smart" they wouldn't be self-defeating or self-destructive. Yet, here again many smart people, Bill Clinton comes to mind here, are very smart and very self-indulgent and destructive.

George W.'s Achievements: Spoiled Ambition or Late Flowering?

Accomplishment is one of the many surrogate indicators of applied intelligence. We assume, often correctly, that if a person reaches a certain position or is known for particular kinds of accomplishments that he reflects a successful application of his capacities and motivational focus. Conversely, we question such accomplishments if the person accumulates them in ways that require less motivation or less successful application of skills and talents.

The children of educated, well-connected parents often represent a difficult case to analyze from these basic frameworks. Such parents often have high expectations and standards for their children. Yet it is also true that such parents often strive, sometimes mightily, to help their children in ways that augment their efforts. A few are willing to substitute their effort and motivation for the child's. In such cases, it is appropriate to speak of spoiled ambition.

Ann Richard's characterization of George Bush as "Prince George " was meant to instil an image of Bush as essentially carried by his wealthy and well-connected family throughout his life. The implication of this line of thinking is that Mr. Bush has not accomplished much on his own, that what he has accomplished has been the result of what others have done for him rather than what he has done himself, and finally that he is by implication not "up to" fending for himself in matters of accomplishment.

George W. Bush attended three top-ranked schools (Andover, Yale, and Harvard Business School) and accumulated solid, but not outstanding grades. He was not sports-minded, but he was people-minded and the center of a web of friendships that have lasted though the years. He chose to move to Midland, Texas, to make his own mark in a very risky business and had some lean years as the market for oil exploration became even more difficult. Yet, he stayed with it and while doing so managed to protect all the people that worked with him, and to make some money in a tricky economic environment. When the chance arose to put together a group to buy a new baseball franchise, Mr. Bush worked hard and eventually the team he had helped create was successful and he eventually sold his interest for a large profit.

Politically, he took on a long-shot race for a Congressional seat, which he lost, but not without working very long and hard at Texas retail politics. He took on another long-short race against a popular incumbent governor and won, and then won re-election. In doing so he was the first modern governor to win two consecutive terms. His work for his father's efforts to gain re-election to the presidency failed but he learned a great deal from the experience.

On the surface, Bush appears to have a mixed record. He has had some setbacks and some solid accomplishments in both business and politics. Certainly, his career has not had the success trajectory of a "star performer," who has had great talent from the start and who deepened and extended his capacities in ever higher levels of accomplishment.

Nor is George W.'s accomplishment trajectory characterized by a steady string of failures in either business or politics that might well cast doubt on his capacities. Very importantly, it is a trajectory characterized at almost all points along the way by hard work and commitment to what he was trying to accomplish. Both Elizabeth Mitchell (2000) and Bill Minutaglio (2000) detail the long hours George W. spent seeking his fortune in the oil business, the long days of campaigning for his Congressional race, the fact that he always stayed every inning of every home game of his baseball team, and the long hours he put into both of his Texas campaigns,[6] and in his work on behalf of his father. It is not the record of a spoiled child with a large sense of entitlement.

George W. chose Texas and the oil business. These were two of the ways in which he followed in his father's footsteps. In doing so he entered a world in which his father had not only succeeded but had built a web of relationships, and, of course, as the son of George Herbert Walker Bush and the grandson of Prescott Bush, he was, at the same time, heir to a family name and a web of relationships that had been built up over decades. It is difficult in such circumstances *not* to find evidence of family connections that have helped or have given the appearance of having smoothed some passage.

Often the evidence is indirect. Elizabeth Mitchell (2000: 263) says of one deal, "Although George W.'s name was probably not the only factor that secured the deal in Bahrain, it is hard to believe that his family connections didn't help him…" It is certainly likely that his name and father's decades-long business contacts helped George W., but it is also difficult to image how, short of going into another line of work in a different location, he could have avoided it.

Nevertheless, these facts have led his harshest critics to portray George W. as a man without accomplishments and, by implication, without much capacity for them. Lars-Erik Nelson, in his review of several Bush political biographies, concludes by saying,

> …the more you look at him the less you see. Every achievement, with the exception of his re-election as governor evaporates on scrutiny, even minor ones like the supposed firing of Sununu or his vaunted Texas tax cuts. …he understands the real world—a world in which the most important question is, "Who are your people?"—better than the rest of us. In his own life so much has been handed to him. Why not the presidency? (2000: 7)

This is surely an overwrought and overdrawn portrait. Certainly, George W.'s win against a popular incumbent governor was an accomplishment of some substantiality. So, too, Elizabeth Mitchell (2000: 248, 273) makes clear that in the cases where George W. might have claimed too much credit, it was clear that he did deserve a substantial amount of it. Moreover, the hard work that all George W.'s biographers note; in connection with his attempt to build his oil ventures business, in his unsuccessful run for Congress, his work on behalf of his father's campaign and his role as manager of the Texas Rangers, and his success as governor—all belies the image of a spoiled narcissist.

The truth is more complicated. George W. grew up in the shadow of a revered and extremely accomplished father in a family in which high achievement, not self-publicity, was expected to reflect your accomplishments. But what if you weren't a superior scholar, sportsman, navy hero, successful business leader, CIA Director, vice president and ultimately president? Yet, what if, at the same time, you elect to follow many of the paths your father had walked?[7] The road to your own consolidated sense of purpose and accomplishment might well have seemed unclear.

Bush himself seems to have been well aware of this dilemma. Reflecting on his role in putting together the Texas Ranger deal he said,

> for those who believe I'm from a pampered lot and have been handed everything, I will never win their vote. That's one of the problems of being the son of George Bush. But open-minded people will realize that the Ranger deal was not an easy thing to put together, nor was it easy to organize my father's campaign. (quoted in E. Mitchell 2000: 249)

Speaking to a reporter about his role as owner/manager of the Texas Rangers he said,

> It solved my biggest problem in Texas. There's no question about it and I knew it all along...my problem was "What's this boy ever done?" I have to make a fairly big splash in the poll for people to recognize me. My poll has been expanded so much because of who my Dad is. The advantage is everybody knows who I am. The disadvantage is that no matter how great my accomplishments may be, no one is going to give me credit for them. (quoted in Minutaglio 2000, 241),

Mitchell makes the point that George W. was very likely helped by his family connections, and he had difficulty acknowledging it. Mitchell (2000: 206, 248, 262) mentions several such instances: the help of his Uncle Jonathan in raising capital for his oil business; the help of Philip Uzielli a friend of James Baker, who helped him out of difficult financial circumstances; the merger with another oil company—Spectrum 7—that family friend Paul Rea had facilitated; the gamble that the Harkin Energy Company took in signing on Mr. Bush, in part because of his family name and connections; and the way in which family connections played a role in acquiring his position as part-owner and general manager of the Texas Rangers baseball team.

Mitchell says (2000: 206; see also 248) that George W., "never seemed to acknowledge adequately the roll of carpet layers in his life." Correspondingly, he had, on occasion, tended to take more credit than was perhaps merited-for example, in connection with putting together the Texas Ranger deal (Mitchell 2000: 248), or in the firing of his father's chief aide John Sununu (Mitchell 2000: 373-74).

Yet, Mitchell also makes a point near the end of her biography that many critics of Mr. Bush either have missed or purposefully overlooked. In a 1999 interview with the *National Journal*, Mr. Bush discussed the success of his bipartisan approach in Texas and was asked (quoted in E. Mitchell 2000: 326) whether he could take his style in Austin up to Washington Mitchell noted that George W.

> seemed almost plaintive in his reply. "It's not just me," he said. "That's the point I'm trying to explain to you. It's an administration."

Nelson (2000: 4) calls George W. "an intelligent man, with a formidable memory, enormous charm and a sense of humor." Yet, in making the case that

George W. has achieved little, and not without substantial help, he misses a deeper, more important and more accurate story. It is not a story of redemption, as those who focus on his decision to stop drinking at forty emphasize. Nor is it a story of a spoiled child who has never had to make his own way, as his critics charge.

Yes, Mr. Bush appears to have taken some time to have found his niche. Others that grow up in intensely successful and political families have as well. Al Gore considered adult life as, respectively, a writer, a journalist, a divinity school student, a homebuilder, and finally as a participant in the calling that had ambivalently framed his ambition-politics. John McCain (McCain 1999) had a set of strong family traditions and his father's expectations to resolve. And he did so by ambivalently embracing a military career as a hell-raising student and Naval Academy graduate who was always close to either flunking out or being asked to leave. John F. Kennedy, too, showed few signs of great-ness or even purpose in what one biography (Hamilton 1992) detailed as his "reckless youth."

The real George W. story is one of a young man struggling to find a place in the world when the most admired figure in your life has already succeeded beyond the possibilities of your wildest dreams in all the places to which you might aspire. The transition was from a brash, undisciplined, unfocused and not wholly attractive young adult to an increasingly focused, disciplined, adult aware of his real abilities and comfortable with his real limitations.

The Public's View of the Issue

The question of whether Mr. Bush was smart enough to be a good president has a legitimacy that transcends partisan politics. The question was obviously raised most often and most loudly by those with more on their mind than refining leadership theory. News reporters making a headline with a "test" that was unfair and indicative of little, other news lemmings trying to divine through books read or précis given whether Mr. Bush was smart enough, and partisan innuendoes by those whose purpose was to cast doubt for their own political advantage were chiefly interested in trying to sway one group—the public.

How did questions about Mr. Bush's intelligence play out there? We get some idea from a Pew study that analyzed the nature of media coverage of this issue as it emerged in the 2000 campaign. The Pew analysis found that a full 30 percent of all the media stories on Mr. Bush, during the five months they col-lected data, were about this issue. Charges that Mr. Bush lacked intelligence accounted for 26 percent of the stories and only 3 percent of them reported he had the requisite intelligence.

And so, does that settle the issue? Not really. Contrary to the "you know" theory where like-minded people repeat to each other what they all "know" to be true, obviating the need for evidence, the Pew study was interested in just that—the nature of the evidence introduced on behalf of these assertions. What was the evidence? Not much.

The Pew study found that

> Usually, this ticklish subject would come in a thinly veiled but unmistakable form...journalists would write about Bush's intellect by talking about how a rival candidate would exploit it. Often, the route was amazingly circuitous. "By invoking the name of Dan Quayle, who as vice president was not known for his experience or substance, and linking it with the presidency of Governor Bush's father, Mr. Gore is trying to conjure up the image of a candidate who is neither ready for the presidency nor capable of sound economic decisions," wrote Katherine Q. Seelye in the *New York Times* in mid-March.

During the period studied, doubts about Mr. Bush's intelligence were more likely to come from journalists themselves (57 percent). Only 4 percent came from voters and only 6 percent came from "experts." Even Mr. Gore and his surrogates accounted for only 25 percent of such accusations. Mr. Gore and his allies clearly had a motivation to make such charges; the news media in theory did not.

So, what evidence did they use? Often none. The study notes,

> Journalists were also more likely than average to simply express an opinion that Bush lacked intelligence rather than cite evidence....Indeed, nearly a third of all the statements about Bush's intellect were unsupported.

When evidence was cited, it came from a variety of sources. However, the most frequent sources of evidence were Mr. Bush's campaign platform (12 percent) and analysis of his tactics/strategy (14 percent). How one would be able to infer a lack of intelligence from Mr. Bush's policy proposals in unclear. They may have been wrong, but they were not unintelligent. As to strategy/tactics, it is hard to credit stupidity to a candidate, who in his campaign challenged an incumbent vice president, who presided over a robust economy during a period of no major foreign conflicts and who enjoyed the active support of a popular president, and still managed to lose the election.

The study concluded its analysis by noting that,

> Perhaps because the evidence is so soft, the idea that Bush may lack intellectual fire-power has not been embraced by the public. Indeed, a slightly greater percentage of Americans actually attribute not being a serious person to Gore than to Bush.

The poll findings on this matter were quite striking. The *Washington Post's* director of polling reported,

> Throughout the primary campaign, the Texas governor was criticized as lacking the maturity or intelligence to be president. The Post-ABC News survey finds that Americans strongly reject both claims. Seven in 10 voters—including six in 10 Democrats—agree that Bush is "mature enough to take on the responsibilities of the presidency." And three in four believe he is "very intelligent," a view shared by

more than two out of three Democrats and independents as well as nine in 10 Republicans. (Morin and Balz 2000)

These findings do not mean that there were not important questions to be answered about Mr. Bush's level of knowledge. Mr. Bush had come to politics late in his life and so did not have the decades of immersion in policy debate that Mr. Gore had acquired over the course of his long political career. Moreover, Mr. Bush, unlike Mr. Gore, did not relish or make use of as an important source of self-validation, the mastery of a wide variety of policy details.

Mr. Bush's leadership style appeared to be one of finding the right people, setting the goals and letting them follow through. Mr. Gore's style, on the other hand, was to keep his own council, rely on a few close advisors and continue to be minutely involved in making and enacting decisions. Keeping in mind the importance of self-help for exercising political leadership that Richard Neustadt emphasized, and my earlier suggestion that this applied as well to presidential decision making, Mr. Gore's style might appear at first to be an advantage and Mr. Bush's a disadvantage.

However, Fred Greenstein (2000) has recently pointed out the distinction between Ronald Reagan's very active stance in setting the tone and agenda of his presidency and in communicating its basic elements to the American public, and compares this to his more hands-off manner in the workings of the office. Greenstein notes,

> As the spokesman in chief and principal negotiator of his presidency, Reagan was unsparing in his efforts. He was more than its star performer however. *He was its producer, setting the tone and direction of his administration's policies.* (2000: 150, emphasis mine)

An "active" *and* a "passive" president! The question that arises here is whether a leadership style that delegates responsibility to others can be very active in the formulation of goals by such a leader. Greenstein's analysis provides a caution to the simple equation of a leadership and decision style which delegates, like Mr. Bush's, and a lack of interest in deciding or leading.

George Bush himself, in commenting on his decision-making style, has appeared to endorse a relationship between how he thinks and how he leads. Asked in an interview how he would decide among conflicting advice from his advisors on economic policy he replied,

> It's just a matter of judgment. It's a matter of a person in my position sorting out, amongst all the voices, who's got the best judgment, who's got the best common sense. (quoted in Shapiro 1999),

The issue of Mr. Bush's intelligence has been raised by his opponents and the press as part of their story line for covering the candidates. However, it has also been fueled by Mr. Bush's periodic mangling of syntax, his mispronouncing of words (e.g., subliminal), his confusion of words (e.g., "presumptive" and "presumptuous") and geography (Slovakia for Slovenia), and his most famous misstep—failing to correctly identify the leaders of several countries during a pop quiz by a reporter early in the campaign.

None of these slips appeared to have much impact on the public's perception of Mr. Bush as smart enough and qualified enough for the office. Presenting the results of a national ABC news poll, Gary Langer (1999) head of that unit reported,

> Nearly six in 10 Americans think George W. Bush knows enough about world affairs to serve effectively as president—whoever Pervaiz Musharraf is. Bush failed in a pop quiz two weeks ago to name the leaders of three foreign nations or republics—Pakistan, India, and Chechnya. He got just one answer right: the leader of Taiwan. He also said Musharraf, who seized power in Pakistan in a military coup, "is going to bring stability to the country and I think that's good news for the subcontinent." While critics pounced, most Americans don't share their concern. In a new ABCNews.com poll, 59 percent of respondents think the Texas governor does have sufficient knowledge of foreign affairs to serve effectively as president; 36 percent think not.

In the end, the public did make specific judgments about Mr. Bush's intelligence and his judgment. In a Pew poll[8] taken in early September 2000, 38 percent thought that George Bush would have good judgement in a crisis [the comparable figure for Al Gore was 44 percent]. By October, 2000 that figure had risen to 43 percent, slightly surpassing the percentage (42 percent) of people who thought so of Mr. Gore.

Smart Scholarship

When we turn to those who might help enlighten us—scholars whose job it is to be more precise—we actually fare no better. Consider in this regard Fred Greenstein's (2000) recent book on the qualities it takes to make a good president and how to identify them. The key to doing so, he briefly suggests, lies in six central qualities. They are (1) the president's proficiency as a communicator, (2) his organizational capacity, (3) his political skill and (4) vision, (5) his cognitive style, and (6) his emotional intelligence, defined as the degree to which a president is able to "manage his emotions and turn them to constructive purposes."

Here, we are most interested in number 5, the president's cognitive style. which Greenstein aptly defines as the ways in which "the president processes the Niagara of advice and information that comes his way" (p.6). This, of course, is definitely related to the question of whether Mr. Bush is "up to the job," although Mr. Greenstein does not deal with the Bush presidency. Yet, in his brief remarks on Eisenhower's cognitive style, Greenstein appears to emphasize intelligence, in the sense of raw intellectual horsepower first, and thereafter his capacity for "wisdom and sound judgment" (p. 57). Certainly intelligence is one, but not the only, ingredient of cognitive style. And good judgment seems a very separable by-product of information, acuity of insight, and emotional balance.

Former President Clinton, too, is given high marks for his cognitive style, again defined in terms of his "impressive intelligence" (p. 187). However, Greenstein also uses Clinton as "yet another indication of the fundamental importance of emotional intelligence in the modern presidency" (p. 188). These examples raise the issue of how each of the six qualities is related to the others. Mr. Clinton, for example, clearly seems to be a president whose intelligence was undone by his psychology.

Greenstein's list does not easily accommodate itself to the insight that many of his six qualities are deeply embedded in a president's interior psychology. Vision is certainly related to the expansiveness of a president's point of view. However, an expansive vision, coupled with untempered personal rather than public-minded ambition, is a recipe for trouble. Vision, information processing, and even keen intelligence are not separable from the purposes to which they are put. All the attention forced to be paid during the 2000 election campaign to Vice President Gore's tendencies to unnecessarily exaggerate suggest anew that being very smart doesn't make one wise.

Raising the issue of the relationship of "smart" to "wise" underscores the obvious: Many smart people behave in ways that are not smart. That is, they behave in ways that are counter-productive to what they say they want and even what they are trying to obtain. And the issue goes deeper here than whether "smart people do counterproductive things." The real issue is the relationship of being smart to having insight into the nature of the problems to be solved and being able develop a judgment that places it into the category it belongs.

In short, the key question may not be whether George Bush is smart, but whether he has a good sense of judgment. The argument could be made that being smart facilitates good judgment. That argument might even be part of a contingent relationship: The higher the candidate's intelligence, the greater his capacity for [actual] good judgment. Yet, here again, we are forced to make some choices, the first of which is how to conceptualize and gain some measurement traction of "intelligence." Do we key in on the general intelligence factor said to be reflected in standard intelligence tests? (Jensen 1998). Or do we try to make use of the newer theories of multiple intelligence argued for in the work of Robert Steinberg (1979) or Howard Gardner? (1993a; 1993b; 2000; see also Goldman 1997).

If we take the route of multiple intelligences we are immediately drawn into the conceptual and evidentiary morass of the many measures' validity. Gardner started in 1983 (see Gardner 1993a, 1993b) with seven such "intelligences"—music, math, language, social practice, naturalism, insight into others, and self-insight. While the idea is educationally and politically appealing (everyone their own prodigy, in some area), evidence for this is scant. In his latest book, Gardner (2000) added at least one, and possibly three new "intelligences" (naturalist, spiritual, and existential). However, since he's not yet sure, he talks in his lectures of seven and one-half intelligences. One is reminded here of the early trait theorists who, in their enthusiasm for the idea, posited a separate one for each behavior.

Gardner said that Mr. Bush had great "people intelligence." However, his greatest weakness was what Gardner called "existential intelligence," meaning the capacity to ask and consider big questions. Who are we? What are good and evil? Will we survive or falter? What should we want from our lives? "So far," Gardner says (quoted in Merida 2000), "George W. seems to be clueless" in this mode of thinking." Gardner's remarks raise the question of whether we should prefer as president a person who is a good judge of people or one who can have an interesting discussion about the meaning of life.

One of Mr. Bush's suite mates at Yale said of him (quoted in Merida 2000),

> He is not the kind of guy you would go back to the dorms and talk about the Reformation with.... It would have been a total surprise if he had turned out to be an English professor.

On the other hand, one reporter (Merida 2000) inquiring into Mr. Bush's intelligence noted that while Bush often does, more often than many, mangle syntax and so on,

> he had the most interesting answer of all at a recent GOP debate. The question was: Which two things would you put in a time capsule to best represent America as it begins the 21st century? Most of his rivals felt compelled to include the Constitution or the Declaration of Independence. Bush's answer: Martin Luther King Jr.'s "I Have a Dream" speech and the microchip—something to "show the heart of America" and something "to show the entrepreneurial spirit of the country."

Candidates may have taken IQ tests sometime in their past; however, no presidential candidate has ever been asked, or volunteered, to release the results. We are thus left to search for proxies of judgment, among which intelligence is a possible—but not necessarily accurate—indicator. What had heretofore been a *possible* correlate of judgment has now become its equivalent.

Saying that intelligence is what IQ measures, without having a test result to guide us forces us back to our understanding of judgment and how the two might be related. In an earlier work (Renshon 1998b: 207-16) I defined judgment as the quality of analysis, reflection, and ultimately insight that informs the making of consequential decisions. Clearly, the analysis part of the definition is related to what is generally understood as intelligence. Individuals with poor analytical abilities, unable to see the constituent elements of an issue and how they fit together would seem to start out with a drawback in reaching a good judgment.

On the other hand, how much analytical ability is enough? Do people with high IQ scores always make good judgments? Bill Clinton, Thomas Eagleton, and Gary Hart are three of many possible illustrations of highly intelligent people making serious mistakes of judgment for reasons that have much more to do with their psychology than with their reasoning abilities. Indeed, in these cases, it is their psychologies that undercut their judgment and trump their intelligence.[9]

One 1988 Democratic presidential candidate Gary Hart, it may be recalled, invited reporters to follow him if they disbelieved his assertions of an affair-free marriage as he flew to Washington to spend a weekend with his girlfriend Donna Rice. Vice presidential candidate Thomas Eagleton failed to disclose to Walter Mondale that he had been hospitalized three times for major clinical depression and this fact helped defeat his party's attempt to gain the presidency. And Mr. Clinton's history is filled with questionable personal and political judgments, in spite of his extraordinary ability to survive the difficulties he creates for himself. Hence, while the ability to analyze is very likely related to good judgment, it obviously doesn't guarantee it. Smart people can be led by their psychologies to make very poor judgments.

There is a further issue as well. Suggesting that good judgment is a result of analytic ability, reflection, and insight raises the question of how intelligence is related to the latter two elements. Can we assume that intelligence is instrumental in reflection, or that it more frequently leads to insight? We simply do not yet know the answers to these questions.

The capacity for reflection seems more closely associated with the capacity to gain appreciation and understanding of the various elements of an issue and their significance. And what does that take? Certainly it takes a capacity to suspend judgment, resist the pressure for action that may arise from many quarters—not the least of which is one's own psychology—and an ability to weigh the alternatives in ways that do justice both to the issue at hand and to those that might arise. Moreover, good judgment entails the capacity to make these evaluations not only on the pragmatic calculus of net gain, but in a way that allows real voice to, and some realization of, key personal values and ideals. Intelligence may well be a necessary instrument for making good judgments, but it is not sufficient.

Intelligence for What: Character and Leadership?

Jonathan Chait relates a revealing anecdote about George Bush. During the campaign, Louis Menand (1999) published a long interview with Al Gore in *The New Yorker*. In that interview Mr. Gore appears to be highly intellectual, but in a profound way personally disengaged. Louis Menand (1999: 66) comments that as a public speaker,

> Gore has only two dials on the console: speed and volume. To convey gravity he slows down; to convey urgency he gets louder. Clinton purrs; Gore disclaims.

In private Menand first notes Mr. Gore's physical solidity (1999: 167):

but the face is unexpectedly pale. The mask is, indeed, a mysterious feature. He inflects with his face, rather than his voice. He grimaces, and though the effect seems self-conscious, it brings out the athleticism. You see the muscular Gore, the super-achiever, the star quarterback who is also captain of the debating team, and invited on Sunday afternoon to have tea with the Dean. But in repose the face sometimes goes completely flaccid, the eyes become hooded, and you see the Vulcan side. The light for the hard drive is on, but there is no message on the screen.

Menand (1999: 170) then asks Gore which thinkers have influenced him and,

> he [Gore] mentioned Reinhold Neibuhr, Maurice Merleau-Ponty and Edmund Husserl. Would that be Merleau-Ponty's "Phenomenology of Perception?" Yes, he said, with a flicker (just a flicker of excitement—did I know it?) He had found the work helpful, he said, "in cultivating a capacity for more refined introspection that gave me better questions that ultimately led to a renewed effort to become involved with the effort to make things better."

Menand adds, "It is a little hard to imagine having this discussion with George W. Bush." Bush, says Chait, has read Menand's article. Was he put off by this slight to his mental capacity? No, not in the slightest. Instead Carlson Tucker, who raised this issue with Bush in an interview, says (1999: 108; see also Chait 1999: 26), "Bush finished the piece convinced that Gore lacks the warmth and personal appeal to win a presidential race."

Chait argues (1999: 26) that the politics of character allowed Mr. Bush to soar upward, propelled by his own weightlessness. The implication of this observation is that there is no substance there or worse, no capacity for it. Perhaps. Yet, although Mr. Bush has not worked his way through Merleau-Ponty or Husserl, his observations on Mr. Gore's handicap in seeking the presidency seem substantively based, and accurately identify a key difficulty in Mr. Gore's candidacy.

In both the Menand comment and the question raised to Mr. Bush directly during the Bedford town meeting, Mr. Bush seems to be providing the raw material which is the basis for David Brooks' (1999: 4) observation that "it could be that a secret of George W.'s political success so far is that in the age of television politics, it is more important to be comfortable with yourself than it is to have built a long string of accomplishments." This is the point, too, of Tucker's controversial interview with Mr. Bush, which presents him as a man proud of his independent thinking even when it's uncomfortable to those who support him. Thus, Tucker reports (1999: 104), when he spoke at a fund-raising dinner of very rich supporters and denounced wealth without purpose—"no one clapped."

In an interview Tucker asked Mr. Bush what rich people say when the man to whom they've just given money tells them getting rich isn't a noble pursuit? Bush (Tucker 1999: 104; see also Kristof 2000: A16) responded,

Doesn't even wait for me to finish the question. I don't care. I really don't care. Does anyone ever say "Fuck you"? "I don't care if they do," he barks. "People have a responsible to give back, affluent people especially. And that's what I tell them."

Nicholas Kristof reports that often,

Bush sounded inclusive themes, mentioning concern for poverty among minorities or single mothers in front of audiences that were virtually all white and well-healed. "The Republican party better have people who not only hear the entrepreneurs, we had better have someone who hears the voices on the outskirts of poverty as well," he told one packed audience at a school. The audience which had been so enthusiastic that it might have cheered Mr. Bush if he had recited pi to 100 decimal places, remained silent.

Mr. Bush, in the words of George Will (1999), is "no intellectual," but then he asks: So what?" David Broder (1999: B07) writes,

I once thought that the smarter a politician is, the better equipped for high office. But voters wisely weigh talents on a different scale. If the presidential candidates in 1980 had been presented with a set of policy documents and a blank sheet of paper on which to summarize the options and recommend a course of action, nuclear engineer Jimmy Carter easily would have outscored former actor Ronald Reagan. But Reagan was a political natural and a gifted leader—one who had clear goals, strong principles and a great gift for translating abstract issues into compelling narratives conveying lessons anyone could grasp.

Nowhere is Broder's point made more clear than in the Mr. Bush's performance after the September 11 terrorist attack. The president responded clearly, forcefully, and comprehensively to that attack, while rallying a shocked and saddened public. Critics were forced to reconsider. Some could still not take in what they had seen.

In 1999, Jacob Weisberg argued in an article entitled, "Do Dim Bulbs Make Better Presidents?" that the answer to that question was "no." Clearly examining then candidate George W. Bush he said,

To be sure, intelligence of the kind that might manifest itself in high SAT scores isn't the most important quality in a chief executive. Leadership, integrity, and determination are all more critical qualities. Dumb luck helps. Dumbness doesn't.

President Bush's performance in the wake of the September 11 attack forced Mr. Weisberg to change his previous analysis, but clearly not his view:

Somewhat inexplicably, Bush does actually seem to have grown a bit more articulate. His intellectual limitations, however, remain firmly in place. Bush continues to exhibit the same lack of curiosity, thoughtfulness, and engagement with ideas that made him a C student. Nuance, complexity, subtlety, and contradiction are not part of the mental universe he inhabits. And curiously enough, it is these very qualities of mind,or lack thereof,that seem to be making him such a good war president. (Weisberg 2002)

In the end, the question is not really whether George W. Bush is smart enough to be a good president. Evidence shows that the answer to that question is: Yes.

Given the choice of a president who already knows it all or a president who can learn, I would choose the second. A president with a strong sense of values and ethics to temper his ambition and adequate but not outstanding intelligence would seem preferable to a very smart, highly ambitious candidate without real convictions or the courage of them. Intelligence, in short, is always encased in a psychology. And when it comes to presidential leadership and judgment, psychology counts.

Notes

1.   Kelly later retracted his view (2001: A23).
2 .   *Time*: So how do you assure folks you're smart enough to be President?
       Bush: I'm confident of my intellect. I wouldn't be running if I wasn't. My job will not be to out-think everybody in my administration. My job will be to assemble an administration full of very capable and bright people.
3.   It is also the title of a book which the publisher assured its readers provides a "witty, trenchant...on target...singularly perceptive and entertaining analysis of George W. Bush." It doesn't. See the book jacket material in Ivins and Dubose (2000).
4.   Interestingly, Maraniss and Nakashimas' informative biography of Al Gore makes use of a similar characterization, the Prince of Tennessee (2000). The Gore biography refers to the fact that Al Gore senior, a United States Senator and his wife had selected a political career for their son Albert, Jr. at a very early age and began training him for it. Mr. Bush also grew up in a family of wealth and privilege, but his family adapted a much more laissez-faire approach to their son's vocational choice.
5.   These incidents parallel others when Mr. Gore denied that he had said that Mr. Bush was not ready to assume the presidency when he clearly had said so. The headline in the *New York Times* accompanying the story read, "Gore Describes Texan as Not Up to the Job" (Seelye 2000). An earlier Gore campaign ad had pointedly asked of Mr. Bush (Marks 2000), "Is he ready to lead America?" Actually Mr. Gore had questioned Mr. Bush's lack of basic knowledge about foreign affairs after he was unable to identify several leaders in a "pop quiz" sprung on him (Neal 1999).
6.   The question of how George W. spent his time while governor requires some explanation. Texas was a "weak-governor" state which meant that the governor didn't have much in the way of formal powers and could lead best by making use of his or her access to the "bully pulpit." The legislature met 140 days every two years. Yet, George W. was governor all 365 days of every year. As a result there was less actual legislative work and thus less day- to- day work for Mr. Bush. Mitchell describes his relaxed daily schedule as governor (Mitchell 1999: 324-25).
7.   The parallels are nothing short of obvious; Andover, Yale, Texas, the oil business, an engagement at the same age as his father's to his mother, service as a pilot, political office, and of course the presidency.
8.   The Pew Center for the People and the Press, " Bush Gains on Personal Qualities," November 1, 2000. http://www.people-press.org/july00rpt.htm (November 20, 2000).
9.   I analyze judgment in each of these cases elsewhere in some detail (Renshon 1998: chapters 6, 9-11).

References

Allen, Mike. "Bush on Stage: Deft or Just Lacking Depth." *Washington Post*, 19 February 2001: A8.

Balz, Dan. "Bush is Already 'Misspoken' for." *Washington Post*, 24 April 1999: A03.

Balz, Dan, and Ceci Connolly. "Excerpts: Post Interview With Gore." *Washington Post*, 13 May 2000.

Begala, Paul. *Is Our Children Learning?: The Case Against George W. Bush*. New York: Simon and Shuster, 2001.

Berke, Richard L. "A Day After the Big Debate, No One boasts of a Big Night." *New York Times*, 5 October 2000c: A1.

_____. "Gore Dots the i's That Bush Leaves to Others." *New York Times*, 9 June 2000b: A1

_____. "In a Fierce Debate, Bush Promises to Cut Taxes, Calling to Mind His Father." *New York Times*, 7 January 2000a: A17

_____. "Some Unease in G.O.P. Over Bush in Debates." *New York Times*, 10 December 1999: A32.

Brooks, David. "Bush Family Values." *New York Times Book Review*, 17 October 1999: 4.

Broder, David S. "A Clear Choice." *Washington Post*, 5 October 2000: A35.

_____. "Smart Versus Shrewd." *Washington Post*, 28 November 1999: B07.

Bruni, Frank. "Jabs by Opponents of Bush Subtly Poke at his Intellect." *New York Times*, 8 December 1999b: A1.

_____. "Pressed by a Reporter, Bush Falls Short in World Affairs Quiz." *New York Times*, 5 November 1999a: A28.

Bruni, Frank, and Eric Schmitt. "Bush Rehearsing for World Stage." *New York Times*, 19 November 1999: A30.

Chait, Jonathan. "Race to the Bottom" *The New Republic*, 20 December 1999: 26-229.

CNN. "*Time* interview with George W. Bush." 1 August 2000.

Dowd, Maureen. "Hainan noon, Starring Gary W. Cooper." *New York Times*, 15 April 2001: wk. 6.

Editorial. "A Pop Quiz for Mr. Bush." *New York Times*, 6 November 1999: A16.

Farnham, Barbara. "Ronald Reagan's Judgment," in Stanley A. Renshon and Deborah W. Larson (eds) *Good Judgment in Foreign Policy: Theory and Application*. Lantham, MD: Rowman and Littlefield, 2002, in press.

Fox News-On Line. "Mom's Endorsement Barbara Bush: George W. 'No Dummy'," *Reuters*, 2 December 1999.

Friedman, Thomas L. "George W.'s Makeup Exam." *New York Times*, 7 November 1999: wk 15.

Gardner, Howard. *Intelligence Reframed: Multiple Intelligences for the 21st Century*. New York: Basic Books, 2000.

_____. *Frames of Mind: The Theory of Multiple Intelligences*. New York: Basic Books, 1993b.

_____. *Multiple Intelligences: The Theory in Practice*. New York: Basic Books, 1993a.

Goldman, Daniel P. *Emotional Intelligence*. New York: Bantam, 1997.

Greenstein. Fred I. *The Presidential Difference: Leadership Style from FDR to Clinton* . New York: Free Press, 2000.

Hamilton. Nigel. *JFK: Reckless Youth*. New York: Random House, 1992.

Harris, John F., and Dan Balz. "Conflicting Image of Bush Emerges :Bush Makes Political Investments, But Will They Make Him?" *Washington Post*," 29 April 2001: A01.

Hunt, Al. "Wednesday's Indecisive Debate Probably Weighs in Bush's Favor." *Wall Street Journal*, 12 October 2000.

Ivins, Molly, and Lou Dubose. *Shrub: The Short But Happy Political Life of George W. Bush*. New York: Random House, 2000.

Jensen, Arthur R. *The G Factor*. New York: Praeger, 1998.

Kagay, Mike. "Poll Watch: Voters Say Gore Won First Debate; Bush Supporters More Enthusiastic." *New York Times*, 11 October 2000.

Kelly, Michael. "Bush's Political Smarts." *Washington Post*, 7 March 2001: A23.

_____. "The Pinhead Factor." *Washington Post*, 14 March 2000a: A18.

_____. "Census and Nonsense." *Washington Post*, 5 April 2000b: A19.

Kinsley, Michael. "The Stupidity Issue." *Washington Post*, 24 October 2000: A27.

Kristof, Nicholas D. "Bush Sticks to Middle to Blunt McCain's attacks." *New York Times*, 29 February 2000: A16.

Langer, Gary. "Public Says Bush Has Smarts to Lead Nation." ABCNews.com, 15 November 1999.

Maraniss, David, and Ellen Nakashima. *The Prince of Tennessee: The Rise of Al Gore*. New York: Simon and Schuster, 2000.

Marks, Pete. "The Ad Campaign: Commercial Attacking Bush is Most Hostile of Campaign." *New York Times*, 3 November 2000.

McCain, John, with Mark Salter. *Faith of My Fathers*. New York: Random House, 1999.

McGeary, Johanna. "How the White House Engineered a Soft Landing: A Carefully Engineered Game Plan Helped Bush Bring the U.S. Flight Crew Home." *Time*, 16 April 2001.

McGrory, Mary. "Caught In The Switch." *Washington Post,* 27 February 2000: B01.

Menand, Louis. "After Elvis." *The New Yorker*, October 26 and November 2, 1999: 165-174.

Merida, Kevin. "George W. Bush: Is He or Isn't He Smart Enough?" *Washington Post,* 19 January 2000: C1.

Milbank, Dana. "Seen But not Heard." *The New Republic*, 8 November 1999: 18.

Millman, Joyce. "President Dumbass." Salon : Arts and Entertainment, 4 April 2001.

Minutaglio, William. *First Son: George W. Bush and the Bush Dynasty*. New York: Times Books, 2000.

Mitchell, Allison. "The Republicans: McCain Turns Up Heat a Notch on Bush." *New York Times*, 31 January 2000.

_____. "McCain is Latest Victim of Pop Quiz." *New York Times*, 20 December 1999.

Mitchell, Elizabeth, and W. Minutaglio. *Revenge of the Bush Dynasty*. New York: Hyperion, 2000.

Morin, Richard, and Dan Balz. "Poll: Bush's Lead over Gore is Gone." *Washington Post*, 12 March 2000: A1.

Neal, Terry M. "Gore Blasts Bush Quiz Answer, Vice President Questions GOP Leader's Foreign Expertise." *Washington Post,* 6 November 1999: A09.

Nelson, Lars-Erik. "Legacy." *New York Review of Books*, 24 February 2000: 4-7.

Nightline. "The Clinton Years: Interview with Leon Panetta." ABC.com (December 27, 2000).

Neustadt, Richard E. *Presidential Power and the Modern Presidents: The Politics of Leadership from Roosevelt to Reagan*. New York: Free Press, 1991 [1960].

Noah, Timothy. "Dubya: Smart? Or Dumb." *Slate*, posted March 13, 2001.

Page, Clarence. "Maybe 'Dubya' Really isn't So Dumb." *Chicago Tribune*, 12 December 1999.

Renshon, Stanley A. "Political Leadership as Social Capital: Governing in a Divided National Culture." *Political Psychology* 21:1 (2000): 199-226.

_____. *The Psychological Assessment of Presidential Candidates*. New York: Routledge Press, 1996 .

Sack, Kevin. "In strategy Shift, Gore Ads Question Bush's Capability." *New York Times*, 23 November 2000.

Sack, Kevin, and Frank Bruni. "As Campaign Spins, Candidates Try to Find Their Edge." *New York Times*, 13 October 2000:A1.

Safire, William. "Bush Wins by Not Losing." *New York Times*, 5 October 2000.

Sanger, David E., and Steven Lee Myers. "How Bush Had to Calm Hawks in Devising a Response to China." *New York Times*, 13 April 2001.

Sawyer, Kathy. "Bush Says Focus is on Substance, Not Quizzes." *Washington Post*, 8 November 1999: A4.

Seelye, Katherine Q. "Gore Describes Texan as Not Up to the Job." *New York Times*, 4 November 2000.

Seelye, Katherine Q., and Richard Prez-Pena. "Gore Team Renews Criticism of Bush as Inexperienced." *New York Times*, 30 October 2000.

Steinberg, Robert J. "The Nature of Mental Abilities." *American Psychologist* 34 (1979): 214-230.

Tucker, Carlson. "Devil May Care."*Talk*, September 1999: 103-110.

Weisberg, Jacob. "How Bush's Shallowness Makes Him a Good War President." *Slate*, 4 January 2002.

_____. (ed.). *George W. Bushisms: The Slate Book of the Accidental Wit and Wisdom of Our 43rd President*. New York: Simon and Schuster, 2001.

_____. "Do Dim Bulbs Make Better Presidents?" *Slate*, 3 November 1999.

Will, George F. "He's No Intellectual—And So What?" *Washington Post*, 23 September 1999: A29.

Von Drehle, David. "Bush Must Deal with a Gray Matter." *Washington Post*, 10 December 1999:A1.

9

Is Al Gore Too Smart to Have Good Judgment?

Can someone be too smart to have good judgment? The idea doesn't seem intuitively correct. After all, it takes some level of intelligence to gather and refine the information that could support good judgment? But does more intelligence result in better judgment? Perhaps it is the case, that all that is necessary to be capable of reaching good judgment is a certain level (not necessarily minimal in the sense of little) of intelligence. Or perhaps more intelligence does lead to an increased capacity for good judgments, up to a point.

The question has rarely been asked, and was never broached during the 2000 presidential campaign because one of the candidates was characterized as smart, while the other was caricatured as dim. Yet, what if the wrong questions had been asked on these matters, and of the wrong candidate? What if Mr. Bush was, as the evidence suggests, perfectly intellectually capable of making good judgments? And what if Mr. Gore, who is certainly the front-runner for the Democratic Party's 2004 presidential race, was the one who escaped any questions regarding this matter, perhaps erroneously?

Here I want to raise and address the question: Is Al Gore too smart to have good judgment? I am aware that the question seems both paradoxical and unnecessary. It is paradoxical because most people assume more intelligence leads to better judgment. And it is unnecessary because Mr. Gore *is* a smart, extremely well-informed man. No dissent from that fact will be put forward here.

Mr. Gore is Smart: How Do We Know?

There is general agreement that Mr. Gore is "smarter" than Mr. Bush. However, how exactly do we know this. This view is not easily supported by the academic accomplishments of the two. Mr. Gore went to Harvard and received so-so grades overall, and Mr. Bush did the same at Yale.[1] Mr. Bush completed a post-graduate degree at the Harvard Business School and Mr. Gore finished neither of his two post-graduate degree attempts [one at Vanderbilt Divinity School, the other at Vanderbilt Law School].

The attribution of intelligence to Mr. Gore is built on his mastery of and immersion in the details of policy, his ability to provide long detailed answers to policy questions on the stump and during the campaign debates, and the missteps of Mr. Bush. These are not "perceptions" with little substantive foundation. On the basic of experience and knowledge Mr. Gore is obviously qualified to be president.

Psychology + Intelligence = Judgment

People who discuss intelligence often treat it is as a trait. One is ordinarily thought to have more or less of it. Critics of standard understandings of intelligence argue that there are many different kinds. They call our attention to the view, not yet demonstrated, that there are" multiple" or domain specific intelligences (see the discussion of Gardner in chapter 8).

What both supporters and critics of traditional views of intelligence fail to consider, however, is that intelligence is always deeply embedded in a person's interior psychology. Regardless of whether there are, or are not a number of different intelligences, their operation is clearly shaped by the psychology that makes use of them. In some cases the relationship is easy to see.

Persons with hysterical elements in their psychology will often make poor judgments, not because they lack intelligence, but rather because their anxiety keeps them from clear or constant focus. Persons whose psychology is permeated by suspiciousness often make bad judgments because their understanding is framed by the certainty that others will traduce them. Bill Clinton was impeached for the series of bad judgments that led him to have an affair with an intern and then lie about it. No one would argue that Mr. Clinton is not a highly intelligent man, only that he lacked sufficient impulse control when it came to his own gratification.

When it comes to his psychology, Mr. Gore is no Bill Clinton. Yet, like everyone else Mr. Gore does have a psychology. And this psychology is the house, so to speak, where his intelligence lives and operates. What, then, can we say about it?

Mr. Gore's Psychology

During the campaign, aides to Mr. Gore told *New York Times* reporter Richard Berke (2000) that Gore "sometimes sees himself as the smartest person in the room, and often he is right." The implications of this view were suggested in a large number of interviews conducted with Gore and White House staff members by David Maraniss and Ellen Nakashima of the *Washington Post* for their book, *The Prince of Tennessee* (2000c) .These interviews are a form of primary data and are striking in the extent to which those interviewed, a diverse group, came to similar conclusion:

Mr. Gore could be both bold and very hesitant. Mr. Gore took a bold stand on the administration's response to the Kyoto conference on Global Warming, but called up his aide Carter Eskew to ask if it would look bad if he baby-sat for his grandson instead of joining his wife and daughter at the Million Mom's March in Washington (*New York Times*, 2000).

Maraniss and Nakashima wrote that,[2]

Those first words of self-doubt that Gore uttered during his 1976 congressional campaign—How'm I doin'? How'm I doin'?—became the private mantra of his political career.

Variations on the theme were recounted by people who worked for him and admired him, yet could recall scenes like this one offered by a former aide: "There was a situation where he was asking me how he did, how he did, how he did, and I guess I was getting annoyed, and he said, 'Don't you know how insecure I am?'" One former advisor reached the conclusion that insecurity was "the seminal force that motivates Gore," a trait, this advisor said, that tended to obscure his better side—"an insightful, intelligent, subtle and well-intentioned person."

So which was it? Gore the partner or Gore the staffer? The bold Gore or the subservient Gore? Those questions go to the struggle within Al Gore that has long been evident—a duality that he brought with him into the vice president's job, that became more pronounced once he was there, and that remained unresolved as he sought to move up to the Oval Office. He was at once competent and self-confident about anything that he could translate into what he considered a question of fact, yet often insecure and plagued by self-doubt when it came to perceptions and emotions and aspects of life that could not be established with mathematical certainty.

This bifurcation between high self-confidence alternating with substantial self-doubt creates difficulties for Mr. Gore's decision-making style, and the quality of his judgments. As one aide comparing Gore and Clinton noted,

Gore is inductive. Once the facts take him to a position, he tends to frame an issue in black and white, at least in his public expressions of it. Clinton is more intuitive, always allowing for more shades of gray.

Facts may be the starting point of judgment, but they are not synonymous with it. The ability to put facts into perspective is a key element of good judgment. Mr. Gore's certainty when he has what he believes are "the facts," and his view that they lead to inescapable conclusions can lead him to take somewhat rigid positions, and also to disparage those who don't happen to hold his view. Several staffers told Maraniss and Nakashima:

While the president and vice president agreed that the White House should offer its own balanced budget in 1995 in the decisive battle with the Republican Congress, once that was done, it was Gore who showed the most resolve, according to aides. Clinton was constantly luring the Republicans with hints of possible compromise, while Gore held an unyielding position from which he hectored his opponents about the waywardness of their reasoning. For Gore it was really kind of simple: "The Republicans were just wrong, so there was no reason to give in to them," said one former top aide. "He really believed it as a matter of fact, not as a matter of faith. Clinton is prepared to compromise off ideology. Gore is less willing to compromise because he thinks his views are fact-based."

The question arises here: Isn't Mr. Gore's position simply a matter of having principles on which you stand? Yes, to some degree, however there is an important difference. Strong adherence to the principle, "I'm certain I'm right," is not the same as standing for a principle with the understanding that others may legitimately differ. Humility leavens hubris.

One of the dangers of high self-certainty is that it is hard to admit when you're wrong. Maraniss' and Nakashimas' interviews with his advisors after Mr. Gore's much criticized remarks on the Joint Chiefs of Staff and policies towards gays in the military suggested,

> a stubborn refusal to acknowledge that he had articulated a damaging position—that such military leaders as Colin L. Powell or H. Norman Schwarzkopf would be ineligible for command in a Gore administration since they believe that allowing gays to serve openly hurts military effectiveness. After two days of internal deliberation, Democratic sources said, Gore grudgingly agreed to state that his original answer had been misinterpreted.

Not surprisingly, Mr. Gore's insistence on being correct leads him to be closed off at times to good advice. The reality is that Mr. Gore is the driving force behind virtually every big decision of his campaign, and many small ones, even in logistical matters. Recently, Berke (2000) noted,

> when he was in a rush to travel from New York to Washington, Mr. Gore announced that he was scuttling Air Force Two because he would make better time on the U.S. Airways shuttle. His stunned military and Secret Service aides knew not to try to talk him out of it.

Joe Biden, Delaware Democratic Senator who supported Mr. Gore in the primaries had this to say about Mr. Gore's open-mindedness:

> Gore comes off to me as a guy who has absolute confidence in what should be done and really isn't all that interested in what you think substantively...Al is interested in getting briefed, forming an opinion and then it's settled. That reflects a political certitude: a guy who will make decisions à la Harry Truman and go home and go to sleep. Except Truman operated on a gut assessment based on a historical context. Al operates on an intellectual assessment that doesn't accommodate much input.

Another analysis in the *New York Times* (2000) detailed the ways in which Gore often asks his chief aides for advice, but ended by noting,

> Mr. Gore's aides could not come up with a major example in which they had persuaded the governor to change his mind. After weeks, the Gore campaign offered only one: The vice president was adamant that he go to the Super Bowl last January to see the

Tennessee Titans. The problem was that the game was on the Sunday before the New Hampshire primary. It took Mr. Eskew and Charles Burson, the chief of staff who is also a Titans fan, to tell Mr. Gore that "it was not the best use of his time," said Chris Lehane, a Gore spokesman. Indeed, the Titans lost the game.

Mr. Gore's tendency to self-certainty when he believes he has "the facts" has another, more troubling side. You can see the results if you examine the transcript of the meeting between Mr. Gore and Mr. Clinton and critics of his initiative on race relations that took place at the White House on Christmas eve in 1997. In it, Gore used moral reproach as a means of discrediting opponents of affirmation action. His opponents were "profoundly wrong," "denied the obvious," and ended by giving those assembled the following glimpse into his view of human nature, that "It is naive in the extreme to assert that there is no persistent vulnerability to prejudice rooted in human nature." "That evil," he continued," lies coiled in the human soul," and to deny that is "just wrong."

Or consider his speech to Atlanta's Ebenezer Baptist Church on Martin Luther King Day in 1998. In it (quoted in Sleeper 1998: 20), he railed against, "modern apostles of apathy" who, "roll [King's] words off their tongues, even as they try to role back equal opportunity" and,

> invoke the phrase "content of our characters"...to pretend that all we need is to establish a color-blind society. They use their colorblindness the way duck hunters use a duck blind. They hide behind the phrase and just hope that we, like the ducks, won't be able to see through it. They're in favor of affirmative action if you can dunk the basketball. But they're not in favor of it if you merely have the potential to be a leader of your community.

There is no doubt this position is politically congenial to some, but there is embedded in it a harsh tone of moral stridency. Mr. Gore's opponents are not merely mistaken, they are devious, hypocritical, wholly opposed to racial progress and increasing opportunity—in short, thoroughly despicable people. Being able to adhere to boundaries of respect and legitimacy for one's opponents might well be an element of good judgment in political leaders, regardless of one's experience and knowledge.

Do Knowledge and Experience Lead to Good Judgment?

In addressing this question, we can begin with a useful distinction between being smart and being well informed. While the two are often used interchangeably, they are distinct, conceptually and practically. Smart generally refers to the capacity to make use of information. Being well informed refers to the range and depth of the information itself. The capacity to be well informed reflects a certain level of intelligence, of course. However, it is the use of that information that truly helps to separate the two concepts.

Mr. Gore's experience and knowledge present a somewhat different frame though which to analyze a set of questions that are related to, but not synonymous with the questions of intelligence discussed above. The Gore competency themes—experience coupled with knowledge—are an obvious outgrowth of his long career in government service. He was elected to the Congress and to the Senate, where he developed an expertise in military and environmental policy. Moreover, he had been a two-term, highly involved, and very influential vice president under Bill Clinton.

Hence, Mr. Gore's competence was an obvious and legitimate theme for news stories about his candidacy. Surprisingly, his competence accounted for only 14 percent of the news coverage themes of him during that period. The Pew study notes,

> Gore's competence was a central message being promoted by his campaign. Sometimes this thread came up in the form of reporters simply summarizing Gore's mindset. "The vice president has great faith in his own national security experience and instincts....The vice president has participated in every major national security debate over the past decade and has access to intelligence and foreign policy expertise throughout the government," noted reporter John Broder in the *New York Times*. Often the praise of Gore came through the coverage of Clinton.

And who raised the theme of Mr. Gore's competence? Gore campaign surrogates were more than twice as likely to plug Mr. Gore's competence than journalists.

Learning from Experience

What is the relationship of experience and knowledge to judgment? Experience in government and in high decision-making circles, as Mr. Gore had, provides a front-row seat and an opportunity to participate in the debates that shape an administration. By all accounts Mr. Gore made it his business to be involved and was. So he was present at most of the administration's policy debates when policy options were suggested and weighed, and when participants sorted through the mix of policy and political considerations that frame most executive policy debates. A seat at such high levels gives one the opportunity to asses other styles of decision-making and the judgments that result. For a person given to reflection, they can provide some insight into one's own decision-making style and the ways in which one reaches a judgment. These can be valuable experiences.

What Mr. Gore did not have in his experience, which Mr. Bush did, was the final authority for making decisions. That experience would be different in important ways from being part of the decision processes. Quite obviously, as part of the decision group you are one of the advisors. As the president, or governor, you are the person with ultimate responsibility. Your role is not as skilful advocate of a position—yours—but as skillful and thoughtful appraiser of others' arguments and their implications.

The two positions are, in important ways, inconsistent with each other. An advocate/advisor's general stance is to discount other options and bolster his preferred one. The leader charged with ultimate responsibility reaches a better judgment by weighing the various advocacies pressed on him before reaching his own position.

There is a final important aspect of experience and the acquisition of knowledge that bears mention. Experience provides not only knowledge, but lessons. I am not referring here to the broad historical kinds that underlie the use of analogy at suitable moments. Nor am I referring to the insights into one's own decision and leadership style that political experience can provide. The lessons I have in mind here are of a more personal, characterological nature.

It is well known that immersion in the routines of an institution or a profession's life can have important consequences. The idealism of young medical students, teachers, and police officers, for example, have all been shown to be responsive to experience in those professions. There is no reason to think political life is an exception.

Mr. Gore has been in political life much longer than Mr. Bush and has had more time to acquire and internalize those kinds of lessons. What kind of lessons might these be? Both Al Gore and George Bush had fathers, whom they loved and (especially for George Bush) idealized, and who lost elections. Both young men took these losses hard. What lessons did they learn here?

Both men had personal experiences with losing races: Mr. Bush in his first political campaign for a congressional seat and Mr. Gore in his run for the nomination in 1998. And Mr. Gore was an instrumental partner for eight years in an administration marked by erratic fortunes and uneven performance. What lessons in leadership and decision-making did Mr. Gore learn in that capacity? And since both were engaged in a brutal, few holds—if any—barred fight to secure the presidency after the vote on November 7, 2000, what lessons did this experience confirm or teach?

Does Knowledge = Understanding? Does Knowledge = Insight?

What of knowledge? How is that related to good judgment? Obviously experience increases knowledge. However, knowledge is not a unitary concept. There are different kinds of knowledge which often get confounded in discussions of experience.

It is important to distinguish between policy *knowledge* and policy *understanding*. We can define the first as a basic building block of understanding. What is missile throw weight? Who is Viktor Chernomyrdin?[3] What are the advantages and disadvantages of allowing people, on a voluntary basis, to invest some of their social security funds in the stock market (Kessler 2000a, b)?

There is no doubt that knowledge can be an important ingredient in reaching good judgments. Yet, how much knowledge and in conjunction with what other elements remains an open question. Familiarity with policy details *may* facilitate good judgment, but that it must necessarily do so isn't true. Recall that numerous times during the tense debates of the Cuban missile crisis, President Kennedy asked for explanations of terms or historical precedents. Keep in mind as well, that a concern with details can often be at the expense of stepping back to see their larger implications. That is one reason, and there are others, why highly obsessive people are not necessarily good decision makers.

Mr. Gore's immersion in the details of the areas that he has selected for specialization is well documented. Indeed, he has been characterized as having "nearly an obsessive hands-on approach" (Allen and Connolly 2000). When he was searching for an issue to make him a player in the Senate, he selected arms control and went about acquiring mastery in a characteristic way (Turque 2000: 142-150). He asked a colleague Edward Boland, Chair of the House Select Committee on Intelligence to recommend someone to help him acquire that knowledge. Boland recommended Leon Furth, who remains a senior Gore advisor.

Gore biographer Bill Turque (2000: 144; see also Zelnick 1999: 117-18) describes the tutorial thus:

> ...for more than a year...Furth tutored Gore in the bleak arcana of throw weights, hard-target kill capacities, and warhead to silos ratios. They met at least once a week, sometimes for four or five hours at a time...

One of those invited to make a presentation to Mr. Gore, then Under Secretary of the Navy James Woolsey (later to head the CIA under President Clinton) said that "he had never had such a detailed technical discussion with a member of Congress."

Mr. Gore's technical mastery of the subject made him a player in the debates on the basing of the MX [multiple warhead] missile system and the deployment of the so-called "Midgetman" missiles, single warhead missiles on mobile launchers (Turque 2000: 142-150; Zelnick 1999: 117-136). His major speech on March 22, 1982, laid out his proposal, which was to convert all the multiple-warhead missiles to single warhead "Midgetman" missiles. Bob Zelnick (1999: 122) says, "there was nothing particularly new about Gore's idea, it had been kicked around for years at Livermore and other Western think tanks." Turque (2000: 145) agrees:

> The centerpiece of Gore's proposal was not an original idea. It had been kicking around the arms control community for years and was certainly well known to Furth.

At first, Gore's idea was greeted with silence, but a series of events over the next year stimulated by the congressional cut-off for funds for the MX missile system revived the idea of the "Midgetman." Yet another commission chaired by former Air Force General Brent Scowcroft recommended the "Midgetman" option, but coupled it with a recommendation to build one hundred MX missiles in hardened silos to prevent U.S. vulnerability in the event of a Soviet first strike. It was this plan that was adopted. In the end, the MX missile was revived by a Senate vote, but the Midgetman program never was developed and ultimately was cancelled. Fifty MX missiles were built and housed.

Turque (2000: 147) calls Mr. Gore's strategy of supporting a revival of the MX a carrot to get the Reagan administration to take arms control seriously, "wishful on two fundamental levels." First, it substantially underestimated the opposition of Reagan senior advisors like Casper Weinberger and Richard Perle. Second, it substantially underestimated President Reagan's preference for a more powerful missile defense, a view that eventually resulted in the push for the Strategic Defense Initiative. Some thought that Mr. Reagan and his advisors had made use of Mr. Gore's personal and policy ambitions to revive the MX missile system (Turque 2000: 148; Zelnick 1999: 123), which they did. Reviews of Mr. Gore's performance (Turque 2000: 149-50) over this debate were mixed:

> Gore's defenders say he stepped into a debate in which few people were making sense and developed a clear workable approach to nuclear stability. The less enamoured saw a hyper-ambitious young man who let his penchant for self promotion and zeal for a place at the table outrun his judgment.

Zelnick notes that Gore saw the Soviet Union as a permanent partner in managing nuclear arms and a great power rival, but Reagan saw the weakness in the Soviet system and was determined to exploit it in order to profoundly change it. His endorsement of SDI helped drive the Soviet Union toward "perestroika" (restructuring) and "glasnost" (openness). Once liberalization started, it could not be stopped or controlled and the Soviet Union as we knew it collapsed.

Zelnick (1999: 125) makes a more profound assertion given our interest in the relationship of knowledge to good judgment. He underscores,

> the irony for Gore is that on nuclear arms control, the issue that turned him from a mildly interesting and promising Tennessee representative to one of his party's premier voices on national security, he was brilliantly, imaginatively, responsibly and valiantly wrong. To Gore, the nuclear issue was part of a relationship with the Soviet Union that had to be managed. To Reagan, it was part of a struggle that had to be won"

Ambition and Good Judgment: The Costs of Scandal

The issue of scandal in relation to the presidential candidates came up early in the 2000 primary season. John McCain, Republican presidential hopeful, admitted that campaign contributions to him as head of an important Senate committee had influenced his willingness to grant access. Appearing with Democratic presidential hopeful Senator Bill Bradley to discuss campaign finance reform he said (quoted in Kunz 1999), "I believe I probably have been influenced because the big donor buys access to my office and we know that access is influence." He took the step of admitting his ethical boundary transgression and then made his admitted lapse the basis of a personal crusade to do away with the influence of soft money contributions.

Mr. Gore's reported lapses were of a different sort and handled in a different way. While there were a number of possible issues that might have been raised in connection with this story line, the Pew study found that, "Usually, the discussion of Gore as scandal tainted came in the form of reminders of Gore's questionable fundraising." When you combined statements that Gore had scandal problems with those statements that said he really didn't, the total made up almost half of the statements (46 percent) of the three themes that the Pew study found being used to characterize the vice president.

The scandal theme was established early in the campaign. Over half, 57 percent, of these assertions appeared in March and another 21 percent in February. Less than a quarter of the assertions of Mr. Gore's problems with scandal came in the last three months, between April and June.

What was the factual basis of such assertions? The Pew study found that,

> The scandal issue was also notable in that there was more evidence for it than any other. Fully 90% of the references offered some form of evidence. Usually—64% of the time—that evidence was interpreting Gore's public record.

Only 8 percent of the scandal assertions were made by an opponent.

Did those raising the issue of scandal link it to judgment? No. The Pew study found:

> Usually they were tied to how he was running his campaign rather than how he might govern the country. Half of the statements about Gore and scandal were tied to his tactics and strategy. Not quite a third (31%) concerned his leadership and just 3% had to do with his relations with voters, or whether it would affect his chances of winning.

On its face value, the association of a presidential candidate with scandal would not appear to be an encouraging sign in the search for good judgment. An involvement in political or personal improprieties is itself an indication that something in the process of making a good judgment has faltered or failed. That something is often the triumph of self-interest over more ethical norms, whether they are those of the community or of the person. Perhaps the person rationalizes his misstep by saying that it will be just this one time. Or perhaps he believes that the stakes are important enough to justify the ethical lapse as an "exception." Perhaps he is subjected to pressures that compete with his moral sense and is unable to resist being pulled off course. Or perhaps a person's ethical standards had always been more forceful in the abstract than in practice. Whatever the reason for it, however, in taking steps away from one's core ethical standards one always runs the risk of being more easily compromised the next time.

Mr. Gore's personal and political circumstances were complex. No hints of scandal were associated with his career or politics before he assumed the vice presidency. He was known as an ambitious, smart, and somewhat inhibited ("wooden") senator, with a reputation for hard work, attention to detail and self-promotion. In short, Mr. Gore had, before he became vice president under Mr. Clinton, a not very out of the ordinary profile that could fit a number of well respected senators or political leaders.

That changed with the complexities of his relationship to Mr. Clinton. Mr. Gore was unusually particular in laying out his demands, insisting that if he and Clinton were elected he be given substantial access and policy responsibility. Mr. Clinton in an equally unusual fashion agreed to do so. As a result, Mr. Gore was not only a uniquely influential vice president, he was for all intents and purposes president in the areas that Mr. Clinton ceded to him. As Maraniss and Nakashima pointed out:

> Al Gore's relationship with Bill Clinton was defined in an agreement they worked out in Little Rock after the 1992 election and before the inauguration...Gore would be a managing partner. He would have an office in the West Wing. Members of his staff would be integrated into the president's staff. The president and vice president would meet for lunch once each week and the meeting would be inviolate, held no matter what else was preoccupying them. And Gore would have what he called spheres of interest in which Clinton would defer to him and let him take the lead for the administration though it was not stated in those terms. Within the White House it became understood that Gore was essentially president of the subjects within his spheres of interest. The list grew over time, as Clinton gave him new assignments at their weekly lunches, eventually including all environmental issues, science, high-tech, the Internet, communications, space, reinventing government, voluntary ratings for network television, the tobacco industry and nuclear disarmament of the former Soviet states. Clinton was willing to cede these spheres of interest to Gore because there were other policy matters that he was more interested in, and because he implicitly trusted Gore to handle them with skill and discretion. (2000a; see also Maraniss and Nakashima 2000b; Broder and Henneberger 2000: A1)

Aside from the unique historical nature of the relationship, their arrangement had a number of obvious psychological results. First, from Mr. Gore's standpoint, it satisfied his personal and political desire to be influential. In short, it satisfied his ambitions. It also created a level of connectedness that was certainly advantageous to him so long as Mr. Clinton had anything resembling a normal presidency.

In exploring the toll that Mr. Clinton's dishonesty about his affair with Monica Lewinsky took on the Clinton-Gore relationship, John Broder (2000: A01) writes,

> Friends and associates say he was angered by Mr. Clinton's deceit, repulsed by his behavior and appalled at his recklessness. Mr. Gore brooded then and afterward about what the episode might mean for his own presidential ambitions. His sense of loyalty struggled against an offended morality, a conflict that, his friends say, has not yet been resolved."

That piece was written on March 3, 2000, and apparently those feelings had been resolved to some degree by December 19, 1998. It was on that day, after Mr. Clinton was impeached, that Mr. Gore, standing with members of the Democratic Congress, said that the vote does a great disservice to a man I believe will be regarded in the history books as *one of our greatest presidents*. There is no doubt in my mind that the verdict of history will undo the unworthy judgment rendered a short while ago in the United States Capital. (Harris 1998: 01; emphasis mine)

Given a number of chances thereafter to modify his glowing assessment of Mr. Clinton, Gore declined. In an interview on *Face the Nation* (transcript 5), the following exchange occurred,

Schieffer: Let's talk about your friend, Bill Clinton. A lot of people remember that Saturday afternoon—I remember it very well—when the House voted to impeach the president. You went to the White House lawn and said, "This president will be remembered as one of the greatest presidents in history." Do you still believe that?

Vice President Gore: Look at the economic record, Bob. We've gone from the biggest deficits to the biggest surpluses. We've gone from a triple dip recession to tripling the stock market. Instead of quadrupling the debt, we've seen the creation of 20 million new jobs.

Schieffer: So you still stand by the statement.

The president's impeachment was not the only problem Mr. Clinton's behavior presented to Mr. Gore. Richard Neustadt (1991[1960]: 169) argues that, "The first eighteen months or more [of a president's term] becomes a learning time for the new President." Certainly Mr. Clinton's first two years in office are consistent with the view. However, Mr. Clinton's uneven performance during this period raised more questions about the president than about Mr. Gore. And, Mr. Clinton did recover his political footing facing a newly elected Republican Congress.

What put Mr. Gore in his predicament was not Mr. Clinton's somewhat erratic political leadership during his first two years of office, but the means by which he carried through his determination to reverse his losses. That entailed winning back Congress as well as his own re-election. And that, in turn, required raising unprecedented amounts of money to begin an early campaign. That effort was critical to Mr. Clinton's re-election chances and therefore to Mr. Gore's as well, but the president's re-election was also critical to whatever ambitions Mr. Gore had to succeed Mr. Clinton.

It was that effort that ensnared Mr. Gore, Bob Woodward (2000a: A01) reports,

In his zeal to raise money and do President Clinton's bidding, Gore took the unusual step of requesting large contributions for the Democratic National Committee—often in private phone calls—with an urgency and directness that several large Democratic donors said they found heavy-handed and inappropriate for an incumbent vice president. Gore became known at the DNC as the administration's "solicitor-in-chief" after Clinton adamantly refused to make direct requests for contributions, according to two senior Democratic officials.

From fall 1995 to spring 1996, Mr. Gore made fund-raising phone calls from the White House using a Clinton-Gore campaign credit card. At first, Gore acknowledged making "a few calls" from the White House for soft money contributions. However, when detailed notes of the solicitations emerged, he acknowledged that he had made eighty-six calls and reached forty-six potential donors (Woodward 1997a). Criticized for doing so, Mr. Gore responded in a hastily called news conference on March 3, 1997, that there is "no controlling legal authority" that prohibited him from making fund-raising phone calls from the White House.

Mr. Gore also got into trouble by attending a high-level meeting at which the money coming into the Clinton-Gore campaign was allocated to hard money/soft money categories.[4] In early August, 1997 when the details of Mr. Gore's fund-raising became a matter of public knowledge, spokesperson for the Democratic National Committee, Amy Weiss Tobe (quoted in Woodward 1997a), said that "the vice president was not aware that money was being designated for the federal [hard money] account." However, a short while later, a memo turned up that contradicted Mr. Gore.[5]

At first Mr. Gore said he wasn't paying that much attention to the discussions in the meeting. However, that was inconsistent with Mr. Gore's generally detailed approach to details and was also contradicted by aides who were present. Then, in an August 8, 1998, FBI interview, Mr. Gore said that because he drank a lot of iced tea and might have needed a rest room break, he could have been absent during key parts of a meeting on fund-raising attended by the president and campaign aides (Lardner 2000: A35). However, former White House Chief of Staff Leon Panetta said in a deposition that he remembers Mr. Gore "attentively listening" to the hard-money conversations, and former White House Deputy Chief of Staff Harold Ickes testified that whenever the vice president left the room, he, Mr. Ickes, stopped the meetings. In light of the evidence, FBI General Counsel Larry Parkinson wrote to the assistant attorney general that there was "sufficient evidence" to prove that the vice president made a false statement to investigators on this matter.

On April 29, 1996, Mr. Gore attended a Buddhist temple fund-raiser where $60,000 in illegal donations was raised and for which he gave several different understandings (Fineman, Breslau, and Isikoff 1997: 77; see also Lewis 2000). On October 22, Mr. Gore said he thought the Buddhist temple event was for "community outreach," not a fund-raiser. Then, in the spring, the vice president conceded that it was "finance-related." Somewhat later his aides described it as an exercise in "donor maintenance." They noted—accurately—that no solicitation was made at the event.

In all those instances, Republicans called for Attorney General Reno to investigate whether the facts warranted an Independent Council investigation. On three different occasions, she concluded that they did not. Some senior members of her staff, notably FBI Director Louis J. Freeh and others, disagreed.

Mr. Gore did not escape unharmed politically however.

There is evidence that all these allegations and Mr. Gore's responses to them did affect him and his candidacy. John Harris and Ceci Connolly (2000: A1) wrote that questions such as whether Mr. Gore lied to FBI investigators,

> strike at places where Gore is already vulnerable. Independent voters who think the Clinton administration has set a low ethical tone, who think Gore is emblematic of Washington politics and its money-chase culture, or who think Gore is not a straight shooter—all their concerns could be exacerbated by the controversy.

The evidence appears to support the view that Mr. Gore's association with questionable fund-raising practices did affect him adversely. At the time the Pew survey was being conducted the campaign had not really commanded the attention of large numbers of voters. Nonetheless, the scandal theme did have some resonance with voters. Another Pew study[6] designed to assess whether voters were responding to the themes raised in the media found,

> Approximately half the public says they would be less likely to vote for the vice president if they heard charges that Gore panders or stretches the truth. Messages that emphasize scandals involving President Clinton or allegations about Gore's own role in illegal fund-raising would turn off about four-in-ten Americans."

"Clinton fatigue" was a real fact throughout the campaign. It was almost certainly an important factor in Mr. Gore' selection of Senator Joe Lieberman, a man who had publicly criticized President Clinton for his "immoral behavior," as his running mate. However, it had a more direct effect on the public's voting as well.

Mr. Gore's Psychology Revisited: Exaggerations, Lies, and Good Judgment

The Pew study also examined the questions that arose regarding Mr. Gore's truthfulness. These concerns took two separate, but related forms. One asked whether Mr. Gore had a tendency to embellish or exaggerate. The other asked whether at times he would "say anything" to get elected.

The Pew study found that,

> more than a third of the Gore assertions studied (34%) were about his tendency to lie or exaggerate.... Once again, Gore's record was often what did him in. More than a third of the statements about Gore's tendency to stretch the truth referred to his public record, slightly higher than for all other themes.... Like his ties to scandal, Gore's honesty problem was hammered at during the key primary battle. In all, 43% of the assertions came in March.

Did the press explore the implications of their story frame for Mr. Gore's judgment? Here, paralleling the failure to do so in the case of the scandal story line, the answer is: No. The Pew study reported that, the press was less likely to explore the implications of this problem on a Gore Administration than to tie the issue to some more immediate concern, such as Gore's campaign. Nearly two-thirds (64%) of the time the assertion was related to how it would affect Gore's tactics and strategy. The press put Gore's exaggerations into the context of his potential leadership just 23% of the time.

It should be clear that exaggeration is related to judgment in a different way than it is to leadership and it is primarily the first that is our focus here. What is the relationship, if any, between exaggeration and judgment? The first step in delineating the relationship is to ask what an exaggeration represents both psychologically and politically.

When someone exaggerates they take a step or more beyond what one can reasonably or truthfully claim. The consequence is to put the exaggerator in a more advantageous position than he would be in were he to stick with a wholly accurate accounting. Exaggeration therefore is a deception with a purpose: to present the person in a way that gives him unwarranted or unearned credit.

An exaggeration is often considered a "harmless" overstatement to which many political leaders are prone (Perry and Cummings 2000).[7] Lyndon Johnson's great grandfather did not die at the Alamo, but peacefully in bed. Ronald Reagan told Israeli Prime Minister Yitzhak Shamir during Mr. Shamir's 1983 visit to the White House that he had been one of the first photographers to take pictures of emaciated inmates of Nazi concentration camps. Mr. Reagan, an Army Air Corps captain attached to the First Motion Picture Unit in Culver City, California, never left the U.S. during World War II. The incident was reported by Reagan biographer Lou Cannon, who speculated that when Mr. Reagan told that story, he probably believed it. The actor had seen films of the death camps, and, Mr. Cannon wrote, films were "real" to him.

In 1988, Senator Joseph Biden Delaware was running for the Democratic presidential nomination. He gave a very moving speech about how he was the first member of his family to go to college. However, much of his speech was lifted word-for-word from a political commercial broadcast by Labor Party leader Neil Kinnock in Britain. Later, Senator Biden claimed that he had graduated in the top half of his law school class; he hadn't.

Mr. Nixon lied when he told the nation he couldn't disclose Watergate details because "national security" was involved. It wasn't. Candidate Lyndon Johnson promised never to send "American boys to fight in an Asian war," at precisely the same time as he was seriously planning to do just that. President Clinton lied when he told the nation he had never had sexual relations in the White House with Monica Lewinsky. He also committed perjury in the same matter before a trial judge for which he was admonished and fined.

Obviously, gross deceptions with large policy or political consequences like those of Presidents Johnson, Nixon, and Clinton are different than padding a resume. In the case of each of these larger lies, the motivation is clear: It is to escape from the negative consequences of one's behavior (Nixon, Clinton) or avoid the negative voting judgments that are likely to occur if you tell the truth (Johnson).

In each of these cases, the president knows that he is lying but puts his own self-interest before the publics'. There are as many ways to rationalize this kind of deception as there are reasons for a leader to think that his self-interest should trump the publics'. However, what is basic to all these cases is that the deceiver never tests his rationalization on anyone other than himself (Bok 1978), who, of course, thoroughly understands and approves of the deceptive steps that had to be taken.

It can be seen immediately that the rational for large lies and exaggerations is precisely the same: To gain unwarranted benefits and/or avoid unwanted consequences. The magnitude of the consequences differs, of course, but not the underlying dynamic.

It also seems clear why lies and exaggerations would be troublesome for political leaders and their leadership. Leadership capital (Renshon 2000) depends on an expectation, and the experiential conformation, of trust between the leader and the public. And that, in turn, rests on a history of honesty.

However, what of judgment? The key question that is raised about judgment from the standpoint of exaggeration, lying and other forms of misrepresentations, is the relationship of ambition and self-interest on one hand to a person's ethical ideals and standards on the other. Do self interest and personal or political ambition trump ethical ideals and standards? Or do ethical ideals and standards provide a stable framework that places limits on self-interest and ambition?[8]

An exaggeration, lie, or other misrepresentation represents the crossing of an ethical boundary. At the same time, it represents a judgment that one's personal self-interest is more important than the normal expectation for honesty and accuracy that others have or depend upon.

One might characterize the relationship between ambition/self interest and personal ethics/community interests *as the* basic judgment framing issue in every important decision a leader makes. Every leader must balance his own personal and political interests with a robust consideration of what's in the public's best interest. Sometimes the two are synonymous. However, most often they are not.

A leader who repeatedly puts his psychological finger on the scales to tip the balance towards his own self-interest has at minimum a weighing bias. He cannot adequately give each element in a decision the weight it might deserve because his self-interest has already tipped the scales. This judgment error is found in the weighing of the evidence elements. However, that is not the only error.

Starting out with a psychologically unbalanced scale is a much more fundamental problem than the plain description above suggests for three reasons. First, it is a primary framing error. That is, it takes place at the very start of the judgment processes. Second, it persists throughout the judgment process. That is, it is not only an error that is committed once, but also each and every time evidence must be considered. And third, it is a systematic motivated error rather than one that might arise from time to time.

Mr. Gore's exaggerations were not at the level of Presidents Johnson, Nixon, and Clinton as already noted. Hence, it is not their magnitude that requires our attention, but their amplitude. Those exaggerations include the following: (1) Mr. Gore said he and his wife Tipper were the models for Erich Segal's novel *Love Story*. The author repeatedly corrected Mr. Gore by pointing out that the male character was a composite and Tipper Gore was never used (Powers 1997; Associated Press 1997); (2) In November 1999, Mr. Gore claimed to be a co-sponsor of the McCain-Feingold campaign-finance reform legislation. But that bill was not introduced until three years after Mr. Gore left the Senate (Bennett 2000: A01); (3) During that same month the vice president claimed to be the author of the Earned Income Tax Credit (Tumulty *Time* Transcript 1999).[9] In fact, the EITC law was enacted in 1975—two years before Mr. Gore entered Congress; (4) Mr. Gore claimed credit for providing major phrases for Hubert Humphrey's acceptance speech at the Democratic National convention in 1968 through his talks with Charles Bartlett whom Mr. Gore described as a major Humphrey speech writer. In subsequent interviews Mr. Bartlett said Mr.Gore had no role in helping Mr. Humphrey write his convention speech (Maraniss and Nakashima 1999: A01); (5) Mr. Gore claimed at a news conference that, "he had been involved in discussions about the strategic oil reserve in its early stages" (Mitchell 2000). Yet the Strategic Oil reserve was established in 1975, two years before Mr. Gore arrived in congress.[10]

There are other examples as well. A claim that his mother-in-law's arthritis medicine cost three times what Mr. Gore paid for the same drugs for his dog turned out to be both inaccurate and untrue. The information had come not from his mother-in-law as Mr. Gore had claimed, but from a Democratic briefing paper and it played loosely with the comparative figures (Robinson 2000). There was artful ambiguity about Mr. Gore's Vietnam experience that left the impression that he had seen combat in the participant sense, rather than having seen the aftermath of it. (Zelnick 1999). And there was Bill Bradley's complaint that Mr. Gore had lied repeatedly about his record (Allen 1999: A01).[11]

Some have argued that Mr. Gore's exaggerations were taken out of context (Perry 2000). However, a closer inspection of the many assertions (e.g., that he had "taken the lead in developing the Internet") all were correctly understood at the time for what they were presented to be: a claim for credit where less was warranted.[12] Mr. Gore's tendency to exaggerate is not a creation of his enemies or itself an exaggeration. The *New York Times* published a memo from Mr. Gore's press secretary, Arlie Schardt, in 1988, warning him "that his main pitfall was exaggeration," and it noted an earlier memo that had warned Mr. Gore of making "remarks that may be impossible to back up." Mr. Schardt (2000) protested the publication of the memo, but not its content.

Establishing a pattern of embellishments is not the same as psychologically accounting for them. That task is certainly possible, but takes us beyond the purposes of this chapter. Rather, I want to turn here to another question, that of consequence.

Did these exaggerations hurt Mr. Gore? There is some evidence that they did. The Pew survey found that,

> Gore's veracity did seem to penetrate to some degree with the public, though not overwhelmingly. The public was noticeably more likely to attribute saying anything to get elected to Gore than to Bush, by a margin of 36% to 25%. And it seems to matter to people. About half of Americans said that Gore's tendency to lie or exaggerate would make them "less likely" to vote for him, compared with 40% who said it wouldn't make much difference.

Conclusion

Yes, Mr. Gore is a very smart man. Yes, he is a well-informed man. And yes, he would be capable, other things being equal, of handling the complexities of policy or crisis. However, while Mr. Gore is do doubt competent, there is less evidence for his keen insights. Mr. Gore understands what he masters, but insight and mastery are not synonymous.

Moreover, his unnecessary embellishments and exaggerations suggest a person who combines strong ambition with substantial personal doubt. One result can be seen in his decision style, which can alternate between certainty that he is right, period—and doubt about whether he is choosing wisely. This is a risky formula for good judgment.

Too much doubt can be paralyzing. Too much certainty can trump prudence. Certainty is a mistake-prone element of psychology. It can lead on one hand to be harsh and overbearing, as with Mr. Gore's comments regarding race, as noted earlier, and his attacks on Mr. Bradley suggest that it is a part of the pattern of his psychology. Certainty is also troubling because it leads one to think that one's convictions are or must be, and that limits listening and learning.

Mr. Gore is smart, well informed, and verbal. The quality of his insights and judgments is less clearly evident. Can a leader be too smart for his, and our own good? Yes, when it leads him to forget that his most important function as a leader is not always to provide authoritative answers, but to help the public to ask the right questions.

Notes

1.   NBC News anchor Tom Brokaw (2000) had this to say about the college careers of both men:

> All of this comes to mind as more stories emerge about the undergraduate years of George W. Bush at Yale and Al Gore at Harvard. For a time, apparently, both men barely kept their heads above water, hovering just at C level. We're told Governor Bush was much more interested in intramural sports and

fraternity social life than the classroom. Classmates of Vice President Gore remember he shot a lot of pool, reportedly smoked a little marijuana, played sports and managed to get a D in one course and not one A during his sophomore year.

2. The quotes that follow are drawn from David Maraniss and Ellen Nakashima (2000a).

3. He is the former Russian prime minister with whom Mr. Gore negotiated and signed a secret arms agreement that became controversial during the campaign (Vita 2000). It was also a name that Mr. Bush dropped "causally" during one of the presidential debates to demonstrate that he was familiar in an easy way with this important official with a somewhat difficult to pronounce name.

4. Soft money is defined as contributions not intended to support individual candidates but to promote "party-building" and other general campaign activities such as television advertising. While it must be reported, it can be given in unlimited amounts. Hard money contributions are highly valued by campaigns because they can be used directly to benefit individual candidates. But federal law places specific restrictions on the solicitation, amount, and use of such contributions. Among those restrictions, the law says that such regulated contributions cannot be solicited on federal property.

5. Grunwald (1998: A1), who reported on the memo stated,

> The memo is potentially damaging to Gore, who has insisted that in making calls to 45 donors during the campaign he only asked for "soft money" that would go to the Democratic Party's general campaign efforts, and not "hard money" specifically for the Clinton campaign. David Strauss, then Gore's deputy chief of staff, scribbled on the November 21, 1995, memo "65% soft/35% hard." The notation is followed by a scrawled definition of soft money: "corporate or anything over $20K from an individual." Those notes, made during a DNC finance meeting attended by Gore, could cast doubt on Gore's protestations that he never intended to solicit hard money, but are not necessarily conclusive, investigators said.

6. The Pew Research Center for the People and the Media, VOTERS UNMOVED BY MEDIA CHARACTERIZATIONS OF BUSH AND GORE, July 27, 2000. http://www.people-press.org/july00rpt.htm (November 20, 2000).

7. The examples that follow, unless otherwise noted, are drawn from this article.

8. I have discussed these matters in details elsewhere (1998a, b) and put forward a theoretical framework with which to analyze them.

9. The transcript reads in part (emphasis mine):

Time: Given how critical Senator Bradley has been of welfare reform, what do you think of the poverty proposals he put forward this week?

Gore: [Bradley's proposals were] an old-style approach that spends a lot of money but doesn't have any new ideas. [He proposes] the expansion of the Earned Income Tax Credit. *I was the author of that proposal. I wrote that,* so I say, welcome aboard. That is something for which I have been the principal proponent for a long time.

10. On ABC's *This Week* the following exchange (Ttranscript 2000) on the subject took place between Cokie Roberts (moderator) and Dick Cheney, Republican vice presidential nominee,

Roberts: You've been making the same kinds of charges. What are you really saying here? Are you saying this man's not fit to be president?

Cheney: I think it raises questions about his—his character. I think he's consistently over the years has a pattern of exaggeration. Turns out he's made statements that are not true, in everything from the Internet to "Love Story," most recently the question of prescription drugs for his mother-in-law and his dog. This week we've had the statement that he was there when the decisions were made on setting up the Strategic Petroleum Reserve; he wasn't.

Roberts: But he was in Congress...

Cheney: He was not in Congress.

Roberts: He was in Congress when the oil was actually put into the reserve.

Cheney: The decisions were made in the Ford Administration. I was there as White House chief of staff, Al Gore wasn't. He wasn't even in Congress yet.

11.   Allen (2000) quotes Bradley as saying, "But I'm afraid he didn't tell you the whole truth about my record–or even half of it," Bradley began. "He said that I proposed raising the eligibility age of Social Security. Not true–he knows it's not true. He suggested I'd cut Social Security benefits and increase Social Security taxes. Not true–he knows it's not true."

12.   As an example of the press misunderstanding Mr. Gore, James Perry (2000) gives the example of his claims about Love Canal. Perry says that the reporter reported Gore as saying "that was the one that started it all," which became transformed to "I started it all." The only problem is that Mr. Gore is really quoted as saying that his hearing on Love Canal "started it all" when, in fact, President Carter had declared Love Canal a disaster area months before Mr. Gore's hearings.

In fact that original story was clear in its quote and in the inference to be drawn from it (Connolly 1999a: A10; emphasis mine):

> Speaking later at Concord High School, Gore boasted about his efforts in Congress 20 years ago to publicize the dangers of toxic waste. "I found a little place in upstate New York called Love Canal," he said, referring to the Niagara homes evacuated in August 1978 because of chemical contamination. "I had the first hearing on that issue." Gore said he first became aware of the problem when a young girl in Tennessee wrote to him about a mysterious illness that had befallen her father and grandfather. Although few remember his hearings on that site in Toone,Tenn., Gore said his efforts made a lasting impact. "*I was the one that started it all,*" he said. Gore's shorthand description of Love Canal—and his failure to note that the hearings he chaired came a few months after President Jimmy Carter declared the neighborhood a disaster area—were reminiscent of earlier attempts to embellish his role in major events.

References

Allen, Mike. "Gore Lies Repeatedly, Bradley Says." *Washington Post*, 3 December 1999: A01.

Allen, Mike, and Ceci Connolly. "Glimpses Show Candidates Cool as Cucumbers." *Washington Post,* 26 November 2000: A12.

Associated Press. "Gore Concedes 'Miscommunication' about 'Love Story' Role." 14 December 1997.

Bennett, William J. "A Lifetime of Lies." *Wall Street Journal,* 11 October 2000.

Bok, Sissela. *Lying: Moral Choice in Public and Private Life.* New York: Pantheon, 1978.

Broder, John. "Clinton's Affair Took a Toll on Relationship with Gore." *New York Times*, 3 March 2000:A1.

Broder, John, and Melinda Henneberger. "Few in No. 2 Spot Have Been as Involved as Gore." *Washington Post*, 31 October 2000: A1.

Brokaw, Tom. "The Gentlemen and Their C's." *New York Times*, 3 April 2000.

Connolly, Ceci. "Gore Paints Himself as No Beltway Baby." *Washington Post*, 1 December 1999a: A10.

Connolly, Ceci. "'New' Gore Bears Striking Resemblance to '88's." *Washington Post,* 11 December 1999b: A08.

Fineman, Howard, Karen Breslau, and Michael Isikoff. "You Can Call Him Caught." *Newsweek*, 15 September 1997: 77.

Friedman, Thomas L. "Foreign Affairs: Yellow Brick Geopolitics." *New York Times*, 5 May 2000.

Grunewald, Michael. "Fund-Raising Memo Leads to New Probe of Gore Role; Aide's Notes Hint at Call Seeking 'Hard Money.'" *Washington Post*, 21 August 1998: A01.

Harris, John F. "Clinton Vows to Finish Out Term President Says He Will Keep Working to 'the Last Hour of the Last Day.'" *Washington Post*, 20 December 1998: A01.

Harris, John F., and Ceci Connolly. "Analysis: Vice President Finds Past Still Perilous." Washington Post, 24 June 2000: A01.

Kessler, Glenn. "Two Visions, Both Quiet on Tough Choices." *Washington Post*, 24 October 2000a: A10.

_____. "Between Bush, Gore Claims is Reality of Social Security." *Washington Post*, 5 November 2000b: A25.

Kuntz, Phil. "McCain's Financing Stance Recalls Keating-Five role." *Wall Street Journal*, 17 December 1999: A16.

Lardner, George Jr. "Public Integrity Chief, GOP Clash on Probes." *Washington Post*, 25 May 2000: A35.

Lewis, Neil. "Gore Fund-Raiser Convicted for Arranging Illegal Gifts." *New York Times,* 3 March 2000.

Maraniss, David, and Ellen Nakashima. "The Bureaucrat vs. the Risk-Taker." *Washington Post,* 12 August 2000a: A01.

_____. "After Careful Courtship, a Natural Affinity." *Washington Post*, 11 August 2000b: A01.

_____. *The Prince of Tennessee: The Rise of Al Gore.* New York: Simon and Schuster, 2000b.

_____. "Senator's Son Feels Pull of Political Life In Caldron of Chicago '68, A Mix of Caution, Ambition." *Washington Post*, 27 December 1999:A01.

Mitchell, Alison. "Bush Attacks Gore, Citing 'Pattern of Embellishments.'" *New York Times*, 24 September 2000.

Neustadt, Richard E. *Presidential Power and the Modern Presidents: The Politics of Leadership from Roosevelt to Reagan.* New York: Free Press, 1991 [1960].

New York Times. "Where the Candidates Turn for Some Advice." 9 June 2000.

Parry, Robert. "He's No Pinocchio: How the Press has Exaggerated Al Gore's Exaggerations." *Washington Monthly*, April 2000.

Perry, James, and Jeanne Cummings. "History Has Shown Politicians Can't Resist a Little Embroidery." *Wall Street Journal,* 11 October 2000: A1.

Powers, William. "For Gore, It Was No Love Story." *National Journal*, 20 December 1997: 2568.

Renshon, Stanley A. "The Comparative Psychoanalytic Study of Political Leaders: John McCain and the Limits of Trait Psychology," in Ofer Feldman and Linda O. Valenty (eds.) *Profiling Political Leaders and the Analysis of Political Leadership: Methods and Cross-Cultural Applications* (Westport, CT: Greenwood, 2001).

_____. "Political Leadership as Social Capital: Governing in a Fragmenting Culture." *Political Psychology* 21:1 (2000): 199-226.

_____. *High Hopes: The Clinton Presidency and the Politics of Ambition* (New York: Routledge Press, 1996.

Robinson, Walter V. "Democrat is Faulted Anew Over Drug Costs." *Boston Globe*, 22 September 2000.

Schardt, Arlie. "My Memo Said What?" *New York Times*, 16 February 2000.

Shapiro, Walter. "Apt Student Bush Making the Grade." *USA Today*, 11 November 1999.

Sleeper, Jim ." Color Bind*." New Republic*, 2 March 1998: 18-20.

Tonner, Robin, and Janet Elder. "An Electorate Largely Split Reflects a Race So Very Tight, *New York Times*, 14 November 2000.

Transcript. NBC's *This Week.* September 24, 2000.

Transcript. CBS *Face the Nation.* October 3, 1999.

Bill Turque. *Inventing Al Gore: A Biography.* Boston: Houghton Mifflin, 2000.

Vita, Matthew. "GOP Uses 1995 Arms Pact to Turn Up Heat on Gore." *Washington Post*, 26 October 2000: A25.

Woodward, Bob. "Gore Donors' Funds Used as 'Hard Money.'" *Washington Post*, 3 September 1997a: A01.

_____. "Gore Was 'Solicitor-in-Chief.'" *Washington Post*, March 2, 1997b: A01.

Zelnick, Bob. G*ore: A Political Life.* Washington, DC: Regnery, 1999.

10

Senator John McCain for President in 2004: Why Not.

There is no passion that so shakes the clarity of our judgment than anger.
—Montaigne

Questions about character in presidential elections are framed by three circumstances. They reflect larger public yearnings stimulated by recent historical presidential experience. They are framed by the state of the country and the public's view of it. And they reflect the public's evaluation of the candidates themselves, their strengths and limitations, the commitments they inspire, and the worries their behavior stimulates.

Character assessments in presidential campaigns, then, reflect several rather than a singular frame of reference. On one hand, they reflect the public's understandings framed through the lens of their own hopes and expectations. Yet they reflect, as well, the real and observable behavior of the candidates themselves.

It would be easier if the public were able to see clearly the real and relevant psychology of the candidates they observe, and evaluate them in relation to their wishes, accordingly. However, there are many reasons why this is not likely, and may not even be possible. The public has different levels of interest: some persons pay more attention to politics and campaigns than others, and few have the training or understanding to do more than make impressionistic characterological judgments. While impressions can sometimes be helpfully accurate, in a democracy accuracy doesn't diminish their impact. One person, one vote is the rule here, regardless of attention, knowledge, or judgment. Strategic self-presentations by candidates, attuned to public wants through polling and focus groups, complicate matters.

Nonetheless, over the course of a campaign, especially one that is contested, an attentive observer can discern patterns and make more informed judgments about aspects of a candidate's psychology. Often, these will conflict with how the candidates may prefer to be seen or may believe themselves to be. Clearly, such was the case with the candidacy of Senator John McCain for the 2000

Republican presidential nomination. His dramatic rise and equally spectacular demise provides an informative and cautionary case study of the intersection of character and judgment.

Senator McCain's well-prepared and not wholly inaccurate persona as a straight-talking heroic maverick fueled his meteoric rise as a candidate. Ultimately, he lost the nomination to his rival George W. Bush because he continued to attract more Independents and Democrats than Republicans. Yet along the way a number of questions were raised about Mr. McCain's suitability for the presidency—questions that appeared to place approval of his character and worry about his temperament on a collision course. In fact, there were reasons to be concerned in both areas. Moreover, these two domains of Mr. McCain's psychology, far from being disparate and contrary elements, were, in fact related elements with important implications for the benefits and risks of a McCain presidency.

These issues, as they relate to Senator McCain are of more than passing historical interest. Since running for the presidency in 2000, Senator McCain has gained national stature and media attention. He was mentioned as a prominent candidate as George W. Bush's vice presidential choice. As the single-minded pursuer of campaign finance reform, he has continued to gain nation attention. And reports have surfaced that Senator McCain is considering leaving the Republican Party and running against Mr. Bush in the 2004 presidential campaign as an Independent. Clearly, Senator McCain is a political force to be reckoned with. The question is: what kind?

In this chapter, relying again on publicly accessible data,[1] I examine the public psychology sources of his surprisingly powerful candidacy. I then examine the questions that were raised about his temperament and the public response to them. In the process, I focus on his own behavior at key points of his candidacy and their implications both for what we came to learn about him and for his suitability for the presidency. I conclude with some observations on the role of McCain's heroic leadership and whether it represented a good fit with the culture of American leadership expectations.

Public Psychology and the McCain Candidacy

Certainly there is ample evidence that Senator McCain's insurgency was fueled by his biography and the public's view of his character. However, there is little evidence it was fueled by the importance of his "signature issue." campaign finance reform. After speaking to many South Carolina voters, Nicholas Kristof (2000) wrote, "Rather than Mr. McCain's stance on the issues, what appears to attract voters is an aura of strength, character and leadership, and above all, his past." These data are born out by surveys. A CNN/USA Today/ Gallup Poll taken January 13-16, 2000, asked voters to note their chief policy concerns. Only 34 percent of American voters saw that issue as "extremely" or "very important." By contrast, of twenty-five issues from which the public could choose, campaign finance ranked next to last. On the other hand, "presidential character and integrity" was very high on the list with 74 percent of Americans choosing it as extremely or very important problem.

McCain's rise in the polls was meteoric. For example, from September 1999 to February 2000 McCain's favorabliity image skyrocketed as ABC poll numbers below indicate.

	2/27	10/31	Change
McCain	60%	36	+24
Bush	49	69	-20
Gore	50	56	-6
Bradley	38	47	-9

Fifty four percent of voters in the same poll agreed with Langer (2000) that, "the more I hear [about him], the more I like him."

McCain's rise was fueled primarily by a palpable hunger on the part of the American electorate to have someone in the oval office who was as honest as he was competent. David Broder (2000), in reporting the views of a number of New Hampshire voters to support this view, says, "that what appeared to be powering McCain over...the other Republicans was the sense of maturity he conveyed, the sense that he had been tested in life, had come to terms with his own strengths and frailties—that he is, in short, a grown-up." These data were confirmed in surveys. A national survey conducted by the *Wall Street Journal* and *NBC News* found (Hunt 1999; see also Berke 2000) that, "eleven months before voters trek to the national election polls for the first time in the new century, people are saying this election is more about leadership than partisanship, more about character and competence than ideology."

McCain voters were overwhelmingly and repeatedly likely to say that character was more important than issues in their judgment.[2] Moreover, in their view, he had the qualities for which they were searching. In the February 24-27 ABC national poll, 67 percent thought that he said what he thought (compared to 53 percent for Bush and 41 percent for Gore), and 64 percent said they thought he was a strong leader (compared to 62 percent for Bush and 45 percent for Gore).[3] A Gallup poll conducted in early February, 2000 found that among the general public sixty-two percent thought him a strong a decisive leader, and among those leaning toward the Republicans that number jumped to 65 percent. Similarly, 54 percent of the American public in a later February Gallup poll found him "a person you admire." and among those leaning Republican that number jumped to 62 percent.[4]

These data, and others that could easily be added, suggest that yes, the public was responding to the McCain candidacy through the lens of their own wishes for a different kind of leader. They were looking for and felt they found a mature, tested and proven leader who was honest and, in the words of one influential newspaper editorial board member (Rabinowitz 2000), an authentic

"American hero." The question I would like to turn to here is not so much whether they were looking for such a leader, but whether in McCain, they really found him.

I want to frame my answer to this question by clearly acknowledging the respect and admiration that Senator McCain earned by his courage and tenacity during his time as a prisoner of war. As is well known, he was shot down over North Vietnam and survived five and a half harrowing years as a prisoner of war, enduring years of solitary confinement and repeated periods of torture.[5] He returned from the war an authentic hero-a brave man, to his captors unyielding and combative. "Yet the question, as Anna Quinlin (2000) has noted, is whether "a temperament invaluable for a POW" is "significantly less useful in a head of state."

McCain, himself, realized early on that his biography was the key to making a successful presidential run. So, from the moment in 1988 when McCain decided to make a run for the White House in 2000, his strategy was to emphasize character [his] and his experience as a prisoner of war (Mitchell 2000). Writing about McCain's use of his biography Jonathan Alter noted (2000), somewhat paradoxically,

> None of this is ever made explicit and that gives it more power. While his ads pound away on the Veteran's angle, McCain wears his mantle lightly and despite the American flags festooning every campaign rally, without the usual patriotic corniness.

While noting that McCain "plays down his valor." Mitchell (1999b) detailed the ways in which "his [McCain's] campaign is relentlessly marketing his life story." As more than one observer noted (Alter 1999; emphasis mine), "McCain skilfully deploys the story by seeming not to exploit it." And in many of the Republican debates Mr. McCain could and often did call on his background to either defend himself or silence his critics.

Yet, the major issue surrounding McCain's authenticity was not his war experience, but his emotional suitability. Senator McCain's psychology became an issue almost as soon as his character and biography began to fuel his political rise. A story in McCain's home state newspaper, the *Arizona Republic*, quoted the state's governor Jane Dee Hull (a fellow Republican) as describing Mr. McCain as someone prone to fly off the handle (Broder 1999). Others, who had dealings with him in both Arizona and the Senate, confirmed that he did indeed have a large temper and often could be publicly humiliating to those with whom he disagreed. For example, George Will (1999) detailed several instances of McCain's temper outbursts that had been reported long before the issue arose in the presidential campaign. He quoted an *Atlantic Monthly*, December 1985:

> Just after the July 4 recess, as freshman Joe Barton was walking down the center aisle of the House to cast a vote, he found himself in the middle of an angry cross fire of epithets between Democrat Marty Russo, of Illinois, and Republican John McCain, of

Arizona. Seven-letter profanities escalated to twelve-letter ones and then to pushes and shoves before the two were separated.

He further reported in an article in the August 6, 1993 issue of the *Boston Globe:*

> McCain came across the Senate floor and while mocking Kennedy, told him to "shut up." according to observers in the chamber. A stunned Kennedy returned the comment, telling McCain to "shut up" and "act like a senator."

Will then went on to quote various current Republican senators, who say many of McCain's outbursts are not about matters of policy ("gross injustices") but about personal pique, speaking off the record with astonishing asperity about McCain, expressing doubts—if not conviction—that his temper is evidence of a temperament unsuited to the presidency. The disqualifying flaw, they say, is characterized by a righteousness that makes McCain disdain the motives of those who differ with him. At this point his temper became a campaign issue (Mitchell 1999a; Kurtz 1999).

At the same time, stories began to appear about a "whispering campaign," questioning whether McCain had emerged from his five plus years as a prisoner of war emotionally damaged (Drew 1999). In fact, Senator McCain himself provided biographical evidence that his volcanic temper had been an issue in his childhood. In his autobiography, McCain (1999) refers to his "outsized temper" as an infant and says that "when I got angry, I held my breath until I blacked out." He further recalls that a doctor told his parents to drop him into a bathtub of cold water when he had these outbursts. Obviously, if McCain had this level of "temper" as an infant, his POW experience could hardly be the primary cause of it.

Discussions of McCain's temper did not harm him, at least at first, with voters. A number took the position of one New Hampshire voter, "I'd rather have a commander-in-chief that loses his temper, than a wuss" (quoted in Rogers 2000). A Republican consultant not affiliated with either the Bush or McCain campaigns said (quoted in Mitchell 2000),

> Most Americans do not expect their presidents to be Casper Milquetoasts. They also don't want him flying off the handle at inappropriate times. And whether or not this matters depends on the example that Senator McCain offers to the American people.

An analysis of his Senate career (Walsh and Dewar 2000; Clymer 2000) suggests that McCain made few friends or political allies. It is also consistent with an interpersonal style that tends to move against others, rather than toward, away, or apart from them. So what? Mr. McCain is certainly not the only candidate or, had he won, president to have a temper. George Washington, Andrew Jackson, Ulysses S. Grant, Theodore Roosevelt, Warren G. Harding, Harry Truman, Dwight D. Eisenhower, Lyndon B. Johnson, and Bill Clinton (Vinciguerra 1999).[6]

Some,[7] including McCain himself,[8] saw the temper issue as a character attack designed to raise questions about his emotional stability and suitability for the presidency. In order to combat "rumors" of his psychological suitability growing out of his POW experience, McCain released over 1,500 pages of his medical records, included post-POW psychological evaluations (Altman 1999b). These records were released in a manner that made them difficult to evaluate fully, but were generally consistent with the view of Mr. McCain having come through his ordeal in fairly good emotional shape.

The picture that emerged from the report was that of a person with above average intelligence, whose ambition is both framed and shaped by a famous and highly successful father, who was, nonetheless, at sea and away from home for long periods of time. Expected to follow in his father's (and grandfather's) footsteps of going to the Naval Academy, he did, but rebelliously. There, he accumulated many demerits, but not enough to be expelled. He also did poorly academically, but not poorly enough to be asked to leave. Generally, he led a somewhat wild and undisciplined life (given his surroundings) of partying and dating attractive women, by which he made clear he was the anti-McCain McCain, a rebel and maverick. Not surprisingly, these are two terms that he uses to describe himself and that have been continually used by others to describe him and his chosen style of political leadership.

A not atypical profile of McCain suggested that he had clearly, "established himself as a maverick messenger." That same profile noted that Mr. McCain's favorite television program was *Maverick,* staring the anti-hero character played by James Garner (Rogers 2000). In another interview McCain was asked whom, besides veterans and students, he planned to recruit to his cause; he answered (quoted in Goldberg 1999), half smiling, "Oh, iconoclasts, mavericks, cranks all of those are part of the coalition we're building here."

A statement released by the McCain campaign by the director of the Center for Prisoner of War Studies[9] who evaluated Mr. McCain, said in part, "Senator McCain had never been diagnosed with or treated for a psychological or psychiatric disorder.... He has been subject to an extensive battery of psychological tests and following his last examination in 1993, we judged him to be in good physical and mental health." Less validly, given the evidence of his post-POW political career, he wrote (quoted in Altman 1999a), "Mr. McCain also learned how to control his temper and not become angry over insignificant things."

The report was clearly wrong. Of course, being judged in "good mental health" is not the same as understanding the elements that constitute a person's psychology, which is precisely the set of questions at the heart of "character issues." However, the report did provide some important clues for the analyst seeking to assemble a portrait of Mr. McCain's psychology. The report spent a substantial amount of time detailing Mr. McCain's "preoccupation" with getting out from under the shadow of his father (a highly successful admiral and

Commander of U.S. Forces), which he felt his experiences as a POW finally allowed him to do. It also details his increasing rebelliousness, doing poorly academically and behaviorally at the Naval academy, a "rebel without a cause" as Mr. McCain described it. Both are consistent with Mr. McCain's descriptions of himself and observations of him by others.

Interestingly, given Senator McCain's behavior during his candidacy, the psychological reports that he released revealed that evaluating psychiatrists used the term "histrionic personality" to describe him. Most reports detailing the release of McCain's medical files either didn't pick up this item or, if they did, confused the term with the question of whether that personality element did or did not represent "mental illness" (Fournier and Neergaard 1999; Dejevsky 1999; Editorial 1999; Associated Press 1999)·

Another typical response to the information was not knowing what to make of it and joking about it. Maureen Dowd wrote a column in which she reported a conversation with Mr. McCain during which they joked about his being the "Manchurian Candidate" (Dowd 1999). In that classic 1962 movie, Lawrence Harvey played a solider captured during the Korean War, returned home, but had been brainwashed to kill his target (the president) on command (when shown the queen of diamonds).

In a discussion on *This Week* (Transcript 1999), co-hosts Sam Donaldson, Cokie Roberts, and Linda Douglas had the following discussion about the report and the term:

Roberts: What is this word "histrionic" that's in here?

Douglas: There is—he is described as having a histrionic pattern of behavior. Our psychiatrist wasn't sure exactly what their psychiatrist meant by that.

Donaldson: Sounds awful.

Douglas: During an interview—well, histrionics can be hysteria. But of course, he was never diagnosed with hysteria, nor was he treated for hysteria nor recommended for treatment. The doctors who treated him in Pensacola say that means he has an outgoing personality (Altman 1999).

Donaldson: Why—"an outgoing personality"?

Roberts: Sam's histrionic.

Donaldson: And you're histrionic? Guilty. Thank you, Linda Douglas. Thank you very much. Well, when we come back, more on Republican politics with candidate Steve Forbes.

More serious were misunderstandings by experts. *Good Morning America* (Transcript 1999) featured one Michael Spodak, a psychiatrist, to discuss Senator McCain's files:

Gibson: Let me ask you about one phrase that appears in those records. "An hist—a histrionic pattern of personality adjustment." What does that mean?

Dr. Spodak: Yeah, basically, I thought of that when I noticed—I—first of all, it's not a diagnosis of any illness, it's simply a description of his trait, and it came, I think, shortly after he started seeking public office. And, basically, it means attention seeking. I suspect that any of us sitting in front of the television could easily be described in the same way as one of the reasons we're doing that is because we have a trait of some degree of attention-seeking behavior. It's really a description of, you know, how you interact with your environment, it's nothing suggestive of anything abnormal or unusual.

Finally, one mass circulation magazine, *Time*, picked up the term, but also had trouble understanding it. The reporter noted (Carney 1999: 43) that there were a few "unflattering disclosures" in the report like "histrionic patterns of personality adjustment" or "mildly hysterical traits" but went on to say,

> the technical terms sound more dramatic than they really are. In essence, the doctors were saying that he was prone to emotional excitability. But they said he could control it.

Well, not quite. Perhaps their confusion is understandable given the characterization of the report by Dr. Michael Ambrose, director of the Robert E. Mitchell Center for Prisoners of War Studies, who released and commented on it. He characterized a "histrionic personality" as essentially "outgoing."

That personality syndrome does appear in the Diagnostic and Statistical Manual of the American Psychiatric Association (DSM IV), and it is worth noting some of its features. The purpose in doing so is not to suggest that Senator McCain has some form of "mental illness." Rather, I want to ask whether some of the characteristics that were evident then to his evaluators will also help us to make sense of Mr. McCain's meteoric rise and spectacular demise.

According to the DSM IV, some[10] of the features of this personality profile are (American Psychiatric Association 1994: 655):

1.   Feeling uncomfortable and unappreciated when they are not the center of attention

2.   Often being lively and dramatic

3.   May initially charm new acquaintances by their enthusiasm and apparent openness...these qualities wear thin as these individuals constantly demand to be the center of attention

4.   Doing something dramatic (e.g., create a scene) to draw the focus of attention to themselves if they are not the center of attention

5.   Using a style of speech that is excessively impressionistic and lacking in detail

6.   Having a tendency to express strong opinions with dramatic flair

7.   Emotional expression that can rapidly shift

8. Being characterized by self-dramatization and an exaggerated expression of emotion

9. A tendency to embarrass friends and acquaintances by an excessive public display of emotions (e.g., having temper tantrums)

It seems clear that some of these characteristics are consistent with aspects of Senator McCain's personal and political career as well as his behavior during the campaign. A large, quick temper is consistent with this psychology, and it was on display a number of times during the campaign. In December 1999 he exploded in very harsh, personal way at a group, Americans for Tax Reform, which questioned his plans for finance reform. According to the report (Neal 1999):

> The McCain campaign struck back in highly personal terms with a blistering attack on ATR and its president, Grover Norquist, calling him "one of Washington's most notorious special interest group leaders" whose only concern was that "the soft money spigot flowing into his group's coffers" would be cut off. But McCain, who is leading Texas Gov. George W. Bush in New Hampshire polls, didn't stop there. He attacked Norquist's character, saying he had lobbied in the past for the "Marxist" president of the Republic of the Seychelles and "against a government crackdown on Internet porn."

His concession speech after his South Carolina defeat was harsh, bitter, personal, and very angry. David Brooks (2000) referred to it as, "one of the most remarkable concession speeches of recent memory, and it was a mistake." Senator McCain's "rage and indignation" came though very clearly and, "he basically called George W. Bush a fraud, a sleaze artist and an empty suit. And, he didn't regret it."[11]

McCain provided his own explanation for his temper, saying in an appearance on *Good Morning America* (Transcript 1999) that yes, he has a temper, however:

> I have gotten angry at people. And I will continue probably to get angry when I see an injustice done. I feel that, as I say, people who are not represented and people who are not well treated, particularly in the legislative process, deserve that kind of attention. And I'll continue to give it.

In other words, his anger is justifiable and in the service of a good cause. A variation of this theme was expressed during a debate among the Republican presidential candidates in which McCain said (*New York Times* transcript 1999):

> Do I feel passionately about issues? Absolutely. When I see the Congress of the United States spend $6 billion on unnecessary, wasteful pork barrel spending, and we have 12,000 enlisted families, brave men and women, on food stamps, yeah, I get angry.

Yet almost all his outbursts are consistent with the observations of his Senate colleagues, many of whom see him as, "sharp-tongued, instinctive and impatient, with a tendency to treat differences of opinion in highly personal terms" (Walsh and Dewar 2000). This characterization was consistent with the concerns raised by others in Arizona that began the national debate on McCain's temperament. Keven Ann Willey, the *Arizona Republic*'s editorial page editor, said (quoted in Kurtz 1999c), "There is a lot to admire in McCain, but we also have a fuller picture of the rest of John McCain." Noting that the senator has "shouted" at her, Willey said, "I've not been called a liar or an idiot, but I've witnessed others [at the paper] being called liars and idiots.... He's quite good at making his unhappiness plain."

A number of his angry charges are vague and impressionistic. Senator McCain's use of the term "reform" and his repeated attacks on the "iron triangle" of "special interests" are cases in point. As Andrew Fergeson (2000) noted,

> The rhetorically extravagant message of a country highjacked by nameless forces of evil ("special interests") may seem far-fetched...McCain's genius has been to understand that it is precisely this affluence and good cheer that make genuine ideas irrelevant...reform...under which people can toss all of their small residual grievances, their nagging unsatisfied wants, whatever they are.

Michele Cottle (2000) made the same point:

> Everyone sees McCain as a crusader—but, depending on their druthers, they see him as a crusader against big tobacco or against gun control or against the decline of the military. Anything you don't like can be labeled a "special interest." It's an ironic strategy for a straight talker.

His vagueness also extends to his discussions of many issues on domestic affairs. As Alison Mitchell (1999) noted, "once off the topics of the campaign finance law or national security policy, he can seem surprisingly uninterested in detail." Until well into his campaign, McCain confused Medicare and Medicaid, using them interchangeably. When asked at some of his forums how he would solve a particular problem he responded by saying he would bring together the best minds to do so, a promise made in 1992 by Ross Perot. Senator McCain's lack of preparation for basic questions about his domestic policy positions is all the more striking because his campaign started in earnest in 1998.

Senator McCain is no stranger to dramatic self-referential statements. During one debate (Transcript, *Larry King Live* 2000), he promised to "fight for reform until the last breath I draw so that we can get the American people back connected with their government." His dramatic and impressionistic characterization of Mr. Faldwell and Mr. Robertson as "evil" falls into the same category (Barstow 2000).

He also has shown a tendency to couple dramatic charges with little substantiation. Shortly before this an important set of primaries' ads appeared attacking Senator McCain's record. The ads' sponsor was initially identified only as Republicans for Clean Air. On Friday, March 3, 2000, Sam Wyly, a wealthy

Texas investment banker with ties to Bush and whose brother and business partner, Charles, is a major Bush fund-raiser, acknowledged financing the ads independent of the Bush campaign (Stevenson with Perez-Pena 2000).

Without offering proof, McCain campaign manager Rick Davis charged that the attacks were being orchestrated by the Bush campaign, which would be a violation of federal campaign laws. Wyly denied the charge, and Bush said he knew nothing about the ads. McCain called the ads "a dreadful thing" and "shameful conduct." He continued (quoted in Walsh and Neal 2000),

> And guess what? Governor Bush says he doesn't know a thing about it. And the guys who are running the ads are cronies of his who have made millions of dollars, guess what from—investing millions of dollars that belong to the University of Texas. So it's wrong, it's wrong, it's wrong.

At a news conference after his temper became an issue Senator McCain charged that George Bush had sent a memo to supporters of his campaign suggesting they attack Mr. McCain on the issue of emotional suitability. When asked about this on *Meet the Press* (Transcript 1999), the following discussion took place:

> *Mr. Russert*: ...you had a press conference at the San Francisco airport. You said, "I guess the memo from the Bush campaign has come out to attack John McCain."

> *Mr. McCain*: I...

> *Mr. Russert*: Was there any memo or do you regret saying that?

> *Mr. McCain*: I regret saying it and that I was speaking metaphorically. And ever since then, I've said, "Look, I have no evidence," and the fact is, it's not something that I can worry about.

McCain's "straight-talk express" and unlimited access on it were also consistent not only with his campaign strategy as an "underdog." but with his psychology and self-presentation as enthusiastically open and accessible.[12] His enthusiasm for his candidacy led reporters to ask how long it had been since "we've had a Happy Warrior on the campaign trail," and to note that "Now a Happy Warrior is plying the roads of New Hampshire in a big white bus that rings with laughter (Von Drehle 2000). His quick change from Happy Warrior to enraged and vindictive losing candidate after his South Carolina defeat raised questions about the depth and staying power of his "happy warrior" persona (Balz and Edsall 2000).

Some critics suggested that McCain's legendary openness was substantially strategic. Ralph Reed, the former Christian Coalition leader who advised Governor Bush, said of McCain's openness (quoted in Henneberger 2000): "He says all the time, 'I was wrong on that vote." McCain has learned the value of winning an argument by conceding the point, but that works better in the cloakroom than in a primary." Some reporters (Kurtz 1999a) wondered whether they were being "spun." Other observers (Alter 2000) agreed "they're right" to wonder whether that was true. It was. As Howard Fineman (2000) noted, McCain's success is,

> the work of a driven and indefatigable campaigner, with a knack for appearing far less calculating than he really is. He has a game plan and a nothing-to-lose attitude to hide it.

Senator McCain sees himself in heroic terms. He also appears to divide the world into good guys and bad guys. For someone who sees himself as the mythical Luke Skywalker,[13] and uses the Star Wars' theme song as his campaign theme song (Mitchell and Bruni 2000), it is not too far a reach to say of himself (quoted in Barstow 2000; see also Broder 2000), "To stand up and take on the forces of evil, that's my job." Nor is it a reach to say as he did (quoted in Von Drehle 2000) while campaigning in New Hampshire, "I feel like Luke Skywalker in the Death Star. We're headed out, after destroying all the bad guys."

Clearly, McCain's life-long (and chosen political) role as rebel and maverick is consistent with his psychology. Being a maverick requires one to take positions that attract attention and controversy and mark that person as a non-ordinary politician. This might be especially attractive to someone whose political career has been somewhat conventional in many respects, and not particularly outstanding.

This, however, is not Senator McCain's view. In the March 3, 2000 Republican debate (Transcript, *Larry King Live* 2000) he said,

> I've had 234 major pieces of legislation and amendments passed while I've been in the United States Senate and Congress. One of the most successful records, whether it be in the area of reform, whether it be in the important issues of telecommunications, such as Y2K product liability, whether it be Internet tax moratorium, or whether it be in every major foreign policy issue that has confronted this country. My credentials are well known.

Asked during one of the debates, what he had accomplished on education across eighteen years in Congress, Mr. McCain had to reach back to his years in the House of Representatives to cite his service on the House Education Committee and spoke vaguely of "being involved in the effort in my state for reform in many ways." The answer was so vague that the Bush campaign promptly put out a statement mocking it (Purdham and Mitchell 2000).

Senator McCain's behavior during the campaign raised questions about his personal commitment to his signature campaign theme, campaign finance reform. Mr. McCain had been implicated, along with four other senators, in an influence peddling attempt (The Keating Five) that resulted in a probe and reprimand by the Senate Ethics Committee. As chairman of the powerful Senate Commerce Committee he had been given large campaign contributions by a number of large companies interested in securing his approval of their plans, a fact acknowledged by him. When Mr. McCain appeared with Democratic presidential hopeful Senator Bradley to discuss campaign finance reform he said (quoted in Kutz 1999), "I believe I probably have been influenced because the big donor buys access to my office and we know that access is influence." Shortly thereafter, letters emerged that Mr. McCain had written on behalf of large campaign contributors to the F.C.C. in an attempt to help his contributors (Labaton 2000a,b; Excerpts, *New York Times* 2000).

Senator McCain has labeled his experience before the Senate Ethics committee as the worst in his life, surpassing even his POW experience.[14] He also said that he had learned from the ethics review experience that it is not just corruption, but the appearance of corruption that mattered. How he could reconcile this view with his acceptance of large corporate campaign donations from the companies he regulated, and his use of private corporate jets for campaign travel,was never resolved.

These were not the only instances of inconsistencies that raised questions. Senator McCain promised to run a "different" positive campaign, but resorted to a harsh personal attack ad that accused George Bush of "twisting the truth like Bill Clinton" (Edsall 2000). Before the Michigan primary the McCain campaign was responsible for placing calls to prospective voters accusing Mr. Bush of being anti-Catholic. When Mr. Bush complained, the campaign and Mr. McCain denied they were involved. After the polls were closed, Mr. McCain admitted that yes, his campaign had placed those calls but then defended them as simply alerting voters to Bush's position (Bruni 2000). During a Republican campaign debate he denied responsibility for an anti-Bush flier that his campaign in fact had distributed (Broder 2000). These and similar episodes were inconsistent with his signature promise that "I will always tell you the truth—no matter what."[15]

Certainly, periodic or chronic displays of temper toward those with whom one works leads to a decreased ability to continue to do so. In McCain's case, however, it is not clear how much a role his temper plays and how much a role his taking positions contrary to the views of his party play in the issues at hand (Mitchell 1999a). Moreover, anger can be an effective tool for chief executives if Richard Neustadt is correct about others always gauging the seriousness of the president's commitments and the consequences for opposing him.

Expectations that Mr. McCain would get testy when confronted with his own not wholly consistent attempts to champion campaign finance reform while writing letters on behalf of large contributors did not materialize, although several commentators did notice the somewhat inappropriate smile that seemed frozen in place when he was asked about these issues.[16] Still, a highly volatile temperament even if held in check publicly, would be inconsistent with arriving a solid judgments on matters large and small, and might well have an adverse impact on a president's ability to form the coalitions necessary to pass legislation or gather public support.

Senator McCain's well-publicized consideration of his possible role as an independent challenger to President Bush in 2004 makes sense from his self-interested political perspective. The news that he was even considering such a move was an important story in many national newspapers and media commentary. It thus, in a stroke, increased both his visibility and possibly his bargaining power. Moreover, the fact that he made clear that "no decision was imminent." insured that speculation, attention and the possible political bargaining power that the comment brought would continue as renewable resources.

Were the senator to actually bolt the Republican Party and run as an Independent, it is extremely difficult to see how he could assemble enough votes, popular or electoral, to win office. He might be as potent as Ross Perot was the first time he ran, but he could well wind up doing worse. In any event, there would be little realistic chance of his winning, but certainly a realistic chance of damaging the re-election candidacy of President Bush.

However, that possibility, while being realistic, is by no means a certainty. Much depends on how George W. Bush conducts his presidency. Recall that Senator McCain's chief hold on the public's imagination was his persona as a straight-talking leader, with a heroic patina. Mr. Bush, too, however, has in his first months in office proved to be a president of strong views and decisive actions. This may capture some of the public sentiment that fueled McCain's rise. Mr. Bush adds to that a political persona with few sharp edges, a reassuring leadership stance.

Senator McCain said that before bolting the Republican Party to run as an independent, he would first assume a leadership position of Republican moderates. His aides suggested that he had in mind a Republican counterpart to the role that the "Democrat Leadership Council" has played in the traditional left-leaning Democratic Party. At a time when the Senate is almost evenly divided and moderates of both political parties are critical to passing any of the president's agenda, such a move would allow Senator McCain increased political and policy influence.

Some analysis has pointed out that the senator has, since his presidential run, become increasing distant from the conservative base that fueled his political career. Some of his new positions are not easily distinguished from liberal democrats. What, exactly, motivated this substantial change of career-long positions is at this point unclear. Certainly, the senator gave no indication during this presidential campaign that he had turned away from the many policy positions with which he had been associated.

Whatever the personal and political considerations that are fueling Senator McCain's new-found position as a born-again, left-leaning Republican, the changes are very consistent psychologically. Mr. McCain has spent a lifetime as a scrappy maverick. He has worn his tendency to go against the grain like a badge of honor. Certainly, it has been a central element of his psychology and self-image.

His ability to provoke has a long history. So does his capacity to endure the consequences. His man-sized temper as a child led to his being given the cold-water immersion treatment. When captured by the North Vietnamese he endured beatings and solitary confinement, but he also took some satisfaction in provoking his jailers. And he has increasingly taken the role—with campaign finance, patients' bill of rights, and gun laws--of a maverick Republican, much to the dismay of his party. Mr. McCain spent his early life, like Al Gore and George W. Bush, in the shadow of a highly successful but somewhat absent father. Like them, he bridled at the future laid out for him even as its psychological gravity propelled him toward it. Like Vice President Gore and President Bush, Senator McCain took some time to find his life's footing. In his case, the stubborn iconoclasm coupled with his heroic determination during his POW captivity gave him a public standing on his return home that fused his psychology as a maverick with a heroic self-image.

That fusion reached its zenith in Senator McCain's run for the presidency. He was widely respected, even honored by a mostly adoring press. He was able to mount a strong challenge to the front-runner, Mr. Bush. And, he was able to place himself where me most prized being, as the highly visible head of a crusade for a cause—campaign finance reform—in which he had come to believe so passionately, if somewhat tardily.

In short, Senator McCain had become a politically prominent maverick with a cause, and a following. In that position he is able to command and receive public attention, a powerful inducement to him psychologically. That, coupled with a view of himself as an embattled individualist perusing a noble and difficult cause, is a powerful emotional combination for Mr. McCain. However, it is a not a particularly effective recipe for governing in a divided democracy.

Moreover, there remains the question of Mr. McCain's capacity for leadership. No, not the leadership that comes in the form of command, but rather through partnerships. Throughout his career, Senator McCain has demonstrated not only that he finds satisfaction in going it alone, but in having it his way. His Senate career is noticeable for its lack of working partnerships, even within his own party.

His recent sponsorship with other members of the Democratic Party (e.g., gun control with Senator Lieberman and patient's rights with Senator Kennedy) appears to, but does not contradict this point. In a closely divided Senate, both of his Democratic partners have many political reasons beyond policy for aligning themselves with Mr. McCain's maverick Republican stance. Whether Mr. McCain would find it possible to build the kind of broad support that governing in such circumstances requires is a very open question.

Mr. McCain sees himself and is in the "heroic" mode of leadership. Yet, he couples that with a somewhat self-righteous view of his positions that allows little space for those who oppose him. As noted, he has a tendency to lash out at others, often in the most personal way. This is not a good recipe for governing in a divided society.

Finally, there is the issue of the relationship between his temperament and his judgment. Mr. McCain's tendency to anger, its often-personal nature, and his insistence on doing things his way, provide fertile terrain for mistakes of judgment. Moreover, the apparent change in his core beliefs raises the question: what deeply held convictions beyond his own self-view as an embattled maverick will temper and anchor his ambitions?

It is possible that Mr. McCain will mount a challenge to President Bush, in part because of a rift–personal and political—between them. The larger possibility, however, is that such a challenge would be fueled by Senator McCain's heart-felt conviction that he, his followers, and his political views have not been given sufficient deference by Mr. Bush. That will be an easily felt view for Mr. McCain, given his psychology, and a difficult political and psychological current for President Bush to negotiate. Senator McCain is very unlikely to be able to win the presidency, but he can help President Bush and his party to lose it.

Notes

1.   See note 3, chapter 6 for an explanation of this term.
2.   And so, when an ABC poll asked which mattered more, character or issues to voters, it recorded the following results (Langer 2000):

Which matters more?

	All	McCain	Gore
Issues	18%	46%	48%
Character	59	79	19
Both equally	23	63	30

3.   Interestingly, respondents seemed to distinguish "having the right personality," a question that did not distinguish among the candidates (McCain-61 percent, Bush-64 percent, and Gore-60 percent), from the more specific questions concerning strength of leadership and political honesty/integrity (Langer 2000).
4.   See Gallup Poll Surveys, February 20-21, 2000 (http://www.gallup.com) March, 1, 2000.
5.   The harrowing details can be found in John McCain (1999: 189-257). His teeth were smashed, his ribs cracked, his arms were tied behind his back and he was suspended, and he was suffering from severe dysentery, Mr. McCain still refused the early release that was offered to him by the Vietnamese in the hopes of securing a propaganda coup.
6.   On Dwight Eisenhower's temper, see Greenstein (1982), on Bill Clinton's temper, see Renshon (1998: 109-111).
7.   Chuck Hagel, Republican Senator from Nebraska and supporter of McCain is quoted (in Mitchell 1999b; see also *Boston Globe* editorial 1999) as seeing the temper issue, "as a not-so-subtle attempt to make a point that McCain's service to his country, five and a half years in a prisoner of war camp, may mean he is not stable enough to be President of the United States."
8.   The issue came up directly in Mr. McCain's appearance on *Meet the Press*;

Mr. Russert: Here's the *New York Times*: McCain releases medical files to counter whisper campaign. What's the whisper campaign?

Mr. McCain: I don't know, and I hope it goes away. But, by the way, it may have the effect of allaying any concerns that people might have. But I had planned on releasing my medical records from the beginning. I thought it was just something that presidential candidates do. And, by the way, it's about 1,500 pages of an orthopedic surgeon's nightmare or dream, depending on how you view it. But I don't know if there's any whispering campaign. It doesn't matter to me. I think the thing is that we need to move forward and I hope that this will be—at least have that beneficial effect.

9.   Only one report looked into the circumstances surrounding the post- POW study group from which McCain's records were released. It noted (quoted in Gamerman 1999), veterans by nature are not a touchy-feely bunch. If they had psychological problems, a military doctor probably would be the last person they would tell. Most people say, "I don't have any problems. OK, see you next year," said Mike McGrath, a former naval aviator, who was held for more than five years in Hanoi and now serves as head of the lobbying group, NAM-POW. "Only the crazy people talk about themselves—you're never going to get a pilot talking to a psychologist. That's wishy-washy."

10. Any diagnostic syndrome or category contains a range of elements, some of which may, and some of which may not, fit a specific individual person. Clinically, the question is whether enough of the major elements that define the category are present to give the clinician a useful understanding of a person. There is no assumption that the person must exhibit all of the diagnostic markers.

11. In an appearance on *Meet the Press,* Mr. McCain refused to entertain the suggestion of Tim Russert that likening Mr. Bush to Mr. Clinton in a commercial had been a "monumental mistake" (Marks 2000).

12. It is very important to note that psychological understandings do not require that one ignore other, political explanations.

13. At a Michigan talk McCain said (quoted in Romano and Neal 2000), "You saw 'Star Wars,' right? I'm just like Luke Skywalker trying to get out of the Death Star. They're shooting at me from everywhere. Everybody's against me. [Michigan] Governor [John] Engler, Governor Bush, all the governors, all the senators. But we're going to kill 'em…we're going to win this election."

In the Republican debate before the South Carolina primary this exchange took place (Transcript, *Larry King Live* 2000):

McCain: Well, I've been labeled everything except—I think they missed fascist. (Laughter) But look, I'm enjoying it. This is a great and exhilarating experience.

King: But you are...

Bush: John, you're...

McCain: I'm Luke Skywalker getting out of the Death Star.

14. Senator McCain later toned down this comparison that he disavowed as "sophistry" (quoted in Walsh 2000). Of course, the too easy, dramatic, but unrepresentative comparison could well be counted as another indication of Mr. McCain's propensity for dramatic self-representation.

Whether the experience was parallel, there is little doubt that given Mr. McCain's concern with honor, the experience wounded his sense of his fidelity to his own ideals. It is thus possible that his devoted concern with campaign finance is related to the blemish on his record that orovided the example of the corrupting influences.

15. In one of his many mentions of this pledge, at the Republican debate before the South Carolina primary, he said (Transcript, *Larry King Live* 2000),

But most of all, I'd like to end up by recounting a story that happened at my 100th town hall meeting in New Hampshire. A lady stood up and she looked me in the eye and she didn't have a question. She said, "Senator McCain, it's vitally important to me that the next president of the United States always tell me the truth." "I promise you as president of the United States, based on my life, my principles and the caution of my old dear friends, I will always tell you the truth, no matter what."

16.   Caryn James (1999; see also Collins 2000), discussing what news clips taken from the Republican presidential debates did and did not reflect, says "what the clips did not reflect was the way in which Mr. McCain suddenly flashed a frozen smile as he trotted out a canned joke about his temper." Discussing his performance during one of the Republican debates, Gail Collins noted that McCain, "trying to fight rumors of a bad temper, had developed a terrible tendency to grin mechanically no matter what he was talking about."

References

Alter, Jonathan. "A Very Human Hero." *Newsweek,* 14 February 2000: 31-32.
_____. "White Tornado." *Newsweek,* 15 November 1999: 45.
Altman, Lawrence K. "Release of McCain's Medical Records Provides Unusually Broad Psychological Profile." *New York Times,* 6 December 1999a: A26.
_____. "McCain Releases Medical Files to Counter Whispering Campaign." *New York Times,* 5 December 1999b: A34.
American Psychiatric Association. *Diagnostic and Statistical Manual of Mental Disorders, Fourth Edition.* Washington, DC: APA, 1994.
Associated Press. "A Look at McCain's Medical Records." 4 December 1999.
Balz Dan,and Thomas B. Edsall. "McCain Struggles to Regain Support, Aide: Senator 'Got Off Message' in S.C." *Washington Post,* 21 February 2000: A01.
Barstow, David. "McCain, in Further Attack, Leaders of Christian Right `Evil." *New York Times,* 1 March 2000:A1.
Berke, Richard. "The New Hampshire Race: Personality, Not Policy, Sways Voters in a Primary." *New York Times,* 13 January 2000:A01.
Broder, David S. "Next Tuesday May Be Senator's Last Chance" *Washington Post,* 1 March 2000a:A07.
_____. "A Winner Once More." *Washington Post,* 21 February 2000b: A27.
_____. "Character Study." *Washington Post,* 8 February 2000c: A23.
_____. "McCain's Past Comes Back to Haunt Him." *Washington Post Weekly Edition,* 6 December 1999: 13.
Brooks, David. "Playing It Safe Works, for Now." *New York Times,* 21 February 2000:A1.
Bruni, Frank. "Bush Angry Over Calls to Catholics." *New York Times,* 23 February 2000.
Carney, James. "The Diagnosis: 'Stable.'" *Time,* December 13, 1999:43.
Clymer, Adam. "The Senate Record: For McCain, Concerns in Senate Are Subtle." *New York Times,* 4 March 2000:A1.
Collins, Gail. "Talk about a Fast Finish." *New York Times,* 7 January 2000:A23.
Cottle, Michele. "Campaign Journal: Open Season." *The New Republic,* 21 February 2000.
Dejevsky, Mary. "Senator Reveals All to Prove his Sanity." *The Independent (London),* 6 December 1999:13.
Dowd, Maureen. "Nuts or Guts?" *New York Times,* 21 November 1999: wk. 15.
Drew, Elizabeth. "Those Whispers About McCain." *Washington Post Weekly Edition,* 29 November 1999: 27.
Editorial. "The Attempt to Smear McCain." *Boston Globe,* 12 December 1999: D6.

Editorial. "Senator McCain's Health." *New York Times*, 7 December 1999: A22.

Edsall, Thomas B. "Negativity Took Toll on McCain Reformer Image." *Washington Post*, 20 February 2000:A10.

Election 2000. The South Carolina Republican Debate, CNN, February 15, 2000. Available at www. CNN/Transcript (February 19, 2000).

Excerpts, "McCain's Letter to F.C.C. and Excerpts from Replies." *New York Times*, 7 January 2000:A 22.

Fergeson, Andrew. "The Message is the Message." *Time*, 14 February 2000: 45.

Fineman, Howard. "The McCain Mutiny." *Newsweek*, 14 February 2000:25.

Fournier, Ron, and Lauran Neergaard. "Doctors Give McCain Clean Bill of Health; Records Said to Rebut 'Whisper Campaign.'" *San Diego Union-Tribune*, 5 December 1999, A-17.

Gamerman, Ellen. "A special breed: Ex-POWs' Medical Examinations Unmask Lingering Trauma of War." *Baltimore Sun*, 6 December 1999: 3A .

Goldberg, Carey. "A Holiday Offers Good News for McCain." *New York Times*, 12 November 1999:A28.

Greenstein, Fred I. *The Hidden Hand Presidency*. New York: Basic Books, 1982.

Henneberger, Melinda. "Growing Pains: The Hobgoblins of Politics: Change and Consistency." *New York Times*, 20 February 2000.

Hunt, Albert Jr. "Voter's Desire for Leadership Gives Bush an Edge." *Wall Street Journal*, 16 December 1999: A9.

James, Caryn."Debate gives Boxing Another Black Eye." *New York Times*, 4 December 1999:A14.

Kristof, Nicholas D. "Leaning Toward Bush But Interested in McCain." *New York Times*, 8 February 2000: A21.

Kuntz, Phil. "McCain's Financing Stance Recalls Keating-Five Role." *Wall Street Journal*, 17 December 1999:A16.

Kurtz, Howard. "Open. Candid. Believable? Who knows." *Washington Post*, 26 December 1999a: B01.

_____. "John McCain: Hero or Hothead?" *Washington Post National Edition*, 8 November 1999b: 13.

_____. "McCain Tries to Temper Reports of His Outbursts Home State Editorial Countered National Raves." *Washington Post*, 2, November 1999c: A03.

Labaton, Stephan. "Issue for McCain is Matching Record with His Rhetoric." *New York Times,* 7 January 2000a: A16.

_____. "McCain Urged F.C.C. Action on Issue Involving Supporter." *New York Times*, 6 January 2000b: A1.

Langer, Gary. "The McCain Phenomenon: John McCain's favorability numbers have soared as those of his opponent, George W. Bush, have sunk." February 28, 2000 (www. ABCNEWS.com).

Marks, Peter. "Bush Barked, but Voters Felt Only McCain's Bite." *New York Times*, 21 February 2000.

McCain, John, with Mark Salter. *Faith of My Fathers*. New York: Random House, 1999.

Mitchell, Alison " McCain, Sure on Military Issues. Is Less Certain on Domestic Ones." *New York Times*, 9 February 2000a: A1.

_____. "The Inside Outsiders Behind John McCain." *New York Times*, 6 February 2000b: A1.

_____. "McCain's Anti-Politics Style is Proving to Be Good Politics." *New York Times*, 30 December 1999a.

_____. "Temperament Issues Poses Test for McCain." *New York Times*, 5 November 1999b: A12.

_____. "McCain Exhorts His Party to Reject Campaign System." *New York Times*, 1 July 1999c: A17.

_____. "The Mantle of the Maverick Suits McCain." *New York Times*, 7 July 1999d: A1.

Mitchell, Alison, with Frank Bruni." Bush and McCain Swap Strategies for Next Battle." *New York Times*, 21 February 2000.

Montaigne. *The Complete Works of Montainge* [translated by Donald M. Frame]. Stanford CA: Stanford University Press, 1948.

Neal, Terry M. "Tax Reform Group Attacks, McCain Fires Back." *New York Times*, 26 December 1999: A32.

Purdham, Todd S., and Alison Mitchell. "The Candidates Return to Familiar Issues: Recriminations and Religious Tolerance. *New York Times*, 2 March 2000.

Quinlin, Anna. "We're Off to See the Wizard." *Newsweek*, 28 February 2000: 76.

Rabinowitz, Dorothy. " Why They Love McCain." *Wall Street Journal*, 10 March 2000: A18.

Renshon, Stanley A. *High Hopes: The Clinton Presidency and the Politics of Ambition.* New York: Routledge, 1998a.

_____. *The Psychological Assessment of Presidential Candidates*. New York: Routledge, 1998b.

Rogers, David. "McCain Mystery is Whether Voter Love Feast will Last." *Wall Street Journal,* 3 January 2000: A20.

Romano, Lois, and Terry M. Neal. "McCain Pulls No Punches in Mich.GOP Establishment Pushes for Bush; Anti-abortion Messages Target Senator." *Washington Post*, 22 February 2000: A01.

Stevenson, Richard W., with Richard Perez-Pena. "Major Bush Donor Reveals He Ran Anti-McCain Ads." *New York Times*, 3 March 2000.

New York Times. "Transcript: Republican Candidates Presidential Debate." 3 December 1999 (http://www.nytimes.com/yr/mo/day/national/index-politics.html).

Transcript. *ABC: This Week*. December 5, 1999.

Transcript. *Meet the Press*. December 5, 1999.

Transcript. *ABC: Good Morning America*. December 6, 1999.

Transcript. *Larry King Live*: Election 2000, The South Carolina Republican Debate, CNN, and February 15, 2000. Available at www. CNN/Transcript (February 19, 2000).

Vinciguerra, Thomas. "Hell from the Chief: Hot Tempers and Presidential Timber." *New York Times*, 7 November 1999: wk. 7.

Von Drehle, David. "Campaign Diary McCain Seeks Favor as Happy Warrior; His Pitch: Straight Talk, Good Times." *Washington Post*, 31 January 2000:A06.

Walsh, Edward. "A Would-Be Admiral Splashes into the Sea of Politics." *Washington Post*, 21 January 2000: A01.

Walsh, Edward, and Helen Dewar. "'Stirring the Pot' in an Elite Club." *Washington Post*, 3 March 2000: A01.

Walsh, Edward, and Terry M. Neal. "McCain Hits TV Ad Blitz from Texas: Voters are Urged to Condemn Bush Backers' 'Dirty Money.'" '*Washington Post*, 5 March 2000: A20.

Will, George F. "The Politics of Sanctimony." *Washington Post*, 14 November 1999: B07.

Part 5

Political Leadership and the Dilemmas of Diversity

11

The Psychology of Courage and the Politics of Truth: Governing a Divided Society

What does it take for a leader to govern effectively in a divided society? The answer is both surprisingly simple yet extraordinarily difficult. It takes a capacity to tell the truth and bear the consequences of doing so.

To tell the truth, one must first know it. Admittedly, this is sometimes difficult. Truth is often complex and sometimes difficult to discern.

Truth is a large word, and I mean no conclusive definition of it here. Rather, I use the term to denote a well realized appreciation of the meaning of the facts as they can be discerned and a competent judgment regarding their importance and implication. In short, truth reflects an understanding that carries logical, empirical, and epistemological weight. There is no implication here that such understandings are the only ones capable of being reached, or that they are necessarily without error, or unrelated to the perspective of the person reaching them. All that is required here is that the person reaching the understanding has the experience, capacity, and motivation to do so.

The paucity of truth among political leaders is not a function of truth's complexity. The problem lies elsewhere. The start of the dilemma is that political leaders are often in the same position as psychoanalysts[1] —they know more than it is prudent to say. One of the clearest reflections of leaderless politics is the incapacity of political leaders to tell the truth, or the capacity and desire of the public to hear it. Knowing the truth is hard, telling the truth is often harder. Why? It can be unsettling to those who hear and costly to those who tell it.

Consider psychoanalytic psychotherapy which consists of assisting the patient to learn about him or herself. This is often not an easy experience. In therapy, patients must eventually face their losses and disappointments. Among these are errors of judgment or actions that have caused oneself or others harm. Mistakes are often difficult to acknowledge; avoidable mistakes even more so. In the therapeutic process individuals often come to see that what looked inevitable at the time was, in fact, a matter of choice—the patient's choice.

The truth telling difficulties of political leadership are more dependent on the circumstances. Political leadership in consensual periods is very unlike the therapeutic process described above. Policy debates about incremental changes do not try to reconcile fundamentally different points of view. When most agree, the work of leadership is expressing, preserving, and perhaps extending that consensus.

However, when there is no consensus the real work of leadership begins. One might say: The greater the lack of basic consensus, the larger the *potential* for political leadership. The leader in these circumstances is easily stuck. Whatever he does will arouse strong feelings. Even doing nothing is not feasible, because all sides who are dissatisfied want change, but in their direction. The obvious need in such circumstances is to develop a new understanding that can serve as building blocks for common purpose.

Nonetheless, it is a difficult position. The leader who may develop such an understanding is now in the position of the psychoanalyst. The psychoanalyst, after some time and thought, may well have arrived at a theoretically informed sense of things about the patient that the patient does not yet realize, or cannot yet acknowledge. There are many individual reasons why such information may be difficult for the patient to accept. In most cases the process of self-understanding and acceptance is neither quick nor easy.

Similarly, even the most modestly intelligent or insightful leader is in possession of far more understanding than he/she is often willing to convey. The reasons for this fact are not obscure. Almost all leaders are educated through college and often beyond. Many have travelled, which broadens perspective. Most have become conversant with different types of social and political issues. And, in the course of their political careers, most leaders have had to address the details of specific policy debates.

I am not arguing that leaders will automatically make *good* judgments about policy or politics. Nor am I arguing that deeply held ideological convictions can't and don't sometimes adversely influence judgment. I am only saying that if anyone were in a position to know "the truth," it would be those who have the education, training, and experience to recognize it as such.

It is certainly possible that there are political leaders who lack the capacity to reach such understandings. Their focus may be too narrow, their experience too limited, or their thinking simply deficient. Yet, many of the those who have sought to lead this country in the last two decades have had their own strong visions, have not lacked for experience, and certainly have given no evidence of being cognitively incapable of reaching understandings to convey to us. No, the problem lies elsewhere.

The analyst faced with the dilemmas between what one knows and what can be usefully told has some tools available to bridge this gap. They are found in the therapist's approach to interventions, be they interpretations, clarifications, or simply framing the issues. Most therapists rarely make direct, authoritative statements. Rather they often rely on statements that are phrased in a conditional or tentative manner. For example, the analyst may say, "I have the sense that...," or "You seem to think that...," or "I wonder if it's possible that you...," and so on.

There is more to this approach than a pro-forma acknowledgement of uncertainty or professional modesty. Rather it reflects the understanding that casting analytic interventions in a directly authoritative way runs several risks. Among the most important for our discussion here is the risk that, even if the intervention is factually correct, it will be too much for the patient to acknowledge and integrate. The clinical and therapeutic responsibility to "tell the truth" is essential to any successful therapy, but working up to the understanding, accepting and building on these truths to effectuate change is a large and important part of that process.

The political leader faced with the same dilemma has few such tools and faces greater difficulties in bridging the gap. Were a political leader to use the same phrasing noted above that analysts use, he or she would be roundly condemned for being equivocal, unsure, and lacking in either knowledge or authority. Worse, unlike the psychoanalysts the political leader cannot count on the underlying alliance that is one foundation of successful analytic relationships. Most people seek analysis because they want to redress an issue that is causing them difficulties in important areas of their lives. So while confronting uncomfortable understandings is not easy, it is made less difficult by the hope that the results will prove worth the distress.

The political leader however, can count on no such alliance. Especially in divided societies the leader can be guaranteed to have many opponents, even enemies, tepid supporters, and friends who may be too politically dispersed to make matters easy. There are no tools or approaches, comparable to the analyst's tentative explorations, to aid the political leader in bridging these gaps. In these circumstances "bi-partisanship" is not a conflict avoidant tool to reach consensus.

Calls for "bi-partisanship" are frequently heard in such circumstances. However, bi-partisanship is most frequently effective when parties agree about fundamental premises. In the circumstances that existed after the 2000 presidential election, bi-partisanship was not a conflict avoidant tool to reach a consensus so much as a continuation of the conflict that follows by other means. Consider for example, the illustration that follows drawn from the first days of the new Bush administration.

In Arsenic, Truth?

Leaders who wish to tell the truth as they see it run the risk in acutely divided societies such as ours of having the opposition characterize their views in harsh, inaccurate, and politically damaging ways. Consider in this regard the flare up over the amount of arsenic that the government would allow in the water. George W. Bush decided to review a regulation put into place at the end of his predecessor's term on the amount of arsenic allowed in drinking water. Since 1942 the allowable level was put at 50 parts per billion. After seven years in office, Mr. Clinton proposed an 80 percent reduction of that figure to 10 parts per billion, although some had argued for an even lower figure of 5 parts per billion.

Now there is no doubt that arsenic is a poison. Yet it is not primarily a problem of industry, but one of nature. That is, arsenic occurs naturally in nature. As a result, it enters the rivers and streams that provide our drinking water all over the United States. Like other aspects of nature, the natural occurrence of arsenic is not evenly distributed. It occurs more frequently in the topological conditions of the Western states, Midwest, and New England states than it does, say in the Northeast. As a result the filtration plants that treat water in the latter areas have less arsenic to remove than do areas where it occurs more readily.

Why should this matter? Well, one fact is that small cities and towns in the areas where arsenic occurs most naturally are also those places in which redesigning their water filtration systems would be a tremendous financial burden. Affected communities would like to see some hard scientific evidence that the financial burden is worth the effort (Egan 2001; Waldman and Fialka 2001), but as detailed below, this is no easy matter. Some say: So what? We know arsenic is a poison so whatever it takes to make drinking water safe should be done.

Yet, it is not that simple. The EPA, charged with the responsibility to set such environmental rules, must do so after conducting a cost-benefit analysis. In this case, the "costs" are the financial and health care costs that must be borne by communities. The benefits are the number of lives saved by the lowering of arsenic levels, which means in essence the revamping of filtration systems to comply with new lower mandated levels. That cost was estimated to be $200 million per year to municipalities, states, and industry (Heilprin 2001). Mr. Bush asked the EPA and the National Academy of Sciences to evaluate the effects of a level of between 3 and 20 parts per billion (Cummings 2001). The National Academy of Sciences had said in 1999 that the level should be lowered from the 50 parts per billion, but did not say to what level (Allen 2001).

How exactly is this analysis done? How do we know how much arsenic per billion is "safe?" The answer is, we don't really know, exactly. All the figures are based on estimates, yet how these estimates are arrived at is of importance in understanding the scientific though not the political debate.

Our lives are priceless, to us, but public health cost-benefit analyses make different assumptions. They are forced to put a value on individual lives, which, of course, will be less that than we would assign to our own. Sebastian Mallaby (2001; see also Kolata 2001) reviewed the methods and found,

In preparing its arsenic rule, the EPA equated one statistical life to ten non-fatal cases of cancer. It then added up the cancer cases it hoped to prevent and estimated that the arsenic rule would save 28 statistical lives each year. Using a value of 6.1 million for each "life" that works out to 170 million worth of expected health benefits from the arsenic rule. But the agency also calculated that the cost of removing the arsenic from water would come to 210 million dollars each year. In other words, costs exceed benefits by $40 million.

Scientists trying to address these issues must rely on estimates and extrapolations (Waldman 2001; Mallaby 2001). There are really two forms of extrapolation. One form consists of generalizing effects from one level of occurrence to another. A first question is whether dose effects are best understood by linear models, e.g., an increase in one unit of x leads to an increase in one unit of y. However, the human body can process low levels of many toxins, including arsenic. So maybe there are threshold effects rather than linear effects.

What are these thresholds? We don't know, and as a result scientists used a linear model to estimate costs. Parenthetically, the one in a hundred estimate used by the National Academy of Sciences as a result of their linear-based estimate does not appear to be consistent with the number of actual cases in localities like New Mexico that have naturally occurring high amounts of arsenic in their water supply. That state ranks forty-eighth in the nation in cases of bladder cancer, a number that is inconsistent with the one in 100 linear estimate.

Geography is the second type of extrapolation. In this instance we find that studies may be done in one place and their data applied in another. What kind of places do scientists look for to estimate the effects of arsenic? Dr. Robert Goyer, an emeritus professor of pathology who led the National Academy committee said (quoted in Kolata 2001), "To determine what levels are dangerous you have to find a population that is stable and that consumes water with a known amount of arsenic." And that, he said, "is hard to do." Why? It's hard in large part because of the enormous geographical mobility of Americans.

So where do you find stable populations with known amounts of arsenic in the water to measure? So far, in Taiwan and in smaller groups in the Andes. In the arsenic debate, several studies conducted in these areas have found a correlation between high levels of arsenic in drinking water and the occurrence of more cancers than would have been expected without it.

Are findings from these applicable to the circumstances in the United States? Studies have found a link between arsenic levels and increased cancer risk in Taiwan and Chile because in those countries the people are exposed to much *higher* levels of arsenic than they are in the United States. The best information comes from Taiwan. There,

...80,000 people consumed 400 to 1000 parts per billion of arsenic in their water, a level 8 to 20 times higher than acceptable in this country....The committee noted that arsenic's effects might vary with genetic makeup, diet and general health.

There are other puzzles as well. Somewhat oddly, "because arsenic hasn't proved particularly toxic in laboratory animals, toxicologists are at a loss of explain its ill effects on humans" (Waldman 2001). To make matters even more complex, it turns out that arsenic is the chief ingredient of a very promising cancer cure. Reviewing the origins of arsenic for this purpose in China and its adaptation by the most prestigious American Cancer treatment hospitals, Elizabeth Rosenthal (2001) says,

> In 1997, doctors at Memorial Sloan-Kettering began their first small study with arsenic trioxide. "It was very, very impressive," says Dr. Steven Soignet of the hospital's department of developmental chemotherapy. "We had these patients who had all relapsed, and many were terribly sick in the intensive-care unit. Their blood pressure was low. They were needing constant transfusions. And we were there pushing arsenic through their IV's. It was very dramatic." The results, too, were dramatic—so dramatic that American specialists are now rethinking the way they treat this disease.

In cost-benefit analysis a primary question for policy makers is: How much is it worth to individuals to reach any particular level? Other questions arise here, too. Could the money be better and more productively spent? One toxicologist who took part in a meeting of the EPA and National Institute of Health about eliminating lead in faucets said (quoted in Kolata 2001),

> ...they're down to very low levels. The economic impact came up at this meeting and it was very large. From my standpoint as a scientist, I realized that well nourished kids absorb less lead. So, being pretty naive, I said, "Why not take the money that the E.P.A. is talking about for lowering lead in drinking water and putting it into nourishing inner city kids?" The E.P.A. said it didn't feed children; the N.I.H. said it didn't have the money. It was a classic federal impasse.

As the issues and complications noted above make clear, the setting of standards for arsenic are riddled with uncertain—of effects, of the efficacy of interventions, and of the price to be paid. The point of this analysis is not that ten parts per billion is "right," and some higher number "wrong." It is that a substantial number of unresolved questions exist and that there is no unanimity of scientific agreement, except at the extremes, which numbers are not an issue here. Mr. Bush did not embrace the number, 50 parts per billion, that the National Academy said should be lowered. What he questioned was whether an 80 percent reduction from this figure was justified.

What Mr. Bush asked for was a review of these questions. It was certainly a legitimate exercise of his executive functions as president. Moreover, given the disagreements noted above, it was reasonable. Yet it was not treated by those opposed to it as either.

A *New York Times* editorial (2001) accused Mr. Bush of taking a position on "poisoned water" that was "aggressively hostile" to environmental concerns. Some pundits were even less restrained. Columnist Richard Cohen while admitting complete ignorance of any of the issues involved in assessing the dangers of arsenic, nonetheless wrote,

> I have no idea, really, whether a teaspoon is sufficient. And I do not know whether the arsenic standards the Cheney administration rescinded are too stringent, as it maintains, or simply prudent. But I do know that an administration about to embark on the wholesale rape and pillage of the land (and the skies) should have waited a bit before becoming pro-arsenic.

Barbara Boxer, California Democrat, accused Mr. Bush of "declaring war on the environment" (quoted in Allen and Pianin 2001). Surveying democratic efforts to attack Mr. Bush, Mike Allen and Eric Pianin (2001) wrote,

> Democrats and major environmental groups have begun gearing up. Senator Joseph I. Lieberman (Conn.), the ranking Democrat on the Senate Governmental Affairs Committee, has launched an inquiry into Bush's decision-making on arsenic, mining and logging. The Natural Resources Defense Council will begin running television ads in Washington and other markets around the country this weekend to criticize Bush's proposal for oil drilling in the Arctic National Wildlife Refuge in Alaska. The Sierra Club is planning a radio and newspaper ad campaign criticizing Bush's stands on arsenic in water and carbon dioxide emissions, while the Audubon Society has run TV ads on Alaska drilling and will hold 30 membership parties throughout the country to drum up resistance to Bush's policies."

However, perhaps the most savage attack came from the Democratic National Committee and its allies which ran a TV ad in which a little girl presents her mother with a glass and asks, "More arsenic please?" a scene the ad depicted as one result of Mr. Bush's stance of the issue. Vice President Cheney said that the recent television advertisement showing a child asking for more arsenic in her water was a "cheap shot" (Kahn 2001).

Character Integrity and the Psychology of Political Courage

No discussion of the nature of the psychology of political courage would be adequate without a focus on character integrity. Elsewhere (Renshon 1998: 188-194), I have defined character integrity as the set of ideals and values by which a political leader says he lives, and his fidelity to them. Both are critical. Cataloguing a political leaders' public expression of the virtues to which they say they subscribe is not enough. None would expect them to say otherwise. Rather, character integrity is to be found in those areas where sticking to conviction entails the possibility of real loss, political and personal. In order for political leaders to have the courage of their convictions, they must have both.

Character integrity provides a clear link between who the leader presents himself to be and who he is. The leader whose persona actually reflects his psychology gathers two critical elements of leadership capital drawn from his interior psychology—integrity and authenticity. This is not a matter of political ideology; leaders of the left, right, and center can have fidelity to their political ideals and values. The critical issue here is the fit, or lack thereof, between what the leader says he stands for and what his behavior reveals about his actual commitment to those ideals and values.

Character integrity is also a resource for a leader in working through the difficult process of deciding and governing. It provides an anchor in a sea of ambiguity and uncertainty. It can sustain a leader's capacity to stay with a problem as well as provide a frame from which to view not only what is politically expedient, but what is personally acceptable. And it can reinforce a leader's personal confidence and sense of personal integrity, themselves important elements of leadership capital and, as well, solace in a sometimes difficult and unforgiving political world.

Truth and Public Consequences

Honesty, integrity, and trustworthiness may well be virtues in themselves, but they are important for the nation's political life. Political leadership involves the mobilization, orchestration, and consolidation of public-mindedness for common purposes. A dishonest political leader forfeits the assumption of public trust that underlies social capital. A president, whose positions do not reflect his convictions, leaves us wondering which, if either, we should credit. And a political leader whose political self-interest can be counted on to supersede his public-mindedness raises the question of whether we are being enlisted for his, or our, purposes. One important function of character integrity, therefore, is to provide an anchor for ambition.

Character integrity does more than anchor ambition or buttress a political leader in the difficult position of making judgments and trying to carry them through. It provides the public with a sense of reassurance that they have given their legitimacy to someone honest enough to deserve it. And, it serves as the basis for extending to the leader the benefits of trust—time in which to complete his work, the benefit of the doubt in conflicted circumstances, and the capacity to tolerate setbacks. In a divided society, character integrity is a critical element of leadership and social capital.

Leadership in times of deep national divisions requires leaders of a particular kind—those who have both courage and convictions, who are not afraid to raise and honestly answer difficult political questions, and make these honest answers the basis of their leadership. To locate such leadership, one must look first to the political leader's interior psychology—his character—and more particularly to the extent to which his principled ideals have developed and provide boundaries and purpose for the exercise of his ambition.

Without honesty from political leaders, promising policy solutions languish and failed policies persist. Yet the damage that leaders do when they fail to speak honestly goes beyond the continuation of failed policies or the delay of promising ones—although these are surely very undesirable outcomes. Leaders who promise more than they can reasonable expect to deliver corrode public trust and social capital, and in the process they use up their leadership capital with all but their most enthusiastic followers.

In times of social and political consensus the results of such a mismatch may be more difficult to see. The same may be true in periods of increasing prosperity, during which the costs of misrepresentation in all its varied forms may not be obvious or, even so, may well be ignored. Nonetheless, the political costs of evasion are no less corrosive for not being immediate.

Leadership, Courage and Candor—The Politics of Deception

It is axiomatic that Americans prefer to be governed from the political center. However, that political space has proved difficult to define. Have candidates and presidents simply been unable to discern the direction or contours of the political center? Do they, as a group, lack the intelligence, political insight or judgment to find it? Some might find this a tempting explanation, but it makes no sense for two basic reasons.

First, if one equates long-standing majority views on such contentious issues as abortion, immigration, and affirmative action with the political center, it is quite clear what the majority of Americans think, and have thought over a long period of time. It does not take a political genius, good judgment, or keen insight to discern these basic facts. Second, most modern presidents have been generally intelligent, some exceedingly so, and would not have gained the presidency without a good appreciation of the country's politics.

The answer lies elsewhere. While leaders of all views define their political aspirations in terms of governing from the center, the reality for many is quite different. One reason for this is found in the mismatch between the ambition that it takes to acquire high office and the moderation that it takes to govern from the political center once you have achieved it. Presidents and candidates have tried to negotiate these treacherous currents for a decade, primarily by trying to finesse rather than engage them. Michael Dukakis famously suggested in 1988 that his presidential campaign was about competence, not ideology. However, his tenure as governor of Massachusetts suggested no lack of ambitious policy aspirations. Bill Clinton ran and won the presidency as a "New Democrat," governed as an old on—and won re-election by declaring, "the era of big government is over," even while copiously adding new programs to it.

Leadership, Courage and Candor—The Politics of Avoidance

President Clinton personified some of the problems that affect our current inability to make progress on the issues that divide us; he is by no means alone. Indeed, for some national leaders, no expressed position seems to be the most politically comfortable one. Consider in this respect former Senator Robert Dole's response to a question asked of him during the third national presidential debate in 1996 with his rival.[2]

He was asked by a woman, a minister with the Universal Fellowship of Metropolitan Community Churches, to explain his reference to being against "special rights," in this case for homosexuals. It was clear from the thrust and tone of the question that the women supported such rights, but regardless of her personal position, it was a fair and reasonable question.

> *Q*: President Clinton perhaps you can help me with something tonight. I've heard Mr. Dole say several times, "all of us together." And when he was asked if he would support equal rights in employment for gay and lesbian people, you said you favored that, and he said that he did not believe in special rights. And I thought the question was equal rights for all people, and I don't understand why people are using the term "special rights" when the question is equal rights. Can you help me in understanding that?

> *President Clinton*: I want to answer your question, but first let me say one other thing [the president goes on discuss school prayer, and declines to characterize Mr. Dole's statement because, "I'd mischaracterize it and try to make you happy."].... Under our constitution, if you show up tomorrow, and obey the law, and you work hard, and you do what you are supposed to do, you're entitle to equal treatment."

> *Mr. Leher*: Senator Dole?

> *Senator Dole*: Well, I hope I made my answer clear. I said I'm opposed to discrimination. You know we've suffered discrimination in the disability community. There are 43 million of us. And I can recall cases where people would cross the street rather than meet someone in a wheelchair. So, we want to end discrimination. I think that answers itself. No discrimination in America. We've made it clear. And I would just say that it seems to me that's the way it ought to be. We shouldn't discriminate—race, color, whatever, lifestyle, disability. This is America, and we're all proud of it. But we're not there yet. What we need is good strong leadership going into the next century. [Mr. Dole then goes on to raise a foreign policy issue with his remaining time].

That question provided a perfect opportunity for Senator Dole to educate the public and specify both where he and the president agreed, being against discrimination and where they didn't (special rights), and why. He might have noted that he worried that some advocates and their allies might make use of these laws in ways which most Americans would not support, for example using the idea of hostile climate to require teaching about gay life-style in public schools to small children. That worry would not have been far-fetched. In New York City public schools a rancorous debate broke out over plans to teach primary school children about homosexual life-styles, and present them as one of a number of equally appropriate family life-style choices. Along similar lines, the Provincetown School Board voted to require teaching pre-schoolers about homosexual life-styles.[3]

Or he might have pointed out that since laws baring discrimination on the basis of sex were already on the federal statue books, he opposed placing additional and unnecessary ones on them. He might have said that he would support the law if it specifically included the idea that the law was a two-way street, that gays and lesbians, who in positions of authority that misused their positions with heterosexual men and women, would be equally subject to the law, the position taken by the Supreme Court in a recent decision.

I don't really know what Mr. Dole would have said, but the point is that neither does anyone else who followed the debate. By either being unclear about the nature of his opposition, or reluctant or unable to express it, he deprived the public of the opportunity to have something to think about.

Joe Lieberman and the Politics of Symbolic Courage

While real courage among political leaders is often in short supply, its symbolic substitutes are not. Symbolic courage, as the term implies, is more concerned with the appearance of courage than its enactment. Apparent courage is easier. First, you select a person or a set of ideas that operate at the most extreme corners of American political experience. Then, you make a point of distancing yourself from such views and receive appreciative approval for taking such a "brave" stand.

The prototype of this symbolic approach can be seen in President Clinton's 1992 presidential campaign. During it, he singled out a then obscure African American singer named Sister Soulja, who advocated taking a day off to kill as many cops as you could. Mr. Clinton denounced such lyrics, much to the consternation of Jesse Jackson, but the widespread approval of almost everyone else. Mr. Clinton had now gone strongly on record as being against murdering policeman, and song lyrics that advocated doing that.

At the time, this was widely viewed as Mr. Clinton taking a symbolic stand against the kind of hard left rhetoric that had gained acceptance in some political circles. It was also seen as a signal that Mr. Clinton would not pander to the "left-wing" of the Democratic Party, and further that he would be tough on crime. As is clear, there was a good deal of meaning read into this singular act, and that is both the nature and the advantage, to the leader at least, of such symbolism.

The actual meaning of such acts only become clear in the context of a leader's other behavior. Mr. Clinton's record of standing apart from the left wing of the Democratic Party on matters related to race was, and remained highly equivocal, at best. True, he could express concern for the country's disunity and initiated a program to restore "One America." However, he framed that initiative in a way, as a black-white problem that guaranteed that it didn't directly address America's real issues with multiethnic, multiracial diversity. (A fuller consideration of this initative is found in chapter 12.)

He could address an African American congregation on Martin Luther King Day and remind them that Dr. King did not sacrifice his life so that blacks could kill blacks and have children and abandon them. However, this statement—his most courageous on race—was generally lost amidst a vast landscape of equivocation, misrepresentation, and reluctance when it came to modifying the special racial preferences built into the structure of American public and private life in the wake of the Supreme Court's Adarand decision.

Senator Lieberman Condemns President Clinton's Behavior as "Immoral"

Sometimes what appears to be an act of courage and conviction suffers in retrospect from being both more and less than meets the eye. Consider in this regard Senator Joseph Liberman's rebuke of President Clinton's behavior with his intern Monica Lewinsky. Mr. Clinton had just conceded in a nationally television address of having an "improper" relationship with her but argued that it was not the public's business but rather between him and his family.

Pressure from the White House to keep upset Democrats rallying around him and his presidency was intense. Mr. Clinton's chief of staff, Erskin B. Bowles and the Democratic leadership had urged him not to speak out, but Mr. Lieberman responded that "the implications for our country are so serious that I feel a responsibility to my constituents in Connecticut, as well as to my conscience, to voice my concerns forthrightly and publicly" (quoted in Berke 1998: A1). Elsewhere he was quoted (in Sciolino 1998: A18) as saying, "I have a loyalty higher that just that of party.... My loyalty is to the public interest."

And so, Mr. Lieberman rebuked the president for behavior that he termed "immoral."[4] The president, in his televised address to the nation, had failed to take sufficient personal responsibility for his own behavior. Senator Lieberman disagreed with the president's assertion that his behavior was a private matter and no business of the public's, and worried about the message the president's behavior would send. Specifically, he said that the president was a role model and worried that his behavior would "compromise his moral authority at a time when Americans of all persuasions agree that the decline of the family is one of the most pressing problems we are facing." Moreover, by being dishonest, he "has hurt his credibility and therefore perhaps his ability of moving his agenda forward."

Senator Lieberman was clearly anguished and conflicted about his speech. He called it a "difficult statement to write and deliver." He expressed the fear that "it will appear unnecessarily judgmental." He said that "only God can judge people [and that] the most we can do is comment without condemning individuals." Moreover, he knew that

> the President is far from alone in the wrongdoing he has admitted. We as humans are all imperfect. We are all sinners. Many have betrayed a loved one, and most have told lies.

Members of Congress have certainly been guilty of such behavior, as have some previous presidents. We must try to understand. We must try to understand the complexity and difficulty of personal relationships, which should give us pause before passing judgment on them.

Among the other factors that had to be considered in the president's behalf was the fact that he

> has shown during the course of his Presidency that he understands the broad concern in the public about the threat to the family. He has used the bully pulpit of his Presidency to eloquently and effectively call for a renewal of our common values, particularly the principle of personal responsibility and our common commitment to family…. Now, all of that makes the President's misconduct so *confusing and damaging.*" (emphasis added)

Hence, to summarize Mr. Lieberman's rebuke: the president's private behavior does have public implications. Having a sexual relationship "with an employee half his age" was "immoral" and sent the wrong message to a public concerned about family values. Moreover, for reasons that are "thoroughly human," "Mr. Clinton had failed to take enough responsibility for this behavior and had perhaps compromised his moral standing and his ability to advance his political agenda.

Had the president lied to the public? Yes. Had the president lied under oath in the sexual harassment suit in which he testified? In other words, had he committed the crime of perjury? Well, his "deception," as Mr. Lieberman termed it, was "intentional and premeditated" and "therefore "particularly troubling." Why particularly troubling? Because "it was not just a reflexive and understandable human act of concealment to protect himself and his family from what he called the embarrassment of his own conduct when he was confronted with it in the Jones case."

Senator Lieberman's moral criticism of the president left many political and legal questions unaddressed. The senator had said that the president had been and ought to be "held to a higher standard." So, again, had the president by engaging in an "intentional and premeditated deception" while giving a deposition before a federal court committed perjury? Although it is clear that he did and that Mr. Lieberman's characterizations acknowledge this fact, Senator Lieberman does not directly say so. Was lying in a deposition consistent with this higher standard?

Did the president, in giving the same deceptive answer to the questions put to him by Mr. Starr commit perjury in a federal grand jury investigation? Mr. Lieberman doesn't say, although by the time Senator Lieberman made his remarks the president's grand jury testimony had already been made public. Was lying and therefore committing perjury before a federal grand jury consistent with that higher standard?

Mr. Clinton's "intentional and premeditated deception" during his deposition was in part a "reflexive and understandable human act of concealment to protect himself and his family from embarrassment." Does that wish constitute a mitigating circumstance available to all who might wish to lie during a court proceeding to so protect themselves? Mr. Lieberman doesn't say.

By placing Mr. Clinton's behavior primarily within a moral framework and avoiding its legal dimensions, Senator Lieberman avoided having to draw some obvious implications, or explain his reasoning if he didn't. Does lying in a federal court deposition and obstructing the administration of justice cross "the high threshold our Constitution rightly sets for overturning the results of a popular election in our democracy and bringing on the national trauma of removing an incumbent President from office?" What if the same president not only did it once in a federal court proceeding, but again in sworn testimony before a federal grand jury inquiring into his conduct in committing perjury and obstructing the administration of justice? Apparently not.

Senator Leiberman voted to dismiss all charges against the president in the Senate trial and before that tried to find a mechanism to make clear that there were not the necessary number of votes in the Senate (67) to sustain a conviction (Kaiser 1999: A29). His reasoning was that although "the president may have committed a crime," it was not "a high crime worthy of impeachment" (Kaiser 1999).

Mr. Lieberman's Courage in Retrospect

Senator Lieberman took a risk in speaking out when he did and making what he presented as a deeply felt, principled statement. The questions are: how much and what kind? Mr. Lieberman did stand the risk of alienating a number of his fellow Democrats. Yet, at the time, some Democrats were torn between being appalled at the president's behavior on a personal level and afraid politically for their president and party if they were too publicly critical.

Senator Lieberman said of himself (quoted in Seelye 1998: A10) in making that speech, "I felt lonely out there." Yet, immediately thereafter Senators Kerrey and Moynihan took the Senate floor to echo and applaud his remarks, and Tom Daschle, Senate Democratic leader, came over and put his arm around him (Seelye 1998). The next day the *New York Times* (Schmitt 1998: A10) published an article entitled, "Many Democrats Concur with Rebuke to Clinton," and began by noting that "Congressional Democrats today began falling in line behind an influential Senator who on Thursday excoriated President Clinton's behavior..."

His Senate speech got coast-to-coast coverage, most of it positive. E-mails and phone calls flooded his office, most of them favorable. He later said (quoted in Kaiser 1999: A29) "the reaction to it was way beyond what I expected." That report, based on extensive post-speech interviews over a ten-month period, said of Mr. Lieberman that, " He came to realize that he was riding the crest of a giant media wave..." and even mentioned, "joking, but not entirely," becoming Al Gore's running mate.

Of course, Mr. Lieberman could not have foreseen all this and it can appropriately be considered due reward for the risks taken. However, this returns us again to the question: What risks? The largest risk Mr. Lieberman's remarks posed was that it would "break the dam," of Democratic Party support for the president and when added to the criticisms of Congressional Republicans, lead to Mr. Clinton's exit or removal from office. But, the democrat's strong showing in the November 3rd elections convinced Mr. Lieberman that Mr. Clinton would escape impeachment. Still, one can reasonably argue that this was November 3rd and Mr. Liberman's speech had been given almost two months before.

Thus, it is instructive to return to that speech and how the decision to give it unfolded. Mr. Lieberman reports (Seelye 1998: A10) being away with his family when Mr. Clinton spoke and becoming increasingly upset at what the president had, and had not said. He was so angry, he said, that he sat down at his laptop and began the first of what proved to be eight drafts of the remarks he finally delivered. In the interview conducted by Ms. Seeyle, the Senator mentioned that the president had called him twice as he was writing the speech. In the first conversation, he told the president he was disappointed and angry with him, and in the second that he was going to make some public comments that "would not be comfortable to hear." In another context, Senator Lieberman said that he had called the president to tell him he was going to deliver a speech about the scandal.

The speech itself, while personally critical of Mr. Clinton's behavior, was not nearly so hard hitting politically. By providing a context of understanding and appreciation of the personal issues that Mr. Clinton faced in deciding on "deception," the Senator's remarks also cushioned him politically. "He called on his colleagues to honestly confront the damage,

> that Mr. Clinton had done over the past ten months, but not to the exclusion of the good that his leadership had done over the past six years, not at the expense of our common interests as Americans.

Impeach the president? "No, because....It seems to me that talk of impeachment and resignation at this time is unwise and unjust. It is unwise because we don't know enough." What should be done? Mr. Lieberman suggested,

> some measure of public rebuke and accountability. We in the Congress...are surely capable institutionally of expressing such disapproval through a resolution of reprimand or censure of the President for his misconduct. But it is premature to do so...until we have received the report of the independent counsel and the White House's response to it.

The Senator's speech gave the president's supporters the perfect response. Yes, his behavior was wrong. No, we don't know whether it crossed the line necessary for it to be an impeachable offense. Yes, public sanction short of impeachment should be considered. Small wonder that Democrats by the score simply summarized their position by saying, "I agree with Senator Lieberman" (Schmitt 1998: A10).

Does the fact that Democrats made use of the Senator's speech necessarily reflect on Mr. Lieberman's courage in making it? Not really, but Mr. Lieberman's own motivations for making the speech turn out to be more than a simple matter of his moral outrage. Mr. Liberman hinted as much in the first interview he gave after the speech. He told Katharine Seelye (1998) that he was "furious with the president, first for bad behavior, second for behavior which undercut the theme of personal responsibility that Mr. Clinton and Mr. Lieberman had advocated over the years they had tried to pull the Democratic Party toward the main-stream values of the political center."

More of Senator Liberman's motivation emerged in a series of interviews conducted by the *Washington Post* (Kaiser 1999: A29). The story reported a speculation by a senior Republican that Mr. Lieberman "had thrashed Clinton to try to help him." Asked about this, Lieberman "demurred, but soon he began to hint that he understood he had helped Mr. Clinton." Asked after the Demo-crats' good showing in the November Congressional elections whether his speech had helped the president by showing that he could be sharply chastised without being forced out of office, Mr. Lieberman replied, "could be."

The report then goes on:

> After the elections, Mr. Lieberman was more forthcoming about the political motiva-tions for his September 3 speech. "The president's August confession," he said, "was a threat to the Democratic Party." "We had worked so hard," he said to demonstrate that Democrats had learned "the difference between right and wrong...[and to] reestablish the party's connection to mainstream values." and, because "Clinton himself was at the center of this transformation, I feared that...we were in danger as a party."

So, Senator Liberman's moral concerns shared motivational space with his more partisan, political concerns. Does this invalidate the praise heaped on Senator Lieberman? No; however it should modify our view of it. There is no doubt that Senator Lieberman was upset with Mr. Clinton's behavior both as a president and as a middle-aged man taking a wholly self-interested advantage of a young woman he should have helped, not used.

Yet, Mr. Lieberman voted against the impeachment of President Clinton. On January 27, 2000, the then senator (Lieberman 1999: S1030; emphasis mine) said it was clear that,

> President Clinton had an extramarital sexual relationship with a young White House employee, which, though consensual, was reckless and immoral, and thus raised a series of questions about his judgment and his respect for the office. *He then made false and misleading statements about that relationship to the American people, to a Federal district court judge in a civil deposition, and to a Federal grand jury....*The question before us now is whether the President's wrongdoing—as outlined in the two articles of impeachment—was more than reprehensible, more than harmful, and in this case, *more than strictly criminal.*

In the end, Senator Lieberman concluded that it wasn't. Sometime later in spite of his statements above about "false' testimony, in an appearance on *Meet the Press* (Transcript, August 13, 2000) Mr. Lieberman was unsure whether Mr. Clinton had lied:

> *Russert*: Do you believe the president lied under oath?

> *Lieberman*: I'm really not in a position to make that legal judgment.

Senator Lieberman's Courage as a Vice Presidential Candidate

No one speech can define a life-long political career. Senator Lieberman has been a reliable stalwart of the Congressional Democratic Party, which is to say that his overall voting pattern is decidedly left of center (Dewar and Pianin 2000) with high yearly ratings from the liberal Americans for Democratic Action (ADA) and 100 percent rating from the NAACP. Yet, he had in some areas tried to help move his party more to the moderate left of center from its less moderate leftward-leaning base. He founded the New Democratic Network in 1996 and was the chairman of the Democratic Leadership Council (DLC) at the time he was selected as vice presidential nominee.

These issues helped to define these two centrist groups and what it meant to be a "new Democrat." He was for, for example, an advocate of experimenting with voucher programs to help stimulate public school reform. He has been an outspoken critic of the tendency of the media to sexualize and debase American culture. He was for the exploration of a space-based missile defense system to protect the United States. He had been a critic of affirmative action programs. And he had supported the idea of some degree of privatization of Social Security investments for younger workers. Senator Lieberman was never a conservative Democrat, but his willingness to be open-minded in several areas earned him a reputation as an independent-minded one. More importantly, it was exactly these policies on which he was open-minded that helped to define the new more moderate stance of the Democratic Party.

Senator Lieberman's policy positions therefore were not only a matter of personal policy positions, but part of a broader movement that he had helped to found and which he represented. However, almost all of these positions were modified, some substantially so, when Senator Lieberman was chosen by Mr. Gore to be his vice-presidential running mate. Mr. Lieberman, of course, faced the dilemma with which most selected for this role must address—how to reconcile their own views with those of the man who has chosen them. It is obviously easier to do so when the two candidates agree, or when the differences are marginal. American political history is full of vice presidents who ran against the person who ultimately became president and were forced to subsume their views to his.

On the other hand, in the past tickets were chosen for ideological as well as geographical balance. And there are examples of presidential candidates modifying their views to get the partner they want on the ticket. Bob Dole modified his stance on tax cuts and economic opportunity in 1996 as an accommodation to the views of Jack Kemp. R.W. Apple (2000: A1) wrote that, "On the basis of his record, some people might have expected something a bit more unconventional from Mr. Lieberman, probably unrealistically."

What makes this particular instance of more than passing interest is Mr. Lieberman's development as a "centrist," and his long history of support for many of the programs and policies he chose to downplay when he ran as a vice presidential candidate in 2000 (critics would say disown, see Cohen 2000; Bennett 2000). Further, he is a pious, observant and devoutly religious man whose temperament in that domain has been central to his established persona in the political domain as well. Mr. Lieberman has always presented himself as a scrupulously moral and thoughtful political leader, one whose positions represent the highest level of candor, reflection, balance and ultimately rectitude. Nonetheless, it became clear in the space of a few days, that a substantial number of the positions through which Senator Lieberman had established his credentials as an independent thinker, "conscious of the Senate," and leader of the "New Democratic" movement, were in jeopardy (Allen 2000a).

Affirmative Action

Like many centrist democrats, Senator Lieberman had become disenchanted with the excesses of affirmative action and a number of its supporters. In 1995 he had said that affirmative action programs that rewarded people strictly because of their race were "patently unfair."[5] He had said, "You can't defend policies that are based on group preferences as opposed to individual opportunity." In August of 1995, the *Hartford Current* quoted him as saying in an interview," many affirmative action programs must change because they are inconsistent with the law and with the basic American value of equal treatment and opportunity."

When he was asked about his views on California Proposition 209 which ended racial preferences, Mr. Lieberman said," I can't see how I would be opposed to it." He said that, "he began at that time to question whether quotas were an acceptable way to achieve equal opportunity." In an appearance on *Meet the Press* (Transcript 2000), Mr. Lieberman defended his position on Proposition 209 by saying,

> I didn't go out there and campaign for it. But at that time, I and a lot of others were raising questions about whether some affirmative action programs had become quotas.

After the senator was selected as the vice presidential candidate, Gore supporters like Clinton Labor Secretary Alexis M. Herman argued that, "Promoters of the referendum used civil rights language to make it sound like it would not dismantle civil rights progress." Herman then went on to say that Senator Lieberman made the statement of support "without knowing the full impact. . .

he did not understand the intent of Proposition 209." Mr. Lieberman agreed when he spoke to the black caucus, saying," There was a misunderstanding" of his views on the subject and that he had supported the proposition based only on its language and not based on details of its implementation. He then summed up his position as follows," "I was for affirmative action, am for affirmative action and will be for affirmative action."

Social Security

For many years, Senator Lieberman had been willing to consider plans to invest a small portion of social security benefits in the market to secure greater returns and thus improve the fund's viability. The centrist leaning Democratic Leadership Council of which Senator Lieberman is a prominent member supported the idea, and he did also. In a 1998 interview with the *San Diego Union-Tribune* Mr. Lieberman said,

> I would support that....We now have decades-long history of an average 10 percent return on stocks.... So, yes, I would support it.... It doesn't make sense anymore not to do that with this enormous investment pool that we're supposed to have for Social Security.... I think in the end that individual control of part of the retirement/Social Security funds has got to happen. (quoted in Kelly 2000)

In a 1998 interview with the *Copley News Service*, Senator Lieberman said that he generally supported the proposition of allowing workers to invest a portion of Social Security savings in stocks. He is quoted (in Mintz 2000; see also Apple 2000) as saying,

> We're going to see again a kind of old Democratic Party/new Democratic Party kind of split on this. I think in the end that individual control of part of the retirement/Social Security funds has to happen.

All of this changed when then presidential candidate Al Gore attacked Governor Bush's proposal to allow some private investments as a "risky scheme." In an interview with Larry King, Senator Lieberman said, "it wasn't true" that he had ever favored privatization of Social Security. Rather, he had merely been "intrigued" by the possibility.

Earlier, Senator Lieberman revealed that in June he had written a newspaper column, which went unpublished, in which he backed away from his support. Why? Always the judicious decision maker, he presented himself as having more closely examined the facts, saying the "more I weighed these facts, the more reluctant I became to tamper with the program's basic structure." However, *Washington Post* (Mintz 2000) reported that, "Lieberman wrote the column after Gore policy advisor Elaine Kamarck asked him and about 20 other Democratic leaders to make statements criticizing Bush's Social Security proposal." Soon after being selected as Al Gore's running mate, Mr. Lieberman was giving a speech before the AFL-CIO in which he said (quoted in Mintz 2000), "Instead of saving Social Security, he's on a course to savage it with a privatization scheme that would take $1 trillion out of the nest egg that belongs to every worker in America, and jeopardize the program's stability and the security of the working future of the American people."

Hollywood

Senator Lieberman had long been a strong voice against "cultural pollution." He had thought up and given the "Silver Sewer Award" to those who egregiously promoted inappropriate materials for under-age audiences. After he had been chosen by Al Gore to be the vice presidential candidate, he appeared on *Meet the Press*, where the following exchange took place (Transcript August 19, 2000):

> *Russert*: But you have been much more outspoken than Al Gore on these issues. In fact, when the president had a summit at the White House, this is the way the "Los Angeles Times" treated the vice president's involvement. I'll put it on the screen. "At the private meeting with potential donors, Gore distanced himself from the federal inquiry into Hollywood's marketing of violent movies launched by President Clinton. Participants said Gore made clear the government study, disparaged by some in Hollywood as a witch hunt, was the president's idea, not his, and was initiated without his input." Will you back down on your criticism of Hollywood now that you're associating with Al Gore?
>
> *Lieberman*: No.

On September 10, Al Gore and his running mate, Joe Lieberman, declared (Sack 2000a) that, "if the entertainment industry did not stop marketing violent films, recordings and video games to children they would propose legislation or new regulatory authority allowing the federal government to sanction the industry." Gore gave the industry leaders six months "to clean up their act"; after that, he said, he would push the FTC to take legal steps against the industry for false and deceptive advertising. "Those who don't like it," said the tough-talking Gore, "well, they don't like it." The *Washington Post* later reported (Neal and Connolly 2000) that the Gore campaign had, "as it has done in the past took pains to privately reassure industry supporters." Earlier, Mr. Gore had called his friends in the movie industry to give them a "heads-up," about the criticism he would deliver.

On September 14, Mr. Gore and Mr. Lieberman attended a large fundraiser held at Radio City Music Hall that netted the Democratic Party $6.5 million (Neal and Connolly 2000). The event was organized by three top Hollywood studio executives, including Harvey Firestone of Miramax pictures,[6] the very people that Mr. Gore and Mr. Lieberman had just threatened with government regulation. An aide to the campaign distinguished between the studio's marketing techniques, with which they disagreed, and the content of the films about which they were not commenting (Sack 2000b).

On September 19, Mr. Gore and Mr. Lieberman attended a $4.2 million fundraiser at the Beverly Hills estate of supermarket magnate Ron Burkle. Mr. Lieberman said (quoted in Allen 2000c), "Al and I have a tremendous regard for this industry..." What of the tough rhetoric of the previous week, and the threats of government regulation? Mr. Lieberman said, "it was all about dialogue and discussion and what was good for the country." He continued that,

> It's true from time to time we have been, will be critics—or nudges, but I promise you this: we will never put the government in a position of telling you by law, what to make. We will nudge you but never become censors.

"Nudge" is a Yiddish word that means gently and indirectly suggest. It is the opposite of a threat to regulate and legislate. Mr. Gore referred "obliquely " to "the controversy of the previous week," without saying anything further about it. A *Times* reporter covering the event wrote (Seelye 2000), "any talk of regulation was gone as was the stern tone."

A *New York Times* reporter (Barstow 2000a,b; see also Allen 2000b) who followed Senator Lieberman around in the days after his selection, noticed "his willingness to tailor his political messages to different audiences." In these talks Mr. Lieberman displayed a competitive streak, "somewhat at odds with his reputation as the conscience of the Senate, as a politician who speaks his mind without regard to the consequences." Senator Lieberman is quoted as telling one group,

> We didn't come to play, we came to win. I'm from the Vince Lombardi School. Winning is the whole deal.

Paradoxically, what might be an act of independence on the part of Senator Lieberman was not reflective of a win-at-any-cost psychology. It took place in the middle of the Florida recount effort by the Gore campaign, a circumstance of the highest political stakes. Diligently searching for additional votes, and for ways to keep Mr. Bush from adding more to his totals, the Gore campaign mounted a challenge to military absentee ballots that were thought to heavily favor the governor (Schmitt 2000).

It was at that point that Mr. Lieberman went to *Meet the Press* and the following exchange took place:

> *Mr. Russert*: Many controversies swirling in Florida. The most recent: Democratic lawyers challenging over seas absentee ballots, some 1,420 were disqualified, more than either Bush or Gore won.

> *Senator Lieberman*: Yeah.

> *Mr. Russert*: Many of them, members of the armed services, and people are very, very concerned. They point to a memo written by Mark Heron, a lawyer who assists the Gore campaign, telling Democratic lawyers, "This is how you knock out ballots from

military people overseas." They don't have a postmark right. They're not dated properly. Technicalities, if you will.

Senator Liberman: Yeah.

Mr. Russert: How can a campaign that insists on the intent of the voter, the will of the people, not disenfranchising anybody accept knocking out the votes of people of armed services?

Senator Lieberman: Tim, I haven't read that memo. That's the first I've actually seen it, though I heard it on the news yesterday. And I spoke with people in the campaign on the recount vote that's now going on in Florida last night, and they told me that this was a memo that was setting out the law for monitors associated with the Democratic Party who are going to be at each of these counties as the ballots were cast. Apparently the Republicans had a similar memo. The decision was made by the local election official, and I presume that the local election officials were calling it real close because of all the focus on every vote in Florida today as this recount goes on. Let me just say that the vice president and *I would never authorize, and would not tolerate, a campaign that was aimed specifically at invalidating absentee ballots from members of our armed services.* And I've been assured that there were more absentee ballots from non-military voters overseas that were ultimately disqualified. We're all about exactly what you said, having every vote counted fairly and accurately, and I think that was the end aim of what happened with the absentee ballots, and it's our aim as the hand counts go on in these three counties in Florida. (Transcript November 19, 2000; emphasis mine)

It is unclear who authorized the Democratic Party's stance toward military absentee ballots, but it certainly was "tolerated," until the Bush campaign made a large public issue of it. That being said, a week later, the Bush campaign withdrew its suit against several local voting boards that had already reversed themselves and agreed to count military ballots (Cooper 2000).

Brief Profiles in Candor and Courage

There are many ways to avoid candor and many political reasons for doing so. Courage, and especially courage that results in loss is not easy or widely practiced. Yet both political courage and candor in politics exist.

The two brief profiles below are not especially seminal events. No heroic heights were reached because of them and no great calamities were avoided. They were not widely remarked upon at the time, but each has something to teach us—the first about the courage of conviction, the second regarding the courage of candor.

Rudy Giuliani and the Politics of Courage

Readers interested in political leadership who are not familiar with New York Mayor Rudy Giuliani are missing an important opportunity to expand their conceptual horizons. He is in many ways an anomaly to his circumstances—a Republican in an overwhelmingly Democratic city, a "Caucasian" ethnic in a city where minorities are approaching majority, and a conservative in a city that is one of the most liberal in the country.

Mr. Giuliani a leader who speaks his mind regardless of whether others like to hear what is being said. He has taken on issues large and small in his quest to reshape and reform the political culture of New York. He has been a champion of immigration at a time when his party was associated with a very different point of view. He has cracked down on rude cabbies and jaywalkers. In a city that is the quintessential explemplar of race and ethnic sensibilities, he has disbanded all city offices designed to serve the many ethnical/racial special interests. He prefers instead to govern under the banner, "one city-one standard" (Gaiter 1997). And, he has extolled the virtues of true welfare reform—returning people to productive personal and work lives—in a city in which that term and spending more money became synonymous.

The political leader who stands against, also stands out. The political leader who stands out and stands against is often lonely. This kind of leader makes himself a target of the forces allied with those political or institutional patterns he is attempting to change. This has certainly been a problem of President George W. Bush, and it is even more of a problem for leaders like Mr. Giuliani with a very combative psychology.

Mr. Giuliani is an extremely blunt man. The mayor has been trying for years to gain control of the vast educational bureaucracy over which he exercise little control but for which he has much public responsibility. During a budget address in which he focused on the dysfunction of city schools in their primary role-that of providing a solid educational foundation for their students, he had this to say:

> I think the Chancellor is working in a system that is dysfunctional. The system is just plain terrible, it makes no sense, and the end result of it is that if this were a business system, it would be in bankruptcy. The whole system should be blown up and a new one should be put in its place. (Quoted in Barry 1999)

Later, in remarks in response to questions after his address, Giuliani told the following anecdote:

> it was candidly admitted to me that there was money in the plan [educational budget] going to boroughs that didn't need that much money, and didn't have that much over-crowding, because they had to get the vote of that borough. And I said, "suppose we just throw it all out and we just look at need? Suppose we look at a plan like that? And, I was told the plan couldn't pass."

As might be expected from the information presented above, Mr. Giuliani is not a man who avoids conflict. Indeed, he embraces it as often necessary to institute real change. However, while being willing to fight for what you stand for is one element of political courage, the willingness to incur some loss, if necessary, is equally important.

In 1999 Mayor Giuliani was deciding whether to run against Hillary Clinton for the Senate seat that had opened up with the announced retirement of Daniel Moynihan. Mr. Giuliani ultimately withdrew from the race after being diagnosed with prostate cancer. But as the Republican Party nominee he had a problem.

A rare supportive editorial in the *New York Times* best summed up Giuliani's stance:

> Most politicians try to side step issues that divide voters along militant angry lines. Rudolph Giuliani firmly rejected this kind of evasion when asked about late-term abortions....the mayor has steadfastly refused to alter his support for abortion rights. What makes the Mayor's stand particularly stalwart is that it could easily jeopardize his nomination by the Conservative Party of New York State. No Republican has won state-wide election in the last 25 years without the Conservative Party line on the ballot...

The arithmetic of election politics in New York is such that since 1974 no Republican has ever won a state-wide race without the backing of New York's small but highly influential Conservative Party (Perez-Pena 1999). The number of registered members of the party is approximately 170,000 or 1.6 percent of the state's population (Perez-Pena 2000) is small, but Republicans who also receive the Conservative Party's nomination can count on about 300,000 votes on that line or somewhere between 4 and 8 percent—enough to make the margin of difference in a close race.

What has made the Conservative Party a real powerbroker in the state is the willingness of the Party and its powerful chairman, Michael L. Long, to run candidates against its more obvious ally, the Republican Party, when they nominate someone not to Mr. Long's ideological liking. Their intervention in the 1980 Republican primary, for example, helped to defeat liberal Republican Senator Jacob Javits and put Alfonse D'Amato in the Senate. In 1990, when polls showed Democratic Governor Mario Cuomo vulnerable to a strong Republican challenge, the Conservative Party ran its own candidate Herbert London who received more that 800,000 votes allowing Mr. Cuomo an easy re-election.

By almost all accounts and poll numbers the Clinton-Giuliani senate race had shaped up to be a very close one. Mr. Giuliani clearly would benefit from having the Conservative Party nomination, but there was one large obstacle. The mayor was a pro-choice Republican, and vocally so—and Mr. Long was a very strongly pro-life party leader in charge of who got his party's nomination. Giuliani had already strained their relationship by allowing the city to recognize same-sex marriages and by supporting a Democrat Mario Cuomo for governor.

The choice Mr. Long posed to the mayor was stark. He must forgo the backing of the State's Liberal Party and, more importantly, change his position and support the ban of late-term abortion. Mr. Giuliani refused. Not only did he refuse, but he did so in a most public way appearing on *Meet the Press* and saying directly he would continue to vote for a woman's right to choose and would attempt to gain the Liberal Party's nomination.

At least one liberal pundit (Tomasky 1999) tried to make the case that by not taking the conservative line, Mr. Giuliani would gain the support of moderates and be harder to label as a conservative by Ms. Clinton. Yet that would still leave him fighting for the moderate political center toe-to-toe with Ms. Clinton. He might well have a chance, but he would by no means be the favorite, which brings us back to the usefulness to him of a conservative line on the ballot which has been worth as many as 800,000 votes.

Even Michael Tomasky (1999: 28) noted that the mayor "is not a man who bends, for anybody...Rudi's inflexibility is often more characterological than ideological, so his position is in truth some combination of principle and stubbornness." Precisely! In one's psychology is exactly where the capacity for courage develops.

John F. Kennedy's Contribution to Understanding Candor

John F. Kennedy's presidency was too short to reach any solid historical judgments. His presidency began with the disastrous set of decisions that culminated in the Bay of Pigs debacle. Nevertheless, as the recently released transcripts of the president and his advisors during the Cuban Missile crisis make clear (May and Zelikow 1997), the president learned from his early mistakes. His performance as a decision maker in that risk-permeated confrontation between the United States and the Soviet Union was truly masterful.

He was very smart, but "bored silly" by the details of government (Doyle 1999: 98). However, when he had to, he could ask questions about the smallest of details (cf., May and Zelikow 1997: 95). He was adverse to political risk, especially when he was up against determined opposition. Perhaps because of the small margin of his election victory, but more likely because of a disinclination to fight to expand his leadership capital, President Kennedy was by nature politically prudent. He told his staff (quoted in Doyle 1999: 97),

> If you're going to have a fight, have a fight about something. Don't have a fight about nothing.

In a discussion with reporters, he said (quoted in Doyle 1999: 97),

> There is no sense in raising hell, and then not being successful. There is no sense of putting the office of the presidency on the line and then being defeated.

Sentiments like these made President Kennedy reluctant to become involved. Sometimes, as with Vietnam, it is possible to see the virtues of such caution. Sometimes, in the case of his response to the Civil Rights movement, it is possible to see its costs. Paradoxically, President Kennedy appears to have shared with President Clinton a tendency toward policy caution, coupled with a substantial lack of it in his personal life.

Kennedy's presidency is now remembered for its youth, its charm, and its tragic promise. But in its short time, it produced something else as well—a president who was willing to say in public what he knew to be true, period. There are a number of examples sprinkled throughout his press conferences, but one is particularly striking.

The situation is that President Kennedy has been forced to call up some units of the National Guard in connection with increased tensions with the Soviet Union over Berlin in the spring of 1963. In that connection the following exchange with a news reporter occurred:

> *Q*: Mr. President, at some of our military camps there have been demonstrations by mobilized reservists, including in one case an attempted hunger strike. I wonder if you couldn't comment on these demonstrations, and couldn't you give the reservists some notion of when they might be released.

> *Mr. Kennedy*: Well, I understand the feeling of any reservist, particularly those who have fulfilled their duty and then they are called back. And they see others going along in normal life, and therefore they feel: how long are we going to be kept?...Now on the question of releasing these reservists, we will release them on the first possible date consistent with our national security. They were called up because of the crisis in Berlin, and because of the threats in Southeast Asia... *Now, secondly, there is always inequality in life. Some men are killed in a war and some men our wounded, and some men never leave the country, and some men are stationed in the Antarctic and some are stationed in San Francisco. It's very hard in military or personal life to assure complete equality. Life is unfair.* But I do hope that in many ways—some people are sick and others are well—but I do hope that these people recognize that they are fulfilling a valuable function and that they will feel, however humdrum it is, and however much their life is disturbed and the years been yanked out of it, they will feel the satisfaction afterwards of feeling that they contributed importantly to their country[7]

Is it possible to imagine many modern presidents saying directly and without obfuscation that "life is unfair?" Which modern presidents come quickly to mind who would publicly justify their policies by national necessity and say forthrightly that policy cannot always be accomplished with "fairness?" And is it possible to imagine a president saying that the real standard in such circumstances is not personal disruptions, but important service to one's country?

Conclusion

The capacity for political candor and courage exists, but it is relatively rare. Many political leaders are torn between what they know and what they feel that can safely say. The responsibility for this lies with them but also with us.

Political leaders faced with tough choices reach a fork in the road and, to paraphrase Yogi Berra, fail to take it. Their methods for doing so are varied. As Lawrence Jacobs and Robert Shapiro (2001) point out in their new book, *Poli-*

ticians Don't Pander: Political Manipulation and the Loss of Democratic Responsiveness, what looks like pandering is, in reality, manipulation. The use of surveys to gauge voters' views is not so much an attempt to follow where the public leads, but to help craft language designed to lead the public to believe that their wishes are being followed.

There is, of course, a question as to whether feeling the need to rephrase your views in acceptable terms isn't really a form of pandering. Jacobs and Shapiro also believe that political leaders don't pander because they ignore overall public opinion in favor of being responsive to their particular constituencies. Again, the finding that political leaders pander to their own constituencies rather than to the general public seems no reason to nominate them for a Profile in Courage Award.

Political leaders may be, as they argue, simply Machiavellian. Yet, what is clear from the concerns of this chapter, pandering to your own group means that you cannot easily stand against it, if necessary. Nor does the tendency for political leaders to craft language that *appears* to put them on the side of the public raise much hope or expectation of frank discussions when they are needed. And in a society permeated by divisions—cultural, political and policy—such discussions are badly needed.

Notes

1. Elsewhere (1998b: 60), I have taken up the issue of what psychoanalysts know and can tell. However, I want to stress here that while there are important parallels (Renshon 1998, 60) to the role of political leaders and analysts with regard to their knowledge and ability to say what others will be able to hear, there are important differences. Political leadership is not therapy.
2. "Presidential Debate in San Diego" (October 16, 1996), Weekly Compilation of Presidential Documents, October 21, 32: 42, pp. 2091-2092.
3   *Washington Times*, 31 August 1997, National Edition: A1.
4. The quotes that follow are drawn from Mr. Lieberman's senate speech (Excerpts 1998: A18.)
5   Unless otherwise noted, this quote and those that follow in the next two paragraphs are drawn from Dao and Sack (2000); Edsall and Harris (2000); and Allen and Edsall (2000).
6   Terry Neal and Ceci Connolly write (2000),
    Mr. Weinstein and his brother Bob produced and distributed some of the most controversial movies of the last decade....By far the Weinsteins' most controversial movie was 1995's *Kids*, which chronicled the lives of a group of skateboard-riding Manhattan teenagers. The movie's protagonist was a teenage boy, Tully, whose specialty is"devirginizing" teenage girls. The movie rating board slapped the picture with an NC-17 rating. Because Disney studios, which owns Miramax, does not release NC-17 movies, the Weinsteins created an independent company, Excaliber, to distribute it unrated. The movie's creators hailed its strong message against sexual irresponsibility and drug abuse. But the cinema verite style and depictions of drug use, sex and profanity led critics of the movie to argue that its message could not be separated from its content.

7.   John F. Kennedy, "Press conference [March 21, 1962]," *Public Papers of the Presidents of the United States-John F. Kennedy, January 1 to December 31, 1962.* Washington, DC: U.S. Government Printing Office, 1963, pp. 259-260 (emphasis added).

References

Allen, Mike. "EPA to Lower Level for Arsenic in Water." *Washington Post*, 19 April 2001: A08.

_____. "Democrats Stroke Hollywood at Dinner." *Washington Post*, 20 September 2000c: A19.

_____. "Reaching Across Liberal-Centrist Lines." *Washington Post*, 18 August 2000b: A28.

_____. "Lieberman Grilled as L.A. Greets Delegates." *Washington Post*, 14 August 2000a: A01.

Allen, Mike, and Eric Pianin. "Democrats See Environment as Bush Liability: Party Using Issue to Energize Base." *Washington Post*, 24 March 2001: A02.

Allen, Mike, and Thomas B. Edsall. "Lieberman Vows Support of Affirmative Action." *Washington Post*, 16 August 2000: A18.

Apple, R.W., Jr. "A Retooled Lieberman Stands by His Master." *New York Times*, 16 August 2001: A1.

Barry, Dan. "Raze School System, Giuliani Says." *New York Times*, 23 April 1999: B10.

Barstow, David . "To Left and Center, Lieberman Revels in 'Love Fest.'" *New York Times*, 18 August 2000b.

Bennett, William J. "I'm Disappointed, Joe." *Wall Street Journal*, 22 September 2000.

Cohen, Richard. "Lieberman Fails a Test." *Washington Post*, 3 October 2000: A25.

Cooper, Michael. "A Tactical Change in Bush Lawsuit Over Military Ballots." *Washington Post*, 26 November 2000.

Cummings, Jeanne. "Bush Will lower Arsenic Standard for Water, but Not Until Next Year." *Wall Street Journal*, 18 April 2001.

Dao, James, and Kevin Sack. "Lieberman Confers with Black Caucus to Seek to Allay Its Concerns about Him." *New York Times*, 16 August 2000.

Dewar, Helen, and Eric Pianin. "Senator's Reform Efforts Sometimes Get Results." *Washington Post*, 9 August 2000: A01.

Doyle, William. *Inside the White House: The White House Tapes from FDR to Clinton.* New York: Kodansha International, 1999.

Editorial. "Mr Bush and Arsenic." *New York Times*, 8 April 2001.

Editorial. "The Mayor's Abortion Stance." *New York Times*, 1 December 1999: A28.

Edsall, Thomas B., and Hamil R. Harris. "Lieberman Stirs Concerns Among Blacks." *Washington Post*, 15 August 2000: A01.

Egan, Timothy. "In New Mexico, Debate Over Arsenic Rules Strikes home." *New York Times*, 14 April 2000.

Excerpts from "Senator Lieberman's Talk on President's Personal Conduct. *New York Times*, 4 September 1998: A18.

Gaiter, Dorothy J. "Color Blind? To Rudolph Giuliani, the Race Issue isn't Much of an Issue at All." *Wall Street Journal*, 19 September 1997: A1.

Heilprin, John. "Bush Defends Arsenic Delay, Promises Reduction." *Washington Post*, 29 March 2001.

Jacobs, Lawrence R., and Robert Y. Shapiro. *Politicians Don't Pander: Political Manipulation and the Loss of Democratic Responsiveness.* Chicago: University of Chicago Press, 2001.

Kahn, Joseph. "Cheney Promotes Increasing Supply as Energy Policy." *New York Times*, 1 May 2001.

Kaiser, Robert G. "The Chronicle of Lieberman: From Key Speech Thrashing Clinton to a Vote for Acquittal." *Washington Post*, 13 February 1999: A29.

Kelly, Michael. "Dumb vs. Dishonest." *Washington Post*, 27 September 2000b: A23.

_____. "Al Gore's Flex-U-Joe." *Washington Post*, 23 August 2000a: A25.

Kolata, Gina. "Putting a Price Tag on the Priceless." *New York Times*, 8 April 2001.

Lieberman, Joseph. "Support of the Motion to Dismiss the Articles of Impeachment Against President Clinton," 106th Congress, 1st (1999), January 27, 1999: S1030-S1031.

Mallaby, Sebastian. "Saving Statistical Live." *Washington Post*, 5 March 2001: A19.

May, Ernest R. and Phillip D. Zelikow. *The Kennedy Tapes: Inside the White House During the Cuban Missile Crisis*. Cambridge, MA: Harvard University Press, 1997.

Mintz, John. "A Passing Exploration of Privatization." *Washington Post*, 10 August 2000: A19.

Neal, Terry M., and Ceci Connolly. "Hollywood Draws Cash for Gore, Ire in GOP." *Washington Post*, 14 September 2000: A01.

Perez-Pena, Richard. "Conservative Party Leader Says Republicans Can Do Better Than Giuliani. "*New York Times*, 8 February 2000: A29.

_____. "Despite Size, Conservative Party is a Force to Be Reckoned With," *New York Times*, 13 December 1999: B1.

Rosenthal, Elisabeth. "Chairman Mao's Cure for Cancer." *New York Times Sunday Magazine*, 6 May 2001.

Sack, Kevin. "Democrats Raise Money, Republicans Raise Hay." *New York Times*, 15 September 2000b.

_____. "Gore Takes Tough Stand on Violent Entertainment." *New York Times*, 11 September 2000a.

Schmitt, Eric. "Many Democrats Concur with Rebuke to Clinton." *New York Times*, 5 September 1998: A10.

Schmitt, Susan. "GOP Complain about Military Vote challenges." *Washington Post*, 19 November 2000: A23.

Sciolino, Elaine. "For Lieberman, 'Loyalty is to the Public Interest'." *New York Times*, 4 1998: A18.

Seelye, Katherine Q. "Before a Hollywood Crowd, Democrats Lower the Volume." *New York Times*, 20 September 2000.

Tomasky, Michael. "Long Shot." *New York*, 13 December 1999: 28-29.

Transcript. "Senator Joseph Lieberman." *Meet the Press*, November 19, 2000.

Transcript. "Senator Joseph Lieberman." *Meet the Press*, August 13, 2000.

Transcript, *Larry King Live*. "Senator Joseph Lieberman." *CNN*, August 8, 2000.

Waldman, Peter. "EPA's Reversal on Arsenic Standards Shows Disagreements among Experts: All Agree Chemical Kills, but Question is Just How Much." *Wall Street Journal*, 19 April 2001.

Waldman, Peter, and John Fialka. "EPA's Move to Rescind Arsenic Standard is Welcomed by Those Facing the Cleanup." *Wall Street Journal*, 21 March 2001.

12

The Politics of Avoidance:
President Clinton's Initiative on Race

As America begins a new millennium, one of the most important domestic questions facing its citizens is whether their political leaders are up to the difficult task of governing a truly diverse, but divided nation. Hopefully the answer to that question is "Yes." However, realistically, the evidence to date would lead one to answer, "Maybe."

However, before we reach any conclusion regarding our leaders and the leadership they provide, we might first begin with some basic questions. Is successful leadership different in divided societies than in harmonious ones? It would seem the obvious answer to that question is Yes. But how is it different? And in what ways does division call for different skills and capacities on the part of society's leaders? Must those leaders have less, or different kinds of ambition? Must they be increasingly empathetic to the many and varied calls for "recognition" (Taylor 1992) that come from advocates of our increasingly diverse population? Are minimalist small-gauge policies an inevitable by-product of our failure to reach or build on common understandings?

One of the characteristics of contemporary American politics is that leaders with both real convictions and the courage to enact them have been in short supply. And it has been thus for some time. Presidents and candidates have tried to negotiate these treacherous currents for a decade, primarily by attempting to finesse rather than engage them. The rise of "New Democrats" and "Compassionate Conservatives" are either artful mixes of political categories designed to escape hard choice, or a truly new categorical blend designed to build on a real vision, with its own hard choices. There is no way to settle which it is a priori. The truth is to be found in the details of the choices that leaders make, or don't make, in the issues that they raise or avoid, and the honesty with which they lay out their views, do their best to explain them, and let the political chips then fall as they may.

In the sections that follow, I examine these issues through the lens of President Clinton's Initiative on Race. I make note of some of the issues that arose as that effort unfolded that compromised its integrity and effectiveness. I conclude with some observations on courage and leadership capital and its implications for One America.

Dissipating Leadership Capital: The President's Initiative on Race[1]

Frank talk about America's racial and ethnic divisions has been noticeably absent in contemporary politics (Sleeper 1990). Harsh accusations have not (Sleeper 1997). Therefore, the President's Initiative on Race, to which the administration gave the hopeful name, "One America," appeared to reflect considerable courage on Mr. Clinton's part.

If there was anyone who might be able to initiate and sustain a frank dialogue on race it was the president. Observers from many points on the political spectrum saw Mr. Clinton as uniquely suited to bridge American's racial and ethnic gaps (however, for a contrary view see Kelly 1997). Peter Baker (1998 10) of the *Washington Post* wrote, "Few doubt the president's sincerity about race, and indeed it is one subject on which he is consistently credited for possessing deep, heartfelt beliefs." The liberal columnist Nicholas Lehman (1997: A17) noted that "the traditional test of racial communication for white politicians is whether they can win an enthusiastic reception from a black audience. "Mr. Clinton," he said, "does that almost effortlessly." Ward Connerly, head of the organization that supported Proposition 209 in California which ended racial preferences, said after his Christmas eve meeting with the president that he, "understands race like no other President, living or dead" (quoted in Bennet 1997b: A1). And, as Michael Frisby (1997: A1) pointed out in a front-page story in the *Wall Street Journal:*

> Not since Lyndon Johnson has an American president devoted such energy to race relations. So for many blacks, particularly outside politics, Mr. Clinton can do no wrong.

On the divisive issue of race, Mr. Clinton had clearly accumulated substantial leadership capital. Whether and how he would use is was a central question. What is clear is that Mr. Clinton understood the stakes.

As he had when he ran for president in 1992, Mr. Clinton showed an accurate understanding of what the country needed, its basic public dilemma.[2] In a talk with reporters he said,

> It is really a potentially great thing for America that we are becoming so multi-ethnic....But it's also potentially a powder keg of problems and heartbreak and division and loss. And how we handle it will determine, really—that single question may be the biggest determination of what we look like fifty years from now...and what the children of that age will have to look forward to. (Clinton 1997a: 509)

Clearly, Mr. Clinton understood the potentially explosive issues that faced this country. Yet there was a critical question that accompanied that understanding. Did color-conscious policies allow America to get "beyond race?" Or did government-sponsored designations of "protected" groups singled out for special and better treatment actually fuel feelings of resentment and entitlement on one side, and just plain resentment on the other?

Mr. Clinton was well positioned to have a frank and helpful conversation. However, he never honestly or effectively engaged that critical question, which is one reason, among several, that few would wind up characterizing his initiative as a major contribution to either the country's engaging these difficult issues, or to President Clinton' legacy. In retrospect, it seems clear that the president failed to use his leadership capital on an issue of signal personal interest to him and one of vast importance for the country. The question before us is: Why?

The Great National Conversation Begins

The original impetus for the initiative came from Jesse Jackson, members of the "Black" Congressional caucus, and similarly minded advocates (Holmes 1995). After a march in October 1995 by the controversial Muslim leader Louis Farrakhan in Washington, they pressed the president to create a presidential commission to address what they saw as the continuing, harrowing plight of African Americans in this country. Several months later President Clinton ordered his staff to find ways for him to "play a prominent role in improving American race relations, a goal that he is trying to make a focus of the legacy of his second term" (Bennet 1996: A4). John Harris (1996: A12) reported at the time that the president was considering a list of "14 pillars" of policy including renewing cities, crime, entitlement reform, and others.

In June 1997 the *New York Times* (Bennet 1997: A22) reported that, "After months of White House debate over how to improve race relations and add heft to President Clinton's second term, Mr. Clinton has decided to hold town meetings and other events on race around the country, appoint a high-powered panel, and write a report next year summarizing "his findings." Then, at the University of California, San Diego, commencement address in June 1977, President Clinton (1997b) announced what he called a year-long national discussion, "a great and unprecedented conversation about race," that would "transform the problem of prejudice into the promise of unity." The president's Initiative on Race was born.

Some questioned whether such a discussion was needed. In their view, the discussion had already been in progress for some time, in many forums—political, legal, and cultural (Baker 1997). Some saw it as part of a discussion that had been part of our national life almost from the beginning. Others thought this conversation had been going on at least since the Eisenhower presidency and certainly by the time of Lyndon Johnson's "Great Society" initiatives.

Others, like Roger Wilkins, long-time civil rights leader, wondered why it had taken the president so long to focus his administration on these issues. He was quoted (in Fletcher and Balz 1997) as saying, "This man has been president for 4/1/2 years, and now he is trying to make civil rights part of his legacy? Isn't that kind of late?"

Even those who supported the proposal questioned whether public, televised forums with hand-picked participants were the best, or most useful venue for conducting such discussions. Orlando Patterson (1998: 1) wrote that, "If what the president proposes is yet another inquiry into America's 'racial dilemma,' his well-meaning initiative is likely to do more harm than good; but if what he has in mind is a debate about how we talk about and evaluate 'race,' it might do some good."

Framing the Issue

In spite of these doubts, Mr. Clinton pressed ahead, convinced, he said, that the country needed such an airing of its conflicts. In his commencement speech introducing the commission he said (1997b: 881),

> What do I hope we will really achieve as a country? If we do nothing more than talk. It will be interesting, but not enough. If we do nothing more than propose disconnected acts of policies, it will be helpful but it won't be enough. But if 10 years from now, people can look back and see that this year of honest dialogue lifted and concerted action helped to lift the heavy burden from our children's future we will have given a precious gift to America.

These are grand, almost heroic visions. And no one with deeply felt commitments to this country and its ideals could disagree with the sentiments, or the hopes the president expressed. The question was, as always with any political leader, to what extent and in what ways would these ideals be translated into civic accomplishment?

More concretely, President Clinton said (1997b: 881) he wanted this panel to

> help educate Americans about the fact surrounding issues of race, to promote a dialogue in every community of the land to confront and work through these issues, and recruit and encourage leadership at all levels to help breach racial divides and to find, develop, and recommend how to implement concrete solutions to our problems—solutions that will involve all of us in government, business, communities, and as individual citizens.

Here, too, the president's stated goals[3] were worthy and desirable. Yet here, too, the question must remain before us: How were these noble goals to be reached? Were the methods selected to accomplish them consistent with their purpose?

Of course, before it is possible to assess whether and in what ways the president (and his commission) achieved the goals he set, another matter must be addressed. That is the basic question of what exactly was the issue that Mr. Clinton wished to address. The answer was far from obvious.

At a press conference on April 11 shortly before he introduced his commission, Mr. Clinton (1997b: 509; emphasis mine) had this to say about framing the issues:

And particularly I feel on this whole issue of how we deal with diversity. It's something...that's dominated my whole life because I grew up as a southerner. But it's a very different issue now. *Its more than black Americans and white Americans.* The majority of students in the Los Angles County schools are Hispanic and there are four school districts in America—four—where there are children who have more than a hundred different racial, ethnic or linguistic backgrounds. So this is a big deal. And every issue we debate whether its affirmative action or immigration or things that seem peripherally involved in this need to be viewed through the prism of how we can preserve one America...

At that press conference, the president was directly saying that the issues arising out of America's unprecedented diversity transcend black-white issues. He said the same thing while introducing the commission and the national dialogue. "To be sure there is old unfinished business between black and white Americans, *but the classic American dilemma has now become many dilemmas of race and ethnicity*" (Clinton 1997b: 878; emphasis mine). Thus, it did not seem far-fetched to expect the president to push for framing the commission's work through the lens of increasing ethnic and racial diversity rather than through the more narrow lens of "black-white relationships." He did not.

One board member, Angela E. Oh, an American of Asian decent and an attorney, urged her colleagues on the panel to "move beyond the 'black-white' paradigm" (quoted in Baker 1997: A4). However, the commission's chairman, Dr. John Hope Franklin, an African American scholar of American race relations, overruled her.

Shortly thereafter in an interview with a correspondent from Black Entertainment Television the following exchange took place (Clinton 1997: 1185):

Mr. Smiley: In the first meeting of your race commission, a small dispute erupted in that the commission chairman, Dr. John Hope Franklin and commissioner Angela Oh, a Korean-American commissioner from Los Angles, had a dispute about the focus, what the mission, the work of the commission ought to be. Dr. Franklin believes that the focus and the mission ought to be around the "black white" conflict, which he sees as the nucleus of every other race problem this country has endured and continues to endure... Commissioner Oh suggests that the work of the commission really ought to be about multiracialism and multiculturalism.

As the leader, as the president who put this commission together, what kind of leadership are you going to provide? How are you going to get them on the right track? If the commission can't have a clear-stated mandate, how do we talk about it as a country?

President Clinton: First, I agree with John Hope Franklin that if you don't understand the black white conflict, you can never understand how race works in America. If you don't know the history and if you don't know what the facts are now, you can never understand the rest.

Thus, from its inception, the president's initiative was misframed by primarily focusing on "black-white" issues of rather than the larger issues many races and multiple ethnicities. Not surprisingly, other ethnic and racial groups felt they were being excluded. Native Americans disrupted one meeting and were quickly rewarded with special meetings called to address their issues. Elaine Chao, a senior fellow at the Heritage Foundation and an invitee to the president's pre-Christmas eve White House meeting with right of center critics, pointed out (in Clinton 1997f, 2090) that the debate had almost entirely left out Asian-Americans. Hispanics were upset about their lack of representation and an Hispanic athlete was quickly added to the list of participants discussing why more managers and owners of professional sports teams were not Americans of African decent, and whether black athletes should have white business managers (Baker and Fletcher 1998: A02).

This was a major, but not the only, problem. The initiative was slow to get started (Baker 1998). Although long in the planning and announced in June, the executive director of the Initiative, Judith Winston, was not hired until August. At first, the White House had no research or senior staff assigned to the effort. After several months spent to not much effect, Mr. Clinton assigned his Chief of Staff Erskin Bowles to bring some focus to the commission.

The lack of advance planning that would have allowed the commission to get off to a fast start was important given that it was scheduled to last only one year. In that time it had a great deal to accomplish, to understate the case. Mr. Clinton's somewhat loose approach to the details of presidential follow through were by this time well known. However, his failure to make an exception in the case of a major initiative that he said was of crucial importance to the country tended to send a mixed message.

Mr. Clinton was aware of the problem. In early September, he said (1997: 1307) that he was "going to try over the next few weeks to increase my public involvement in this racial dialogue that I called for..." Two weeks later, he was gently trying to nudge his commission towards a more active stance. Appearing at their first public meeting, the president (1997 1462) gave them several ideas for going forward before saying, "finally, and in the end, we have got to decide what we are going to do."

The causes of the commission's diffused focus were numerous. Critics from both the left and right criticized both the slow start and the lack of focus (Holmes 1997e: A17). Others noted that Mr. Clinton himself had not given the panel any clear direction (Holmes 1997d: A23) However, a more accurate description would be to say that Mr. Clinton had given them too ambitious an agenda rather than a unclear one.

Early on, one White House aide noted that the commission was still differing over what it was trying to solve, racism or poverty. That aide was also quoted as saying, "There is no consensus that the issue is fundamentally about race, or about equality of opportunity and education" (quoted in Holmes and Bennet 1998: A01; see also Blow 1998). Some aides felt the initiative should suggest specific remedies, others believed the goal was to spur talk about race. The president urged his aides to do both (Holmes and Bennet 1998) . At the same time (January 1999), civil rights leaders had urged the president to narrow the initiative's focus, yet that conversation itself revealed the fluidity of the commission's own view of its mandate.

There were other substantive divisions in the commission as well. How much "white racism" could be held responsible for the contemporary plight of some groups of Americans of African decent? How much responsibility did individuals share for their circumstances? Had there been significant progress, or was there still very far to go in making any?

Divided views permeated not only with the commission members, but also with White House staff members. Holmes and Bennet (1998: A1) report that,

> On the Saturday after Labor Day, members of the Advisory Commission Staff met with more than 20 aides from the White House ...hoping to get a clearer idea of what they would do. Instead, minority members of the White House Staff talking about personal experiences with racism took much of the time up. "We got a recantation of why it was important to have the initiative, rather than what the initiative was supposed to accomplish."

There were also issues of budget and cost connected with any major new initiatives and issues of political support (Branegan 1999: 73). Finally, there had been the issue of how closely the president ought to be identified with his initiative, lest they compromise the president politically by introducing controversial suggestions. One set of such suggestions appeared early on in the form of suggestions that the president apologize to the African American community for slavery and that he consider sponsoring reparations.[4] As a result of all these problems, the initiative which had made headlines when it was introduced..."promptly dropped off the radar screen and ran into trouble" (Frisby 1997: A24).

As late as December 1997, six months after the initiative had been formally announced, the impression of disarray persisted. At first, in the privacy of a one-on-one interview with a reporter for the Knight-Ridder news service, the president acknowledged that the initiative had gotten off to a slow start and that he was partially responsible (Clinton 1997: 1943-44). However, several weeks later at his national televised news conference on December 16, the following testy exchange occurred on the issue (1997: 2053-54),

> *Q*: Mr. President, reports from the frontlines of your race initiative suggest that the initiative is in chaos, it is confused. The Akron town meeting was little more than a Presidential "Oprah." Some people involved are beginning to—
>
> *President Clinton*: That may be your editorial comment. That's not my report. I've received scores of letters, including letters from ordinary people, who said that they loved it, and they thought it was important. So, if that's your opinion, state it is your opinion, but—
>
> *Q*: It's an opinion, sir, that I'm hearing from others who are beginning to question whether simply talking—

President Clinton: Who are they? Name one. Just one. Give me a name. All this "others" stuff—you know, its confusing to the American people when they hear all these anonymous sources flying around.

Q: I don't want to get them fired by you, sir, so [laughter] but they are people who are involved in the process, who are beginning to question whether simply talking is enough.

Almost one month to the day after that exchange, the commission's chairman Dr. Franklin (in Clinton 1998b: 54) was urged the president to strongly publicize actions and events relating to the race initiative "because that had not attracted much media attention, thus far." And Mr. Clinton was promising, in response to a reporter's question (1998a: 25-26) to "do more and more visible things."

"The Great National Conversation": Honesty and Its Barriers

If framing the issues was a core requirement for the commission's success, the nature of the conversation was critical. An "honest dialogue" was central to the president's presentation of the initiative's purpose. It was also central to his more concrete goals of educate "Americans about the facts surrounding issues of race, to promote a dialogue in every community of the land to confront and work through these issues" (1997b: 881). There obviously could be no working through of these difficulty issues without the honest and respectful engagement of differences.

The president himself emphasized this point, saying

We must begin with a candid conversation on the state of race relations today and the implications of Americans of so many different races living together and working together.... *We must be honest with each other.* (1997b: 880; emphasis added)

Later, in the same address, he noted

Honest dialogue will not be easy at first. We'll all have to get past defensiveness and fear and political correctness and other barriers to honesty." (1997b: 881)

Elsewhere he had said (Clinton 1997e: 1302) that his race initiative was meant, "above all, to bring Americans of different backgrounds together to face one another honestly across the lines that divide us." Commenting on the first meeting of his advisory board, the president (1997d 1094) said it was full of "lively debate and honest disagreement."

I like that. We should discover quickly that people who are honestly committed to advancing this dialogue will have honest differences and that they ought to be aired.

The president's concerns were well founded. Arthur Levin (1999: 7), president of Columbia University reports that in group interviews on twenty-eight college and university campuses, conducted by a team of which he was a member between 1992 and 1997,

> ...students were more willing to talk about intimate details of their sex lives than to discuss race relations on campus....The usual response in heterogeneous focus groups was silence, their body language changed, smiles vanished, and students stared at the table rather than talking to each other. What followed was either a long painful conversation with many pauses or an attempt to gloss over the topic.

That discussions of race are more sensitive than those regarding sex is not wholly surprising. In many ways explicit public images have become commonplace and, as a result, sex has become deprivatized. That fact does not explain, however, why race has replaced sex as a taboo subject.

One piece of evidence on the subject comes from a national survey study conducted by Public Agenda (1998 a, b) on views among Americans of African and Caucasian decent on a range of difficult school issues. That survey was supplemented by eight focus groups in different parts of the country to give nuance and depth to the survey instruments.[5] Of relevance to us here is the statement put to all of the 1,600 respondents: It is hard for whites to talk honestly about problems in the black community because they are afraid that someone will accuse them of being racist.

Seventy two-percent of the "white" respondents agreed with that statement (Public Agenda 1998b: 17). Very interestingly, 73 percent of the 'black" parents agreed with them!

The same surprising convergence showed up in another statement which also bears on this matter: Blacks are sometimes too quick to believe negative things happen to them because of their race. Seventy-nine percent of the "white" respondents agreed with that statement. However, so did 75 percent of the "black" respondents (1998b: 17).

Clearly though, Caucasians feel more at risk and their discomfort is validated by Americans of African descent. The study noted (1998a: 23) that "to whites, discussions about race carry considerable risk—they may say the wrong thing, be misunderstood, or worse, be accused of racism—so a more common response is to keep quiet or tread carefully." When asked why the conversation about race was uncomfortable, one respondent said "Anytime you talk about back and white, there will be trouble. "Another said, "Whites have to walk on egg shells (when discussing race)."

This study was not alone in its findings of what it called "reluctant discussion." The study (1998a, 21-22) noted,

> Focus groups conducted for this and previous Public Agenda projects show that white parents are very reluctant to talk about education in racial terms, even in groups with no African Americans present. White parents in every part of the country and from every income and educational level would circle warily around the issue for a half an hour or more, resisting discussions about categories of people...the reluctance was especially strong when the subject was academic under achievement among African American

students, When the moderator persisted, the discomfort was clear and the reluctance to engage palpable.

"The Great National Conversation": Dialogue or Monologue?

Randall Kennedy wrote that the country had not yet had, and needed, an examination of racial issues that would clarify what we know and where we do or do not agree. However, he added,

> The peril is that Clinton and his aides will squelch the possibilities for an informative, intense and surprising discussion and instead sponsor a series of scripted, pseudo-events devoid of the candor and contentious frankness required for any serious attempt to grapple with the race question. Given that a honest, respectful discussion was the foundation of all Mr. Clinton said he hoped to accomplish, it is a legitimate question to ask how, as the leader in charge, he handled it. (1997: C01)

Given that an honest, respectful discussion was the foundation of all Mr. Clinton said he hoped to accomplish, it is a legitimate question to ask how, as the leader in charge, he handled that task. One place to begin looking is at the composition of the commission itself. Its members were certainly distinguished enough and they were ethnically and racially diverse.[6] However, they seemed to be less diverse in their political views than they were on the issues they were examining. One board member, former New Jersey governor Thomas Kean, commented (in Clinton 1997l: 2093) later that he, too, believed, "that the board had been too narrow." The decision not to include any persons with views from the from the moderate/conservative side of the political spectrum as commission members was an obvious attempt to narrow the range of views represented.

The "national conversation" was meant to bring all sides together to discuss the issues that divided them. However, critics noted that from the start those with views were absent from the debate (Holmes 1997e: A17). This was a central criticism of the commission from its inception.

Early initiative events were marked by platitudes and the avoidance of anything that might give offense. Bland, but carefully chosen personal narratives meant to highlight experiences that might lead to a consensus about what "needs to be done" predominated. In this light, an adolescent minority youth related an experience of taking his mother's check to the bank and being asked for identification. This, he submitted, was an example of the special burdens placed on those like himself. No one, including the president who served as moderator, pointed out that trying to cash a check made out to someone else at a bank where you are not personally known might lead to questions for anyone. One news reporter characterized the public meetings as, "a hodge podge of personal anecdotes of grievances that did little to steer the conversation towards broad-based conclusions or recommendations" (Babington 1999: 29).[7]

At the first "Town Hall" meeting held in connection with the president's initiative on September 27, 1997 the subject was race and the public schools. It "produced near unanimity of opinion among those gathered...and those who took part by satellite in 20 other cities" (Holmes 1997c: A28). The report (italics mine) continued that participants agreed:

> public schools had a responsibility to foster understanding...they argued for more money for public education and called for training to make teachers more sensitive to students of different backgrounds. They supported bilingual education and denounced attacks on affirmative action. *But because the gathering lacked dissenting voices, no questions were raised about whether school diversity should be the goal of blacks and other minorities and no arguments were made for such issues as English-only classes or school vouchers.*

One participant (quoted in Holmes 1997c: A28) said, "We seem to be preaching to the choir."

The criticism that the president's initiative on race lacked a diversity of views *within* the commission now broadened to concerns that the national public dialogue itself suffered from the same problems. Secretary of Transportation, Rodney Slater, an African American, took part in a racial dialogue that "pointedly excluded whites" (Hunt 1997: A23). However, that criticism came into sharper focus at the November meeting of the committee at the University of Maryland to discuss how to achieve diversity on college campuses.

The chair of the Committee, Dr. Franklin, said he saw no need to invite persons with different points of view about the value of diversity. In particular, he said he saw no reason to invite Ward Connerly, who led the fight against preferences at the University of California, to the meeting. Why? Because, he said,

> The people whom we did invite had something special to say about how to make universities more diverse than they are. The people in California that advocate Proposition 209, for example, are not addressing the subject of how to make the university more diverse. Consequently, I'm not sure what Mr. Connerly could contribute to this discussion. (Quoted in Holmes 1997f: A24; see also Holmes and Bennet 1998)

The subject in Dr. Franklin's mind was *how* to create more diversity, not whether there might be some serious issues associated with such efforts that ought to be examined. An administration official, asked if he was disappointed about the make up of the discussion, replied, "we believe we had a good group of people for what we were trying to achieve, to teach about the value of diversity."

Mr. Connerly for his part, said that he, "found it astounding that the President's race panel believes that it can have a national dialogue that we have been discussing in America for four years now, without involving those of us who represent a point of view that is shared by probably 60 percent of the people in the nation." A *New York Times* editorial (1997b, A34) pointed out:

Many Americans were skeptical when Bill Clinton called for a "national dialogue on race," but then delegated responsibility to a panel that has been slow to get started. The skepticism deepened this week when the panel held a hearing on diversity but declined to hear the opponents of affirmative action. This does not make for much of a dialogue.

Speaker of the House Newt Gingrich was sharply critical of the composition of the board for not including dissenting views. He asked,

When did your call for a dialogue become a monologue? Is your panel interested in educating our citizens or indoctrinating them?" (Holmes 1997g: A30)

This angered White House officials who noted that the board's chairman, Dr. Franklin, had written to Mr. Gingrich on July 7 seeking his advice and suggestions. They said he never responded. Mr. Gingrich, however, then produced a copy of a detailed letter that had been sent to all the commission members dated, September 29, 1997, suggesting a ten-point program to help close the racial divide.

The initiative began to look more and more like a poorly managed soliloquy than a real dialogue. The commission's executive director denied that the board had deliberately eschewed the views of conservatives; she acknowledged there was a "perception" that it was not seeking a variety of views (quoted in Holmes 1997f: A24).

Yes or No? Yes or No!

In response, the president decided to engage the commission's critics, but did so in a way that appeared to undercut his aim of a frank dialogue. The president announced that he would meet with critics of his racial policies (Holmes 1997d: A23) at the White House. That meeting, it turned out, was held on the last Friday evening before Christmas when it would receive almost no public attention (Bennet 1997a: A1; Clinton 1997l: 2085-2093; Excerpts 1997: A24; see also Begard 1997). Only one member of the president's commission, Governor Kean, was present.

In the meantime, the president invited one prominent critic of his racial preference programs, Dr. Abigail Thernstrom, to the nationally televised town meeting scheduled for Akron, Ohio. The president said that the decision to include a critic was made before the controversy surrounding Dr. Franklin's pointed exclusion of critics, but that a particular person had not been selected before the announcement (Holmes 1997h: A29).

The Akron town meeting, with one notable exception, was much like other such forums. The one exception to polite, serial monologue was the exchange between the president and Dr. Thernstrom. At 6' 3", the president towered over the petite and seated Dr. Thernstrom.

President Clinton: Abigail, do you favor the United States army abolishing the affirmative action program that produced General Colin Powell—yes or no? Yes or no? (Applause). I get asked all these hard question all the time. I want to do it. (1997I: 1968)

Dr. Thernstrom: I do not think that it is racial preference that made Colin Powell—

President Clinton: He thinks he was helped by it.

Dr. Thernstrom:—The overwhelming majority of Americans want American citizens to be treated as individuals. And we've heard the voices here of—

President Clinton: Should we abolish the Army's affirmative action program—yes or no?

Dr. Thernstrom: We should—the Army does one thing very, very right—it prepares kids—it takes kids before the Army and it prepare them to compete equally. That's what you're talking about when you are talking about American education. Let us have real equality of education. These preferences disguise the problem. The real problem is the racial skills gap, and we ignore it when we—

President Clinton: Well, then, the real problem may be the criteria for how we admit people to college, too, how we do it.

This small exchange was much larger in what it revealed, both about the dialogue and the president's approach to using his leadership capital. Certainly, a president who had spent so much time touting the virtues of a honest dialogue and noting how difficult it would be to achieve it, did nothing to help that cause in the exchange. Nor, could his hectoring tone and style, repeating "yes or no," "yes or no" several times, give others with somewhat different views the reassurance they might need to speak honestly.

Nor, it turned out, was this a spontaneous exchange. The day after the debate, it emerged that, "Mr. Clinton had been urged by aides to provoke such an exchange…"(Bennet 1997a: A1). As Hanna Rosin commented (1997, 28), "it was the meeting's only tense moment, but all it really showed was how willing the president was to score points at the expense of real debate."

Moreover, as almost every commentary on the exchange pointed out, the president's question could hardly be answered by either a yes or a no (Greenfield 1997: 84; Rosin 1997: 28; Hunt 1997: A23; Review and Outlook 1997: A18; Thernstrom 1997: 35; Editorial 1997a: A30). Abigail Thernstrom (1997: 35) pointed out that the army had an equal opportunity program, not a preference program, a point backed up by the *New York Times* (1997a: 30) and the *Wall Street Journal* (Review and Outlook 1997: A18). In his own book, Colin Powell (1999; emphasis mine) states,

Equal rights and opportunity mean just that. They do not mean preferential treatment. Preferences, no matter how well intentioned breed resentment among the non-preferred....The present debate has... a lot to do with deficiencies. If affirmative action means programs that provide real opportunity, then I am all for it. If it leads to preferential treatment or helps those who no longer need help, I am opposed. *I benefited from equal opportunity and affirmative action in the army, but I was not shown preference.*

Some found the exchange not only flawed in execution and, as a matter of fact, but disquieting in its assumptions as well. Rosen (1997: 28) pointed out that "the president's suggestion that Powell was 'produced' by affirmative action was simplistic and very nearly offensive." The respected columnist Meg Greenfield (1997: 84) wrote,

> Bill Clinton, who understands these things better than that exchange would show, knows that affirmative action does not "produce" anyone. Given at least a fighting chance, people produce themselves. Colin Powell produced Colin Powell. His story— and his views— would be an excellent starting point for a revised national argument.

The Akron meeting drew its model from the "The Coming Together Project" that had been established in Akron after the Rodney King incident (Holmes 1997I: A26).[8] Meant to foster racial dialogue, it may have complicated Mr. Clinton's efforts. There were moments when Mr. Clinton (1997i 1962) seemed to show a measure of impatience with the kind of touchy feely efforts that bring people together, but do not necessary result in social change. After two ministers joked and talked about their mutual efforts the president said that he would "be the cynic now just for purposes of argument":

> I'll say, okay this is really nice. You've got two churches, and you pray on Sunday and everyone is nice to each other....We do all that kind of stuff.... How does it change these people's lives? How is it changing the life in Akron? How does it result in less discrimination in the workplace? Or in the school, or people helping each other to succeed in school or at work? Can you give us any other examples about what it's done other than make people feel good about themselves for an hour on Sunday or some other church event?

In the end, as one observer (Lee 1997) noted of the Akron meeting:

> It may have been honest, but it wasn't dialogue. Like much of America's discussion of race, it was a serial monologue, an airing of grievances and personal perspectives. Two Hispanic women complained about being compared to the sort of character played by Rosy Perez. A bi-racial student said people perceived only half of who he was...it limped politely along to the end: a jumble of policy prescriptions and anecdotes.

The President's Initiative—A Postscript

After fifteen months of hearings, on September 18, 1998, the commission presented its report to the president. The *New York Times* headlined its coverage with the title, "Clinton Panel on Race Urges Variety of Modest Measures" (Holmes 1998b). The commission had compiled suggestions that had been made during the hearings yet, "many of the suggestions were endorsements of policy positions—like money for school construction projects in minority areas that the administration has already made"(Holmes 1998b: A1). Its boldest, though not necessarily groundbreaking, proposal was for the president to establish a permanent Presidential Council on Race. This idea was later abandoned.

The president downgraded this recommendation and decided instead to establish an Office of Race Relations within the White House (Ross 2000). One official (quoted in Ross 2000) said the fact that the president chose to set up an office on a smaller scale did not mean the effort was being given a lower priority. A further indication of its status was the appointment of a deputy director of outreach. The office set up was similar to the White House Office for Women's Initiatives and Outreach, which Clinton established in 1995 to ensure smoother handling of their concerns. In short, the president's grand plan for a national dialogue on race had devolved into a White House interest group outreach effort.

Asked in March 1999 when he expected to complete his report to the nation on his race initiative, Mr. Clinton replied (1999: 480; see also Babington 1999; Baker 1998), "I hope it will be ready sometime in the next couple of months." As of January 2002 the country still awaited the president's major statement, in book form, of his summing up of the initiative's efforts and its implications for "One America."

President Clinton's Other Race Initiatives

It seems clear that the president's ambitious hopes for his race initiative went unrealized. The question is: Why? Were his ambitions for the initiative too large? Perhaps; yet the importance of the subject would seem to suggest that it is better to fail nobly than never to attempt the difficult.

Was the matter too difficult to engage publicly? Surely, the matter is sensitive. Nevertheless, the national conversation on race produced moments of real clarity. This happened in the town meeting, held in Annandale, Virginia, on bridging the racial divide in primary and secondary schools. Here, knowledgeable and articulate individuals with diverse views discussed their positions on one (vouchers) or a focused set of issues (standards) with the result that the issues were laid out squarely for all to engage (Holmes 197Ij: A24). It also happened, in a less public way, in the Christmas eve White House meeting with critics of the president's racial policies.

Thus, discussion that informed and honestly laid out the bases of the different views on a focused set of questions or problems could have been one of the initiative's valuable contributions. Yet, it wasn't. Part of the problem lay in the premature and shallow consensus the initiative often produced because of the way it had been structured.

Those problems began with the lack of true diversity on the board the president appointed. The board had not one person who disagreed with the administration's basic policies. As a result, the mindset was pre-cast and the result was that the commission set out with a set of like-minded truths, not open-minded questions.

It seems clear, too, that the televised forums of average citizens sharing their very subjective experiences, each of those unique, can take public clarity and understanding of the complicated issues involved only so far. These experiences did provide important lessons, as I will argue at the conclusion of this essay, but not in the way they were put to the initiative's use. As they were presented, they represented diverse experiential elements that were difficult to use in accumulating either increased understanding or common ground.

Certainly, little evidence emerged that these disparate personal stories were very useful for those in attendance, those who watched, or those who thought about these matters on a more regular basis. Moreover, there was never any sense of how the public forums with their less focused remarks which had difficulty adding up to a true dialogue could be integrated with the more focused professional presentations that, at their best, did clarify and sometimes even refine. Could all the different conversations—some televised-some not, over more than a year, in different localities, by different kinds of people, some on national TV, some on local TV, some on sports cable networks [ESPN, Clinton 1998d: 642-648), some on PBS, on a wide range of topics—ever become a real national conversation about so diverse and sensitive a set of issues as are contained in the word "race?"

I think not. The attempt to reach into different venues had some initial appeal. Yet it ran the risk of giving the public a very thin slice of the overall conversation. One lesson of the race initiative may be that in a highly differentiated "public education market," sustained and focused efforts may be more successful than varied and diffuse ones. However, in some ways, this observation misses a core reason why the initiative floundered and that reason is the ways in which the president chose to carry out his initiative.

Honesty and Race: The President's Leadership as a Model

The president, as noted, had substantial leadership capital on the race issue. Certainly any fair reading of his more substantive discussions on the issue with his conservative critics (1997l), Jim Lehrer of PBS (1998), or his analysis of the issues in bi-lingual education (1998b, 56) would show a man well versed in the details of the various issues involved in the debates. However, it would also show a president equally adept at agreeing with every side of any issue, at least while he was talking with the group with whom he expressed agreement.

Consider the debate about whether the race initiative should focus on black-white relations or focus more specifically on the larger issues of diversity raised by immigration and the mixed-race/mixed ethnic identities. One of the commission's members, Angela Oh, had opted for the later, but had been overruled by the chairman, Dr. Franklin, long-steeped in the former. Asked about it at a news conference. Mr. Clinton sided with Dr. Franklin. However, consider the following exchange between the president and Richard Rodriguez of the

Pacific News Service on the McNeil-Lehrer show (1998e: 1336):

> *Mr. Rodriguez* [paraphrased by transcriber]: asserted his belief that race issues in the country have become more complicated and that the national discussion unified under "One America: The President's Initiative on Race" and its chair John Hope Franklin, has not kept pace with that complexity.

> *President Clinton*: Well, I basically agree with you about that.

One wonders why, if the president agreed with that sentiment, he did not do more to help frame the discussion in those terms either through the composition of the board or its focus. Or consider the question of class versus race in the dilemmas that the commission addressed. The following dialogue is between the president and Cynthia Tucker (1998e: 1337), a reporter for the *Atlanta Constitution*:

> *Ms. Tucker* [paraphrased by transcriber]: suggested that what many consider racial differences are actually class differences, that disproportionally poor blacks resent whites, and that working-class whites with stagnant or declining incomes blame blacks and immigrants.

> *President Clinton*: There's no doubt about that.

And so, it is class not race. Well, not quite. Consider the exchange that followed (1998e: 1337) with Kay James, Dean of the School of Government, Regent University:

> *Mr. Lehrer*: Cynthia, is the unfinished business still black and white?

> *Ms. James* [paraphrased by transcriber]: answered that no matter how middle class a person becomes, if that person is black, he or she will experience discrimination. She suggested that topics of poverty and class are worthy topics, but they should not take precedence over discussions of racism in America.

> *President Clinton*: Well, obviously I agree with that, or I wouldn't have set up this initiative.

Here is the president agreeing that racism is so ingrained in American life that even middle-class blacks will experience discrimination as a matter of course and that it is the racism of this country that led him to set up the initiative. This is an extraordinary statement. Does the president truly believe that all or most middle-class blacks experience discrimination? Does he really believe that it is America's continuing racism that is the basic reason why the country needs a national conversation on race?

Even in these more substantive and focused settings, the president seemed to exempt himself from his call for frank honest discussion. Earlier in January

1998 the president and Mr. Lehrer (1998c: 112) had this exchange on blunt talk and race:

> *Mr. Lehrer*: Why are you having trouble getting some blunt talk started on this?
>
> *President Clinton*: I don't know—we finally got some blunt talk on affirmative action. And there were some pretty compelling stories told in Phoenix the other day. But I would like to see some blunt talk.
>
> *Mr. Lehrer*: On affirmative action?
>
> *President Clinton*: Well, we had some blunt talk on affirmative action.

This exchange took place after the president's widely discussed demand for a "yes or no" answer from Abigail Thernstrom to a complicated affirmative action question in his Akron national forum. That exchange could hardly have encouraged those with different views to speak out.

Mr. Clinton seemed to lay great stress on the "compelling stories" [of discrimination] told at the Phoenix public forum. Yet, given this emphasis, his response to another such story, from Elaine Chao, former head of United Way, during the later Lehrer PBS special (1998e: 1338) was extremely odd. This exchange occurred just after the one noted above between the president and Cynthia James on racism in America:

> *Mr. Lehrer*: Elaine Chao, where do the Asian Americans—what kinds of obstacles do they start out with compared to white Americans, or Native Americans or black Americans, whatever?
>
> *Ms. Chao* [paraphrased by transcriber]: noted the increased strain in relations between races due to feelings of unequal treatment and the Asian American community's under-representation in the minority figures.
>
> *President Clinton*: Give us an example.
>
> *Ms. Chao* [paraphrased by transcriber]: noted the story of an Asian-American single mother in San Francisco whose son was denied admission into a school, despite high test scores, because it already had "too many Asian Americans."
>
> *President Clinton*: Let's go back to what Kay said. What do you think the roots of racism are?

Apparently, some stories are more compelling than others.

Roy Wilkins had criticized the president for his late start in beginning this initiative. However, a late start is not the same as a bad idea. Others noted that the race initiative was part of an effort by the president to burnish his legacy and reputation. While that doubtlessly played a role, it is not in itself a valid criticism of the effort. Portions of self- and public interest are certainly compatible in a political leader.

The larger problem is that the president was not forthright about some very divisive racial issues both before and after the initiative. Consider the case of affirmative action. Perhaps nowhere was the president's tendency to be on many sides of an issue more evident, and be less than straightforward, than in his remarks on affirmative action.

What is very striking in reading through the president's views on these issues is how extreme some of them are. Why was the president in favor of affirmative action? Because (1997b: 879) "It has given a whole generation of professionals in fields that used to be exclusive clubs, where people like me got the benefit of 100 percent affirmative action." Translation: Any white could get into any school or profession simply because they were white.

Or consider the president's undeniably correct assertion that many affirmative action students "work hard, they achieve, they go out and serve the communities that need them for their expertise and role models." However, he continues (1997c, 879) we must "not close the door on them..." Does that mean that if the relatively few schools that have high standards for admission take only those who qualify and not use a race-related criterion, minorities will be denied a place in a college or university?

Even worse, the president (1997b, 880) added,

> minority enrollments in law school and other graduate programs are plummeting for the first time in decades. Soon, the same will likely happen in undergraduate education. We must not resegregate higher education...

If non-affirmative action minority students get into undergraduate and graduate schools, does that mean the affirmative-action minority students will be able to do neither? Of course not. The overwhelming evidence is that there is ample room in American undergraduate and graduate programs of all types for students who wish to pursue their interests. The specter of resegregation is a strong symbol to raise. Modifying affirmative action is hardly a parallel to the Jim Crowe laws that governed the Southern racial caste system.

Mr. Clinton was certain (1997b: 880) that "the vast majority" of those who voted against preferences in California, "did it with the conviction that discrimination and isolation were no longer barriers to achievement." Or perhaps they were concerned about the ways in which racial preferences appeared to trump considerations of merit. Or perhaps they felt uncomfortable with giving some groups preferences, which had an adverse effect on other, non-covered groups.[9]

The president was not beyond introducing more sinister motives to those who didn't agree with his views. Asked about the vote to stop granting racial preferences in California higher education, the president replied (1997d: 1097), "I don't know why the people who promoted this in California think it's a good idea to have a segregated set of professional schools."

Oddly, enough the president was aware that many of the criticisms made of affirmative action by its critics were right. At the outreach program the president held with critics of his policies, he listened to them the whole evening and then recounted his own efforts as governor to develop and enforce standards. He then said to his critics (1997l: 2092; emphasis mine), *"I basically think all that stuff you said was right.* Earlier (1997l: 2088; emphasis mine), he had said to them in response to a number of points they had raised, " But let me just say, first of all, *I think what you generally just said is absolutely right."*

Was this an example of the president's well- known tendency (Renshon 1998b: 114-115, 315-16) to strongly agree with an opponent's position while he is present? Perhaps. However, the president is too well versed and intelligent not to know that his critic's arguments have substantial substantive merit. No, the answer lies elsewhere.

Why does he say he supports affirmative action, given that he agrees with his critics? His answer (1997l: 2092) :

> The reason I have consistently supported affirmative action programs—[is that] I am sick and tired of people telling me that poor minority kids who live in desperate circumstances, that they can't make it...I think we should give them a hand up to make it. The reason I have supported affirmative action programs is...I don't want to see all these kids be sacrificed to a principle that I agree with, because the practice of life could not be fixed in time to give them a chance.

This is a noble sentiment, but it actually contradicts something the president had said a little earlier. Responding to a number of points made by his critics, the president said (1997l: 2088) that as he saw it the major problems with his administration's economic affirmative action plans was that it was hard for those in business who had been helped by special preferences to "graduate out" from dependence on government preferences. A second problem he saw was, "it doesn't reach the vast majority of the people who have a problem because it doesn't reach down into basically the isolated urban areas with people in the underclass." These are exactly the same arguments made by critics of preference policies in higher education.

Elsewhere (1998e: 1340) the president had given a different basic reason:

> The reason I've supported affirmative action...is that I think number one, test scores and all those so-called objective measures are somewhat ambiguous, and they're not perfect measures of people's capacity to grow. But secondly, and even more importantly, I think our society has a vested interest in having people from diverse backgrounds.

The president introduced his plan for a nationwide, honest conversation about race with a criticism of those, "who would argue that scores on standardized tests should be the sole measure of qualification for admission to colleges and universities." Few argue that, but on the usefulness of such tests, the president had this to say 1997l: 2091) in his conversations with his critics about test scores, "As a matter of fact, the test scores were—[inaudible]—they have been a pretty good rough indicator."

Diversity is a laudable goal. It also has some advantages. However, the Supreme Court has ruled that it cannot be used as the basis for preferential public policies.

The president (1997b: 880) called on opponents of affirmative action to "come up with an alternative...I would embrace it if I could find a better way." In a later set of remarks he raised the bar considerably. On affirmative action he said (1997c: 889; emphasis mine):

> Look if I didn't think we needed it, I'd be happy to shed it. If someone could offer me a credible alternative, and *then test it for a year or so, and prove that it worked*, I'd be happy to shed it.

This would seem to be a formula for keeping the status quo.

Other Presidential Race Initiatives

A president's credibility and leadership capital rests not only on on what he says but what he does. Mr. Clinton's words therefore must be considered in the context of his actions. I do not want to take up the argument here that the president's credibility in matters pertaining to his relationship with Ms. Lewinsky created a pall on his policy credibility, although I think that was accurate. What I wish to consider here is the president's policy integrity and truthfulness. In this respect, not only were the president's words contradictory, but his actions tended to be at variance with his stated beliefs.

The president (1997a: 509) noted that divisive issues like affirmative action, "need to be viewed through the prism of how we can preserve one America." He had given an impassioned plea for the need to "mend, not end" affirmative action. He realized, he said, that affirmative action had not "been perfect" (1997b: 879) but pointed to his efforts to fix it.

One of these steps was taken after the Supreme Court limited the use of preference programs unless a demonstrated history of past discrimination could be sustained. One step President Clinton did take was a program to open minorities to set aside contractual bidding to qualified disadvantaged "white"-owned businesses (Holmes 1997a: A1; see also Editorial 1997: 11). How could "whites" qualify? They had to have a net personal worth of less than $250,000, excluding their homes, and had to *prove* that they had been victims of chronic discrimination to qualify as "economically disadvantaged" for purposes of Section 8A affirmative action based Small Business Awards. I emphasize the word "prove" because other already "protected groups" were presumed to have met this criteria regardless of their personal experiences or economic circumstances.

Or consider the administration's program to revise the rules that funnelled billions of dollars in federal contracts to "small disadvantaged businesses."

The proposed revisions would rely on a sector-by-sector analysis of the "available minority firms" ("capacity") in relation to the amount of dollars given to those firms ("utilization"). If there are more such firms than dollars given, those firms will be given bidding preferences (Broder 1997: A1).

The fallacy of this approach was quickly pointed out by critics of such policies (Sullivan and Clegg 1998: A13). First, it assumes that any disparity is the result of discrimination. It may well be a result of other factors, for example, under-capitalization or thin experience. Second, this approach assumes that the only way to fight discrimination is by adding in preferences. Critics point to other problems as well.

Among the other issues noted are these: (1) the program aggregates all racial and ethnic minorities and assumes if one is discriminated again, they all must be, (2) "availability is treated differently for whites and blacks, the former must have already bid on a project to be included in the "capacity" part, the former need not, (3) the rules ignore subcontracting, a prime source of participation for new companies, which many minorities firms are [the supreme court ruled this kind of information must be taken into account when seeking evidence of discrimination], (4) the rules assume that all members of minorities are "socially disadvantaged" regardless of education, income, family background and so on, (5) the system aims for racial balance, not the end of discrimination, and (6) the program awards preferences no matter how slight the disparity.

The president had aptly warned Americans that their growing diversity is "potentially a powder keg of problems, and heartbreak and division and loss." He concluded (1997a: 509).that "how we handle it (our diversity) will determine, really—that single question may be the biggest determinant of what we will look like 50 years from now and what our position will be in the world." Three months later the Clinton administration decided against adding a "multiracial" category to the 2000 Census (Office of Management and Budget 1997). In doing so, the administration preserved untouched for another decade at least, increasingly divisive single race/ethnicity categories. And in the process, it took a step away from helping to nurture a "group that is quintessentially American—emphasizing the melting pot quality of the population rather than the distinctions (Eddings 1997)—the very outcome that the president had said he championed.

President Clinton's legitimacy as a national leader of a frank dialogue was further compromised by the almost dizzying succession of his positions on the Taxman affirmative action case settled by affirmation action advocates before the Supreme Court could render its decision. He holds the unique and, from the perspective of principle and candor, dubious distinction of heading the only administration ever to submit three distinct briefs to the Supreme Court, each taking a decidedly different position.

Susan Taxman, who is white, brought suit against a board of education that fired her to maintain diversity. President Bush originally entered into case on the side of Ms. Taxman's position. When he became president, Mr. Clinton reversed that position and had the Justice Department enter on the side of the board and against Ms. Taxman.

After two lower courts decided in favor of Ms. Taxman, the administration changed course, this time submitting a brief urging the Supreme Court not to hear the case because its circumstances made it unusual and a poor vehicle for fashioning an important decision in this area. The court decided to take the case anyway and the Clinton administration then submitted its third brief in the same case—this time on Ms. Taxman side, but with a twist.

The administration then argued that only in cases of a proven history of discrimination could the desire to increase diversity be a legitimate standard to use, but it also argued that it might also be used in the absence of such a proven history when there was a tangible purpose for doing so, such as with a police or corrections department that might wish more diversity to better accomplish its mission. Eventually, the case was settled out of court by affirmative action advocates funding the settlement with Ms. Taxman.

The President's Initiative on Race suggests that a symbolic focus on hard issues is no substitute for real and honest engagement. Lofty aspirations don't automatically translate into leadership capital. Rather, the PIR example suggests that it is in the *how,* not necessarily in the *what,* that leadership capital is accumulated. President Clinton's multiple, conflicting, and seemingly strategic positions in this case made it hard to know just which conviction he was demonstrating the courage of.

One America: In Retrospect

The President's Initiative on Race was an idea with a laudable purpose. It is questionable whether it could have succeeded in the form it took, even without the flaws in framing and process that became clear as it unfolded. Certainly, the many problems of the initiative were compounded by the president's failure to be honest with the public about what he truly believed.

If he understood the flaws in affirmative action programs, why not tell the public so that the debate could begin from a different starting point? By not doing so, and being inconsistent and sometimes evasive, his conversation began and stayed at the same level of impasse while advocates and foes debated if there were problems, and if so, what they were.

If he understood that the issue facing America was more than "black-white" relations, why not say so and move the debate on to those more immediate, pressing, and relevant issues? By not doing so directly and consistently, the president allowed those issues to be muddled, not clarified. As a result, the conversation never reached the level of clarity that was one of its main goals.

If the president really wanted an honest dialogue, why didn't he model it with his own appointments to the board and his own treatment of his opponents? Did confronting Abigail Thernstrom on national television with his "yes or no" demands of a single answer to a complex question, model respect for opposing views that he had said he wanted? Did it give others who might hold different views than those expressed the sense that it was safe to dissent?

There is one other fact that needs to be mentioned here and that is the president's impeachment. I am not referring here to his relationship with Ms. Lewinsky, but to the fact that the report from his commission was given to the president almost at the same time that his four-hour videotaped grand jury testimony about lying under oath in the Monica Lewinsky case was aired to the nation. That same day more than 3,000 pages of documentation from the Independent Council's investigation were released by Congress (Simpson, Taylor, and Rogers 1998: A3).

The president's initiative was unfolding while, behind the scenes, the president was fully engaged in saving his presidency. One of the linchpins of this effort was the overwhelming support he received from Americans of African decent (Sack 1998: A1). The figures are startling. In February 1997 as the events leading to his impeachment were unfolding, 93 percent of African American approved of the president's job performance, while 63 percent of "whites" did. Ninety-one percent (91 percent) of African Americans had a favorable view of Mr. Clinton, 52 percent of "whites" did. Only 5 percent of African Americans thought the president was to blame for his problems, while 85 percent said they were the fault of his enemies. The respective figures for "whites" were 38 percent and 51 percent. Finally, and perhaps most puzzling, 80 percent of African Americans thought the president had the "moral values that most Americans try to live by," while only 34 percent of "whites" thought so.

I am not imputing cynicism to the president, but I think it fair to say that President Clinton has always had a very high level of self-interest. Even under normal circumstances, there have been many questions raised about his tendency to put his own self-interest before the public's, or to mask the former by appeals to the latter. It is certainly understandable that in fighting for his political life, he would put his own interests before those of having a successful commission. It would be a great deal to ask of any leader and, perhaps, particularly Mr. Clinton to put the work of the commission, however laudable, ahead of his political survival.

One America = The Voices of Individualism?

Paradoxically, there were some important things to be learned from the public forums that were critized as "Oprah-like." The Akron town meeting is a good case in point. Woven throughout the tales and complaints of unfair treatment, was another, equally compelling set of narratives, perhaps more in keeping with the traditions of the country.

There is Vanessa Cordero asking the group to remember that, "this is not black and white in America...it's hurt me all these years that I've been in the United States, since 1957, that all I hear is black issues and white issues."

Another young lady of Hispanic descent has a similar concern. Using the segregation she witnesses on her campus, she comments, then asks,

> white people hang out here and black people hang out there. And as a Hispanic and coming from a Mexican background, where does that put me? I'm neither one.

There is McHoughton Chambers, the bi-racial child of a mixed marriage, struggling to find his identity. He expresses his concern that people only see half of who he is, and that they often neglect to see the other side of his bi-racial makeup. Another student, Erika Sanders, eloquently evokes (Transcript 1997; emphasis mine) her experiences as a black student in an all-white school:

> ...I feel like I live in two different worlds, When I go to school, sometimes *I feel the burden to speak for all of black America*. And slowly, *I'm helping my classmates to realize that I'm not all of black America, I'm Erika.*

Anna Arroyo recalled her experience as a Puerto Rican in a college course on Latin America. She related that her classmates thought that because of her origin she should be able to speak authoritatively on all Latin cultures. However,

> What people don't understand is that I'm not Peruvian; I'm not Mexican. I don't understand their culture. I'm Puerto Rican and all I know is Puerto Rico.

What does all these narratives have in common? These individuals share something extremely basic, yet very profound. They are all asking, each in their own way, to be taken as the unique persons that they are. They do not ask to be representatives of groups. Ms. Sanders does not want to have to speak for all African Americans; she would much prefer that her friends get to know her as who she is—Erika. Ms. Arroyo does not wish to be known by the fact that she is an Hispanic, but by rather her *particular experiences and identification.* Mr. Chambers does not wish to be known for one-half of his bi racial identity, whichever half is emphasized. He wants to be known as who he is, in total.

Perhaps paradoxically, it appears that the road to One America lies through the path of individualism.

Notes

1. The case material and analysis in this section draws on a variety of data including event transcripts, news accounts, survey data, and the words of the principles themselves. For a detailed consideration of the advantages and imitations of each kind of data and their usefulness in a composite analysis, see Renshon (1998a: 405-408).
2. Elsewhere (Renshon 1998b: 3-33), I have described the basic public dilemma as a fundamental unresolved question concerning public psychology and governance facing the president on taking office. It is not a specific question about public policy, but rather the public's psychological connections to its institutions, leaders, and

political process. This unresolved public concern underlies and frames more specific policy debates.

3.   White House material accompanying the initiative lists a fifth purpose, " to articulate the President's vision of a just, unified America." See "Background and Points of Progress" (Office of the White House, Washington, DC., no date).

4.   The questions had comes up in various forums, but were put to the president directly in an interview (1997: 1187-88) in the initiative's early days:

Mr. Smiley: Your challenge to America to have a conversation about race has certainly spun out a number of conversations, including conversations about slavery and reparations. And I'm wondering, since you've had more time to reflect, do you think an apology to African Americans is warranted? And specifically, what do you think of at least having a commission to study the feasibility of reparations, regardless to what [*sic*] your opinion is?

PresidentClinton: Well, I don't believe that—what I think I should do now is let the advisory board do its work and see what they have to say about the apology issue and all the related issues.

5.   I am indebted to Dr. William Friedman of Public Agenda for making these data available.

6.   They included former governors Thomas Kean of New Jersey (Republican) and William Winter of Mississippi (Democrat), Linda Chavez Thompson of the AFL-CIO, the Reverend Suzan D. Johnson Cook, a minister from the Bronx, New York, Angela Oh, a Los Angeles attorney and community leader, and Robert Thompson, CEO of Nissan, U.S.A., and the chair Dr. John Hope Franklin of Duke University.

    In the descriptions of the panel members and some excerpts from their remarks during the first meeting (Holmes 1997b: A1), it is clear that there is very little divergence in basic views among the board members.

7.   In fact this proved to be truer of the community meetings than it was of meetings that focused on particular issues, like health or poverty. Yet even in the latter those invited to speak were skewed in the direction of the commission's basic assumptions and preferences regarding the issues.

    On the difference between community based meeting and those with more specialized audiences compare the Community meeting which took place in Phoenix on the morning of January 14, 1998, with the more focused meeting on race in the workplace that took place that afternoon. Transcripts of those meetings and the other public meetings of the Race Initiative can be found online at: http://www.whitehouse.gov/Initiatives/OneAmerica/america.html (November 1, 2000).

8.   A somewhat sobering, some would say chilling, observation about the program can be found in Rosin (1997: 29). Hanna Rosen reports that the program was coercive and measured "change in results in a desired direction." What is the desired direction? Rosen writes,

One question measured support for affirmative action. If, by the end of the program you showed stronger support that meant you had changed in the desirable direction. If by the end of the program you showed less support for affirmative action, but loved your fellow man even more, well, that just didn't count as a better attitude.

9.   The president made the same kind of characterization of those who opposed bilingual education in California. Speaking of that referendum, he said (1998b: 56):

Now, in the initial polling…it is deeply troubling to defenders of bilingual education because the initial polling has 70% of Hispanic voters voting for the initiative. Now, what does that mean? That doesn't mean they necessarily understand the implications of this initiative and that they want to vote for it.

References

Babington, Charles. "A Grand Plan Loses Steam." *Washington Post-Weekly Edition*, 28 June 1999: 29.

Baker, Peter. "An Initiative That's Going Nowhere Fast," *The Washington Post Weekly Edition*, October 13 1998: 10.

_____. "A Splinter on the Race Advisory Board." *Washington Post*, 15 July 1997: A04.

Baker, Peter, and Michael A. Fletcher. "Clinton's Town Hall Taking Discussion of Race into Sports Arena." *Washington Post*, 14 April 1998: A02.

Baker, Russell. "We've Got to Talk." *New York Times*, 17 June 1997: A21.

Begard, Paul. "Clinton Sets Up Session on Race with Critics." *Washington Times*, 11 December 1997:A1.

Bennet, James. "Clinton, at Meeting on Race, Struggles to Sharpen Debate." *New York Times*, 4 December 1997: A1.

_____. "Clinton Debates 9 Conservatives on Racial Issues." *New York Times*, 20 December 1997b: A1.

Blow, Richard. "Race Wars at the White House." *George*, March 1998.

Branegan, Jay. "Bill's Block." *Time*, 13 December 1999, 73.

Broder, John M. "U.S. Readies Rules Over Preferences Aiding Minorities." *New York Times*, 6 May 1997: A1.

Charles, Mark. "Americans Remain Wary of Washington. "*Wall Street Journal*, 23 December 1997: A14.

Citrin, Jack, Beth Reingold, and Donald P. Green. "American Identity and the Politics of Ethnic Change." *Journal of Politics* 52:4 (1990): 1124-1154.

Clinton, William J. "Remarks and Question and Answer Session with the American Society of Newspaper Editors," (April 11 1997). *Weekly Compilation of Presidential Documents,* 14, April, 33:15 1997a, 501-510.

_____. "Remarks at the University of California at San Diego Commencement Ceremony," (June 14, 1997). *Weekly Compilation of Presidential Documents*, 23, June, 33:25, 1997b, 876-882.

_____. "Remarks at a Democratic National Committee Diner," (June 16, 1997). *Weekly Compilation of Presidential Documents*, 23, June, 33:25, 1997c, 883-894.

_____. "Remarks and Question and Answer Session with the National Association of Black Journalists in Chicago, Illinois," (July 17, 1997). *Weekly Compilation of Presidential Documents*, 21, July, 33:29, 1997d, 1092-1101.

_____. "Interview with Tavis Smiley of Black Entertainment Television," (August 4, 1997). *Weekly Compilation of Presidential Documents*, 11, August, 33:32, 1997, 1184-1189.

_____. "Remarks at American University," (September 9, 1997). *Weekly Compilation of Presidential Documents*, 15 September, 33:37, 1997f, 1296-1308. .

_____. "Remarks at a Democratic Business Council Diner," (September 9, 1997). *Weekly Compilation of Presidential Documents*, 15, September, 33:37, 1997g, 1304-1308.

_____. "Remarks Prior to a Meeting with the President's Advisory Board on Race," (September 30, 1997). *Weekly Compilation of Presidential Documents*, 6, October, 33:40, 1997h, 1462-1463.

_____. "Interview with Jodi Enda of Knight-Ridder Newspapers," (December 1, 1997). *Weekly Compilation of Presidential Documents*, 8, December, 33:49, 1997i, 1943-1948.

_____. "Remarks in a Roundtable Discussion on Race in Akron," (December 3, 1997). *Weekly Compilation of Presidential Documents*, 8, December, 33:49, 1997j, 1959-1969.

_____. "The President's News Conference," (December 16, 1997). *Weekly Compilation of Presidential Documents*, 22, December, 33:51, 1997k, 2049-2069.

_____. "Remarks in an Outreach Meeting with Conservatives on the Race Initiative," (December 19, 1997). *Weekly Compilation of Presidential Documents*, 22, December, 33: 51, 1997l, 2085-2093.

_____. "Remarks and a Question and Answer Session at a Democratic National Committee Dinner," (January 8, 1998). *Weekly Compilation of Presidential Documents*, 12, January, 34: 2, 1998a, 21-27.

_____. "Remarks on an Outreach Meeting on the Race Initiative," (January 12, 1998). *Weekly Compilation of Presidential Documents*, 19, January, 34: 3, 1998b, 50-57.

_____. "Interview with Jim Lehrer of the PBS 'News Hour,'" (January 21, 1998). *Weekly Compilation of Presidential Documents*, 26, January, 34: 4, 1998c, 104-115.

_____. "Remarks at the ESPN Town Hall Meeting on Race Relations in Houston," (April 1, 1998). *Weekly Compilation of Presidential Documents*, 20, April, 34: 16, 1998d, 642-648.

_____. "Remarks in the 'Presidential Dialogue on Race' on PBS," (July, 13, 1998). *Weekly Compilation of Presidential Documents*, 8, July, 34: 28, 1998e, 1336-1344.

_____. "The President's News Conference," (March 26, 1999). *Weekly Compilation of Presidential Documents*, 19, March, 35: 12, 1998, 471-484.

DiMaggio, Paul, et al. "Have American Attitudes Become More Polarized?" *American Journal of Sociology* 102:3 (1996): 690-755.

Eddings, Jerelyn. "Counting a 'New' Type of American: The Dicey Politics of Creating a "Multiracial Category in the Census." *U.S. News and World Report*. 14 July 1977.

Editorial. "Stifling the Race Debate." *New York Times*, 21 November 1997a: A34.

Editorial. "Talking About Race in Akron." *New York Times*, 5 December 1997b: A30.

Editorial. "Whitewash." *The New Republic*, 22 September 1997: 11

Excerpts from Round Table with Opponents of Racial Preferences. *New York Times*, 22 December 1997: A22.

Fletcher, Michael A., and Dan Balz. "Race Relations Initiative May Pose Risks for Clinton." *Washington Post*, 12 June 1977: A01.

Frisby, Michael K. "White House Reworks Troubled Race Initiative as President Heads for a Town Meeting in Ohio." *Wall Street Journal*, 3 December 1997: A24.

_____. "Race Course: Clinton Stays Popular with Blacks in Spite of Fraying of Safety Net." *Wall Street Journal*, 13 June 1997: A1.

Greenfield, Meg. "The Colin Powell Test." *Newsweek*, 15 December 1997: 84.

Harris, John. "What's a President to Do?" *Washington Post*, 15 September 1996: A12.

Holmes, Steven A. "Race Advisory Panel Gives Report to Clinton." *New York Times*, 19 September 1998a: A1.

_____. "Clinton Panel on Race Urges Variety of Modest Measures." *New York Times*, 18 September 1998b: A1.

_____. "U.S. Acts To Open Minority Program to White Bidders." *New York Times*, 15 August 1997a: A1.

_____. "Scholar Takes on His Toughest Study of Race." *New York Times*, 28 September 1997b: A1.

_____. "Talks About Race Get an Early Start." *New York Times*, 28 September 1997c: A28.

_____. "President Nudges His Race Panel to Take Action." *New York Times*, 1 October 1997d: A23.

_____. "Critics Say Clinton Panel About Race Lacks Focus." *New York Times*, 12 October 1997e: A17.

_____. "Race Panel Excludes Critics of Affirmative Action Plans." *New York Times,* 19 November 1997f: A24.

_____. "Clinton Panel on Race Relations is Itself Biased, Gingrich Says." *New York Times*, 21 November 1997g: A30

_____. "Policy Opponent to Join Clinton at Race Forum." *New York Times*, 27 November 1997h: A29.

_____. "In Akron, Dialogue But Few Changes." *New York Times*, 4 December 1997i: A26.

_____. "Conservatives' Voices Enter Clinton's Dialogue on Race." *New York Times*, 17 December 1997j: A24.

_____. "Clinton to Meet Conservatives." *New York Times*, 11 December 1997k: A23.

_____. "After March, Lawmakers Seek Commission on Race Relations." *New York Times*, 18 October 1995: A1.

Holmes, Steven A., and James Bennet. "A Renewed Sense of Purpose for Clinton's Panel on Race." *New York Times*, 14 January 1998: A1.

Hunt, Albert R. "The Race Initiative: Tough but Worth the Effort." *Wall Street Journal*, 11 December 1997: A23.

Kelly, Michael. "The Great Divider." *The New Republic,* 7 July 1997: 6, 41-42.

Kennedy, Randall. "Clinton Must Resist Impulse to Control the Race Debate." *Washington Post*, 15 June 1997: C01.

Lee, Felicia R. "The Honest Dialogue That is Neither." *New York Times*, 7 December 1997: wk. 5.

Lehman, Nicholas. "Clinton the Great Communicator." *New York Times*, 20 January 1997: A17.

Levin, Arthur. "President's Essay." In Teacher's College Annual Report: Diversity 1999, Columbia University, 1999.

Neal, Terry M., and Ceci Connolly. "Hollywood Draws Cash for Gore, Ire in GOP." *Washington Post*, 14 September 2000: A01.

Nye, Joseph F. Jr., Philip D. Zelikow, and David C. King (eds). *Why People Don't Trust Government*. Cambridge, MA: Harvard University Press, 1997.

Office of Management and Budget. Recommendations from the Interagency Committee for the Review of the Racial and Ethnic Standards to the Office of Management and Budget Concerning Changes to the Standards for the Classification of Federal Data on Race and Ethnicity; Notice. *Federal Register* Vol. 62, No. 131 (July 9, 1997), pp. 36873-36946.

Pew Center for People and the Press. "Deconstructing Distrust: How Americans View Government." March 10, 1988.

Powell, Colin. *My American Journey*. New York: Random House, 1999.

Public Agenda. "Time To Move On: African American and White Parents Set an Agenda for Public Schools." New York, 1998a: 1-51.

Public Agenda. "Time to Move On: Technical Appendix." New York, 1998b: 1-48.

Rosen, Hanna. "Small Talk." *New York*, 15 December 1997: 28-29.

Ross, Sonya. "President to Establish Race Office." *Associated Press*, 4 February 1999.

Sack, Kevin. "Blacks Stand by a President Who 'Has Been There for Us.'" *New York Times*, 19 September 1997: A1.

_____. "Gore Takes Tough Stand on Violent Entertainment." *New York Times*, 11 September 2000:A1.

Simpson, Glenn R., Jeffrey Taylor, and David Rogers. "New Evidence Complicates Clinton Case." *Wall Street Journal*, 23 September 1998: A3.

Sleeper, Jim. *Liberal Racism*. New York: Penguin, 1997.

_____. *The Closest of Strangers: Liberalism and the Politics of Race in New York*. New York: W.W. Norton, 1990.

Sullivan, John, and Roger Clegg. "More Preferences for Minority Business." *Wall Street Journal*, 24 August 1998: A13

Taylor, Charles. *Multiculturalism and the "Politics of Recognition."* Princeton, NJ: Princeton University Press, 1992.

Thernstrom, Abigail. "Going Toe to Toe with Bill." *Newsweek*, 15 December 1997: 35.

Wayne, Steven G., C. MacKenzie, D. M. O'Brien, and R. L. Cole. *The Politics of American Government*. New York: St. Martin's Press, 1999.

Wolfe, Alan. *One Nation After All*. Chicago: University of Chicago Press, 1998.

Part 6

Presidential Leadership in the New Millennium

13

George W. Bush's Mandate:
Governing on the Razor's Edge

The 2000 presidential election marked the culmination, and perhaps the most concrete expression of a trend that had been gathering momentum since 1964. The 1964 presidential election gave Democratic Party nominee Lyndon Johnson a landslide victory and a majority in both houses of Congress. Thereafter, Americans apparently began to see the advantages of divided government.

Lyndon Johnson did not stand for a second term, and Republican Richard Nixon took his place. Nixon, however, did not finish his second term and Republican Gerald Ford took his place, only to be dispossessed by Jimmy Carter, who, in turn, was beaten by Ronald Reagan. Mr. Reagan won two terms, but had to contend with a Democratic Congress in both of them, as did his one-term successor George Bush.

Bill Clinton won the presidency with less than 50 percent of the votes cast in 1992, but he began with a Democratic Congress. However, his lurch to the left after promising to govern from the center, cost him and his party control of both houses of Congress, a condition that continued through his second term. George W. Bush had a Republican Congress for a few months, but a party switch by one senator brought America back to divided party rule. Looking back, that makes over thirty-seven years, with modest exceptions, since the Congress and the presidency were in the hands of one party. For how long and with what results are open questions.

The 2000 presidential election was anomalous in a number of important ways. It was an election whose closeness widely confounded pundits. Scholars who study and predict elections were not only wrong in picking Mr. Gore as the winner, but very wrong in predicting his margin of victory. It was an election in which an extremely able, sitting vice president, running with the strongest American economic performance in modern memory, lost to a relatively inexperienced novice in national politics. It was an election in which the American public rated one candidate, Mr. Gore, as much better on the issues, and the other, Mr. Bush, better on leadership and values. It was an election with a climatic, traumatic and, by the time it was over, anti-climatic ending—one that stimulated ferocious partisan feelings overlaid on top of already raw political and cultural divisions. And, it was an election in which the winner began to govern as if he had received a mandate much to the outrage of those who were certain that he hadn't.

Why Did Al Gore Lose?

The election was Al Gore's to lose,[1] and he did. That was the conclusion not only of reporters who covered the campaign, but of a number of political scientists who study and try to predict national election outcomes. At a panel that took place at the American Political Science Association Meetings in September 2001, every expert on voting predicted unequivocally that Mr. Gore would decisively beat Mr. Bush. The forecasts ranged (Clymer 2000; see also Wlezien 2001: 27-Table 3) from 52.8 forecast by James E. Campbell, to 60.3 expected by both Thomas M. Holbrook and Brad Lockerbie, with the others between.[2] The predictions were made even during periods when Bush was up in the polls by as much as nine points (Wlezien 2001: 27).

Modeling forecasts generally make use of two major elements to predict presidential election outcomes. Almost all use some measure of *economic performance* and some measure of public opinion—usually focused on judgments of *sitting presidents and their public approval ratings*.[3] Surprisingly, the elements that news reporters write about and the basis on which people say they are judging the candidates are no where to be seen in most of these models. That said, however, over the past thirteen years such models have done very well, with some notable exceptions, in predicting final results of presidential elections.

Does this mean that economics trumps policy, or that presidential popularity trumps psychology? Probably not. Presidential performance measures are themselves summary variables whose elements certainly include aspects of presidential psychology, for example, policy judgment and leaderships skills. Economic prosperity is a part of economic policy and related to presidential performance evaluations as well.

In the 2000 election these models were clearly wrong. In a series of papers, a number of those whose predictions were wrong tried to explain why. Authors of at least one paper argued in spite of the results that they had been right all along.[4] Their efforts are instructive. All involved reassessing the models and assumptions that formed the basis of their predictions. And all the reformulations suggest that even when the models are working well, it is important to understand clearly the human behavior on which these models are built.

Some writers looked to refine their economic indicators. Larry Bartels and John Zaller (2001: 14), for example, argued that income *growth* would have been preferred over growth in economic output in their irregression models. Michael Lewis-Beck and Charles Tien (2001) suggested that for non-incumbents economic evaluations are prospective, whereas for incumbents they are retrospective. Christopher Wlezien (2001) examined a range of forecasts at different periods before and leading up to the elections. Looking over the different models that were used Wlezien concluded that those who relied on

"objective" measures of economic performance outperformed models that used "subjective" measures of economic performance. Yet, while this explains why some did better than others, it does not explain why all were wrong.

The problem, of course, is that the models "are premised on the idea that one of the candidates will find it in his interest to emphasize the economic record" (Campbell 2001: 37). Holbrook agrees (2001: 40), noting that,

...one of the assumptions that underlie the forecasting model is that the two major party candidates will both run effective and relatively balanced campaigns. In regard to claims about the economy, this means that the incumbent-party candidate runs on and takes credit for good economic times...

How well did Mr. Gore's behavior conform to the assumptions of the prediction model that saw him winning? Not well at all.

Wlezien considers other factors, for which there is some evidence.[5] However, he notes that Mr. Gore did not adequately campaign on the robust economy. He writes,

...Gore did not take credit for the economic and policy performance of the last four years, and so he did not get credit, at least fully. Instead, he stepped away from this arena, where he was advantaged, to one where he was on more equal footing—the policy future. This is a tempting explanation and there is some basis for it...the success of forecasting models in previous election years probably tell us as much about what the candidates did in their campaigns as it does about the importance of the economy and other aspects of presidential performance. Credit for a good economy does not happen magically, candidates make it happen. (2001: 28)

James Campbell agrees. He writes (Campbell 2001: 37), after analyzing why the predictive models were so inaccurate in the 2000 election, "Gore badly misplayed what appeared to be a winning hand." Others (Holbrook 2001: 39-40) conclude that Gore's failure to emphasize the good economy as an important element in his loss. These analyses seem to severely undercut Bartel and Zallers' view (2001: 18) that appeals to election specific explanations (e.g., Gore's and Bush's actual campaigns and their skills in mounting it) are "quite superfluous."

Perhaps the most noted line of Mr. Gore's acceptance speech (Transcript 2000) before the Democratic Convention was his assertion that, "I stand here tonight as my own man." It is a phrase with many meanings. At one level, it is the strategic claim of a man who has been the second in command of a generally popular leader with an excellent economy, serving as proof to many that he is an effective president. Yet there is also another strategic and, perhaps, a more deeply personal, claim being made here as well. It is a disclaimer—that he is not like Mr. Clinton, and ought not to be tarnished by his association with a president and administration whose ethical lapses were frequent, publicly and personally damaging, and in several instances criminal.

Mr. Gore made it quite clear that he was not running on his partnership with Mr. Clinton and the robust economy that had developed during their terms of office. Moreover, he was also very clear in asking the public not to judge him by the economy. In his words (Transcript 2000; emphasis added) he left no margin of error for himself and others when, at the very start of his acceptance speech he said,

> But now we turn the page and write a new chapter. And that's what I want to speak about tonight. *This election is not an award for past performance. I'm not asking you to vote for me on the basis of the economy we have…*

If the public was not to judge him on the economy, or more generally what many people saw as a successful administration partnership, what were they to judge him on? The answer, I think, was a tremendous political misjudgment, given Mr. Gore's psychology and a public anxious to leave divisive partisanship and rancor behind. He said (Transcript 2000; emphasis added),

> To all the families in America who have to struggle to afford the right education and the skyrocketing costs of prescription drugs, I want you to know this: I've taken on the powerful forces, and as president, I'll stand up to them and I'll stand up for you.

This is not the only possible cause for Mr. Gore's loss,[5] but it does appear to be a substantial one.

The Razor's Edge: Some Figures

That brings us to 2001 where, for the first time since Jimmy Carter had the advantage for four years and Mr. Clinton for two, a president entered office with his party in control of Congress, though barely. That didn't last long. However, that control was razor thin, fifty-fifty in the Senate, and very vulnerable to a defection—as happened, or the mid-term elections (2002). In 2002, twenty-three Republican Senate seats are up for reelection and only fourteen Democratic seats.

The 50-49-1 Senate split means that the president is dependent on Senate democrats for passing his agenda. In the House, the margin is less narrow, but not much more robust—221 versus 212 seats, with two independents (Eilperin 2000: A05). The last time control of the Congress was so evenly divided was in 1953-55 when Republicans had a 49 to 46 Senate edge, and a 219-215 edge in the House (Clymer 2000, A1).

About 51.2 percent of the nation's 200 million eligible voters cast ballots in the 2000 election, marginally greater than the rock-bottom level seen in 1996, but significantly lower than the 1992 level (Dreazen 2000; Associated Press 2000). In 1996, only 49 percent of those qualified to vote actually did so, the lowest turn-out since 1924. By contrast, some 55 percent of the electorate went to the polls in 1992's close race between Bill Clinton and President George H.W. Bush. In that election, Ross Perot ran as the Independent Party candidate and Mr. Clinton won a plurality, not a majority of votes cast.

George W. Bush's victory was extremely narrow in a number of important respects. Out of more than 105 million votes cast, Mr. Gore received 50, 996, 064 votes or 48.39 percent, George Bush received 50, 456,167 votes (a difference of 539, 947) or 47.88 percent, while Green Party candidate Ralph Nader received 2, 864, 810 votes or 2.72, percent and Independent Party nominee Patrick Buchanan received 386, 024 votes or .037 percent.

Combining Mr. Gore's left-of-center candidacy with Mr. Nader's very-left-of-center insurgency, this election revealed a just over 50 percent plurality for left-of-center candidates. Exit polls supported this. Barnes (2000: 17) notes that exit polls show that compared with 1996, 2 percent more voters self-identify as liberal, and 3 percent less self-identify as conservative.

The electoral college vote was narrow as well. Mr. Bush won 271 votes there, one more than necessary and Mr. Gore won 266, having received one less than he won because of a protest vote by a District of Columbia elector protesting the "colonial status" of the district (Stout 2000). Mr. Bush won 30 states, Mr. Gore 20. A look at the electoral map suggests that each candidate's strength was geographically concentrated.

Figure 13.1
2000 Electoral Votes

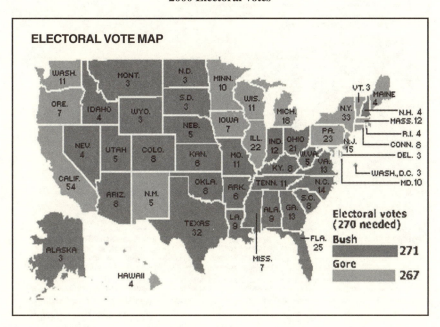

This map has led some to question whether geography is indeed becoming political destiny. Terry Teachout (2001: 242) argues,

> Look at the national map. Except for Alaska and New Hampshire, all 29 states won decisively by Bush are geographically contiguous, forming a vast L-shaped curve that sweeps down from the Rocky Mountains across the great Plains, then through the Midwest and the South. By contrast, except for California and Washington, most of the states won decisively by Gore are bunched tightly around the urban and industrial centers of the Northeast and Great Lakes.

In line with this, Brooks (2000: 26) notes that "each party is getting more dominant in its home base."

Yet a slightly different pictures emerges if one examines the election results at a more micro level. If you examine the vote at the county level, a different picture comes into focus, and a different psychological sense of the closeness of the outcome. Mr. Gore won 676 counties across the United States, while Mr. Bush won 2,436 counties according to preliminary final results. If you look at the square miles of the counties won, Mr. Gore won 575,184 and Mr. Bush, 2,432, 456. In terms of the population of the counties won, those that went to Mr. Gore contained 127 million, those that went to Mr. Bush, 143 million.

Figure 13.2
2000 Election Vote by County

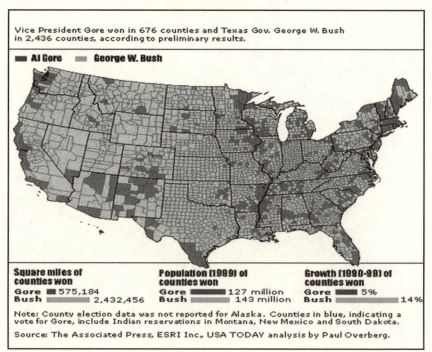

Vice President Gore won in 676 counties and Texas Gov. George W. Bush in 2,436 counties, according to preliminary results.

■ Al Gore   ▨ George W. Bush

Square miles of counties won	Population (1999) of counties won	Growth (1990-99) of counties won
Gore ■ 575,184	Gore ■■■ 127 million	Gore ■■■ 5%
Bush ■■■■ 2,432,456	Bush ■■■ 143 million	Bush ■■■■ 14%

Note: County election data was not reported for Alaska. Counties in blue, indicating a vote for Gore, include Indian reservations in Montana, New Mexico and South Dakota.

Source: The Associated Press, ESRI Inc., USA TODAY analysis by Paul Overberg.

Finally, if one looks at the growth of population for 1990-99 of the counties won, Mr. Gore's counties increased 5 percent and Mr. Bush's increased 14 percent.

Overall (Connelly 2000), a majority of women, older voters, Democrats, liberals and blacks, Hispanic and Asian voters cast their ballots for Mr. Gore. Mr. Bush captured the votes of most men, "whites," conservatives, Republicans, Southerners and "white Protestants." Ralph Nader did well among Independents, especially liberal ones and among young men.

These differences show up in more detailed analysis (Pomper 2001). Gerald Pomper finds (2001: 137) that the difference between the Gore and Bush votes in a large number of social/political categories is quite striking (Gore favoring groups first, Bush favoring groups listed second): between poor and rich a 14 point difference; single and married people, 13 points; working women and homemakers, 14 points; gays and straights, 23 points; non-believers and frequent church-goers, 25 points; Catholics and white Protestants, 15 points; Jews and white Christians, 40 points; other voters and the religious rights, 36 points; high school drop-outs and college graduates, 14 points; union members and non-union members, 18 points; and "blacks" and "whites," 48 points. Pomper (2001: 137) concludes his analysis with the decided understated truth, " In 2000, the United States was not united."

The Razor's Edge: Two Cultures/Two Nations—One Country?

Teachout (2001: 24; see also Himmelfarb 1999; 2001), examining the political implications of geography in the 2000 presidential race, clearly has more than geography on his mind:

> ...the voting populations of these two geographical entities are, taken together, almost identical in size. Yet, they are very different places. On one side of the fence is an urban- and suburban-based congeries of government employees, union members, blacks, and those highly educated comparatively affluent "knowledge workers" known to political scientists as the New Class. On the other side is the contemporary equivalent of what H.L. Menchen dubbed the Bible Belt...in which rural and small town America have joined forces with the fast growing group of Americans who live in "exurbia," the new middle-class communities that are springing up beyond the rim of the older suburbs.

The result is that, "what the recent election indicates is that Himmelfarb's 'one nation, two cultures' is splintering still further, this time into two geographically and culturally distinct units—call them 'Democratic Nation' and 'Republican Nation'—that are competing for control of the country as a whole." Gertrude Himmelfarb, whose two-culture thesis (1999) is the basis for Teachout's analysis, does not disagree (2001). Hendrick Hertzberg's (2000: 91) ringing affirmation that Bill Clinton, "through unheralded perseverance and political skill had succeeded in freeing the country from the fiscal (and ideological bonds) that constricted political possibility for a generation," was obviously premature.

Teachout (2001: 26) is well aware that one must be cautious in ascribing uniform views since neither area is wholly homogeneous. However, his point is that while the election may have been very close when viewed through the traditional lens of states won and electoral votes gained, the election was not at all close when viewed through the lens of distinct political groups. Hence, for example,[6] the more regularly you attend the church, the more likely you were to vote for Mr. Bush. Sixty-one percent of voters who never go to church voted for Mr. Gore.

Americans of African decent voted nine to one for Mr. Gore, while 60 percent of Caucasian men voted for Mr. Bush. More men than women voted for Mr. Bush, he gained 53 percent of married women's votes, while Mr. Gore received 57 percent of unmarried women's votes. Mr. Bush received 56 percent of the votes of those women who are married with children. Of the 4 percent of voters who identify themselves as homosexual, 70 percent chose Mr. Gore.

Of the 16 percent of voters who belong to unions, 62 percent voted for Mr. Gore. In some states the combination proved even more potent. John Judis (2000: 18) points out that exit polls in Michigan show Mr. Gore winning 91 percent of the African American vote, 64 percent of the union vote, which makes up more than a quarter of the electorate there. He also won a majority of votes of those with advanced degrees and those making more than $75,000 per year. Those with incomes under $15,000 were strongly in favor of Mr. Gore (57 percent to 37 percent), as were 58 percent of working women. He received 79 percent of the Jewish vote, but only 42 percent of the Catholic vote. Finally, Mr. Gore received 70 percent of the votes among those who thought abortion should always be legal.

Consistent with Figure 13.1 and Mr. Teachout's analysis, 29 percent of the 2000 voters lived in a city setting and 61 percent of them voted for Mr. Gore. Forty-three percent lived in suburbs and the candidates split this vote (47 percent Gore, 49 percent Bush). And, 28 percent of 2000 election voters lived in rural settings and 59 percent of these voted for Mr. Bush.

There are other sharp difference that could be noted. However, I think the point is clear: Mr. Gore and Mr. Bush appealed to two very different constituencies—geographically and categorically. The question to which we turn in the next section is whether the candidates approached their leadership roles in a way that gives any support for the distinctions drawn between reflective and heroic styles.

Election "Mandates": Narrow Victories, Diminished Ambitions?

It is obvious that large electoral victories provide large mandates. Certainly FDR's sweeping electoral victory was a vote to "fix" America's economic system. Ronald Reagan's forty-nine-state victory over Walter Mondale in 1984 surely reflected the public's desire to move the government to a more right of center, rather than a left of center stance. Sometimes, however, the meaning of the term "mandate" is not always clear. Lyndon Johnson's sweeping 1964 victory over Barry Goldwater was certainly a vote for the continuation of a Democratic administration in the aftermath of John F. Kennedy's tragic death. It was also quite clearly a vote for the candidate that was viewed as the "more moderate" of the two running. Yet whether it was a specific vote for the large policy ambitions that came to be known as the "Great Society" is another matter entirely.

Winning elections by narrow margins represents an issue of a wholly different kind. On what basis can a political leader claim a "mandate," if his margin of victory is razor thin? What if he actually were to lose the popular vote, but win the electoral vote? What if, like Bill Clinton, he failed to gain a majority of the votes cast?

Mr. Clinton won both of his elections, in 1992 and 1996, by a plurality of the votes cast. Mr. Clinton's solution? In 1992, he added the votes of his opponent, Ross Perot, to his and claimed that both groups "had voted for change" and he, therefore, had his mandate.

John F. Kennedy won the presidency with the smallest popular vote margin in history. Mr. Kennedy was a policy moderate and politically cautious. He responded to his narrow victory with a sense that, as a result, he could ill afford large policy ambitions. His Secretary of State Dean Rusk recalled (quoted in Doyle 1999: 97), "He did not feel that he had a strong overwhelming mandate from the American people, and so he would rather be careful about the issues on which he wanted to make a fight."

George W. Bush is obviously another illustration of a president who has won office by the slimmest of margins, after losing the popular vote. Yet his response has been quite different than that of John F. Kennedy's or Bill Clinton's. He has not claimed some overarching principle that unites his opposition with his camp as Clinton did. Nor has he adopted a strategy of scaled-back ambitions. On the contrary, he has proceeded as if he has a mandate, or as one reporter (Babington 2001) put it, "in landslide fashion."

President Bush's Mandate

The title of this section may appear anomalous. After all, Mr. Bush certainly received no popular mandate, if size of the popular vote is the measure. And his electoral vote was only one more than necessary to win election. Yet, I want to argue that Mr. Bush did receive a mandate, and it is a mandate that allows him to lead.

What is that mandate? It is not, obviously, the mandate that comes with a sweeping electoral victory either in the popular vote or Electoral College. It is not even one that comes with a convincing or even clear victory in either of those areas. Yet, it is a mandate nonetheless.

Obviously, this is not the same kind of mandate that comes with a sweeping victory, as Ronald Reagan's or Lyndon Johnson's did. It is not even the kind of mandate that comes with winning the Electoral College vote by a wide margin although not gaining a majority of the popular votes cast as was the case for Bill Clinton in 1992. So, just what kind of mandate is it?

One way to address this question is to distinguish between a numbers mandate and a *legitimacy mandate*. The former rests on the margins by which you win, the latter on the fact that you did win. The *legitimacy* mandate accrues to a leader by virtue of the fact that he did win a victory, of whatever magnitude, so long as that victory was a result of the rules and standards in place at the time of the election. Simply put, the mandate is this: if you have won your victory fairly in accordance with the rules in place at the time, you are accorded legitimacy, and hence a mandate.

However, to say a person has earned a mandate leaves unanswered the question: To do what? One obvious answer is that any mandate involves the responsibility of governing. Governing requires setting priorities and carrying out policy responsibilities. Setting priorities, in turn, requires some things to be chosen, some to be delayed, and some never to get started. This is one essential element of the role of leadership: to choose.

Yet leadership also is to be found in the second major aspect of all governing, solving problems. When a leader publicly points to what he sees as a problem, he takes on political responsibility for addressing and trying to resolve it. That too, requires proposing policy.

Obviously, political leaders often differ in the problems they see and the solutions they propose. Sometimes this takes the form of specific policies. Sometimes it takes the form of more general approaches to problems. In either case, the leader who has earned the legitimacy mandate from his victory, has also earned the right to *try* and put his vision and policies into effect.

I emphasize the word *try*, not because the outcome is in doubt, although it is. I emphasize the word because the real mandate that a leader gains on winning is the right to try to convince us that his views and policies ought to be the ones that govern. The legitimacy mandate without a numbers mandate, implies no assumption that the leader's views must prevail, only that he should have the opportunity to try and convince us that they should.

This is the cornerstone of the relationship between the legitimacy mandate and political leadership.

Legitimacy Mandates and the Political Center

The political center is the Holy Grail of American politics, the Archimedean point at which North/South/East/and West, men and women, urban and suburban, left and right, and race and ethnicity are in harmonious political balance. It is the fulfillment of the modern alchemist's dream of transmutation—of views into votes, and political conflicts into public consensus. But it appears increasingly difficult to discern, much less to lead, from the political center in contemporary American politics.

One reason for this is to be found in the lack of conceptual clarity and clear political thinking about the term. How best can we understand the nature of the political center? Is it Arthur Schlesinger's (1968) "vital center," Stanley Greenberg's (1998) "new American majority," Richard Nixon's "silent majority,"[7] or Pat Robertson's (1993) "moral majority"?

What is the *political location* of the political center? Is the center economically conservative, socially progressive as Paul Tsongas (1995) argued, or is it wholly "progressive," as Stanley Greenberg and Theda Skocpol (1997) have argued? "Is there," as Joe Klein (1995; see also Halstead and Lind 2001) has argued, a "radical middle," or as Richard Darman (1995) has argued a "sensible center? Or is John Judis (1995) correct in arguing that the political center contains both?

Is the political center non-partisan, synonymous with bi-partisanship, or even non-ideological? Or is the political center more moderate or even conservative?

How does one divine the political center? Is it the sum of political extremes, divided in half? Is it reached by small incremental policies on divisive issues, or are bold historic compromises a better model? What role, if any, should principles play?

The Principled Political Center

The single largest error made by those analyzing the nature of the contemporary political center has been to equate it with consensus, without first examining the difficult and conflictual process by which political centers become "consensual." That point is well captured by an interview with the combative former mayor of New York, Rudy Giuliani:

> Q: "To get that reform, why is it necessary to challenge the power structures...rather than actually working with them? So many times we see you being critical of those groups rather than trying to work closely with them.

> *Mayor Giuliani:* ...We brought more change in the last 18 months than this city has had in a very long time...and there's no way you can do that without controversy. It just can't happen. You can't take two, three, four billion dollars out of the budget without major controversy.

> *Q*: Isn't there any room for political consensus with your opponents, as opposed to the usually confrontational incidents that frequently occur with people who stand in your way?

> *Mayor Giuliani:* I think there are some confrontations Most of them get resolved. And then nobody pays attention to the resolution of them...if you are proposing things, and there are a significant group of political figures in the city who have consistently throughout their career opposed doing those things, they're going to oppose you when you do it.... *politics is not all about harmony...specifically when you're going through*

an era of change and difficulty....In the negotiating process, you've got to be willing to take the heat for a while to get to the final result."

It might be objected that this is too conflictual a view of the political center. "Deliberative models" of political consensus (Fishkin 1997) emphasize rational arguments—their articulation and acceptance. Yet most of these models are drawn from specially set up and monitored forums in which rules of civility are expected and enforced. They hardly reflect real political life.

A political center does exist, although not in the form that it has been variously proposed. It is "vital," though not in Schlesinger's sense of an active alternative to communism, on one hand, and fascism on the other. It has been quiet, but not "silent"—it's voice having been hard to hear over the shrill accusations and demands of advocates. It is majoritarian, though its majority status is quite equivocal, achieved through conflict, and unrelated to religion. It is "sensible," but not necessarily common sensical, and because it is often arrived at through conflict is often characterized in shrill, extreme language. And, contrary to neo-liberals, like Greenberg and Skocpol, it is neither "radical," nor "progressive." It is not even economically "conservative," but "socially progressive."

A focus on the search for a viable "political center" has obscured the fact that the political center is primarily cultural. Historically, there have been several different spheres in which a political center has developed in modern American history. Further, such centering has only emerged after a period of protracted conflict, punctuated by a major crisis. In each historical circumstance, the center was consolidated by a president with a particular ability to blend principle and leadership.

The political center has undergone three overlapping transformations in American history. Each raised and ultimately settled fundamental national public understandings that govern us, although in each case not without a public crisis of historic proportions. I characterize them, respectively, as the search for a principled national political center in three major spheres of public life: political, economic, and strategic. I argue that we are in the midst of a fourth transformation at present whose nature has been profoundly misunderstood.

The first, and fundamental set of issues, concerns the shaping of a *principled national political center*. The basic issues fought through were the shape and operation of our national political culture—our institutions and practices, the basic political understandings that we agreed would govern us. These were largely settled in the period following the Civil War, but it took that war to do it.

The second recentering concerned the search for a *principled national economic center*. These coincide roughly with the rise, consolidation, and expansion of large commercial institutions. The relationships of these to each other, and to the public and government, respectively, was the fundamental question shaping the search for a consensual center. That period extended from the late nineteenth century on through the mid-twentieth century, and was essentially resolved by the series of new partnerships (the New Deal, Fair Deal) between business, government, and the public in the aftermath of the Great Depression. But again, as in the first case, it took a traumatic event, the Depression, to consolidate the understandings of how we would henceforth govern our economic life.

The third set of issues to frame the search for a *principled national strategic center* concerned America's role as a world leader in the Cold War. From Washington's advice to avoid entangling alliances to the sharp, but limited conflicts that accompanied manifest destiny, America has been a country more comfortable at home than abroad. It was a late and reluctant ally in World War I, and an unavoidable but reluctant partner in World War II. By 1948 America, alone, had the capacity to meet the challenges of Communist expansion, first in Europe and then in Asia and Africa. The great question that framed the next four decades of American public life was whether this country and its leaders had the will. They did, having in the process survived the wrenching setback to a successful containment policy in Vietnam. The collapse of the Soviet Union during the Reagan presidency marks the successful conclusion of this, the third fundamental policy issue in search of a consensual center.

We are now in the middle of the political center's fourth transformation. In some respects it is the most complex. Like the first, it certainly has profound implications for the country's politics. Like the second, it has implications for the country's economic life. It also has barely recognized and little discussed implications for the third, strategic, transformation of the American political center.

However, unlike the first and even the second and third, the fourth transformation has to do with our way of life, our values, our basic societal beliefs and the fundamental understanding of our national identity. It is, in reality, not a search for a political center, but rather a search for a *principled national cultural center.*

The basis of finding and leading from the political center is not now principally a matter of resolving political or policy confrontations, although those are certainly rampant. Rather it is, at base, an expression of deeper cultural values, of which these policy conflicts are a reflection. Therefore, the major question that faces those interested in forging a contemporary "political center" is whether Mr. Bush can reconcile conflicting cultural understandings with a strong principled statement of national cultural understanding and leadership. His task is to reestablish our contentions with each other and our government through the force of his character, the candor and courage of his leadership, and an honest and open-minded approach, coupled with real convictions of policy choices.

It is a very large and daunting task.

Notes

1. In a post mortem on election forecasting errors in *PS: Political Science and Politics*, March 2001, almost all the contributors concluded that the election was Gore's to lose, although they offered different explanations of why he did so.
2. For an exception, see Bartels and Zaller (2001).
3. The only exception is the work of Norpoth (2001) which relies primarily on the primary performance of the incumbent party candidate. These measures, do however, correlate (.78) with presidential approval ratings in election years.
4. Bartels and Zaller (2001: 9; emphasis mine) begin their analysis by writing, "Most political scientists, *including us*, believed that peace and a booming economy would give Gore a significant advantage in the 2000 presidential race." Yet, almost in the same breath they argue that, "the election outcome was well within what one would expect if both candidates ran more or less equally competent campaigns." And, later (2001: 19) they say they find, "little to be surprised by in the outcome of the 2000 presidential election."
5. Wlezien (2001) considers several possible explanations for Gore's loss including factors from " outside" the model, the standard one relying on the economy and approval ratings of the sitting president. He considers the impact of Ralph Nader, who did take votes from Gore, but that only decreases the forecast of the over-all percentage by 1 percent, still not enough to bring them into line with results. A second factor he considers is that Gore was not an incumbent president. Yet, historically, incumbency, independent of the other elements of the model doesn't help to explain very much.
6. The figures that follow are drawn from Teachout (2001), the CNN national exit polls: http://www.cnn.com/ELECTION/2000/results/index.epolls.html (December 28, 2000).
7. Richard Nixon's view of the "Silent Majority," or "New Majority," as he sometimes referred to it is contained in his November 3, 1969, address to the nation at the height of the anti- Vietnam war movement. Nixon had used similar terms—"the silent center," the new majority," and the "quiet majority"—in several 1968 presidential campaign speeches. Vice President Spiro Agnew had later used it several times in a May 1969 speech. On the politics of the term, see William Safire (1994: 171-180). Safire sees Nixon's speech as "historic and tide-turning" (p.175) and provides an important insight into the psychology of its power.

References

Associated Press. "Report: Gore Won Popular Vote by 539, 987." *Washington Post,* 21 December 2000: A09.

Babington, Charles. "Bush Moving in 'Landslide' Fashion." *Washington Post,* 16 May 2001.

Barnes, Fred. "Call It the Flyover Party." *The Weekly Standard*, 4 December 2000: 17-18.

Bartels, Larry M., and John Zaller. "Presidential Vote Models: A Recount." *PS Political Science and Politics* 34:1 (2001): 9-20.

Brooks, David. "An Emerging Democratic Majority? *The Weekly Standard,* 26 December 2000: 26-29.

Campbell, James E. "The Referendum That Didn't Happen: The Forecasts of the 2000 Presidential Election." *PS: Political Science and Politics* 34:1, 33-38.

Clymer, Adam. "Political Memo: And the Winner is Gore, If They Got the Math Right," *New York Times*, 4 September 2000a.

_____. "G.O.P. Clings to Control, but Democrats Gain in Both Chambers." *New York Times,* 8 November 2000b.

Connelly, Marjorie. "Who Voted: A Portrait of American Politics, 1976-2000." *New York Times*, 12 November 2000.

Darman, Richard. *Whose in Control? Polar Politics and the Sensible Center*. New York: Simon and Schuster, 1995.

Doyle, William. *Inside the Oval Office: The White House Tapes from FDR to Clinton*. New York: Kodansha International, 1999.

Dreazen, Yochi J. "Voter Turnout Remains Low, Despite Ad Barrage, Close Race." *Wall Street Journal*, 9 November 2000.

Eilperin, Juliet. "GOP Gains in House After Concession." *Washington Post*, 13 December 2000.

Fishkin, James S. *The Voice of the People: Public Opinion and Democracy*. New Haven, CT : Yale University Press, 1997.

Greenberg, Stanley A. *Middle Class Dreams: The Politics and Power of the New American Majority*. Revised and updated edition. New Haven, CT: Yale University Press, 1998.

Greenberg, Stanley B., and Theda Skocpol (eds.). *The New Majority: Ttoward a Popular Progressive Politics*. New Haven, CT: Yale University Press, 1997.

Halstead, Ted, and Michael Lind. *The Radical Center: The Future of American Politics*. New York: Doubleday, 2001.

Hertzberg, Hendrick. "Both Sides Now." *The New Yorker*, 16 & 20 October 2000: 91-92.

Himmelfarb, Gertrude. "Two Nations or Two Cultures." *Commentary*, January (2001): 29-30.

_____. *One Nation. Two Cultures*. New York: Alfred A. Knopf, 1999.

Holbrook, Thomas M. "Forecasting with Mixed Economic Signals: A Cautionary Tale." *PS: Political Science and Politics*, 34:1 (2001): 39-44.

Judis, John B. "For Richer and Poorer: How George McGovern Won Election 2000 for the Dems." *The New Republic*, 4 December 2000:18-19.

_____. "Off Center." *The New Republic*, 16 October 1995.

Klein, Joe. "Stalking the Radical Middle." *Newsweek*, 25 September 1995.

Lewis-Beck, Michael S., and Charles Tien. "Modeling the Future: Lessons from the Gore Forecast." *PS: Political Science and Politics*, 34:1 (2001): 21-23.

Pomper, Gerald. "The Presidential Election," in Gerald Pomper, Anthony Corrado, E. J. Dionne, Kathleen A. Frankovic, Paul S. Herrnson, Majorie Randon Hershey, William G. Meyer, Monia L. McDermott, and Wilson Cary McWilliams. *The Election of 2000*. New York: Chatham House, 2001.

Norpoth, Helmut. "Primary Colors: A Mixed Blessing for Al Gore." *PS: Political Science and Politics* 34:1, 45-48.

Robertson, Pat. *The Turning Tide*. Dallas, TX: World Books, 1993.

Safire, William. *Before the Fall*. New York: Doubleday and Co., 1974

Schlesinger, Arthur Jr. *The Vital Center: The Politics of Freedom*. New York: Da Cap Press. 1968 [1949].

Stout, David. "The Electors Vote, and the Surprises are Few." *New York Times,* 19 December 2000.

Teachout, Terry. "Republican Nation, Democratic Nation?" *Commentary*, January (2001) 23-29.

Transcript. "Text: Gore's Acceptance Speech at the Democratic National Convention." *Washington Post*, 17 August 2000.

Tsongas, Paul E. *Journey of Purpose: Reflections on the Presidency, Multiculturalism, and Third Parties*. New Haven, CT: Yale University Press, 1995.

Wlezien, Christopher. "On Forecasting the Presidential Vote." *PS Political Science and Politics*, 34:1 (2001): 25-31.

14

Governing a Divided America in the Aftermath of September 11: Heroic versus Reflective Leadership*

Americans at century's end live in a time of unprecedented prosperity. Yet, before September 11, they continued to be uneasy about the quality of their leaders, the competence of their institutions, and the larger meaning of their lives. They live in a country where there is increasing interconnectedness, but far less relatedness. They live in a country where indicators of economic and cultural well being go in opposite directions. And they live in a country where, in spite of its success, many—in most polls a majority—of its citizens were profoundly troubled by the direction in which it appears to be going (Wysocki 1999; Pew Research Center 1999).

The 2000 presidential election further deepened the political divides that separate Americans, and these were in addition to the already substantial cultural divides that separate us. How can Mr. Bush, or any leader, govern under these circumstances? I begin to answer that question by drawing a distinction between *reflective and heroic* leadership and suggest that in countries, such as the United States, which are deeply divided, it is the former type of leadership, not the latter which best fits our times. The nature of leadership in the United States is changing and a new form *emerging*. America is now poised, perhaps stuck, between two very different understandings of that critical term. It is one more way in which America seems to be divided, and it is as yet unclear how the resolution of this dilemma will unfold, or be resolved, if it is.

Heroic versus Reflective Political Leadership

There are two very different templates of leadership competing for public support in America at the turn of the twenty-first century. In the modern presidency, one is traditional and well known; the other is emerging and not yet well articulated. These models of leadership are, respectively: the *heroic* and the *reflective*.

327

Heroic leadership in American society is the traditional. Its archetype is Franklin Roosevelt, its metaphor the hierarchy, and its motto: decide and command. The task of the heroic leader is to convince the public of what it is that he already thinks they *must* do. It envisions the leader as struggling against, and overcoming through determination, courage or even artifice the circumstances he must surmount. He is known for his authoritative views and acts, not his accessibility. He makes no concessions to the illusion of public intimacy, because the heroic leader stands above, and beyond, his supportive publics.

Some sense of the kinds of leaders who typify this model are found in James McGregor Burns' (1978: 1) lament:

> One of the universal cravings of our time is a hunger for compelling and creative leadership. Many of us spent our early years in the era of the titans...Mao and Gandhi, Churchill and Roosevelt, Stalin and Hitler and Mussolini....These giants strode across our cultural and intellectual and political horizons. We—followers everywhere—loved or loathed them. We marched for them and fought against them. We died for them and we killed some of them. We could not ignore them.

Reflective leadership, on the other hand, is personal and diffuse. It draws its authority not by being beyond people, but by being of and like them. It draws its legitimacy not by gathering up all available power, but by dispersing it. Its prototype, but not its archetype, is Bill Clinton. President-elect Bush may prove to be its exemplar. Its metaphor is the prism, and its motto is: select and reflect. It is not reflective in the introspective sense, but rather in the sense of radiating outward.

The task of reflective leadership is to gather the disparate elements of a frayed or fractured political and cultural consensus and mirror them so that publics can see the basis for their common purposes. The reflective leader tries to diffuse conflict, not sharpen it. It is leadership whose purpose is not to choose and impose, but to engage and connect. It is in a basic sense in democracies, restorative—although this need not make it conventional.

And, it is profoundly interpersonal in nature. Freud believed that when crowds (publics) were beset by anxiety they turned to leaders, but that in the process group members became disconnected from each other. In these circumstances, Freud (1920) argued, group members were only indirectly allied to each other and then, only through their joint connection to the leader. This is one drawback of heroic leadership.

Reflective leadership, unlike heroic leadership, seeks to develop common horizontal ties, not direct and hierarchical ones. The reflective leader does not bend the public to his will, but rather leads by serving as an expression of a more common one. He does not so much command as explain. He does not so much demand as ask. And, he is not so much the author of the publics' common interests, as their reflection.

Reflective leadership is not passive, nor is such a leader essentially a "clerk" (Neustadt 1960). His agenda is common purpose and the circumstances that give rise to this kind of leadership will no doubt require the leader to fight vigorously for it. What kinds of circumstances give rise to such leadership?

Several points seem immediately clear. Countries in which there are no great mobilizing crises, but which are, nonetheless, deeply divided seem ripe for reflective leadership. Add to these two factors, citizens who feel separated from their major institutions and each other, and who technologically and socially have decreased needs to be so connected. The result is a political culture and system in which the domestic issues that divide the country are less responsive to traditional heroic leadership.

Technology is part of the reason that reflective leadership has been gathering momentum. Bennett (1988) sees economic dislocation and anxiety as the cause of the publics' disconnection from traditional means of civic engagement. Geographical, occupational and other forms of mobility also add to the loosening of traditional ties. Robert Lane (1978), in his prescient early paper referred to this as "sociological release." the freeing of people from formerly restricting, but also connecting categories. He also worried that the "colder" market of exchange had increasingly supplanted the domain of community. Communications, mirroring politics, have become decomposed into niches (Blumer and Kavanaugh 1988). And, of course, the rise of the Internet certainly allows and may facilitate social disconnection from common purpose (Shapiro 1999: 118-120).

There are other factors to consider here as well. The rising idea of candidate-centered politics (Wattenberg 1991) and the parallel decline of party-centered politics (Wattenberg 1990) is a well-established fact of modern American political life. Less commented upon in relation to these developments is the function that party-centered politics played in forging horizontal ties among the public to each other, as well as vertical ties with the leader. With traditional party politics, selected candidates were broadly reflective of the party's position and less directly reflective of the candidates' idiosyncratic personal characteristics. Of course, personal characteristics did matter to some degree, but they were reinforced and were consistent with the party as a major organizing frame of reference, and did not supplant or transcend it. As a result, supporting publics were connected primarily to each other via the party, not the candidate.

In the world of party-centered leadership, there was no expectation that publics would be connected directly and psychologically with the leader. There was no expectation that the leader would strive for intimacy, or the illusion of it, with party supporters. It was enough that he or she represented their broad party-related interests and views.

With the decline of party-centered politics and the rise of candidate-centered politics that balance shifted. Voter attachments came to be more connected with individual candidates and their specific formulation of policies, and secondarily to the party. Democrats (Republicans) were still Democrats (Republicans), of course, but the particular personal characteristics of the candidates began to assume increasing importance. Changes in party nomination rules (especially among Democrats) made insurgency (e.g., non-party regular) candidates viable and successful.

These developments accelerated the ascendancy of persona over party. George McGovern in 1972 and Walter Mondale 1988 ran as unabashedly liberal democrats, a stance which pleased a well-defined-but-narrow base of party activists, but not the general public. Jimmy Carter ran and won on his plain-spoken honesty and his blend of conservative and progressive views, not on his long and successful association with the Democratic Party. Bill Clinton ran and won office as a Democrat who repudiated the narrow liberalism of past party stalwarts and a person whose deeply effective charm appeared to trump his character.

Paradoxically, the rise of candidate-centered and "personal" politics has not led to more trust between candidates and their publics. On the contrary, the more we get to know about some leaders, the more they need to reassure us that what we think we know isn't necessarily true, or at least irrelevant to our larger concerns.

Bennett (1995: 94) captures this paradox precisely:

> In this climate of anger, suspicion and restlessness, politicians must continually work up new strategies to keep themselves on the good side of the public, as the Clinton campaign illustrates so vividly. In the current electoral environment, candidates must manufacture short-term images and feed them back continually to skeptical voters in as intimate a style as electronic media permit.

In short, as political parties ceased to stand for broad inclusive views and policies, and as each new candidate refined party principles in their own idiosyncratic and politically self-interested way, there were less stable and consistent principles for supporters to attach themselves to, and a corresponding rise in the number of independent voters. One consequence of this was not only the consolidation of candidate-centered politics and a corresponding rise in voters' connection to individual leaders and their specific personas and policies, but also a dramatic rise in the transience of voters' attachments. You might be a Democrat and like Jimmy Carter but not Walter Mondale. You could like Bill Clinton but not Al Gore. If you were a Republican you could like George Bush better than you liked Bob Dole.

Candidates would and did cater to segmented political markets. The capacity to reach targeted audiences, along with candidate-centered politics, led voters to expect that their specific, individual views would not only be considered, but enacted. And candidates rushed to reassure voters, through the symbols of intimacy like town meetings and policies derived from intensive use of focus groups, that they were doing so. As Bennett (1995: 92) has insightfully noted, the combination of unrealistic public expectations of familiarity coupled with shallow political attachments gives rise to candidacies that focus on "responsiveness, intimacy (no matter how contrived) and continual reassurance."

Heroic and Reflective Leadership in the 2000 Presidential Campaign

As leadership theorists repeatedly point out, there is a close connection between the leader and the times. Dire circumstances call for heroic leadership. Americans flirted with heroic leadership in the 1992 and 1996 presidential campaigns with Ross Perot and Pat Buchanan. Both articulated, encouraged and tried to make use of grievance, coupling it with their own strong claims for heroic leadership status. Pat Buchanan in 1992, like Alan Keyes in the 2000 campaign, ran on the premise of his own strong ideological consistency. Whether leading a "pitchfork revolt" (Buchanan), or finding dignity in a mosh pit jump (Keyes) neither candidate could promise Americans more than uncompromising conflict in a society already weary of it. In 1992 and 1996, Ross Perot emphasized "straight," but not particular insightful, talk coupled with a promise to open up the hood of government and get in there and fix it—period! Having come from the quintessential command and control experience (his own company), he was ill prepared, ill suited and, in the end, mismatched for the position to which he aspired. Americans may have been responsive to his apparent but limited candor, but not at the price of his temperament and control. And, in the aftermath of September 11 George W. Bush has offered a new, hybrid version of heroic and reflective leadership.

Bill Clinton: Reflective Leadership Harbinger?

Bill Clinton was successful in both elections because he represented a new, less sharp-edged leadership. He was certainly the harbinger, and to that point the best example of reflective leadership. His reflective style is easily documented. He promised to "put people first," and seemed to care and connect with many Americans. They, in turn, connected with him.

His was a very personal candidacy. Questions about his behavior required him to share and explain more of his personal life than had been the case for other candidates. Yet he was also personal in another very direct and important way. He was the candidate who said, "I feel your pain"—a statement of direct, personal, even intimate connection. During one 1992 presidential debate, he was asked by a woman to comment personally on how the problems of the national debt affected the economic problems of common people. The question could have been rephrased: Are you one of us? He responded by saying that as governor of a small state he *personally* knew people who had been affected and tried to help them.

Mr. Clinton did not promise to command, but to respond. He would "focus like a laser" on the economy if that was what many Americans wished, since they were worried. He reassured the public that as a leader he would not aspire to grand plans, but rather sensible policies. His political stance as a "New Democrat" promised to heal the cleavages that permeated our society and do so in a way that would bring left and right, Democrat and Republican, together in new common efforts. In short, he was the prototype, until he was forced to work with a Republican Congress, and became, ultimately, a flawed exemplar of a new leadership style that had been building in this country for several decades.

It is now clear in retrospect that Mr. Clinton adapted a reflective style to mask some very basic heroic tendencies. For example, in the same State of the Union Address that told the American public that the "era of big government was over," he also spent almost all his time laying out an unusual number of new government initiatives. When *Washington Post* correspondent John Harris raised the inconsistency with him, Mr. Clinton bridled and lashed out at him (Harris 2000: B01). As a result of many such inconsistencies, Mr. Clinton, far from diminishing political and cultural conflict, helped to escalate it. Far from bringing people together, he divided them. During his administration the country may have been prosperous, but it was not at peace.

That was part of his legacy as Al Gore and George W. Bush campaigned to take his place. If this analysis is correct, a number of Americans were not looking for a fighting leader, but a leader who could, but only if necessary, fight. They preferred someone who reconciled rather than divided, and they preferred someone with common plans, not large ones.

Al Gore's Heroic Leadership Style

Viewed from this perspective, Al Gore's psychology and campaign may well have represented a mismatch between him and the new, emerging climate of American leadership. Vice President Gore was very programmatic, a reflection of his interest and experience in government. His strong support of government programs reflected a very robust view of their role. Although he is most often viewed as coming out of the Clinton small-bore program mold, and was criticized by Mr. Bradley for lacking "big ideas," Mr. Gore put forward many, potentially large-scale program initiatives during the primaries. He proposed $115 new billions for education (Seelye 1999: A1), $7.1 new billions for a "Democracy Endowment" that would have the federal government fund all elections (Connolly 2000: A06), $2 new billions more on parks (Associated Press 1999: A02), and so on.

During a campaign debate with his rival Bill Bradley, the vice president said (quoted in Harris and Allen 2000: A01), he believed the next president could and should seek to do many things. "I have different models for the presidency—leaders like Franklin Roosevelt, John Kennedy and Lyndon Johnson," Gore said. "They knew that we had to proceed on all the great unfinished business of our society."

This is heroic leadership with a decidedly large "H." For all the moderation that is a key element of Mr. Gore's political persona, his was still, basically, a command and control model. Had Mr. Gore been elected president, there would have been a basic clash between his large-scale policy aspirations and his capacity to carry them. Consistent with the heroic leadership aspirations associated with doing more, CNN exit polls found that of the 43 percent of the public who wanted the government to do more, 74 percent voted for Mr. Gore. And of the 53 percent who wanted the government to do less, 71 percent voted for Mr. Bush.

Mr. Gore's relentless pursuit of traditional Democratic constituencies and his inability, or disinclination, to distance himself even symbolically from his core constituencies raises the issue of how fairly Mr. Gore would have represented groups across the board and not only the constituent pillars of the Democratic party. Mr. Clinton had Sister Soulja, Mr. Bush warned the Republican Congress against balancing the budget on the backs of the poor. There was not even such symbolic space between Mr. Gore and his traditional Democratic party supporters.

Here, too, one can see differences between *reflective* and *heroic* leadership styles and also a mismatch for both candidates. Recall that personal intimacy, no matter how contrived, is part of what voters want to feel from candidates. A candidate like Bill Clinton who says he feels your (personal) pain is much more in keeping with the "intimacy" of reflective leadership, than one who will fight for particular groups. Mr. Gore's campaign theme "fighting for you" represented a good fit between his psychology and leadership style, but it was sometimes done in a harsh way. It was consistent with the wish of many Americans who wanted calming not strident leadership.

Promising to fight, as Mr. Gore did, against those "large forces arrayed against you" appeals to an individual's sense of anxiety and grievance, but not to their sense of intimacy. Someone who says he will fight battles for you that you are powerless to win, doesn't foster a sense that he is like you. It is also instructive to consider the stylistic differences of leadership style embodied in signature phrases. In using his signature phrase, "I feel your pain." Mr. Clinton signaled a very personal, intimate, and responsive leadership style. In using his signature phase, "I'll fight for you," Mr. Gore signaled that standing apart from the public he saw what it needed and would, through his own heroic efforts, get it for them.

Vice President Gore was a candidate whose determination and earnestness could easily shade off into insistence. He is a man who *very* much wanted to be president and gave the impression of being willing to do almost anything to get it. In one article Mr. Gore was quoted as saying, "you have to rip your opponent's lungs out and then move on." He is also very easily drawn to harsh demagoguery. In a relatively peaceful period in which the public said it was tired of intense conflict, this might well have been a drawback.

Mr. Gore's Intimacy Problem

Mr. Gore and his campaign realized early on that an inability to easily connect with other people presented an "intimacy" problem. This, in turn, led to a search for symbolic manifestations of connections with ordinary people. Mr. Gore's long and public kiss of his wife before a national television audience awaiting his acceptance speech can be seen from this perspective and was somewhat successful.[1] Other efforts were less so.

In the first presidential debate Mr. Gore used two people to make a policy point. In the first instance he said,

I'd like to tell you a quick story. I got a letter today, as I left Sarasota, Florida....His name is Randy Ellis, he has a 15-year-old daughter named Kailey, who's in Sarasota High School. Her science class was supposed to be for 24 students. She is the 36th student in that classroom, he sent me a picture of her in the classroom. They can't squeeze another desk in for her, so she has to stand during class. I want the federal government, consistent with local control and new accountability, to make improvement of our schools the number one priority so Kailey will have a desk and can sit down in a classroom where she can learn.

The trouble with this story was that it was highly misleading. The girl was without a desk for one class period (Kennedy 2000; see also Sack 2000) and the reason, according to the school's principal, was that it was the first day of class and,

Sarasota High School is typical of most American high schools. At the start of the school year, schedules are in flux. Students and furniture are moved about the campus to accommodate learning needs.

The second incident occurred when Mr. Gore raised the issue of one Winifer Skinner:

...here tonight from Iowa. I mentioned her earlier. She's 79 years old, she has Social Security. I'm not going to cut her benefits or support any proposal that would. She gets a small pension. But in order to pay for her prescription drug benefits, she has to go out seven days a week, several hours a day, picking up cans. She came all the way from Iowa in a Winnebago with her poodle in order to attend here tonight.

The trouble with this story was that Ms. Skinner was, it turned out, somewhat eccentric, she preferred to search for cans even though her son was a well-to-do professional who was well able to, and did, provide his mother with economic assistance. And, of course, few asked how a woman who needed to collect cans to pay for prescription medicine could afford a Winnebago or the gas money to get from Iowa to Boston.

There was also the story of Mr. Gore's mother-in-law and his assertion that she paid more for her prescription arthritis medicine (Lodine) than it cost for his dog. This story turned out to be inaccurate in several respects, the most important to our concerns here, is the fact that he didn't actually know what his mother-in-law paid and had never spoken to her about it (Associated Press 2000a).

In all three of these stories there is the issue raised of Mr. Gore's tendency to exaggerate, but they also reflect a lack of knowledge about each of the persons that he cited. In all of these stories, what seemed to be first-hand individual knowledge turned out to be inaccurate, thus further emphasizing the actual distance from the people he had presented as knowing. Mr. Gore's public relations effort to enlist a group of "real people" to advise and accompany him as he prepared for his first debate (Connolly 2000b) did little to dispel this impression. In reality, Mr. Gore spent almost all his time with his real advisors behind closed doors.

George W. Bush: A Reflective Leader

George W. Bush, before and to some degree still after September 11, represents a different kind of leadership. He is certainly not as programmatic as Al Gore, and assuredly not as well versed on the details of policy complexities. Perhaps as a result of having entered politics later in life, he is not a man of large personal political agendas. That is a decided drawback to those who look to government to solve the host of problems we confront. Yet such a position basically represents a heroic view of leadership. So, too, Mr. Bush's commitment to facilitating institutions in the "civil society" to stimulate horizontal public connections is certainly more consistent with *reflective* than *heroic* leadership.

As noted in chapter 6, reflective leadership is not necessarily passive or conflict avoidant. Mr. Bush's cabinet selections confirm he is comfortable being at the center, but doesn't need to be "on top." And his decision against hiring Dan Coats as Secretary of Defense demonstrates he is not, as critics charge, a rubber stamp for his advisors. His willingness to go forward with his agenda in the face of his narrow victory, suggests as well, he will not wither in the face of loud complaints that he is not "bi-partisan" enough, which is to say governing as if he were a Democrat.

George W. Bush is scrappy and can bristle when challenged on something he feels he is being inappropriately asked. Appearing before 700 students at Newberry College, Bush got angry when asked if he was attempting to co-opt Senator McCain's agenda with talk of being a reformer. Bush told the student to "sit down," words he often used when faced with questions he doesn't like. Bush went on to say that most GOP senators had rejected McCain's push for campaign finance.

As noted earlier, he can also be tough, as his ads on John McCain's votes against pork, which included money for cancer research, showed (Levy 2000). Yet, as one reporter noted, surprisingly Mr. Bush appears squeamish and uncomfortable with the politics of insult—and not very good at it. He notes that when Mr. McCain used the slur "gooks" to refer to his North Vietnamese guards when he was a prisoner of war (Mr. McCain later apologized), Mr. Bush had a perfect opportunity to criticize his opponent. But when the issue arose at Mr. Bush's daily press conference, this was this exchange (Kristof 2000: A23):

Q. "Is that appropriate language for someone running for president?"

A. "That is going to have to be up to the people. You know, it's amazing. I haven't seen that in the press yet. I appreciate you bringing that up."

Q. (inaudible)

A. "I better not say anything about it, lest I be accused of negative campaigning."

Q. "Do you have an obligation as a leader to take a stand on that kind of language?"

A. "He has an obligation as a potential leader to explain what he meant."

At base, Mr. Bush is a person who moves toward people, not against them. Generally, the evidence is that he is more a conciliator than a divider. After watching him over time on the campaign trail, one *New York Times* reporter (Kristof 2000: A23) wrote,

> Mr. Bush is a natural politician—far more so than the vice president—with a down-home, one-of-the-guys charm that puts people at ease. He loves the crowds, relishes the limelight and invariably comes across to audiences as likable, funny, sincere and decent.

Mr. Bush is certainly intelligent enough, but not as versed or as immersed in policy detail as Mr. Gore. He is as interested in building relationships as building policy monuments. On domestic policy, he cares deeply about education and as one observer noted "running against the sixties." However, no one can reasonably argue that he sees himself proposing, much less providing a solution to every problem the country faces. Mr. Bush envisions a government of limits and that reflects something about his ambitions for accomplishment in office. It also suggests a view that is consistent with the American public. Overall, CNN exit 2000 election polls showed that the public preferred the government do less (53 percent) than more (43 percent).

Mr. Bush may also be better at providing reassurance to the public than he is at providing "intimacy" and immediate responsiveness. He is well known, like his father, to deeply dislike introspective questions about himself. And, he does not easily share the personal details of his life. On the other hand, Mr. Bush is a leader who may provide a different kind of intimacy—one rooted in authenticity. Mr. Bush is a man who wears his emotions on his sleeve, so to speak. He is not good at hiding what he feels. When he is unsure, he doesn't mask it. When he feels confident, it is obvious. When he is moved, it is clear. When he is angry or upset, you know it. There may well prove to be a form of public intimacy in knowing that what you see is truly what there is. This was certainly the case for Ronald Reagan. And while such clarity may not be profound it does seem to have been critical to his (Reagan's) connection to the public and its confidence in American leadership institutions during his administration.

Public Views of Heroic and Reflective Leadership: Significant Questions, Fewer Answers

If heroic and reflective leadership are viable substantive categories, we should see some evidence for them in choices that voters make in what voters find important in making those choices. One place to begin the task of attempting to see if they do is by examining the reasons given for their votes. Exit polls, while providing some data, appear to generate more questions than answers. In this section rather than attempt to explain the sometimes anomalous, findings I would like to use them to sharpen the questions we might reasonably and usefully ask.

One reason for caution in interpreting these data is that some questions that would seem very relevant to the distinctions between heroic and reflective leadership are simply not asked. I've not seen any specific attempts yet to measure a candidate's expansiveness of vision. A second, major problem is that the arguments that partisan supporters have used (and their candidates have made) might well shape the pattern of responses. This can occur regardless of whether these characteristics would be theoretically or ordinarily associated with either type of leadership.[2]

Thus, for example, the category "cares about people" was chosen as important by about 12 percent of the respondents. Of those, 64 percent chose Mr. Gore as doing so and 31 percent choose Mr. Bush. Mr. Gore's major campaign theme "fighting for you" may well have led his backers to view him as "caring for people." Yet it is unclear just what these findings suggests for the two templates of leadership style. Can heroic leaders still "care about people?" Perhaps they can. Would a question that asked whether the heroic leader "cared about people *like me*" elicit the same response? If it did, it would suggest that both heroic and reflective leaders could share a sense of personal connection to their followers.

If reflective leaders establish more of a personal connection with their followers does it mean that they are better liked? Perhaps. Only 2 percent of the poll respondents chose being "likable" as an important quality, an indication that is not highly relevant. However, among those who did, 59 percent thought Mr. Bush was likable and only 38 percent thought that of Mr. Gore.

Other exit poll data raise larger questions regarding the nature of the reflective or heroic leader's ties to the public. For example, consider the question of "strong leadership." We might ordinarily associate that with heroic leaders, but I have also suggested the reflective leaders need not be clerks or conflict avoidant. Being a strong leader was selected as important by 14 percent of respondents. Thirty-four percent of those who so chose, said Mr. Gore was such a leader, while 64 percent thought that applied to Mr. Bush. If Mr. Gore is indeed out of the heroic mold and Mr. Bush is helping to define the reflective, it is clear that we will have to think further about our understandings of what constitutes "strong leadership."

One promising conceptual path for doing this is found in the domain of honesty and trustworthiness. Consider a "strong leader" in the sense of having large plans and high self-confidence about them, who, nonetheless, is seen as having personal ambition trump the public's ability to count on him. This seemed to be the case in the 2000 campaign with Mr. Gore. Of course, Republicans made Mr. Gore's "willingness to say or do anything to get elected" a campaign issue, but that message seems to have fallen on receptive ears. A very high 74 percent of CNN exit poll respondents thought Mr. Gore would "say anything." There was, of course, a partisan split in these numbers with 39 percent of Mr. Gore's supporters saying it was not true and 58 percent of Mr. Bush's supporters agreeing. Still, the numbers, even among Gore supporters, suggest the extent to which this was a problem.

Consider further the qualities that Americans find important in a leader. The item that garnered the highest percentage of mentions was honesty and being trustworthy. Twenty-four percent of respondents thought it important, and of those only 15 percent thought the characteristic fit Mr. Gore, while 80 percent thought that it fit Mr. Bush. Does the view that you are "willing to say anything to get elected" undercut a claim on "strong leadership?" It seems likely on theoretical grounds that it would. Hence, that might be one plausible explanation of how you could have a heroic leadership style yet not be seen as a strong leader.

What of the role of experience and "understanding the issues." Do either of these have a solid theoretical tie to either reflective or heroic leadership? The answer to that question is unclear. Presumably, experience would be relevant to both leadership types, although it might be argued that the more heroic the changes a leader wants to make, the more prepared by virtue of experience he ought to be. The same could be argued for "understanding," since reflective leaders might have to understand *and select* from among the disparate elements they mirror. Yet, while success in achieving heroic aspirations might be tied to "understanding" and "experience," having those aspirations in the first place would seem to have much more to do with a leader's level of ambition, self-image, and self-confidence.

Two questions having to do with experience and understanding distinguished the reasons given for voting for Mr. Gore as opposed to Mr. Bush. Among those who selected "understanding issues" (13 percent), about 75 percent chose Mr. Gore and 19 percent chose Mr. Bush. Among those voters who thought experience important (15 percent), 82 percent chose Mr. Gore and 17 percent chose Mr. Bush. It seems clear that Mr. Gore had substantially more political and executive experience than Mr. Bush, and his advocates voted, in part, on the basis of that fact.

Finally, we turn to a basic question about reflective and heroic leadership, which has to do with the relative importance of personal qualities and the issues in making leadership choices. While leadership of both kinds has become more personal, is reflective leadership more so? The reflective leader is not chosen so much on the basis of his policy depth as on his interpersonal skills in bring disparate elements or groups together. Knowledge of the issues has been a continuing theme in modern elections, and the 2000 election was no exception. Sixty-two percent of the public thought that knowledge of the issues was more important than the personal characteristics of the candidate.

However, here too, we can see a split between Bush and Gore voters. Fifty-five percent of the latter thought that issues were more important while 40 percent of the Bush supporters thought so. The larger split came with differences on the importance of personal qualities versus issue knowledge with 62 percent of Bush supporters saying personal characteristics were more important, and 35 percent of Gore supporters so thinking.

Presidential Leadership—Before and After September 11: American Politics Transformed?

The new millennium began as a paradoxical time for American politics. While America had unparalleled status and influence abroad, it was beset domestically by fractious disagreements about its values, history, culture, and policies. They show no signs of abating even though a majority of Americans find a consensual range of agreement on many of these issues (DiMaggio, Evans, and Bryson 1996; Wolf 1996, 1998).

The 2000 election pitted not only two men, but also two different styles of leadership—the *heroic* and the *reflective* (Renshon 2001; 2002). What kinds of circumstances give rise to such leadership? At the time of the election, it seemed clear that countries such as the United States, in which there are no great mobilizing crises, but which are, nonetheless, deeply divided, were ripe for reflective leadership. Adding to the impetus for reflective leadership was the fact that until the terrorist attack of September 11 many citizens felt separated from their major institutions and from each other. As a result, the country seemed psychologically and structurally less responsive to traditional heroic leadership.

All of this changed dramatically as a result of the terrorist attack on the morning of September 11, 2001. Americans were traumatized and the circumstances of the Bush Presidency were transformed. What had been a presidency struggling to implement its agenda in the face of a divided public and a contentious Congress was now a wartime presidency. It was immediately clear to observers from across the political spectrum that this was a defining moment for both Mr. Bush and his presidency (Beschloss 2001; Seib 2001; Editorial 2001; Broder 2001; Fineman 2001), and for Americans. The crucial question, given the questions that had been raised about Mr. Bush's readiness for the presidency, was quite simple and profound: Would he measure up?

The answer appears to be "yes." He rallied a stunned nation and effectively capitalized on the "rally effect" to mobilize Congress for a true bi-partisan effort around the issues of American domestic and international security. After a difficult beginning, many—but not all—observers praised Mr. Bush for his forceful, steady response. R. W. Apple (2001) wrote that the presidency seemed to gain legitimacy. From a solid, steady, but hardly robust public approval level in the low to mid-fifties, President Bush has surged to unprecedented heights of public approval—at least for the short term. Whether, and for what reasons, he might be able to maintain a strong level of public support through difficult times is a critical question for his presidency and for the public's relationship to it.

It is clear that the Bush presidency has been transformed, but specifically how and with what implications for the future of the presidency? There is evidence that Mr. Bush himself has been changed and some argue transformed (Sanger and Bummiler 2001; Sanger and VanNatta 2001), but if so, exactly how? Has the public's relationship to this country, its institutions, and its politics been transformed, and if so how? Dana Milbank (2001b) of the *Washington Post* reports on the changes in President Bush's leadership style based on interviews with White House aides. Jeanne Cumings and Neil King (2001) have reconstructed an element of the Mr. Bush's decision process and his rejection of a military plan that he thought too tepid in response to the attack. Dick Cheney has given details of the administration's decision-making processes in an interview with Jim Lehrer (Transcript 2001). What are the implications of these transformations, if they are real, for Mr. Bush, presidential leadership, and the public's relationships to its leaders and institutions?

President Bush—Before and After

The circumstances of Mr. Bush's election created substantial controversy. His policy ambitions once in office created more. Mr. Bush appeared unbowed by his narrow victory margin. He began his administration with a number of far-reaching proposals, initiatives whose scope and nature were far more consistent with a robust numerical mandate than the razor-thin margin by which he gained office.

It was widely noted during the campaign that Mr. Bush was a leader who liked to focus on articulating a few policies and then pursue them relentlessly. As evidence, proponents of this view pointed to his campaign for governor, which featured four prominent themes—education, tort reform, strengthening the criminal justice system, and welfare reform (Minutaglio 2000: 277-279; Mitchell 2000: 304-305). And it is true that in his first campaign for, and in his first term as governor, he did do that. Yet his behavior on reaching the presidency was quite different.

A superficial look might indicate that Mr. Bush was going to repeat his governor's strategy in the White House. He announced on September 1, 2001, that his four priorities for the fall were "the economy; education; opportunity, including his 'faith-based' legislation; and security, including defense, Medicare, and Social Security." Ari Fleicher, Mr. Bush's spokesman, promised that the president "is going to focus like a laser" on his four categories (quoted in Allen 2001: A1).

Yet in reality this list did not add up to four. Only two of items, the president's education bill and his faith-based bill, were embodied in a single bill. The others involved more than one initiative. Mr. Bush's major tax cut, for example, was viewed as the first in a series of steps. The fourth area, security, contained three very major legislative initiatives of which defense strategy and reorientation were only the start. Additionally, Mr. Bush wanted to undertake a revamping of Social Security and the Medicare program, two politically sensitive and difficult undertakings.

Small wonder that David Broder (2001: B07) of the *Washington Post* questioned whether Mr. Bush wasn't trying to do too much with too little political capital. Mr. Broder noted that Mr. Bush had actually added to his "to do" list a comprehensive energy plan, itself made up of a number of far-reaching and controversial parts, an HMO reform bill, and a trade bill to give the president "fast-track" authority (Cooper 2001). To this he might have added an unexpected and controversial initiative to "regularize" the status of millions of illegal immigrants in this country (Schmitt,2001); a major plan for a "new federalism" (Allen and Balz 2001); a new initiative to provide housing for the disabled (Allen 2001a); a new plan to enforce and refine gun control (Lichtblau 2001); a "New Freedom Initiative" to help the disabled (Hunt 2001); and a review of a host of regulatory rules in areas including ergonomics (Dewar and Skyrzycki 2001), medical records privacy (Pear 2001), and a number of areas in environmental enforcement including air pollution (Pianin and Mintz 2001), land usage and control (Jehl 2001), and the Endangered Species Act (Seelye 2001).

Far from presiding over an administration of limited policy ambitions, Mr. Bush, even before the terrorist attack of September 11 was a president of robust policy ambitions. It appears there were *heroic* elements in what looked like a *reflective* leadership style.

The events of September 11 transformed the Bush presidency from one struggling, not always successfully, to create bi-partisan majorities on each piece of its legislative agenda to wartime president with all that that entails. It also appears to have brought about changes in his leadership style (Milbank 2001a). What might in retrospect be described as a mixed heroic/reflective style has been transformed to one that is more fully and explicitly heroic. Yet it is a style in which reflective elements, like his "plain talk" remain.

President Bush said that his administration was now wholly refocused on the worldwide fight against terrorism. And, indeed, Dana Milbank (2001b) reports that almost the entire White House staff switched from whatever they were working on, to responding to the attack. Just how long such a single-minded focus on this set of issues can be maintained is an open, but important question. By January of 2002, Mr. Bush had turned his attention to the economy and the Democrats.

Mr. Bush, himself, is said to be transformed. He has used protean language casting this struggle as a "war." a "crusade." and a stark confrontation between "good and evil." These are mighty terms reflecting large tasks and large ambitions. Whether and how he will be able to fulfill them is a question that is critical to his presidency.

American Politics and Social Capital—Then and Now

A central question of presidential leadership in the aftermath of the September 11 terrorist attacks is the public's view of and response to it. The last three decades have been difficult ones for American political culture. Americans have lost regard for their leaders, their institutions—with a few exceptions—and levels of civic engagement have declined.

These trends have been studied under the rubric of social capital. The term capital, as in social (Coleman 1987, 1988, 1990; Putnam 2000) or leadership (Renshon 2000) capital, suggests a surplus—something that you have beyond sufficiency that enables you to do something else of value. Leadership capital and how to earn and expend it in a still divided culture and society, but newly united country, are central questions in the aftermath of the terror attack.

As America began its twenty-first century it was clear that its politics were as divided as its culture. The famous red and blue 2000 election map (see chapter 13) reflected a country split along several deep fault lines—cultural, political, and psychological. Before the attack, a conflicted and hostile stalemate permeated our politics. And a motivated avoidance characterized much of our civic life. Calls for "bi-partisanship" often masked partisan agendas. Indeed, in a country so deeply divided it was hard to understand exactly what bi-partisanship meant or how it could be implemented.

The terrorist attack pushed "normal" politics to the periphery, and the politics of unity to the fore at least for awhile. Yet many divides remain. Republicans and Democrats have disagreed about the nature of the economic stimulus package and whether airline security should be totally federalized. Republicans and Democrats have joined together against others in their respective parties on issues of balancing the need for wider government powers to address domestic security issues and a concern with civil rights. And, of course, many contentious issues still remain—on judicial appointments, energy policy, and missile defense.

In theses circumstances it is important to ask, and attempt to answer, the question of where the American political center now lies and how it is related, if it is, to previous understandings of "bi-partisanship." Will domestic and national security issues continue to be the frame or prism through which most politics are viewed and conducted in the United States? Is this finally the post-New Deal realignment for which political scientists have been searching the last fifty years in vain? If not, what will the current focus on security gradually be transformed into, and with what implications for presidential leadership and governing thereafter?

The terrorist attack has changed American political culture—at least temporarily. Government is now seen as essential, certainly in the most basic areas of American domestic and national security. Trust in government, long in decline, has surged (Morin and Deane 2001). In April 2000, only 4 percent of the public thought you could trust the government to do what is right "almost all of the time." and only 26 percent thought you could do so "most of the time." In a poll taken by the *Washington Post* on September 27, 2001, the respective figures were 13 and 51 percent! Certainly, these figures are consistent with and perhaps are a result of support of President Bush's performance to date. Mr. Bush's father enjoyed similarly high support after the Gulf War, but failed to make good use of his leadership capital, and was not re-elected. What will George W. Bush do with his?

There are also reasons to be cautious in over-generalizing a new "era of good feelings." The general rise in trust in government, like its counterpart in the fleeting comity of bipartisanship, masked substantial divisions. A poll conducted by ABC news (Langer 2002) found that

> The public by a wide margin does trust the federal government when it comes to handling national defense and the war on terrorism, the poll finds. But when it comes to handling social issues, Americans' distrust of the government remains high.

More specifically, 68 percent of the public trusted the government to handle national security issues well, but only 38 percent thought the government could be trusted with social issues. Not surprisingly, given the divisions in the country, party identification played a large role in these views. Almost 80 percent of Republicans thought the government could be trusted on national security issues, while only 62 percent of Democrats thought so, and 72 percent of independents did. On social issues, 48 percent of Republicans thought the government could be trusted while 32 percent of Democrats and 37 percent of independents thought so.

Finally, it is clear that American political culture is now experiencing a surge of strongly explicit and expressive patriotism. Attachment to and support of country have, for the present, displaced the politics of identity (Sengupta 2001), which is a development of potentially enormous significance. Can a newer national identity be forged in which attachment to country exists harmoniously with the many other attachments that are possible in a multicultural democracy? Will the president recognize the implications of this development and guide it in constructive ways that extend its benefits? Will such a "new identity" make the politics of the political center clearer? Will it facilitate the emergence of real bi-partisanship to replace the masked partisanship it covered before the attack? These are critical questions for American society and politics, and their answers await us.

Americans' Choice: Reflective or Heroic Leadership?

At the beginning of this twenty-first century it is clear that America's politics are as divided as its culture. Al Gore and George Bush not only represented two different political parties and two different philosophical views, but two vastly different approaches to leadership and governing.

Mr. Bush assumed the presidency with some groups highly suspicious and antagonistic towards him. In such circumstances it is not clear what all the calls for "bi-partisanship" really meant. For those who opposed him, the phrase seemed to be a demand that he act in accordance with their wishes, not the principles and programs on which he campaigned. Yet Mr. Bush campaigned on a platform of uniting Americans, and promised on election to be president of "all the people." These are reflective leadership themes.

Mr. Bush appears to be a conservative pragmatist and one whose pragmatism and moderation is a reflection first of his psychology, and thereafter of his strategy. However, he began his presidency in a political world in which public patience was mercurial and trust in leaders of whatever style had been stretched thin. Yet many still looked to leaders for heroic answers and saw no limits on what they could reasonably expect or ask.

The magnitude of the tasks that Mr. Bush and this country face in the aftermath of the terrorists' attack is daunting. And his rhetoric in addressing them seems certain to stimulate heroic expectations. In such circumstances President Bush's capacity to govern effectively will tell us a great deal about the powers, and limits, of reflective and heroic presidential leadership. Yet, most of all it will tell us something very important about us, as citizens and Americans, and about our prospects as a viable democracy and country.

Notes

*   This analysis draws on, and build upon Renshon (2001). Research for this paper was facilitated by a research fellowship from The Joan Shorenstein Center on the Press, Politics and Public Policy, Kennedy School of Government—Harvard University, and a grant from the Horowitz Foundation for Social Policy.

1.   Dennis Farney (2000) noted that,

> The one Al Gore planted on his wife Tipper at the Democratic National Convention seems to have packed a political wallop. That is the message from a focus group here in the St. Louis suburbs — swing voters in a swing state. Because of the vice president's uncharacteristic show of emotion, along with a fatherly hug of his daughter Karenna and a solid convention speech, the group is re-evaluating him in a whole new light. "Al Gore really surprised me. I didn't know he could be so passionate." said Jim Baker, a 54-year-old political moderate who remains undecided but now leans toward Mr. Gore.

New York Times reporter Carolyn James (2000) wrote of the kiss,

> But instead of letting go, as nice politicians are supposed to, he wrapped her tighter in his arms, closed his eyes and gave her a full-mouthed kiss that lasted an exceptionally long time. (Actually three seconds; we have tapes; we've counted.) When he remembered where he was—on national television about to accept his party's nomination for president—he backed away and went on with his business. Of course, he could not really have forgotten the cameras for a second, and soon commentators were speculating about how calculated the kiss was. Mrs. Gore had spent days on the talk show circuit trying to humanize her husband's

image, after all. And here was the living proof of his humanity, and a photograph the papers couldn't resist.

2. Some characteristics were important to both candidates. For example, good judgment was chosen by about 13 percent of the voters, and among those so choosing there was no appreciable difference between those voting for Mr. Gore (48 percent) and Mr. Bush (50 percent). Other characteristics did distinguish support for the candidates.

References

Allen, Mike. "Kennedy Joins Bush in Unveiling Aid for Disabled." *Washington Post*, 2 February 2001a: A02.

Allen, Mike, and Dan Balz. "Bush Unveils 'New Federalism.' "*Washington Post*, 27 February 2001:A10.

Apple, Jr., R.W. "Bush Presidency Seems to Gain Legitimacy." *New York Times*, 16 September 2001.

Associated Press. "Report: Gore Won Popular Vote by 539, 987." *Washington Post*, 21 December 2000: A09 .

Associated Press. "Gore Campaign Is Distracted By Flap Over Family Drug Costs." *Wall StreetJournal*, 20 September 2000a.

Associated Press. "Gore Urges $2 Billion Park Efforts." *Washington Post*, 15 November 1999: A02.

Bennett, W. Lance. "The UnCivic Culture: Communication, Identity, and the Rise of Lifestyle Politics." *PS: Political Science and Politics*, December (1988) 741-761.

_____. "The Clueless Public: Bill Clinton Meets the New American Voter in Campaign '92." in Stanley A. Renshon (ed.) *The Clinton Presidency: Campaigning, Governing, & the Psychology of Leadership*. Boulder, CO: Westview Press, 1995.

Berke, Richard L., and Katherine Q. Seelye. "With a Convert's Passion, Gore Pledges Campaign Finance Reform." *New York Times*, 12 March 2000.

Beschloss, Michael. "Bush Faces the Greatest Test." New York Times, 17 September 2001.

Blumer Jay G., and Dennis Kavanaugh. "A Third Age of Political Communications: Where is it Heading?" Paper presented to the Roundtable on Seeking Responsibilities for Political Communication, London, 1988.

Broder, David S. "A New Reality for George W. Bush." *Washington Post*, 13 September 2001:A31.

_____. "Now Comes the Hard Part." *Washington Post*, 2 September 2001: B07.

Bruni, Frank. "For Bush, A Mission and a Defining Moment." *New York Times*, 22 September 2001.

Burns, James MacGregor. *Leadership*. New York: Harper and Row, 1978.

Coleman, J. S. *Foundations of social theory*. Cambridge, Mass.: Harvard University Press, 1990.

_____. Social capital and the creation of human capital. *American Journal of Sociology* 94, 1988, S95-S120.

_____. "Norms as social capital, " in G. Radninsky and P. Bernholtz (eds.) *Economic Imperialism: Economic Method Applied to Fields Outside of Economics*. New York: Paragon House, 1987.

Connolly, Ceci. "Analysis" Finance Plan May Reform Gore's Image." *Washington Post*, 28 March 2000a: A06.

_____. "'Real People' Advise Gore to Stay Loose." *Washington Post*, 2 October 2000b: A10.

Cooper, Helen. "New Trade Representative Faces An Old Obstacle: Fast-Track Fight." *The Wall Street Journal*, 6 April 2001.

Cumings, Jeanne, and Neil King, Jr. "Military Response by U.S. is Broader Than Plan Originally Proposed to Bush." *Wall Street Journal*, 8 October 2001.

Dewar, Helen, and Cindy Skyrzycki. "Workplace Health Initiative Rejected." *Washington Post*, 7 March 2001: A01.

DiMaggio, Paul, John Evans, and Bethany Bryson. "Have Americans Social Attitudes Become More Polarized?" *American Journal of Sociology* 102 (1996): 444-96.

Editorial. "Demands of Leadership." *New York Times*, 13 September 2001.

Farney, Dennis. "Gore Gains Ground in Missouri, Partly Due to Convention Kiss." *Wall Street Journal,* 25 August 2000.

Fineman, Howard. "End of Innocence: Can Bush Lead America through This Nightmare? *Newsweek*, 11 September 2001.

Freud, Sigmund. *Group Psychology and the Analysis of the Ego* (1920) in *Standard Edition,* Vol. 18. London: Hogarth Press, 1974.

Greenstein, Fred I. *The Hidden-Hand Presidency*. New York: Basic Books, 1982.

Harris, John. "Clinton Never Liked the Media. But Don't Ask him Why." *Washington Post*, 31 December 2000.

Harris, John F., and Mike Allen. "Democrats Sketch Shapes of Prospective Presidencies Bradley Envisions a Cleansing, Gore a Big Agenda." *Washington Post*, 4 January 2000: A01.

Hunt, Albert. "An Army of Opposition to Disability Rights." *Wall Street Journal*, 15 March 2001.

James, Carolyn. "When a Kiss isn't Just a Kiss, *New York Times*, 20 August 2000.

Jehl, Douglass. " White House Considering Plan to Void Clinton Rule on Forests." *New York Times*, 2 May 2001.

Judis, John B. "For Richer and Poorer: How George McGovern Won Election 2000 for the Dems." *The New Republic*, 4 December 2000: 18-19.

Kristof, Nicholas D. "Political Memo: Rival Makes Bush Better Campaigner, *New York Times*, 3 March 2000: A23.

Kurtz, Howard. "What Bush Said and When He Said It." *Washington Post*, 1 October 2001: C01.

Ladd, Everett C. *The Ladd Report*. New York: Free Press, 1999.

Lane, Robert E. "Interpersonal Relationships and Leadership in a 'Cold' Society." *Comparative Politics*, July (1978): 443-460.

Langer, Gary. "Water's Edge, Greater Trust in Government Limited to National Security." ABC.com *(http://abcnews.go.com/sections/politics/DailyNews/poll0120115.html)*, 21 January 2002.

Levy, Clifford J. "The Ad Campaign: Making Breast Cancer a Political Issue Against McCain." *New York Times*, 4 March 2000.

Lichtblau, Eric. "Gun Policy Faces Major Bush Revamp." *New York Times*, 26 July 2001.

Milbank, Dana. "Crisis Brings Shift In Presidential Style." *Washington Post*, 14 September 2001a: A01.

_____. "White House Staff Switches Gears Response to Attacks is Now Focus of Almost All Presidential Aides." *Washington Post*, 17 September 2001b: A25 .

Milbank, Dana, and Bradley Graham. "With Crisis, White House Style is Now More Fluid: Faster Decision Making Has Its Flip Side: Confusion." *Washington Post*, 10 October 2001: A04.

Minutaglio, Bill. *First Son: George W. Bush and the Bush Family Dynasty*. New York: Times Books, 2000.

Mitchell, Elizabeth. *W.: Revenge of the Bush Dynasty*. New York: Hyperion, 2000.

Morin, Richard, and Claudia Deane. "Poll: Americans' Trust in Government Grows Confidence in Government More Than Doubles Since April 2000." *Washington Post*, 28 September 2001.

Murray, Charles. "Americans Remain Wary of Washington." *Wall Street Journal,* 23 December 1997: A14.

Neustadt, Richard. *Presidential Power.* New York: John Wiley and Co., 1960.

Pianin, Eric, and John Mintz. "EPA Seeks to Narrow Pollution Initiative Utilities Fight Clinton Rules on Coal-Fired Power Plants." *Washington Post*, 8 August 2001: A01.

Pew Research Center for the People and Press. "Technology Triumphs, Morality Falters." 13 July 1999.

Renshon, Stanley A. *The Psychological Assessment of Presidential Candidates.* New York: Routledge, 1998.

_____. "Political Leadership as Social Capital." *Political Psychology* 21:1 (2000):199-22.6

_____. "Political Leadership in a Divided Electorate: Assessing Character Issues in the 2000 Presidential Campaign." The John F. Kennedy School of Government, Harvard University, 2001. (http://www.ksg.harvard.edu/presspol/publications/pdfs/renshon2.PDF)

_____. "American Political Leadership at Millennium's End," in Ofer Feldman and Linda O. Valenty (eds.) *Political Leadership for the New Century: Lessons from the Study of Personality and Behavior Among American Leaders.* Westport, CT: Greenwood, 2002 .

Sack, Kevin. "Gore Says He Makes Mistakes, but He Does Not Exaggerate." *New York Times*, 8 October 2000.

Sanger, David E., and Don Van Natta. "Four Days That Transformed a President, a Presidency and a Nation, for All Time." *New York Times*, 16 September 2001.

Sanger, David E., and Elisabeth Bumiller. "The President: In One Month, a Presidency Transformed." *New York Times,* 11 October 2001b.

_____. "The Planning: Quietly, Carefully, President Worked Toward a Decision." *New York Times*, 8 October 2001a.

Seib, Gerald F. "Attack Hits Bush with Severe Test of His Untested Leadership Skills. *Wall Street Journal*, 12 September 2001.

Seelye, Katherine Q. "Gore Proposal Would Create $115 Billion Education Fund." *New York Times,* 16 December 1999: A1.

Seelye, Katherine Q. "A Deal Protects Species from Wrangling, for Now." *New York Times*, 30 August 2001.

Sengupta, Somini. "September 11 Attack Narrows Racial Divide." New York Times, 10 October 2001.

Shapiro, Andrew L. *The Control Revolution: How the Internet is Putting Individuals in Charge and Changing the World We know.* New York: BBS, 1999.

Transcript." Interview with Vice President Dick Cheney-Part III." *Jim Lehrer NewsHour*, 12 October 2001 *http://www.pbs.org/newshour/bb/terrorism/july-dec01/cheneyc_10-12.html* (10/12/01).

Wattenberg, Martin P. *The Decline of American Political Parties: 1952-1988.* Cambridge, MA: Harvard University Press, 1990

_____. *The Rise of Candidate Centered Politics: Presidential Elections of the 1980's.* Cambridge, MA.: Harvard University Press, 1991.

Wayne, Stephen J. , et al. *The Politics of American Government,* Second Edition. New York: St. Martin's Press, 1997.

Wolfe, Alan. *Marginalized in the Middle.* Chicago: University of Chicago Press, 1996.

_____. *One Nation After All.* Chicago: University of Chicago Press, 1998.

Wysocki, Bernard, Jr. "Americans Decry Moral Decline." *Wall Street Journal*, 24 June 1999: A9.

Subject Index

Name Index